Plato's Divine Dialogues: Together With The Apology Of Socrates

Plato, Socrates

o

PLATO'S DIVINE DIALOGUES,

TOGETHER WITH THE

APOLOGY OF SOCRATES,

TRANSLATED FROM THE ORIGINAL GREEK,

WITH

INTRODUCTORY DISSERTATIONS AND NOTES

FROM THE FRENCH OF M. DACIER.

SIXTH EDITION,

CAREFULLY REVISED AND CORRECTED FROM

SYDENHAM AND TAYLOR.

LONDON:

HENRY WASHBOURNE, NEW BRIDGE STREET,

BLACKFRIARS.

1851.

INTRODUCTORY DISCOURSE

ON THE

WRITINGS OF PLATO.

WHAT is every day seen to befal the noblest houses whose great names are usurped by obscure families, ha been the fate of *philosophy*. A great number of arts, which indeed may be of use in their places, but are worthy only to be the slaves of that science which can alone render our lives equally good and happy, have seized on this magnificent name, and made it contemptible in the eyes of men. We have no idea of a true philosopher, since this august title is lavishly bestowed on a sort of curious experimentalists, who, chained down to the earth, spend the whole of their lives in making experiments on the weight of the air, and the virtues of the loadstone This name has been still more degraded, in being given to those, whose insatiable avarice binds them day and night to a furnace;* as if gold, the greatest quantity of which is not comparable to the least virtue, were the end of philosophy. In fine, men are not content with having given it such blemishes as these, but have also rendered the name odious, in throwing it away on those libertines, who, by a pretended *force d'esprit*, which at bottom is no better than weakness and ignorance, live rather like beasts than men. Is it then to be wondered at, that philosophy is mistaken and neglected, and that men no longer pay her that respect and veneration, which she formerly excited in their minds? Ashamed of being confounded with the daughters of the earth, she is reascended to heaven, from whence Socrates brought her.

The Athenians heretofore by a public decree forbade that the names of Harmodius, and Aristogiton, who had deli-

---

* Alchymists; the object of whose vain research, was to convert the baser metals into gold.

vered their country from the tyranny of Hippias and Hipparchus, should ever be given to slaves : for they thought it a horrible indignity, by so shameful a communication, to blast those names that were devoted to the public liberty. Philosophy is another deliverer, she triumphs over vices, overthrows impiety, and confounds the wisdom of the world.   It is somewhat greater than the arts, and than what men commonly call the sciences ; it is the love of true wisdom, the knowledge of Divine and human things, that is to say, the science of God, a science which teaches us to know the relation which our souls necessarily bear to their Creator, and by and in him to all rational creatures, and which produces the certain knowledge of all our duties, toward God, our neighbours, and ourselves.

To be truly a philosopher, is to have temperance, justice, and fortitude, to love the truth, to avoid sensual pleasures, to despise riches ; to weaken, as much as may be, the bands that fasten the soul to the body ; to hate and contemn this body, which is always opposing wisdom ; to renounce all our desires, to fear neither the poverty, nor shame, nor reproach we may be exposed to, for the sake of righteousness and truth ; to do good to mankind, even our very enemies ; to have nothing in view, but how to die well ; and for this end to renounce one's self and every thing else.   This is the idea the wisest heathens had of philosophy.

This being supposed, nothing can be more useful, than to follow the certain and visible progress which they made in their research after those truths, and to see to what degree of knowledge it pleased God to lead them.   If we do not make such an examen this, we cannot speak of them with judgment, and without falling into a false account of things, as it has often happened, and still happens every day to the most learned men. Whenever they speak of the heathens, they bear witness against themselves that they never well read them, and that they have only an imperfect idea of them ; for they impute such sentiments to them as they never had, and deny them others which they had in reality ; which is a great piece of injustice : nay, it seems (if I may so speak) to diminish somewhat from the mercy and justice of God, not to acknowledge all the testimonies he was pleased to give of himself among the Pagans, in

those times that were corrupted with the most abominable
idolatry, in order to reduce them to the true religion.

This negligence is the more blamable ; in that a man
needs only to read *Plato*, to be perfectly informed of the
extent of their knowledge ; for his writings have amassed
together all the truths that were scattered up and down in
the works of other philosophers ; and with the advantage
of new discoveries of his own, they compose as it were a
body of doctrine, which contains the highest perfection of
knowledge to be found among the heathens.

Let a man read ever so little of him with attention, and
reflect upon what he teaches, and he will easily discern,
that God, to stop the mouth of incredulity, was long since
preparing the way for the conversion of the heathens,
which had been so often predicted by the prophets : for
was it not the work of God, and a kind of preludium of
their conversion, that a heathen in the most idolatrous city
in the world, and almost four hundred years before the
light of the Gospel illuminated the universe, should declare
and prove a good part of the truths of the Christian religion !

The circumstance of the time is remarkable, for Plato
began to write immediately after the three last prophets
that were in Israel. So that as soon as the prophets cease
among the Jews, God raises up philosophers to enlighten
the Gentiles; and divers of the principles of the Gospel are
taught at Athens.*—Instance the following particulars :

* Both Justin Martyr and Athenagoras believed that the Greek
philosophers had a certain measure of inspiration, whereby they
were enabled to arrive at those parts of their systems which are in
accordance with the Scriptures. " One article of our faith," says
Justin Martyr, " is that Christ is the first begotten of God, and we
have already proved him to be the very LOGOS, or *universal reason*
of which makind are all partakers ; and therefore, those who live by
reason are in some sort *Christians*, notwithstanding that they may
pass with you for *Atheists* : such among the Greeks were Socrates,
Heraclitns, and the like ; and such among the Barbarians were Abra-
ham, and Ananias, and Azarias, and Misael, and Elias, &c.—So on
the other side ; those who have lived in defiance of *reason* were *un-
christian* and enemies to the LOGOS ; but they who make reason the
rule of their actions are Christians." (Reeves's translation of Justin
Martyr, vol. 1. p. 83.)—So also Clement of Alexandria. " This philosophy they received from the fertilising influences of the LOGOS or
Divine wisdom, which descended at the same time upon the Jews,
giving them the law and the prophets : and upon the Gentiles, giving
them philosophy, like the rain which falls upon the house tops, as

"That there is but one God; that we ought to love and
serve him, and to endeavour to resemble him in holiness
and righteousness; that this God rewards humility, and
punishes pride.

That the true happiness of man consists in being
united to God, and his only misery in being separated
from him.

That the soul is mere darkness, unless it be illuminated
by God: that men are incapable even of praying well,
unless God teaches them that prayer, which alone can be
useful to them.

That there is nothing solid and substantial but piety;
that this is the source of virtues, and that it is the gift of
God.

That it is better to die than to sin.

That we ought continually to be learning to die, and
yet to endure life, in obedience to God.

That it is a crime to hurt our enemies, and to revenge
ourselves for the injuries we have received.

That it is better to suffer wrong than to do it.

That God is the sole cause of good, and cannot be the
cause of evil, which always proceeds only from our disobedience, and the ill use we make of our liberty.

That self-love produces that discord and division which
reign among men, and is the cause of their sins; that the
love of our neighbours, which proceeds from the love of
God as its principle, produces that sacred union which
makes families, republics, and kingdoms happy.

That the world is nothing but corruption, that we ought
to fly from it, to join ourselves to God, who alone is our
health and life; and that while we live in this world we
are surrounded by enemies, and have a continual combat
to endure, which requires on our part a resistance without

---

well as in the fields." (1 Strom. § 7.) In another place he argues
thus: "All virtuous thoughts are imparted by divine inspiration;
and that cannot be evil, or of evil origin, which tends to produce good.
The Greek philosophy has this virtuous tendency: therefore the
Greek philosophy is good. Now God is the author of all good; but
the Greek philosophy is good: therefore the Greek philosophy is
from God. It follows that the law was given to the Jews, and philosophy to the Greeks, until the advent of our Lord." (6 Strom. § 17.)
where see more to the same purpose. Justin Martyr flourished
A. D. 140, Athenagoras 170, St. Clement of Alexandria 190.

intermission ; and that we cannot conquer unless God or angels come to our help.

That the Word (Λόγος) formed the world, and rendered it visible ; that the knowledge of the Word makes us live very happily here below, and that thereby we obtain felicity after death.

That the soul is immortal, that the dead shall rise again, that there shall be a final judgment both of the righteous and of the wicked, when men shall appear only with their virtues or vices, which shall be the occasion of their eternal happiness or misery."

But I forbear to proceed, that I may not repeat that here, which will be found elsewhere. Yet I cannot choose but add, that Plato had so great and true an idea of righteousness, and was so thoroughly acquainted with the corruption of mankind, that he makes it appear,* that if a man perfectly righteous should come upon earth, he would find so much opposition in the world, that he would be imprisoned, reviled, scourged, and in fine crucified by such, who, though they were extremely wicked, would yet pass for righteous men. Socrates was the first proof of this demonstration. For, as St. Justin says, the Devils seeing this philosopher made their nullity appear by the discovery of the truth, and that he endeavoured to reclaim men from giving them religious worship ; these malicious spirits so ordered the matter by means of men who were corrupt and took pleasure in vice, that this righteous man was put to death as if he had been an impious person, that lived without God in the world, and introduced new Gods.

There are some who pretend the above-mentioned passage of Plato is a prophecy, because the terms do not agree with the circumstances of Socrates, who was put to death only by a draught of poison, but precisely suit with those of the Saviour of the world, who was both scourged and crucified.

But we shall not presume to make a prophet of our philosopher, from whom reason alone, when moved by the injustice of men, might extort such exaggerated expressions ; but shall content ourselves to inquire what there

---

* In the second Book of his Commonwealth, Tom. 2.

may be in his writings conformable to the designs of God, who always desired the salvation of men, and often made use of the pagans for the execution of his eternal decrees.

We understand by the Holy Scripture, which is the only lamp of truth, that natural religion was the first use men made of their reason; that lust and irregular passions having corrupted their reason, they abandoned themselves to the sacrilegious worship of idols; and that God, to stop the course of this abomination, made himself known a second time, and gave the Jewish law; which, as it revived in the minds of men the principles of the law of nature, so it promised a more sacred and perfect covenant which the righteous were to expect, and which alone was capable of triumphing over death; and so alone able to conduct men to a glorious immortality.

Plato seems to have been acquainted with the Divine conduct in this matter, and to endeavour to reclaim the heathens by the same means.

He endeavours to re-establish natural religion, by opposing paganism, which was the corruption of it.

He gives a law, which in its principal heads is entirely conformable to the tradition of the Hebrews, and the precepts of Moses and the prophets; from whom he has borrowed that which is most rational and substantial in his works.

And he supports this law by a great many principles more sublime than those of natural religion, and of the law of Moses; and by clear and express promises of spiritual and eternal blessings, which the Christian religion alone can make men enjoy, and which Moses and the prophets only promised under the veil, and figures of temporal enjoyments. So that Plato is not content to give a testimony only to natural religion, and the Jewish law, but also in some sort pays homage to Christianity; in piercing, by a supernatural light, into a part of those shadows and figures that covered it; and in proposing most of the greatest motives, and glorious objects, which it has always employed to raise men above themselves, and to make them masters of their passions.

"A happy immortality (says he) is a great prize set

before us, and a great object of hope, which should engage
us to labour all the time of our life to acquire wisdom and
virtue." This the reading only of this small volume will
completely set in its true light.

It is commonly inquired on this subject, how the books
of Moses and those of the prophets could come to Plato's
knowledge. I will not undertake to prove that there were
Greek translations of them before that of the Septuagint;
it is too difficult a matter to support that supposition, and
I must confess I can find no solid foundation for it. But
I will declare what seems most probable to me.

After the departure of the Israelites out of Egypt, they
almost always continued their commerce with the Egyptians. They traded in their country, they sometimes desired their assistance against their enemies, and often entered into treaties and alliances with them. By these
means the memory of all that had happened to their nation
was easily preserved among those people. * The captivity
of king Jehoachaz, whom Pharaoh Necho carried away prisoner about the beginning of the forty-second Olympiad;
and † the dwelling of the prophets Jeremiah and Baruch
in Egypt some years after with the miserable remainder of
the Jews, that the king of Babylon had left in Judea,
could not suffer the Egyptians to forget these things.

About this time Pythagoras travelled into Egypt, from
whence he brought those traditions into Greece; his disciples communicated them to Socrates, who acquainted
Plato with them; and he, to be more perfectly instructed
in them, went to the same place, where he might see not
only the grandchildren, but the children of such as had
conversed with the fugitives that retired thither with
those prophets. And, perhaps, it is no ill-founded supposition, that by his frequent conversation with them he
learned enough of their language to read those originals
himself, of which the Egyptians, who were a very curious
people, might have copies. But whether he read them,
or knew nothing of them, but what he learned in conversation, it is certain he could draw that tradition, which he
calls *sacred*, from no other source. For he harmonizes so
well with those originals in many things, not only in re-

* 2 Kings 23.   † Jer. 43.

spect of the truths themselves, but, moreover, in the very
manner of his expressions, that one would often think he
translates them.   From whom, unless from the Hebrews,
could the Egyptians have a tradition containing such wonderful doctrine, and of which never any other people had
heard, before the peculiar people of God were instructed
in it?

But it is said there are many errors intermixed with the
writings of Plato ; that in his explication of the greatest
truths, he is full of doubt and uncertainty ; and it is observed that Socrates constantly professes that *he knows
nothing :* What advantage can be received from a man that
knows nothing but his own ignorance?   And it is fit
these objections should have an answer.

It is certain Plato is not without his errors ; but when
they come to be strictly examined, there are to be found
in them some traces of ancient traditions and predictions
of the prophets : and if these traces are compared with
the doctrine of the Holy Scripture, one may discover the
source of those errors, which by this means become one of
the proofs of the truth of the Christian religion.   For we
must be forced to acknowledge that the heathens had a
dim sight of divers great truths, which, because they were
not to be fully unveiled till the coming of the Messiah,
were involved in darkness too thick to be penetrated by
their eyes.   And this was predicted by the prophets, who
all declared, " that Christ should be the light of the world."
None but Jesus Christ was able to discover to them those
mysteries, which were to be kept secret before his coming.
Therefore it is no very surprising thing, that such persons
as attempted to penetrate * those mysteries, only by the
light of their reason, did evaporate into vain imaginations.
And for this reason we ought not to pretend to give a
clear explication of the truths of religion by the notions of
this philosopher ; but, on the contrary, should explain his
notions by these truths : this is the way to display light
every where, and dissipate all errors.   And when his principles accord well with these truths, we may with very
good advantage make use of the proofs he has given of
them.

* Such as the doctrine of the Trinity, the Resurrection, the Fall of
Man, and the Creation of the Souls of Men before their Bodies.

The doubts and uncertainty of which he is reproached about the most essential points, are so far from shaking his principles, that they only give the greater confirmation to them ; and one may say that certainty and conviction spring from these very doubts. For instance, in his *Phædon,* where he is treating of the great objects of our hope in the other life, he insinuates that it is a very difficult matter certainly to know the truth of these things, while we live here; and that how strong soever the proofs are, on which we may found an expectation of a happy eternity, the greatness of the subject and the natural *infirmities* of man are inexhaustible springs of doubts and uncertainties; for these spring up in multitudes from the stock of corrupt nature, which opposes the most manifest truths, and resists the most evident proofs which reason can produce. What was to be done then to dissipate these doubts ? The prophets had spoken, but their oracles were yet obscure, and men might not discern in their words the Divine Spirit that animated them. It was necessary that God himself should speak. Nothing less than an express promise, nothing less than a plain Divine Revelation could entirely disperse the clouds of ignorance and incredulity, and convert these doubts into certainties. This is what * Plato confesses in express terms. For he brings in some philosophers that render homage to God, calling his promises "the vessel in which no danger is to be feared, and the only one in which we can happily accomplish the voyage of this life, on a sea so tempestuous and full of rocks." Thus we see where his doubts terminated ; they led men to acknowledge the need they had of a God, to assure them of the reality of the great blessings for which they hoped. And this is accomplished in the Christian Religion ; which as it is the only religion that has God for its teacher, so has it also the promises of eternal happiness, of which the prophets spake, and of which Plato had a glimpse ; and for which the word of this God, by the confession even of these pagans, is a most certain security. So that, by the acknowledgment of the most enlightened heathens, there are now no reasonable doubts concerning the truth of the Christian Religion; that being the only

* In his Phædon

vessel in which we can never be lost. And this is what the prophets predicted, that in Jesus Christ. life and immortality should be brought to light, and that he should be the desire of nations.

It is not only in these principal points that Plato doubts, but almost in every thing; and his doubts have given occasion to many to make a wrong judgment of the Academic philosophy; for it has been imagined that it asserted nothing, but accounted all things equally uncertain, which is a very unjust supposition. Socrates and Plato were not of the number of those philosophers, whose fluctuating minds kept them continually wandering, so that they had no fixed and steady principles. This was their principle and rule: They taught that men could not of themselves have any opinion but what was founded only on probabilities; but that when God enlightened them, that which was no more than opinion before, now became science. And this they explained by a pretty comparison: Dedalus made two sorts of statues that could walk, with this difference, the one sort had a spring which stopped them when one pleased, and the other had none; so that when they were let go, they run along to the end of their line, and could not be stopped. The latter were not of so great a price, but the former were very dear. Now Socrates and Plato compared opinion to these statues that could not be stopped; for opinion is not stable, but is subject to change. But when it is restrained and fixed by reasoning drawn from causes which the Divine Light discovers to us, then opinion becomes science, and is fixed and steady, like those statues which had that governing spring added to them. So that their meaning was, that opinion turns only on probability, which is always like moving sand; but that science rests on certainty and truth, which are a firm foundation. Thus Socrates and Plato disputed about every thing, while they had only opinions; but when these opinions, after serious researches and long labour, were become science by the Divine Light, then they affirmed what they knew. Till then all was doubtful and uncertain to them. But these doubts were more wise and safe than the arrogance of those positive philosophers, that rashly affirmed every thing, and always took opinion for science.

The third objection against Socrates, "That he only

knew that he knew nothing." is no more solid than the former; and is to be answered by the same principle: and if I am not mistaken we shall find in this ignorance a marvellous fund of knowledge.

There are two sorts of ignorance, the one natural, which is good or evil, according to the good or ill use that is made of it; and the other acquired, and always good: for this latter is the ignorance of those who after they have learned all that men can know, are convinced that they know nothing. This was Socrates's ignorance, it was * *a learned ignorance that knows itself.* He had run through astronomy, geometry, physics, metaphysics, poetry, polite learning, &c., and saw the vanity of them. He even undertakes to prove that all these sciences are either useless or dangerous, and that nothing but the knowledge cf God can make us happy; that where this divine science is not, there can be no good, and consequently that there is a sort of ignorance more useful than the sciences; for this ignorance seeks not for knowledge in itself, well knowing it has none, but only in God who is pleased to fill its vacuum. It was for this reason Socrates always began his instructions with an affirmation that he knew nothing. By this he signified that our souls have no true knowledge of any thing, any farther than they are enlightened by God: that they should always look on that piercing light, in which alone they can see light; and that when they turn their looks another way, they necessarily fall back into obscurity, and produce nothing but the works of darkness. Let the proud wise men of the world appear, and compare themselves with this ignorant man.

So much for one of the uses that may be made of Plato's writings, which ought to be looked upon as so many titles belonging to Christianity, found long ago among the pagans, and are so much the more venerable, in that so much as is found in them is faithfully copied from those which the prophets have left us; and in that which we find altered and corrupted, we may, however, discover the vestiges of those truths which irreproachable witnesses published.

The second use that may be made of them, and which is

---

* It is an expression of Socrates, which states two sorts of ignorance, one that is ignorant of itself, and the other that knows itself.

no less considerable than the former, is that by this means we may be confirmed in the knowledge of a great many Christian truths, which are proved in them with such a strength and evidence, as no reasonable man can resist.

Religion only proposes them; for it belongs not to the majesty of a God to prove the necessity, justice, and truth of all he commands. He makes men love what he requires, and that is more than to prove it to be reasonable. But a philosopher, who has no authority over us, any further than he persuades us by his reasons, is obliged to give proofs of every thing he advances; and this Plato does, and his proofs cannot choose but be very agreeable to them that believe, and very useful to unbelievers, if they are but willing to attend a little to them for their instruction.

Some learned and zealous person, who is well read in ecclesiastical history, will perhaps say, If Plato be so useful, whence come those thundering censures, which some of the fathers of the church, and, above all, St. Chrysostom, have let fly against him? It would be a sufficient answer to this, should I only oppose to it those great praises which other fathers have given him, especially St. Augustin. But is it to be imagined, that the same principles that charmed St. Augustin, were displeasing to St. Chrysostom? No, certainly: the Spirit of God is not divided, and truth always appears to those whom God is pleased to illuminate. I will therefore endeavour to shew from whence this difference of their sentiments proceeded.

The philosophy of Plato was looked on two different ways, which have given occasion to two very opposite opinions concerning it.

Christian philosophers looked upon it as a doctrine, which by its principles naturally led to the Christian religion.

And pagan philosophers considered it as a doctrine, which contained morals as perfect as those of Christianity, and which might even take place of this holy religion.

In the first respect it was worthy of all the encomiums that have been given it by the greatest doctors of the church, who came out of his school.

And on the second account it deserved the greatest anathema. The defects of this philosophy could not be too much aggravated, nor could those haughty philosophers that valued themselves so much upon it, be too much abased; for the wisdom of the wise, and the knowledge of the learned, are no better than folly, if they lead us not to the knowledge of Jesus Christ. Plato himself, by his principles, would furnish us with arms, to oppose those of his admirers, that should be so senseless, as to take up with his opinions, and shut their eyes against the bright truths of religion.

But this difference is now ceased: there are now none of those ignorant persons. Nobody is so blind to prefer, or even compare Plato and Socrates, I will not say to the evangelists or apostles, but to the meanest Christian. So that there is no danger in setting a value on those truths which are found in Plato, and in rendering them all the honour they deserve. They are not the less worthy of our respect because they proceed from the mouth of a heathen. Did not God take Balaam from among the Gentiles to communicate his spirit to him? When we render homage to the truths foretold by that covetous and corrupt prophet, we do not honour the prophet, but Him by whom he was inspired. For, as St. Ambrose says, "It is not the desert of him who prophesies, but the oracle of him who calls, and which the grace of God reveals." St. Ambr. Lib. 6, Epist. 37. The greater the darkness was that benighted those times, the more esteem we ought to have for Plato and Socrates, whom God seems to have chosen to be the first heralds of those great truths, and if I may venture to say it, the forerunners of St. Paul, in the most superstitious and idolatrous city in the world. It was the doctrine of these philosophers that had produced and cherished those sparks of knowledge which this great apostle found in the hearts of some of the Athenians, concerning the resurrection of the dead and the immortality of the soul.

What respect we have for this doctrine, will turn to the glory of the Christian religion: for if the conformity of a part of Plato's opinions, with what is revealed to us in the Gospel, has so raised this philosopher's name, that he is called the "divine philosopher," what esteem and veneration do they deserve, whose minds and hearts are filled with all the truths of Christianity, and who are fed with the celestial doctrine, which our Lord Jesus Christ learned of God the Father, and came himself to teach us?

This conformity of Plato with the doctrines of the

Gospel, last year engaged a learned and pious ecclesiastic, to give a small extract of it, which was very well received by the public. This extract, which was made in the palace, and under the eye of one of the best and most learned archbishops God has given his church, is a great eulogium on the doctrine of this philosopher. What greater approbation can it have, than that of a prelate, who so strongly adheres to the word of truth, and is so diligent in instructing the people in it himself, as well as in causing others to instruct them?

Another great advantage to be gained out of Plato's writings, is, that a man may form his judgment by them; and acquire that justness of mind, and accuracy of reasoning, which are necessary in all conditions of life, in order to discern truth from error, that he may take the right side in all affairs that occur. For, the philosophy of Socrates is the source of good sense, as Horace* himself acknowledges.

There is no work in the world that teaches so well as this, the art of confuting sophists, who, by their poisonous maxims, labour to corrupt the minds of men, and to destroy truth and good sense. As there will always be such impostors to be found, this art will always be of very great use, and there is no man teaches it like Plato. There is nothing more complete than his logic, which infallibly gains its point in every thing it undertakes; it is impossible for a man to defend himself from the force of it. It may be compared to the sun, which, when it rises, scarce makes us feel its heat, but gradually increases it, so that at length it becomes too hot to be endured.

I shall not speak of the charms of his dialogues, which are inexpressible: there are no satires or comedies that come near them. We can no where find such sharpness of wit, so many graces, and decent turns of thought, nor so much variety either of conceptions, or expressions: nor were ironies ever so finely managed; so that it is not so much an entertainment of reading as an enchantment.

I have elsewhere sufficiently exposed to view the advantages of dialogue above all other ways of treating a subject. I shall here only add, that that which contributes most to render it so agreeable and useful, is that truth comes gra-

* In Arte Poetic, v. 310.

dually out of the bowels of the dispute ; just as when pictures are unrolled we see the persons represented rise up by degrees, till at last they appear in their full proportion : and there is nothing more agreeable to the mind than the springing up of truth after this manner, the insensible progress of which even leaves the soul time to be before-hand with it, and to foresee its appearance. Now a truth which our minds have as it were divined, pleases us much more than that which has been formally proved to us, which most commonly only irritates and makes us uneasy.

These dialogues have been the admiration of all ages : in the reign of Trajan they were still so much esteemed at Rome, that they occasioned the introducing of a custom which was received with great applause ; they used to choose the finest of these dialogues, and make their children learn them by heart, that so they might at their feasts recite them at table, with those different tones and gestures that were suitable to the manners and characters of the different persons whom Plato brings in speaking.

It is true, this custom lasted not long ; but that which put an end to it was no less honourable than that which introduced it. For the philosophers that condemned and abolished it, did so only because they accounted Plato too sublime to be so used, and because they could not endure that dialogues so serious and solid should serve for a divertisement at table, and be heard amidst the merriment, noise and tumult of a feast. And this sentiment of theirs was supported by the authority of Plato himself, who, in his Banquet, being to speak of the end of man, of the sovereign good, and other theological matters, does not push on his demonstration very far ; he does not, according to his ordinary custom, imitate a vigorous wrestler, who never lets go his hold, and who locks his adversary so closely that he cannot escape him ; but he softens his proofs and makes them pleasant, and attracts his auditors by the insinuation of fables and examples, which seem to be contrived not so much to convince as to divert them. For no questions ought to be started at table but such as may move the soul after an agreeable and useful manner, and such as every one may easily understand ; and those ought to be banished (to use the words of Democritus) that are thorny, and out of which it is difficult to extricate one's self. The discourse at table ought to be for every one, like the wine ; and such as propose there abstracted and difficult questions, banish thence this kind of community, and renew the feast of the fox and the crane.

If I had only considered the eloquence, the strength and harmony of these writings, I confess I should never have had the courage to translate them ; in doing which, either through my own defect, or that of the language in which I write, I have had the uneasiness of finding myself unable to preserve a multitude of beauties and elegancies that render these dialogues masterpieces, not to be equalled. But I considered, that seeing they contained matters of so great importance and necessity, it would be a great piece of folly, to be so superstitious about terms as to deprive mankind of so great an advantage. And by good hap, that which is the most useful cannot be hurt by my translation. It preserves the art of logic, and all the truth which Socrates proves by that means, and that is enough. Those beauties which consist only in expression are not so necessary, and we may easily forego them, provided we enjoy others ; and not do like a certain writer of the last age, who, after he had made many good reflections on Socrates, and had acknowledged him to be an admirable pattern in all great qualities, amuses and perplexes himself with trouble, that a soul so lovely had met with a body so deformed, and disagreeable to its beauty. Which is as if a soldier, in reading the great actions of Cæsar or Alexander, instead of taking advantage of his reading, and learning the art of war, should distress and afflict his mind, because one was bald, and the other inclined his head on one side.

But it may be I have less reason to fear how it will go with my translation, than how Socrates himself will escape. Our age so much resembles that wherein this philosopher lived, that in all appearance, if this wise man now finds some intelligent judges who will do him justice, he will find a greater number of persons extremely prejudiced, who will be sure to condemn him. In an age wherein nothing is esteemed but riches ; wherein that slavery, which leads to wealth, is preferred to liberty, and men choose rather to nourish the vices of others by their flatteries, than to augment their own virtues by their labour; the temperance, frugality, fortitude, justice and liberty of Socrates will be laughed at; and this will be but the accomplishment of what he predicted : * " If my fellow-citizens (says he) have not been able to endure my maxims, much less will they be tolerable to strangers."

The greatest part will not give themselves so much trouble as to read him. † They will much sooner read the Milesian fables, as St. Jerom says ; that is, such pieces as corrupt the heart and mind, than dialogues which inspire nothing but wisdom. And among those that will read him, many will do it out of curiosity ; for in our time we may make the same complaint that was made heretofore by Taurus, the philosopher, an ancient commentator on Plato. One asks for "Plato's Dialogue of the Banquet," to have the pleasure of seeing the excesses of Alcibiades. Another for his "Phædrus," because it is a treatise of criticism, and the oration of Lysias is examined in it ; and others desire those dialogues which have the greatest reputation, and are accounted the best penned, only for a frivolous pleasure : and not one of all these thinks of embellishing his mind by reading of these books, so as to become more modest, temperate, just, patient, and pious.

But those who will prove the least favourable to Socrates, are a sort of men who highly value themselves upon their refined wit ; and a great many of those who are taken with the pomp and gay appearances of the world.

The former not having eyes piercing enough to discover the secret light of those hidden beauties that adorn these dialogues, will count Socrates a dull and languid author, because he has no witticisms, nor genteel turns. An obscure person who never did anything worthy to be read, shall call in question the reputation of Socrates, a person who has been an honour to human nature by the excellency of his understanding ; and shall prefer himself to him, trampling under his feet ‡ "the testimonies which all the learned men of antiquity, and all Greece have rendered him, that for good sense, wit, pleasantness, subtilty,

* Apology 69.
† Multoque pars major est Milesias Fabulas revolventium, quam Platonis Libros. St. Jerom in the Preface of his 12th book on Isaiah.
‡ Cicero in his 3rd Book of Oratory.

strength, variety and abundance, he excelled all that ever
had appeared in the world." A man must, indeed, have a
high opinion of himself, to appeal from so solemn a judgment, and to make his appeal to himself too.

The latter are commonly corrupted by reading frivolous
books, which are wholly composed for ostentation, and, as
Montagne says, cannot perceive riches unless they make a
pompous show, and so have a disgust for every thing that
is plain and simple ; being persuaded that what is natural
and easy, is akin to dulness and stupidity. These will
think it below them to attend to a philosopher who entertains them only with such discourses as they count vulgar
and trivial, who is scarce ever to be found out of shops ;
who talks only of husbandmen, smiths, masons, carpenters,
shoemakers, and tailors, and is eternally hammering on the
same subjects, and representing the same images.

There are not wanting good reasons to prove to them,
that as a man sometimes is thought plump and in good
case, when he is only swelled and bloated ; so that which
is frequently taken for accuracy of judgment, is the effect
of some distemper, and not at all the mark of a nice and
fine relish. The highest and most sublime conceptions are
often hid under a form that appears vile and contemptible.
Are not the most celestial truths proposed to us in the
Gospel under popular images and modes of expression, like
those used by Socrates ? That which creeps on the earth,
is no less capable than that which is raised to the heavens,
of serving for a representation to let the greatest secrets,
both of nature and grace, into our understanding. Nay,
many times the most simple and common ideas, are the
most proper to impress truth on the minds of men ; for
besides that these are more proportionate to us, they do
not transport us out of ourselves, as the most magnificent
ideas do. If none but great and dazzling images could
strike us, God would not have failed to have constantly
employed them ; and since it is no more difficult for him
to change men than to illuminate them, he would have
been so far from making his Spirit stoop to the manners
and customs of those whom he inspired, that, on the contrary, he would have transformed their manners and customs, to subject them in some sort to his Spirit ; and yet
he did not do this. When he inspires Daniel, he leaves

him to speak like a man educated in a royal court, he uses
only great and magnificent ideas; and when he inspires a
shepherd, such a one as Amos, he leaves him to explain
himself by such terms as were most familiar to him : but
the truth is every where equally sublime, and as it receives
no accession to its lustre by the majesty of figures, so neither does it lose anything of its glory by their simplicity.
Socrates was so well persuaded, that this simplicity was
alone capable to move and correct the minds of men, that
when Critias, the most cruel of the thirty tyrants, commanded him to let all the artificers alone, and talk no more
of them, he answered; * "I must then let all those consequences alone too, which I draw from them, and must
speak no more, either of holiness or justice, or any other
duties that become a good man."

But, perhaps, our censors will have less deference for
the authority of reasons, than for that of examples; it is
therefore necessary to give them an account of what passed
in the time of Socrates himself; and to shew them the
characters, both of his friends and enemies.

On the one side were the most stupid and most corrupt
among the people, some of whom, through ignorance,
laughed at his morality, and the manner of his behaviour :
others, through the corruption of their hearts, could not
endure his generous liberty.

On the other side, persons of the greatest honour, and
of chief note in the commonwealth, Pericles, Nicias,
Xenophon, Apollodorus, Criton, Critobulus, Æschines,
Antisthenes, &c. These found infinite charms in his conversation. Who is it that is ignorant of Alcibiades! No
man had more wit, or a truer gust of things; he was one
of the best made, bravest, most gallant, most magnificent,
most ambitious, and nicest men in the world; he was at
the head of the Athenians, he commanded their armies, he
had won several battles, he had glittered in the courts of
kings, and had not been rudely treated by queens. According to the maxims of the world, there is nothing more
bright and illustrious than such a man as this. Yet this
same Alcibiades, amidst all this glory and pomp, is so far
from being offended at Socrates' way and manner of de-

Xenoph. in the 1st book of the Memorable Things of Socrates.

portment, which were so opposite to his own, that he no
sooner became acquainted with him, but he was struck
with such a sense of his merit, and the solid gracefulness
of his conversation, that he knew not how to leave him;
he was enchanted with his discourses, which he preferred
to the most excellent music; * he confesses, that a man
could neither hear him speak, nor even hear others repeat
what he had said, without being transported. The force
and truth of his words drew tears from him, and made
him even leap for joy. He compared him to certain
statues of Satyrs and Silenes, which were made to open
and shut: to look on the outside of them, nothing was
more ugly; but when they were opened, all the deities
were found in them together. He hardly loved or respected
any one besides him, and he never met with him, but he
took off from his own head the crown, which he, according
to custom, wore on days of ceremony, and put it on the
head of Socrates.

Therefore there is no medium, we must judge of Socrates,
either as the worst and meanest of the Athenians did, or
like Pericles and Alcibiades: We may make our choice.

All these contradictions which I have foreseen, and
which indeed may make these Dialogues become to the
greatest part of readers † "like those exquisite dainties
that were formerly set on tombs," have not discouraged
me, but only convinced me that a bare translation, though
ever so exact and faithful, would not make a sufficient
impression on the minds of some men, if it were not
supported by something, that might prevent all these
inconveniences, or, at least, a good part of them; and I
could think but of two ways to succeed in this.

The first was, to place an argument at the head of every
dialogue, to explain the subject of it, to unfold the art and
method of it, and to take particular notice of every thing
in it of the greatest importance. The arguments of Marsilius Ficinus do not go to the matter of fact; besides,
they are too abstracted, and are abundantly more difficult
to be understood than the dialogues themselves. And
those of De Serres are too wide and indefinite, they never

* In the Dialogue of the Banquet.
† Quasi oppositiones Epularum circumpositæ Sepulchro. Ecclesiastic. 30. 18.

well fix the state of the question, or the quality of the
proofs ; nor do they ever explain either Plato's design, or
his address. Now an argument ought to be a faithful
guide always to attend the reader, to conduct him where-
ever he goes, and always to set him into the right path.

The second way was to make remarks to elucidate the
principal difficulties, to render the hidden beauties discern-
ible, to explain the train of reasoning, and the solidity of
the principles and proofs, and to help to discover what is
false, from that which is true.

Marsilius Ficinus did not so much as think of this ; De
Serres, on this account, is more useful than he ; for by
his marginal notes he at least hinders you from losing the
thread of Plato's reasoning, and makes you comprehend the
train and progress of his proofs : but yet he abandons
you in the greatest difficulties.

In the time of Maximus Tyrius, that is, in the second
age, it was very earnestly desired, that some one would
undertake to elucidate those obscure and knotty passages
of Plato; above all, in what respects his opinions in theology: and many philosophers laboured in this work, as
may be seen in his life ; but with so little success, that
instead of resolving the difficulties, they have increased
them. They have scarce assisted me once or twice in all
the dialogues which I have translated ; and they would
very often have led me into mistakes, if I would have followed them.

The cause of their errors was, that they did not draw
from the true fountain, and had a mind to explain Plato by
Aristotle's principles, which are very different from those
of Plato. The latter is most commonly conformable to
sound theology, or may be very easily reduced to it by his
own principles well explained : but it is otherwise with his
disciple ; and where Plato may be once corrected by Aristotle, Aristotle may be corrected a hundred times by Plato.

I do not presume so much on my own ability, as to
think I have filled up all the devoirs of a good interpreter;
without doubt some difficulties will yet be found in that
which I have translated, but perhaps all of them ought
not to be imputed to me. Obscurities ordinarily arise
from three causes, from the sublimity of the subject, from
the ignorance of the interpreter, and from the incapacity

or inattention of the reader.   It will be reasonable for the
reader to accuse me of some of them ; but let him also
sometimes accuse either the subject or himself : if this
conduct be observed, I may venture to hope for the diminution of these difficulties.

I might here have a fair occasion to answer the invec-
tives that have been made against Plato in our time, but
since they come only from such persons as never read so
much as one of his Dialogues ; perhaps they will change
their sentiments when once they have read him.   Besides,
it is wasting one's time to defend Plato ; for he sufficiently
defends himself : and that may be said of him with yet
more justice, which the greatest of the Latin historians
said of Cato, equally ridiculing the praises Cicero had given
him, and the satires Cæsar had made on him ; * "None
could ever augment the glory of this great man by his
praises, nor diminish it by his satires."

* Cujus gloriæ neque profuit quisquam laudando, nec vituperando
quisquam nocuit.   *Titus Livius.*

THE FIRST ALCIBIADES: .

OR,

OF THE NATURE OF MAN.

THE ARGUMENT.

In this Dialogue, which is entitled, "OF THE NATURE OF MAN," Plato attempts to cure our pride and self-love, by setting the infirmities and defects of human nature in the clearest light; and by prescribing the means which ought to be used to reform it, with the care we ought to take of ourselves. The matter in question, therefore, is to know what we ourselves are; and that part of the Dialogue which treats of this, appears little less than divine. For here Plato teaches that man is the reasonable soul, which participates of understanding, and makes use of the body. The soul, as reasonable, makes use of her reason to reflect on herself, and to know her own necessities: as she participates of understanding, she makes use of this to raise her up toward God, and to know herself in that resplendent light, in which only we can be able perfectly to view ourselves; and to know what is good, profitable, lovely, just; in a word, the true Good, of which that is the fountain: and it is this knowledge alone that sets us right; and which, by directing our actions, renders them useful both to ourselves and others. But that it may not be thought that it absolutely depends on us to acquire this perfection, he assures us, that all our efforts will be useless without the assistance of God. We shall find here, besides this, other truths as surprising in a pagan: for instance, that which he says of the two sorts of ignorance, one of which is good, and the other evil: and what he teaches us concerning particular things, that the knowledge of these is not sufficient to produce the peace and union of states and families; and that we have need of the knowledge of universal things, which alone produces charity, the mother of union. It is not necessary here to set off all the beauties of this Dialogue. I shall only remark, in general, that all these Dialogues are as so many pieces of the theatre: comedy reigns in some of them, and tragedy in others. This is of the latter kind, and in some sort resembles Sophocles's Œdipus. For, as in that piece, we see a prince who, from the highest pinnacle of grandeur, and after he had been looked upon as a god, falls into a most deplorable state of misery : we here, in like manner, see Alcibiades, after having been counted worthy of the greatest honours, obliged to acknowledge, that he deserves only to be a slave. They who are shocked at the passionate manner in which Socrates speaks to Alcibiades at the beginning of this Dialogue, will cease to be offended when they have read it out ; for they will then see it is a very innocent passion, designed only for the advancement of virtue. Young people would be very happy, if they always found friends that loved them as truly and piously as Socrates loved Alcibiades : for, as Plutarch says, " He did not seek with him an effeminate pleasure unworthy of a man, but cured the corruptions of his soul, filled the void of his mind, and repressed his extravagant vanity." He endeavoured to lead him out of darkness, and conduct him to the true light. It is not difficult to fix the time in which Plato supposes this Dialogue to have been made, since he tells us Alcibiades was then in the 20th year of his age ; it must have been, therefore, in the third year of the eighty-seventh Olympiad, one year before the death of Pericles.

This Dialogue is μαιευτικὸς ; that is, Socrates so manages the matter, as to make Alcibiades of himself find out the truths which he has a mind to teach him.

SOCRATES, ALCIBIADES.

Socrates. O son of Clinias, you are without doubt surprised, that since I was the first that followed you, I should also be the last; and that whereas others have pursued you with their importunities, I have been so many years without speaking to you. It is no human consideration that has retained me, but a regard altogether * divine ; which I will explain to you hereafter. At present, while that God who conducts me lays me under no restraint, I make use of the permission he gives me to accost you ; and I hope our conversation for the time to come will not be disagreeable to him. I have hitherto observed in what way you have conducted yourself towards my rivals : among that great number of proud and haughty men who have adhered to you, there is not one whom you have not shocked

* [A regard altogether divine.] He means he was not willing to speak to him without the permission of God, under whose conduct he is ; and that God would not suffer him to speak during the great tenderness of Alcibiades' youth, which would have rendered all his instructions useless. See the argument of the APOLOGY about the Genius that conducted Socrates.

by your lofty carriage.   And I am now willing to tell you the cause of the contempt you have had for them.   You think you have no need of any man; so liberally has nature, as you suppose, indulged you with all the goods both of body and mind.   First of all, * you think yourself to be one of the finest and best made men in the world: and in this it is probable you are not mistaken.   In the second place, you are sensible of the advantage of † your birth; for you are of the most illustrious house of Athens, which is the most considerable of all the cities of Greece. On your father's side, you have a great many powerful relations and friends to support you on all occasions.   You have no less number, nor less considerable in quality, on your mother's side.   And that which you think yet more augments your reputation, is, that your father left you Pericles for your guardian; whose authority is so great, that he does what he pleases not only in this city, but likewise in all Greece, and among the most powerful of the barbarous nations.   I might also speak of your riches, if I did not know that these are the least occasion of your vanity.   ‡ All these great advantages have inspired you with so much pride, that you have despised all your admirers as so many inferiors, not worthy of attention. Accordingly they have all left you, and you have very well observed it; therefore I am very sure you cannot sufficiently wonder what reasons I can have to continue in my former passion; and are considering what hope I can have yet to follow you, after all my rivals have retired.

Alcibiades. But one thing which without doubt you do not know, Socrates, is, that you have prevented me but a moment, and that I designed to speak to you first, to ask the reason of your obstinacy.   What do you mean? or what

* Plutarch reports that the beauty of Alcibiades kept in a florid state through all the ages of his life; and that the saying of Euripides that the autumn of handsome men is gay, was verified in him.

† On the side of his father Clinias, he descended from Eurysaces, the son of Ajax; and on the side of his mother, Dinomache, he was Alcmæonides, and descended from Megacles.

‡ The most noted and strongest passions Alcibiades had, were a boundless vanity, which made him endeavour to carry all before him with an air of haughtiness, and an unlimited ambition, which made either a superior, or equal, always seem intolerable to him: this made Archestratus say, Greece could not bear two Alcibiades's.   *Plutar.*

is it you hope for, that you trouble me after this manner, using your utmost diligence continually to attend me in every place whither I go? For, in fine, I cannot enough wonder at your deportment; and you will do me a pleasure to tell me once for all, to what you pretend.

Socrat. That is, you will freely hear me, seeing you have a mind to know my thoughts. I shall therefore now speak to you, as to one who will have patience to hear me, and will not take occasion to get away from me.

Alcib. Yes, you may.

Socrat. Consider well to what you engage yourself; that you may not be surprised, if I find it as hard for me to make an end, as it has been to begin.

Alcib. Speak, Socrates; I will give you as much time as you please.

Socrat. Well, then, I will obey you; and though it be a very difficult thing for a man to speak to a person he loves, who yet does not love him, I must take the courage to tell you my thoughts. For my part, Alcibiades, if I had always seen you devoted to your vanity and grandeur, and in the design of living, as you have hitherto done in your luxury and softness, I should also have long ago renounced and forsaken you; at least, I flatter myself that I should have done so. But now I am going to discover to you your own thoughts, which are very different from those you have had formerly; and by this you will know that the reason of my obstinate persisting in following you up and down, was, to study you. I am ready to think, that if some God should all on a sudden say to you, Alcibiades, would you rather choose to live with all the advantages you have at present, or to die; if you were withal forbidden to aspire to the possession of yet greater for the future: I am ready to think, I say, that you would choose to die. So that this appears to be the hope with which you flatter yourself, and which makes you in love with life. You are persuaded, that you shall have no sooner harangued the Athenians, and that will be within a very little time, but you will make them sensible you deserve to be honoured more than Pericles, or any of our greatest citizens; that you shall soon be master of this city; and that your power shall extend over all the cities of Greece, and over the barbarous nations that inhabit our continent. And if this

God should farther say, Alcibiades, you shall be king of all Europe, but you shall not extend your dominion over the provinces of Asia; I believe you would not be willing to live for so small an empire, unless you could fill the whole world with the noise of your fame. You esteem none but Cyrus and Xerxes: and as you are charmed with their glory, you propose them as patterns for your imitation. These are the views you have. I know it, and it is not mere conjecture. You very well know I say nothing but the truth; and therefore, perhaps, you will ask me: What respect, Socrates, has this preamble of yours to that you had a mind to say, to explain to me the reasons you have to follow me every where? I will immediately satisfy you of that, O son of Clinias. It is because the * great projects you form in your head can never be put in execution without my assistance; so much power have I over all your affairs, and over yourself too. And hence it is, without doubt, that the God who governs me, has never suffered me to speak to you till now, and I have been long waiting for his permission. Now, therefore, as you hope that when you have convinced your fellow-citizens that you are worthy of the greatest honours, they will make you master of their fortunes; I also hope you will make me master of your conduct, when I have convinced you, that I am more worthy of this honour than any other person, and that you have neither guardian, friend, nor brother, that can give you that great power to which you aspire: there is none but I who can do it, with the help of God. While you were younger, and had this great ambition, God was not pleased to suffer me to speak to you, that my words might not be thrown away. Now he gives me leave to break silence; and you are indeed in a better disposition to hear me.

Alcib. I confess, Socrates, † you seem to me a more strange person since you have begun to speak, than while you were silent; though, indeed, I have always taken you for an odd sort of a man. It seems, then, you know my

* The designs of the ambitions cannot succeed but by the counsels of the wise.

† The wisdom of Socrates could not but seem mere folly to Alcibiades, especially while Socrates promises him such great things, which he could not tell how to comprehend.

thoughts perfectly well; so let it be : if I should tell you the contrary, I should have enough to do to convince you. Yet I pray tell me, how you will be able to prove that with your assistance, I shall effect the great things I am projecting, and that I can do nothing without you?

Socrat. Do you ask me if I am capable of making a long discourse, * as they do whom you are wont to hear? You know that is not my manner. But if you would (though ever so little) comply with my way, I will do all I can to convince you, that I have advanced nothing but what is true.

Alcib. I am willing to comply with it, provided it be not very difficult.

Socrat. Is it so difficult a matter to answer a few questions?

Alcib. No ; if that be all, I am willing to do it.

Socrat. Answer me then.

Alcib. Well, interrogate me as soon as you please.

Socrat. May we not suppose that you have always those great thoughts which I have attributed to you?

Alcib. I agree to it: I shall at least have the satisfaction of hearing what you have to say to me.

Socrat. I believe I am not mistaken ; you are preparing to go in a few days to the assembly of the Athenians, to make them participate of the knowledge and skill you have acquired. And if I should meet you at that instant, and ask you, Alcibiades, what are the matters about which you are going to advise the Athenians? Are they not such things as you know better than they? What would you answer me ?

Alcib. Without doubt, I should answer, it is about such things as I know better than they.

Socrat. For you would not know how to give good counsel but in matters that you know.

Alcib. How should any one give it in other things ?

Socrat. And is it not certain, that you know nothing but what you have either learned of others, or what you have found out yourself?

Alcib. What can one know otherwise ?

Socrut. But have you learned anything of others, or

* He reproaches him for abusing himself too much in hearing the long discourses of the sophists. For Alcibiades pretended much to eloquence, which made him so much relish those studied discourses.

found out anything yourself, when you have neither been willing to learn nor search into anything?

Alcib. That cannot be.

Socrat. Have you ever thought it worth your while to endeavour to find out, or learn, what you believed you already understood?

Alcib. No, certainly.

Socrat. There was a time then, in which you thought yourself ignorant of what you now know?

Alcib. That is very true.

Socrat. But I pretty well know what are the things you have learned. If I forget any one of them, mention it to me. You have learned (if my memory do not deceive me) to read and write, to play on the harp, and to wrestle: but as for the flute,* you did not value it. This is all you understand, unless you have learned some other thing that I never knew of. And yet † I do not think you have gone abroad either day or night, but I have been a witness to the steps you have taken.

Alcib. It is very true, these are the only things I have learned.

Socrat. Will you then, when the Athenians enter into a deliberation about writing, to know how that art ought to be practised, rise up to give them your advice?

Alcib. No, surely.

Socrat. Shall it be when they consult about the different tunes in music?

Alcib. A fine consultation indeed!

Socrat. Nor are the Athenians used to deliberate on the various turns used in wrestling?

Alcib. No, certainly.

Socrat. What is it then you expect they will consider, wherein you may give them advice? It must not be about the manner of building a house neither; the meanest

---

· * He looked upon it as an ignoble instrument, and unworthy of the application of a freeman. But the principal cause of this aversion was, because it spoiled the graceful air of his countenance.

† Alcibiades was besieged night and day by a corrupt sort of men, who made it their constant endeavour to seduce him. But Socrates, like a good father, kept him always in his sight, to secure him from all those dangers, well knowing that none but himself was capable of preserving him from so great perils.

bricklayer would be able to advise them how to do that better than you.

Alcib. He would so.

Socrat. Nor must it be about any point of divination, you are not so well acquainted with that business as every diviner is, let him be small or great, handsome or ugly, of high or low birth.

Alcib. What does all that signify?

Socrat. Nor is it any matter whether he be rich or poor, for good counsel proceeds from knowledge, and not from riches.

Alcib. That is easily granted.

Socrat. And if the Athenians should take into consideration the ways and means of recovering their health; do you think they would not send for a physician to consult him, without giving themselves any further trouble?

Alcib. No doubt of it.

Socrat. When is it then, do you think, that you will rise up with any colour of reason to give them good advice?

Alcib. When they deliberate on their affairs.

Socrat. What, when they consult about the building of ships; to know what sort of vessels they should make?

Alcib. No, not that.

Socrat. For you never learned to build ships; that is the reason, I suppose, you will not speak of that matter; is it not?

Alcib. To be sure, I will say nothing on that subject.

Socrat. When is it, then, that their affairs will be so deliberated, that you will put in for a speech?

Alcib. When they have before them the business of peace and war, or any other thing belonging to government.

Socrat. You mean, when they consider with what nations it is proper for them to make war or peace; and when and how it ought to be made?

Alcib. You hit it.

Socrat. Peace or war ought to be made with those nations with whom it is best to make either one or the other; and when the best occasion offers, and also after the best manner; and as long as it continues to be best.

Alcib. True.

Socrat. If the Athenians should consult with what wrestlers it is best to take the lock, and what others it is best to deal with * at arms-end without closing in to them, and when and how these different exercises ought to be performed, should·you give better advice in these matters than the master of the wrestling ground ?

Alcib. No question but he would give the best counsel in this case.

Socrat. Can you tell me what this wrestling-master would principally regard in giving instructions, with whom, when, and how, these different exercises ought to be performed ? Would he not have respect only to what is best ?

Alcib. Without doubt, he would.

Socrat. Then he would order them to be performed as often as it should be best so to do ; and on such occasions as should be most proper.

Alcib. Very true.

Socrat. He that sings ought sometimes to join his voice with the harp ; and sometimes to dance as he plays and sings, and in all this he should conduct himself by what is best ?

Alcib. That is most certain.

Socrat. Seeing then there is a best in singing, and in playing on instruments, as well as in wrestling, how will you call this *best* ? For, as for that of wrestling, all the world calls it the most *gymnastic*.

Alcib. I do not understand you.

Socrat. Endeavour to follow me ; for my part I should answer, that *this best* is that which is always the best ; and is not that which is *always the best*, that which is most according to the rules of the art itself ?

Alcib. You have reason.

Socrat. What is this art or wrestling ? Is it not the gymnastic art ?

Alcib. Yes.

Socrat. What I have been saying, is, that which is best in the art of wrestling, is called the most gymnastic.

Alcib. This is what you have already said.

Socrat. And this is right.

Alcib. Very right.

* It is a kind of wrestling Hippocrates speaks of in his 11th book of Diet. Chap. 11. To wrestle only with the arms without taking hold of the body, makes one lean, and draws the flesh upward.

Socrat. Come, then, do you also endeavour to give me a right answer. How do you call that art, which teaches to sing, to play on the harp, and to dance well? Can't you tell me that?

Alcib. No indeed, Socrates.

Socrat. Try if you cannot hit on it in this way. How do you call the goddesses that preside over this art?

Alcib. You mean the Muses.

Socrat. Very well. Let us see what name this art has derived from them.

Alcib. O, it is music you speak of.

Socrat. Very right: and as I told you that which was performed according to the rules of the art of wrestling or of the gymnasium, is called gymnastic; tell me also how you call that which is according to the rules of this other art?

Alcib. I call it musical, and say such a thing is done musically.

Socrat. Very good. And in the art of making war, and in that of making peace, what is that which is best, and how do you call it? Seeing as to those two other arts, you say:that which is best in the one, is that which is most gymnastic, and that which is best in the other, is that which is most musical; try now, in like manner, to tell me the name of that which is best in the arts we are now upon.

Alcib. Indeed, Socrates, I cannot tell.

Socrat. But if any one should hear you discoursing, and giving advice about several sorts of food, and saying that is better than this, both for the season and quality of it; and should ask you, Alcibiades, what is it you call better? Would it not be a shame if you could not answer, that you mean by better that which is more wholesome? Yet it is not your profession to be a physician. And is it not yet a greater shame that you know not how to give an answer in things you profess to know, and about which you pretend to give advice, as understanding them better than others? Does not this cover you with confusion?

Alcib. I confess it does.

Socrat. Apply your mind to it then; and endeavour to give me an account what is the design of that better thing, which we seek in the art of making peace or war with those with whom we ought to be either in war or peace.

Alcib. I know not how to find it out, what effort soever I make.

Socrat. What, don't you know, that when we make war we complain of something that has been done to us by those against whom we take up arms? And are you ignorant of the name we give to the thing of which we complain?

Alcib. I know on such occasions we say, they have deceived us, they have insulted us, they have taken away our property.

Socrat. Very well, when one of these things befalls us, I pray explain to me the different manner in which they may happen.

Alcib. You mean, Socrates, that they may befall us justly or unjustly.

Socrat. I do so.

Alcib. And that makes an infinite difference.

Socrat. Against what people, then, shall the Athenians declare war by your advice? Shall it be against those who follow the rules of justice, or such as act unjustly?

Alcib. A pretty question, Socrates! if any one should be capable of thinking it needful to make war with those that follow the rules of justice, do you think he would dare to own it?

Socrat. Because, you will say, that is not conformable to the laws.

Alcib. No, doubtless; it is neither just nor honourable.

Socrat. You will always, then, have justice in view in all your counsels.

Alcib. That is very necessary.

Socrat. But is not that *better thing* about which I was just now inquiring of you on the subject of peace or war, viz. to know with whom, when, and how, war and peace should be made, * always the most just?

Alcib. I am of that mind.

Socrat. How comes this to pass then, my dear Alcibiades? Is it that you perceive not that you are ignorant of what is just, or is it that I perceive not that you have learned it, and that you have secretly attended some master who has

---

* It is not sufficient to know what is just, we should know what is most just: and this point is very difficult to be found. This is not within the reach of little politicians. *M Le Fevre.*

taught you to distinguish well between what is most just, and what is most unjust? Who is this master? I pray tell me, that you may put me under his care, and recommend me to him.

Alcib. These are your common ironies, Socrates.

Socrat. No, I swear it by that God who presides over our friendship, and whom I would least offend by perjury, I very seriously entreat you, if you have a master, tell me who he is?

Alcib. And what if I have none, do you think I could not otherwise know what is just and unjust?

Socrat. You know it, if you have found it out yourself.

Alcib. Do you think I have not found it out?

Socrat. I am persuaded you have found it if you have sought for it.

Alcib. Do you think I have not sought for it?

Socrat. You have sought for it, if you have believed yourself ignorant of it.

Alcib. Do you then imagine that there was not a time when I was ignorant of it?

Socrat. You speak better than you think; but can you then precisely assign me the time, when you believed you did not know what was just and unjust? Let us see; was it the last year that you sought for the knowledge of this, being thoroughly convinced of your ignorance in this matter? Or did you then think you knew it? Tell the truth, that our conversation may not appear vain and trifling.

Alcib. The last year I believed I knew it.

Socrat. And did you not think the same, three, four, or five years ago?

Alcib. Yes.

Socrat. And before that time you were no more than a child, were you?

Alcib. Very true.

Socrat. And at that time when you were but a child, I am very sure you thought you knew it.

Alcib. How are you so sure of that?

Socrat. Because during your childhood, when you were with your masters and elsewhere, and * when you played

* See what Alcibiades did one day as he was playing at dice, as it is reported by Plutarch in the beginning of his life.

at dice, or any other play, I have very often observed you did not hesitate to determine what was just or unjust; and to tell the first of your playfellows that offended you, with a great deal of plainness and assurance, that he was base and unfair, and did you a great deal * of injustice. Is not this true?

Alcib. What should I have said then, do you think, when any injustice was done me?

Socrat. If you were ignorant that what was offered you was unjust, you might then have asked what you should have done.

Alcib. But I was not at all ignorant of that; for I very well knew the injustice that was done me.

Socrat. By this you see then, that when you were but a child, you thought you knew what was just and unjust.

Alcib. I thought I knew it; and so I really did.

Socrat. At what time did you find this out? for it was not when you thought you knew it.

Alcib. No, doubtless.

Socrat. At what time then do you think you were ignorant of it? Consider: reckon. I am much afraid you will not be able to find that time.

Alcib. Indeed, Socrates, I cannot give you an account of it.

Socrat. Then you have not found out of yourself the knowledge of what is just or unjust.

Alcib. So it seems, Socrates.

Socrat. You just now acknowledged that you had not learned it of others neither: and if you have neither found it out yourself, nor learnt it of others, how came you to know it? whence had it you?

Alcib. But perhaps I mistook myself, and did not answer you well, when I told you I had found it out myself.

Socrat. How did you learn it, then?

Alcib. I learned it as others do.

Socrat. Then we are to begin again: tell me of whom you learned it?

Alcib. I learned it of the people.

---

* When children tricked one another in their play, the ordinary term they used at Athens was ἀδικεῖς, you do me injustice; or, as we say, you do me wrong. There is a very express instance of it in Aristophanes' Clouds. *M. Le Fevre.*

Socrat. Now you quote a bad master.

Alcib. What! are not the people capable of teaching it?

Socrat. So far from that, that they are not capable of teaching one to judge right * of a game at tables; and that is much less important and less difficult than to understand justice : don't you think so as well as I?

Alcib. Yes, without doubt.

Socrat. And if they know not how to teach you things of little or no consequence, how should they teach you things of this importance and solidity.

Alcib. I am of your mind : yet the people are capable of teaching a great many things much more solid than any thing that belong to this play.

Socrat. What are those?

Alcib. Our language, for instance : I learned that only of the people; I cannot name you any one single master I had for it; I am altogether obliged to the people for it, whom yet you account so bad a master.

Socrat. This is a very different case. † In this the people are a very excellent master; and we have always reason to apply ourselves to them on this account.

Alcib. Why?

Socrat. Because they have every thing that the best masters ought to have.

Alcib. Why, what have they?

Socrat. Ought not they who would teach others any thing, first to know it well themselves?

Alcib. Who doubts it?

Socrat. Ought not they who know any thing well, to agree about what they know, and never dispute about it; for if they should dispute about it, would you believe them to be well instructed in it? and could they be able to teach it to others?

Alcib. By no means.

* This play was neither our draughts, nor chess; but a more philosophical game : for it taught the motions of the heavens, the course of the sun, that of the moon, the eclipses, &c. Plato says, in his Phædrus, it was invented by the Egyptians.

† This was true at Athens especially, where all the citizens speaking prefectly well, and there being no different use of words, as now-r-days among us, the people were an excellent master for the ground of the language. Therefore, Aristophanes says, the first corner was a child's master.

Socrat. Do you see the people disagree about what a stone and a stick is? Ask all our citizens that question, they will answer you alike: and when they go about to take up a stone or a stick, they will all run to the same thing; and so of the rest. For I understand this is what you mean by knowing the language; all our citizens constantly agree about this, both with one another, and with themselves. Of all our Greek cities, there is not one that disputes about the signification and use of words. So that the people are very good to teach us the tongue; and we cannot do better than to learn of them: but if instead of desiring to learn what a horse is, we would know what a good horse is, would the people, do you think, be capable of informing us?

Alcib. No, certainly.

Socrat. For one certain sign that they do not know it, and that they know not how to teach it, is, that they cannot agree about it among themselves. In like manner, if we desire to know, not what a man is, but what a sound or unsound man is; would the people be in a condition to teach us this?

Alcib. Still less than the other.

Socrat. And when you should see them agree so little among themselves, would you not judge them to be very bad instructors?

Alcib. Without any difficulty.

Socrat. And do you think the people agree better with themselves. or others, about what is just and unjust?

Alcib. No, indeed, Socrates.

Socrat. You believe then they agree least of all about that?

Alcib. I am thoroughly convinced of it.

Socrat. Have you ever seen or read, that to maintain that a thing is sound or unsound, men have taken up arms against each other, and knocked one another on the head?

Alcib. What a folly must that be!

Socrat. Well, if you have not seen it, at least you have read, that this has happened to maintain that a thing is just or unjust. For you have read Homer's Odyssey and Iliad.

Alcib. Yes, certainly.

Socrat. Is not the difference men have always had about

justice and injustice, the foundation of those poems? Was it not this difference that caused so many battles and slaughters between the Greeks and Trojans? Was it not this that made Ulysses undergo so many dangers, and so much toil, and that ruined Penelope's lovers?

Alcib. You say right.

Socrat. Was it not this same difference that destroyed many Athenians, Lacedemonians, and Bœotians, at the famous * battle of Tanagra, and after that again at the † battle of Coronea, where your father was killed?

Alcib. Who can deny this?

Socrat. Shall we then dare to say, the people know a thing well, about which they dispute with so much animosity, that they are carried to the most fatal extremities?

Alcib. No, certainly.

Socrat. Very good! and yet are not these the masters you cite, when at the same time you acknowledge their ignorance?

Alcib. I confess it.

Socrat. What probability then is there that you should know what is just and unjust, about which you appear so uncertain and fluctuating; and which you confess you have neither learned of others, nor found out yourself?

Alcib. According to what you say, there is no probability of it at all.

Socrat. How! according to what I say? You speak not right, Alcibiades; say, rather, it is according to what you say yourself.

Alcib. What! is it not you that say, I know nothing at all of what belongs to justice or injustice?

Socrat. No, indeed.

Alcib. Who then? is it I?

Socrat. Yes, it is yourself.

Alcib. How so?

Socrat. I will tell you how so; and you will agree with

* This great battle was fought the last year of the eightieth Olympiad. The Athenian Captain who gained it was named Myronides. Socrates was then twelve years of age, or thereabout.—*M. Le Fevre.*

† This battle of Coronea was fought the second year of the eighty-third Olympiad. Here the brave Tolmides was killed: after which the Athenians were driven out of Bœotia. Socrates was then twenty-two years of age. This battle of Coronea has often, through mistake, been confounded with that of Cheronea.—*M. Le Fevre.*

me. If I should ask you which is the greatest number, One or two? you would immediately answer, Two. And if I should again ask you, how much greater this number is than the other? you would likewise answer, that it is greater by one.

Alcib. Very true.

Socrat. Which of us two would it be then that would say two is more than one? Would it be I?

Alcib. No, I should say it.

Socrat. For it was I that asked, and you that answered. Is it not the same thing in the present question?

Alcib. That is certain.

Socrat. If I should ask you, what letters compose Socrates's name, and you should tell them me one after another; which of us two would tell them?

Alcib. I should do it without doubt.

Socrat. For in a discourse which is spent in questions and answers, he that asks never affirms, but always he that answers. It is I that have asked you, and it is you that have answered: it is you therefore that have affirmed the things you have said.

Alcib. This must be granted.

Socrat. It is yourself that have said that the fine Alcibiades, the son of Clinias, not knowing what is just and unjust, and yet thinking he knows it very well, is going to the assembly of the Athenians, to give them his advice about such things as he knows nothing of. Is it not so?

Alcib. It is even so.

Socrat. One may then apply to you, Alcibiades, that saying of Euripides; "It is thyself that has named it." For it is not I that have spoken it, but yourself; and you are to blame to charge it on me.

Alcib. You have reason.

Socrat. Believe me, Alcibiades, it is a wild enterprise to have a mind to go teach the Athenians that which you do not know yourself, and about which you have neglected to inform yourself.

Alcib. I fancy, Socrates, the Athenians, and all the rest of the Greeks, very rarely examine in their council, what is most just or unjust; for they are satisfied that is very evident. And therefore, without amusing themselves with this vain inquiry, they only consider what is most advan-

tageous and useful: and utility and justice are very
different things; since there have always been people in
the world that have found themselves very prosperous in
the commission of great injustice; and others who have
succeeded very ill in the exercise of justice.

Socrat. What!do you * think then, that if what is useful and what is just are very different, as you say they are
you know what is useful to men, and why it is so?

Alcib. What should hinder me, Socrates; unless you
would ask me of whom I learned this too? or how I
found it out myself?

Socrat. Is your proceeding just, Alcibiades, supposing
what you say is not right, as that may very well be; and
that it is very easy to refute you by the same reasons
which I have already employed? You would have new
proofs, and fresh demonstrations, and treat the former as
old clothes, which you are not willing to wear any longer.
You are still for having something entirely new: but for
my part, without following you in your stragglings and
escapes, I shall ask you, as I have already done, whence
you came to know what utility is? and who was your in-
structor? In a word, I ask you all I have asked you
before. It is very certain you will answer me too after the
same manner you have done, and that you will not be
able to shew me either that you have learned of others to
know what is useful, or that you have found it out yourself. But, because you are very nice, and do not love to
hear the same thing twice, I am willing to drop this question, whether you know what is useful to the Athenians
or no. But if what is just and what is useful are one and
the same thing; Or if they are very different, as you say;
why have you not proved it to me? Prove it me, either
by interrogating me, as I have dealt with you; or in making me a fine discourse, which may set the matter in a
clear light.

Alcib. But, Socrates, I know not whether I am capable
of speaking before you.

* If what is useful, and what is just, were different things, yet if
one knew what is useful, one might also know what is just: for we
know contraries by their contraries. But they are not different, and
Socrates is going to prove it. Alcibiades knows no more what is
useful than what is just.

Socrat. My dear Alcibiades, imagine me to be the assembly; suppose me to be the people. When you are among them, must you not endeavour to persuade every one of them?

Alcib. Yes.

Socrat. And when a man knows a thing well, is it not equal to him to demonstrate to this and that person one after another, or to prove it to divers persons all at once? as one that teaches reading or arithmetic, can equally instruct one or more scholars together.

Alcib. That is certain.

Socrat. And consequently, of whatsoever you are capable of persuading many, you may very easily persuade one single person. But of what can a man persuade others? Is it not of that which he knows himself?

Alcib. Without doubt.

Socrat. What other difference is there between an orator that speaks to a multitude of people, and a man that discourses with his friend in familiar conversation; but that the former persuades a great number of people at once, and the latter persuades but one?

Alcib. It is likely there may be no other difference.

Socrat. Come then: since he who is capable of proving what he knows to many, is by a much stronger reason capable of proving it to one single person; display here all your eloquence to me, and endeavour to shew me that what is just is not always useful.

Alcib. You are very urgent, Socrates.

Socrat. I am so urgent, that I will presently prove to you the contrary of that which you refuse to prove to me.

Alcib. Do so.

Socrat. Only answer me.

Alcib. Ha! nothing but questions: let me entreat you to speak yourself alone.

Socrat. What, are you not willing to be convinced?

Alcib. Yes, with all my heart.

Socrat. When you yourself shall grant, and affirm to me, that what I advance is true, will you not be convinced?

Alcib. I think I shall.*

* Alcibiades is afraid of Socrates's questions; which shews this to be the best method to convince and refute.

Socrat. Answer me then; and if you yourself do not say that what is just is always useful, never believe any man living that shall tell you so.

Alcib. Agreed; I am ready to answer you, for I shall receive no damage by it.

Socrat. You are a prophet, Alcibiades; but tell me, do you think there are some just things which are useful, and others which are not so?

Alcib. Yes, certainly.

Socrat. Do you think too that some of them are comely and honourable, and others quite the contrary?

Alcib. How do you say?

Socrat. I ask you, for instance, if a man who does an action that is shameful, does an action that is just?

Alcib. I am very far from such a thought.

Socrat. You believe then that whatsoever is just is comely.

Alcib. I am entirely convinced of that.

Socrat. But is every thing that is comely and honourable, good? or do you think there are some comely and honourable things that are good, and others that are evil?

Alcib. For my part, Socrates, I think there are some honourable things that are evil.

Socrat. And by consequence that there are some shameful things that are good?

Alcib. Yes.

Socrat. See if I understand you well. It has often happened in battles, that one man in attempting to succour his friend, or relation, has received a great many wounds, or has been killed; and another, by abandoning his relation or friend, has saved his life: is not this your meaning?

Alcib. It is the very thing I would say.

Socrat. The succour a man gives to his friend is a comely and honourable thing, in that he endeavours to save one whom he is obliged to save: and is not this what we call valour?

Alcib. Yes.

Socrat. And this very succour is an evil thing, in that it is the cause of a man's receiving wounds, or of being killed?

Alcib. Yes, without doubt.

Socrat. * But is not valour one thing, and death another?

Alcib. Yes, certainly.

Socrat. This succour then that a man gives to his friend is not at the same time an honourable and an evil thing ⸪ the same respect.

Alcib. So I think.

Socrat. But observe, if that which renders this action comely, is not that which also renders it good; for you have yourself acknowledged that in respect of valour this action was comely. Let us now examine whether valour is good or an evil: and I will shew you the way to make his examination aright. Do you desire for yourself goods r evils?

Alcib. Goods, without doubt.

Socrat. And the greatest?

Alcib. Yes, you may be sure of it.

Socrat. And you would not suffer any one to deprive a of them :

Alcib. Why should I suffer that?

Socrat. What do you think of valour? at what rate do value it? Is there any good in the world for which would be deprived of it?

lcib. No, not life itself. What, to be a coward! I ld a thousand times rather choose to die.

crat. Then cowardice seems to you the greatest of ils?

cib. Yes.

rat. And more to be feared than death itself?

ib. Most certainly.

rat. Are not life and valour the contraries to death wardice?

ib. Who doubts it?

at. You desire the former, and by no means wish latter; is it not because you find those very good, se very evil?

. Yes, doubtless.

at. You have yourself acknowledged, that the suc-

ates means, that valour and death being two very different is ridiculous to judge of one by the other: but each of them be examined by itself. The former of these is the thing bate, and not the latter. This is extremely ingenious; and s did not expect such a very quick repartee.

cour a man gives to his friend in battle is a comely and
honourable action; if it be considered with respect to
the good that is in it, which is valour.

Alcib. I have acknowledged it.

Socrat. And that it is an evil action, when considered
with respect to the evil that attends it; that is, wounds
and death.

Alcib. I confess it.

*Socrat.** Then it hence follows, that we ought to call
each action according to what it produces; we ought to
call it good, if good springs from it; and evil, if evil arise
out of it.

Alcib. So it seems to me.

Socrat. Is not an action comely in that it is good, and
shameful in that it is evil?

Alcib. That is beyond contradiction.

Socrat. When you say then that the succour a man
gives his friend in a battle is a comely action, and at the
same time an evil action, it is as if you should say, it is
evil though it be good.

Alcib. Indeed, I think what you say is true.

Socrat. Then there is nothing comely and honourable
which is evil, so far as it is comely and honourable; nor
is any thing which is shameful good, so far as it is shameful.

Alcib. So I think.

Socrat. Let us seek for another proof of this truth. Are
not all that do good actions happy? Can they be happy,
unless it be by the possession of good? Is not this possession of good, the fruit of a good life? And consequently, is not happiness necessarily for them that do
good actions.

Alcib. Who can deny it?

Socrat.† Then happiness is a comely and honourable
thing. Hence it follows that what is comely and what is
good are never two different things, as we just now agreed;
and that whatsoever we take to be comely, we shall also
take to be good, if we look narrowly into it.

---

* This maxim is false in Alcibiades' sense, but very true in that of
Socrates; for nothing can ever spring from a good action, but good;
as nothing but evil can spring from an evil one.

† And consequently happiness cannot be the fruit of an ill life and
of ill actions.

Alcib. This is absolutely necessary.

Socrat. What do you say then, is that which is good useful, or not?

Alcib. Yes, it is useful.

Socrat. Do you remember what we said when we spoke of justice, and about what we agreed?

Alcib. I think we agreed that all men that do just actions, must needs do what is comely and honourable.

Socrat. Then that which is comely is good?

Alcib. Yes.

Socrat. Then that which is good is useful?

Alcib. That is certain.

Socrat. And consequently whatsoever is just is useful?

Alcib. So it seems.

Socrat. Take good notice that it is yourself who affirm these truths; for I, for my part, only ask questions.

Alcib. I acknowledge it.

Socrat. If any one then thinking he well understood the nature of justice, should go into the assembly of the Athenians, or Parthians if you please, (to lay the scene more remote) and should tell them he certainly knows that just actions are sometimes evil, would not you laugh at him who have just now granted and acknowledged that justice and utility are one and the same thing?

Alcib. I solemnly protest to you, Socrates, that I know not what I say, nor where I am; for these things appear to me sometimes one way and sometimes another, according as you interrogate me.

Socrat. Do not you know the cause of this disorder?

Alcib. No, I know nothing at all of it.

Socrat. And if any one should ask you if you have three or four hands, do you think you should answer sometimes after one manner and sometimes after another? or would you not answer him always after the same manner?

Alcib. Though I begin to be diffident of myself, yet I think I should always answer the same thing.

Socrat. And is not this because you know very well you have but two eyes and two hands?

Alcib. I think so.

Socrat. Since then you answer so differently whether or no about the same thing, it is a certain sign that you are ignorant of it.

Alcib. So one would think.

Socrat. You confess then that your thoughts are uncertain and fluctuating about what is just and unjust, honourable or dishonourable, good or evil, useful or the contrary. And is it not evident from hence, that this uncertainty springs only from your ignorance?

Alcib. It is evident.

Socrat. Then it is a certain maxim, that the mind is always fluctuating and uncertain about every thing it does not know?

Alcib. It cannot be otherwise.

*Socrat.** But do you know how to mount up to heaven?

Alcib. No, I protest.

Socrat. Are you in any doubt, or does your mind fluctuate about this?

Alcib. Not in the least.

Socrat. Do you know the reason of this, or would you have me tell it you?

Alcib. Tell it me.

Socrat. It is because as you do not know how to mount up to heaven, so you do not think you know it neither.

Alcib. How is that?

Socrat. Let you and I examine this. When you are ignorant of a thing, and you know you are ignorant of it, are you uncertain and fluctuating about this? For example, about the art of cookery—do not you know you are ignorant of it? Do you then amuse yourself in reasoning about the manner of dressing meat, and speak sometimes one way, and sometimes another? do not you rather suffer the cook to take his own way?

Alcib. Yes, certainly.

Socrat. And if you were on board a ship, would you concern yourself to give advice to turn the helm to the right or left? and when you do not understand the art of navigation, would you speak about it sometimes after one fashion, and sometimes after another? Would you not rather be quiet, and leave the pilot to steer?

Alcib. To be sure I should leave that to him.

* After he had shewn Alcibiades that ignorance is the cause of all the errors of mankind, he goes about to prove to him, that men ought not to be accused of ignorance in general, for if one kind of it is evil, there is another kind good, and this he maintains very solidly.

Socrat. Then you are never fluctuating and uncertain
about things you do not know, provided you know that
you don't know them?

Alcib. So it seems.

Socrat. By this then you very well discern that all the
faults we commit proceed only from this sort of ignorance,
which makes us think we know that of which we are indeed
ignorant.

Alcib. How do you say?

Socrat. I say that which induces us to attempt a thing,
is the thought we have that we know how to do it; for
when we are convinced that we do not know it, we leave
to others.

Alcib. That is certain.

Socrat. Thus they who are under this last sort of ignorance never commit any fault, because they leave to others
the care of such things as they know not how to do themselves.

Alcib. That is true.

Socrat. Who are they then that commit faults? It is
not they that know things.

Alcib. No, certainly.

Socrat. Seeing it is neither they that know things, nor
they who while they are ignorant of them, know that they
are ignorant; it necessarily follows, that it is they who
while they are ignorant of them, yet think they know
them: can it be any others?

Alcib. No, it is only they.

Socrat. Well, then, this must be the ignorance which is
hurtful, and the cause of all evils.

Alcib. True.

Socrat. And when this ignorance happens to be about
things of very great consequence, is it not very pernicious
and very shameful?

Alcib. It cannot be denied.

Socrat. But can you name me any thing that is of
more consequence than what is just, what is honourable,
what is good, and what is useful?

Alcib. No, certainly.

Socrat. Is it not about these things that you yourself
are fluctuating and uncertain? Is not this uncertainty a sure sign, as we have said already, not only that

you are ignorant of these things that are so great and important, but also that while you are ignorant of them, you think you know them?

Alcib. I am afraid this is but too true.

Socrat. Oh, Alcibiades! in what a deplorable condition then are you! * I dare not mention it, yet seeing we are alone, it is necessary I should tell it you. My dear Alcibiades, you are under a very shameful kind of ignorance, as appears by your words, and your own testimony against yourself. And this is the reason you throw yourself with so much precipitancy into the government, before you are instructed in what belongs to it. But you are not the only person who has fallen under this unhappiness; it is common to you with the greatest part of those who have intermeddled with the affairs of the commonwealth. I can except but a small number. Nay, it may be your tutor Pericles is the only person that ought to be exempted.

Alcib. And, Socrates, it is likewise said he did not become so accomplished of himself; but that he had a great deal of conversation with many great men, such as Pythoclides, and Anaxagoras; and to this very day, as old as he is, he spends whole days with † Damon, to inform himself still more and more.

Socrat.‡ Did you ever see any one who perfectly knew a thing, and yet could not teach it another? Your reading-master taught you what he knew; and taught it whom he pleased. And you that have learned of him might teach it another. The same may be said of a music-master, and of a master of exercises.

---

* He does not mention it immediately. Alcibiades is not yet in a condition to bear the horror of it. But he will mention it at length when he has disposed and prepared the young man to receive his thunder clap.

† This is he of whom Plutarch speaks in the Life of Pericles; under the specious veil of music he hid his profession, which was to teach politics. The people perceived this, and banished him with the sentence of the ostracism.

‡ Upon what Alcibiades had just said, that Pericles had rendered himself accomplished by the conversation of philosophers and sophists, Socrates would intimate to him that this conversation was very useless for the acquiring of virtue, in which true accomplishment consists. And this he ingeniously proves by the example of Pericles himself, who had not been able to teach his own children any thing; a sure sign that he had learned no great matter of his sophists.

Alcib. This is certain.

Socrat. For the best sign that one knows a thing well, is to be in a condition to teach it others.

Alcib. So I think.

Socrat. But can you name me any one whom Pericles has accomplished? Let us begin with his own children.

Alcib. What does this prove, Socrates, if Pericles' children were blockheads?

Socrat. And your brother Clinias?

Alcib. A fine proof, indeed! you talk to me of a fool.

Socrat. If Clinias is a fool, and the children of Pericles are blockheads, how came it to pass that Pericles neglected such good natural parts as yours, and taught you nothing?

Alcib. I am the only cause of it myself, in not attending well to what he said to me.

Socrat. But among all the Athenians and strangers, whether freemen or slaves, can you name me one whom the conversation of Pericles has rendered more accomplished? as I will name you a Pythodorus, the son of Isolochus, and a Callias, the son of Calliades, who became great men in Zeno's school, at the expense of a hundred Minas.

Alcib. I cannot name you one.

Socrat. † That's very well; but what will you do with yourself, Alcibiades? will you continue as you are, or will you at last take some care of yourself?

Alcib. It is a general affair, Socrates, and concerns me more than others. For I understand all you say, and agree with you. Yes, all that concern themselves with the affairs of the republic, are a company of ignorant people, excepting a very small number.

Socrat. And what then?

Alcib. ‡ If they were men of great accomplishments, it would be necessary for one that should pretend to equal or

---

about £200. sterling.

.tes is not willing now to push on this question which he has whether virtue may be taught. The question is too general Il treat of it elsewhere; here he keeps close to his subject, to confound the pride of Alcibiades.

entiment of Alcibiades is that which still to this day ruins young men.

surpass them, to learn, and exercise himself, and after that to enter the lists as wrestlers do; but seeing they do not fail to intermeddle with government, though endued with very indifferent and common qualities, what need is there for a man to give himself so much trouble in learning and exercise? I am well assured, that with the assistance of nature alone, I shall excel them all.

Socrat. Ah, my dear Alcibiades, what have you now said? what sentiment is this so unworthy of that noble air, and all the other advantages which you possess?

Alcib. What do you mean, Socrates, when you speak thus?

Socrat. Alas! I am inconsolable, both on your account and my own, I have so great an affection for you, if——

Alcib. If what?

Socrat. If you think you have only such kind of people to contest with, and to surpass.

Alcib. Whom then would you have me strive to surpass?

Socrat. Again! Is this a question becoming a man of a great spirit?

Alcib. What do you mean? Are not these the only persons I have to deal with?

Socrat. If you were to guide a * man of war, which was to fight in a little time, would you be content if you were more expert in navigation than all the sailors you had on board you? Would you not rather propose to yourself to acquire all necessary qualities, and to surpass all the greatest pilots on the enemy's side, without measuring yourself as you do now with those of your own party, above whom you should endeavour to raise yourself to that degree, that they should not have so much as a thought of disputing any advantage with you, but finding themselves absolutely inferior to you, should only think of fighting under your command? These are the sentiments that should animate you, if you designed to do any thing great, and worthy. both of yourself and your country.

Alcib. Why, this is all I design.

Socrat. This must needs be a glorious thing indeed, Alcibiades, to be a braver man than our soldiers! Ought you not rather constantly to set the generals of our enemies

---

* An admirable lesson, which Socrates gives Alcibiades.

before your eyes, that you may excel them in capacity and greatness of courage ? And should you not study and labour to this end, always endeavouring to equal the greatest persons ?

Alcib. Who, then, are these great generals, Socrates?

Socrat. Do not you know our city is almost continually in war, either with the Lacedemonians, or with the * great king ?

Alcib. I know it.

Socrat. If then you think to put yourself at the head of the Athenians, you must also prepare yourself to receive the attacks of the † kings of Lacedemonia, and of the king of Persia.

Alcib. You may be in the right.

Socrat. No, alas ! no, my dear Alcibiades. ‡ You have only to think of excelling a Midias, who is so accomplished a man for feeding of quails, and others of the same rank, that seek to intrude themselves into the government; who by their stupidity and ignorance shew (as good women would say) that they have not yet quitted the slave, but retain him still under their long hair; and who with their barbarous language are come rather to corrupt the city by their servile flatteries, than to govern it. These are the people you must set before you without thinking of yourself; that when you are to engage in such great battles, you may go without having ever learned anything of what you ought to know, without being exercised and without making any preparation; in a word, that without having ever given yourself the least trouble, you go in this condition to put yourself at the head of the Athenians.

Alcib. Socrates, I believe all you say is true. Yet I think the generals of Lacedemonia, and of the king of Persia are like other generals.

* king of Persia.
† there were two at a time.
‡ Plutarch is of use to make us understand the bitter satire that is under these words, for he informs us that Alcibiades applied himself to feed quails, like this Midias; witness that which he let fly out of his bosom in an open place, and which was caught again by a master of a ship, named Antiochus, who had the favour of Alcibiades so far, insomuch that he left him the command of a fleet in his absence, which had like to have ruined the affairs of the Athenians.

Socrat. Ah, my dear Alcibiades, pray observe what an opinion that of yours is.

Alcib. Why so?

Socrat. * In the first place, which of these two opinions do you think will be most advantageous to you, and will engage you to conduct yourself with the greatest care; whether to form to yourself a great idea of those men, which may render them formidable, or to take them, as you do, for ordinary men, that have no advantage above you?

Alcib. Doubtless that of forming to myself a great idea of them.

Socrat. Do you think then it is an evil for you to conduct yourself with care?

Alcib. On the contrary, I am persuaded it will be a very great good.

Socrat. Then this opinion which you have conceived, already appears to be a very great evil.

Alcib. I confess it.

Socrat. But besides this it is false, and I will presently demonstrate this to you.

Alcib. How so?

Socrat. Whom do you account the best men; those who are of high birth, or such as are of mean extraction?

Alcib. Without doubt, those who are of high birth.

Socrat. And do not you think, they that have had as good education joined to their high birth, have every thing that is necessary for the perfection of virtue?

Alcib. That is certain.

Socrat. By comparing therefore our condition with theirs, let us see first of all if the kings of Lacedemonia, and the king of Persia, are of meaner birth than we: do not we know that the former descend from Hercules, and the latter from † Achemenes, and that Hercules and Achemenes descend from Jupiter?

Alcib. And does not our family, Socrates, descend from Eurysaces, and does not Eurysaces carry his line up as far as Jupiter?

---

* What Socrates is now going to say, is one of the finest things antiquity has left us.

† Achemenes, the son of Perseus.

Socrat. * And does not ours, my dear Alcibiades, if you take it that way, descend from Dedalus? And does not Dedalus likewise carry us back as far as Vulcan, Jupiter's son? But the difference between them and us is, that they re-ascend as far as Jupiter by a continual gradation of kings without any interruption: the former have been the kings of Argos and Lacedemonia, and the latter have always reigned in Persia, and have often possessed the throne of Asia, as they do now, whereas our ancestors were only private persons like us. And if to do honour to your ancestors you were obliged to shew Artaxerxes the country of Eurysaces, or that of Æacus, which is still more remote, what occasion of laughter would you not give him in pointing out to him two little† islands not much bigger than one's hand? Since then we are obliged to give place in point of birth, let us see if we are not like-wise inferior to them in respect of education. Have you ever been told what great advantages the Lacedemonian kings have in this, whose wives are kept publicly by the ephori, that they may be certain, as much as it is possible, that they produce no princes but of the race of Hercules? And the king of Persia is so far beyond the kings of Lacedemonia in this respect, that it has never yet been so much suspected that the queen could have a child that might be the king's son. Therefore she is not guarded; all guards she has are terror and majesty. When she is delivered of her first son, who is to succeed to the crown, the nations that are spread over that great empire cele-brate his birth; after which, that day is annually one of their greatest festivals; in all the provinces of Asia there is then nothing but sacrifices and feasts; whereas when we are born, my dear Alcibiades, that expression of the comic poet may be applied to us:

The news scarce to our nearest neighbours comes.

When the young prince is weaned, he is not left in the hands of women, but is committed to the care of the most virtuous eunuchs of the court, whose business it is to form and fashion his body, that he may be brought to the best

† this is a piece of raillery of Socrates, as we shall see when we come to his Eutyphron.
† Ægina and Salamina.

shape that can be; and this employ brings them abundance of honour. When the prince is seven years old, he is put into the hands of the gentlemen of the horse, who begin to carry him a hunting: at fourteen years of age, he comes under the charge of those who are called the king's preceptors: these are the four greatest lords, and the most accomplished men of all Persia; they are taken in the vigour of their age; one passes for the most learned, another for the most just, the third for the wisest, and the fourth for the most valiant. The first teaches him the magic of * Zoroaster the son of Oromazus, in which is comprehended all the worship of the gods; he teaches him likewise the laws of the kingdom, and all the duties of a good king. The second teaches him always to speak the truth, though against himself. The third instructs him not to suffer himself at any time to be overcome by his passions; that he may always maintain his freedom and his royalty, in having constantly an absolute dominion over himself, as well as over his people: and the fourth teaches him not to fear either dangers or death; because if he should become timorous, from a king he would degenerate into a slave. Whereas, Alcibiades, for your part what preceptor have you had? Pericles left you in the hands of Zopyrus, a vile Thracian slave, who was indeed unfit for every thing besides, because of his old age. I would here recount to you all the consequent matters relating to the education of your antagonists, but that I should be too long; and the specimen I have given you is sufficient to make you easily judge of the rest. † No person took care of you at your birth more than of any other Athenian; nobody takes any pains about your education, unless you have some one who concerns himself with it, because he sincerely loves ‡ you. And if you consider the riches of the Persians, the magnificence of their habits, the prodigious expense they make in perfumes

* Zoroaster was a Magus, and king of Bactriana; he wrote divers volumes on magic, which contained religion, physic, and astrology. He lived in the time of Ninus, and of Noah.

† It is certain the Athenians gave their children no governors, but slaves, or such as were enfranchised; this appears by the Greek comedies which are left us, and by the comedies of Plautus and Terence. *M. Le Fevre.*

‡ Socrates means himself.

and essences, the multitude of slaves that surround them,
all their luxury, finery, and politeness, you will see yourself
so little, that you will be quite ashamed of yourself. Will
you but cast your eyes on the temperance of the Lacedemonians, on their modesty, easiness, sweetness, magnanimity, their good disposition of mind under all the accidents of life, their valour, firmness, and constancy in
labours, their noble emulation, and love of glory; in all
these great qualities you will find yourself a child in comparison of them. Again, if you would have us take notice
of their riches, and think yourself something under this
head; I am willing to speak to it, to make you remember
who you are, and whence you came: there is no comparison between us and the Lacedemonians; they are
abundantly more wealthy. Shall any of us dare to compare our lands with those of Sparta, and Mesene; which
are much larger and better, and maintain an infinite number of slaves, without counting the Helotes? Who can
number that excellent race of horses, and those other sorts
of cattle which feed in the pastures of Mesene? whereas
we inhabit a dry and barren country. But I pass by all these
things. Would you speak of gold and silver? I tell you,
all Greece together has not near so much as Lacedemonia
alone; for the money of all Greece, and very often that of the
barbarians too, has for several ages gone into Lacedemonia,
and never come out again. So that one might very well
say, in allusion to what is said by the fox to the lion in
Æsop's fables, " I see the track of all the money that is
gone into Lacedemonia, but I see no track that signifies
there is any gone out from thence." It is certain, the commons of Lacedemonia are richer than any other commons
of Greece, and the kings are richer than all the rest of the
Lacedemonians put together; for these pay their kings
immense taxes, which extremely augment their revenues.
But if the wealth of the Lacedemonians appears so great in
comparison of that of the other Greeks, it is nothing when
compared with that of the king of Persia. I heard a man
worthy of credit, who had been one of the ambassa-
dors that was sent to that prince, say, he had travelled a
long way in a very fine and fruitful country, which the inhabitants called the Queen's Girdle; and that he made
another long journey in another country as pleasant,

which they called the Queen's Veil; and that he passed
through a great many other fine provinces that were destined only to furnish that princess with clothes, and had
their several names from the things they were to provide.
So that if any should go, and say to Amastris, the wife of
Xerxes, the king's mother; "There is at Athens a citizen
whose whole estate is not above three hundred acres of
land, which he possesses in the town of Erquies, and who
is the son of Dinomache; whose clothes and jewels all together are scarce worth fifty * minæ; this citizen is preparing to make war with your son." What do you think
she would say? "This man founds the success of his
designs on his application, experience, and great wisdom;
for these are the only things that make the Greeks
esteemed in the world." But if one should say to her,
"This Alcibiades is a young man, not yet twenty years of
age, who is very ignorant, has no manner of experience,
and who, when a certain friend of his, whom he passionately loves, represents to him, that he ought above all
things to cultivate himself, to labour, meditate, to exercise
himself; and after having acquired the capacity that is
necessary, might engage in war with the great King; will
not believe a word of the matter, and says he is fit enough
for this as he is already." How great would be the wonder
of this princess? Would she not ask, "On what then
does this young giddy-brains depend?" And if we should
tell her, "he depends on his beauty, his fine shape, his
nobility, and fortunate birth;" would she not take us for
fools, considering the great advantages the kings of Persia
have in all this above us? But, without going any higher,
do you think Lampyto, the daughter of Leotichydas, the
wife of Archidamus, and mother of Agis, who were all
born kings of Lacedemonia, would be less astonished, if
one should tell her, that as ill educated as you have been,
you do not scruple to trouble your head with a design of
making war with her son? Alas! is it not a horrible
shame, that the very women among our enemies know
better than we what we ought to be, to undertake to make
war with them with any likelihood of success? Follow my
advice then, my dear Alcibiades, and obey the precept

* About £100. sterling.

which is written on the gate of the temple of Delphos,
" Know thyself." For the enemies you have to deal with
ire such as I represent them to you, and not such as yo_
magine them to be. The only means of conquering them
re application and skill. If you renounce these so neces-
ary qualities, renounce the glory too, of which you are so
assionately ambitious.

Alcib. Can you then explain to me, Socrates, how I
ight to cultivate myself? For no man whatever speaks
ore truly to me than you.

Socrat. I can, without doubt, but this does not respect
u alone; this concerns us all, how many soever we are.
ought to seek the means of making ourselves better:
I I speak no more on your account than on my own,
o have no less need of instruction than you, and have
y one advantage above you.

llcib. What is that?

ocrat. It is this: my tutor is wiser and better than
cles, who is yours.

lcib. Who is this tutor of yours?

crat. It is God, who never permitted me to speak to
before this day : and it is in pursuance of his inspira-
that I tell you, that you will never arrive at the
tation you desire, but by me.

cib. You jest, Socrates.

crat. It may be so. But, in fine, it is still a great
, that we have great need to take care of ourselves.
en need this, and we yet more than others.

ib. You speak no untruth, so far as it concerns me,
tes.

rat. Nor in what concerns me neither.

ib. What shall we do then?

at. Now is the time to throw off laziness and softness.

b. It is very true, Socrates.

at. Come then, let us examine what it is we would
. Tell me, Would we not render ourselves * very

---

there are many different sorts of goodness, and upon this
is going to enlarge. For the word good in Greek signifies,
ished, excellent, improved in any art or science, or virtuous.
word evil, by the rule of contraries, has as many significations.
ark is necessary for the understanding of what follows.
                                                        M. Le Fevre.

Alcib. Yes.

Socrat. In what sort of virtue?

Alcib. In that virtue that renders a man good and fit.

Socrat. For what?

Alcib. For business.

Socrat. What business? The managing of a horse? It cannot be for that, for that belongs to equerries. Is it Navigation? nor that neither, for that belongs to pilots. What business is it then?

Alcib. The business in which our best Athenians are employed.

Socrat. What do you mean by our best Athenians? Are they the prudent or imprudent?

Alcib. The prudent.

Socrat. So that, according to you, when a man is prudent in any thing, he is good and fit for that thing; and the imprudent are very bad for it.

Alcib. Without doubt.

Socrat. A shoemaker has all the prudence necessary for making shoes. And therefore he is good for that.

Alcib. It is right.

Socrat. But he is very imprudent for making of clothes, and consequently is a bad tailor.

Alcib. That is certain.

Socrat. That same man then is both good and bad?

Alcib. So it seems.

Socrat. It follows from this principle, that your Athenians whom you call good and honest men are bad too.

Alcib. That is not what I mean.

Socrat. What do you mean then by the good Athenians?

Alcib. They that know how to govern.

Socrat. To govern what? Horses?

Alcib. No.

Socrat. Men?

Alcib. Yes.

Socrat. What sick men, pilots, or mowers?

Alcib. No, none of these.

Socrat. Whom then? those that do something, or those who do nothing?

Alcib. Those that do something.

Socrat. Those that do what? Endeavour to explain yourself, and make me understand your meaning.

Alcib. Those that live together, and make use one of another, as we live in cities.

Socrat. According to you then, the good Athenians are such as know how to command such men as make use of men.*

Alcib. I mean so.

Socrat. Is it those who know how to command the masters of gallies, who make use of rowers?

Alcib. No.

Socrat. Because this belongs to pilots. Is it then those at know how to command the players on the flute, who ake use of musicians and dancers? No, doubtless, for s belongs to the masters of the choirs.

Alcib. That is certain.

Socrat. What do you mean then by knowing how to ommand such men as make use of other men?

Alcib. I mean, it is to command men that live together ler the same laws and polity.

Socrat. What is this art then that teaches to command n? If I should ask you what is the art which teaches ommand all the rowers of the same vessel, what answer ld you give me?

Alcib. That it is the pilot's art.

Socrat. And if I should ask you what is the art that es to command musicians and dancers?

Alcib. I would answer you, it is the art of the masters e choirs.

Socrat. How then do you call this art, which teaches to and those who make the same politic body, and live er under the same government?

Alcib. It is the art of giving good counsel.

Socrat. How! what then is the art of pilots the art of bad counsel? Is it not their design to give good?

Alcib. Yes, certainly, to save those that are in the ship.

Socrat. You say very well: of what good counsel then speak? and to what does it tend?

Alcib. It tends to preserve the city, and to make it policied.

Socrat. But what is it that preserves cities, and makes etter policied? What is it that ought or ought not

politicians command the magistrates, and these the rest of ons.

to be in them? And if you should ask me what it is that ought or ought not to be in a body to make it sound and in good health, I would immediately answer you, That that which ought to be in it, is health; and that which ought not to be in it, is sickness: do not you think so as well as I?

Alcib. I think the very same.

Socrat. And if you should ask me the same thing of the eye, I should answer you after the same manner, That the eye is in a good condition, when it has all that is necessary for sight, and when nothing hinders it from seeing. And the very same of the ears, that they are very well, when they have every thing they need to hear well, and no disposition to deafness.

Alcib. True.

Socrat. And now for a city, what is it which by its presence or absence makes it to be in a better condition, better policied, and better governed?

Alcib. I think, Socrates, it is when amity is well established among the citizens, and hatred and division are banished out of the city.

Socrat. What do you call amity? is it concord or discord?

Alcib. It is concord certainly.

Socrat. What art is that which makes cities accord; for example, about numbers?

Alcib. It is arithmetic.

Socrat. And is it this that makes particular persons accord one with another, and each one with himself?

Alcib. Without doubt.

Socrat. And how do you call that art which makes each one agree with himself about the length of a span or cubit? Is it not the art of measuring?

Alcib. Yes, doubtless.

Socrat. Then cities and particular persons accord by means of this art. And is it not the same thing about weight?

Alcib. The very same.

Socrat. And what is that concord of which you speak, in what does it consist, and what is the art that produces it? Is the concord of a city the same that makes a particular person accord with himself and others?

Alcib. I think so.

Socrat. What is it? Do not be weary in answering me, but charitably instruct me.

Alcib. I think it is this amity and concord that makes parents agree with their children, one brother with another, and the wife with her husband.

Socrat. But do you think a husband can agree well with his wife, and that they will accord perfectly about the tapestry which she works, and he knows not how to make?

Alcib. No, certainly.

Socrat. Nor is there any need of it; for it is the women's work. No more is it possible that a woman should agree with her husband about the use of arms; for she knows not what belongs to it, this being a science which appertains only to men.

Alcib. It is true.

Socrat. You agree then that there are some sciences which are destined only for women, and others which are reserved for men.

Alcib. Who can deny it?

Socrat. It is not possible that women should accord with their husbands about all these sciences.

Alcib. That is certain.

Socrat. And consequently there will be no amity, seeing amity is nothing but concord.

Alcib. I am of your mind.

Socrat. So that when a woman does what she ought to do, she will not be loved by her husband; and when a husband does what he ought to do, he will not be loved by his wife.

Alcib. This is a certain consequence.

Socrat. Then that which makes cities well policied, is for every one to follow his own employment in them.

Alcib. However, Socrates, methinks ——

Socrat. How do you say? Can a city be well policied without having amity in it? Are we not agreed that it is by amity that a city is well regulated; and that otherwise there is nothing but disorder and confusion?

Alcib. But yet, methinks, it is this very thing that makes amity, namely, That every one mind his own business.

Socrat. You said the contrary but just now. But I

must endeavour to understand you; what do you say? That concord well established produces amity? What! can there be concord about things which some know, and others do not understand?

Alcib. That is impossible.

Socrat. When every one does what he ought to do, does every one do what is just, or what is unjust?

Alcib. A pretty question! every one then does what is just.

Socrat. Hence it follows, that when all the citizens do what is just, yet they cannot love one another.

Alcib. *The consequence is necessary.

Socrat. What then is this amity or concord, that can accomplish and make us capable of giving good counsel; so that we may be of the number of those whom you call your best citizens? for I cannot comprehend what it is, or in whom it is to be found. Sometimes it is to be found in certain persons, and sometimes it is not to be found in them, as it seems by your words.

Alcib. Socrates, I solemnly protest to you, I know not what I say myself; and have run a great risk in being a long time in an ill condition, without perceiving it.

Socrat. Do not be discouraged, Alcibiades, if you should not perceive in what condition you are till you are fifty years of age; it would be a difficult matter for you to recover yourself out of it, and to take care of yourself: but now, at your years, it is the fittest time for you to feel your distemper after the manner you do.

Alcib. But when a man feels his distemper, what must he do?

---

* This consequence is very certain; Alcibiades acknowledges it, but he does not yet understand the reason of it. I have given a hint of it in the Argument; but it is fit to explain Socrates' thought here at length. His design is to shew, that when men precisely do only their own business, they only take care of what belongs to themselves, and so limit themselves to the knowledge of particular things, and do not rise up to that of the essence of universal things, which is the only knowledge that produces union and concord; whereas the knowledge merely of particular things produces disorder and division. Therefore, to make concord reign in a state, it is not enough for every one to take care of what he has; he must take care of himself too. This care will teach him to love his neighbour as himself; and it is only this love which has God for its principle, that can produce concord and union.

Socrat. You need only answer to some questions, Alcibiades; which, if you do, I hope, by the help of God, both you and I shall become better than we are; at least, if my prophecy is to be believed.

Alcib. If there needs nothing but to answer you to bring it about, I will promise you your prophecy shall prove true.

Socrat. Come then; what is it to take care of one's self so, that when we think we take care of ourselves the most, may so happen to us without our knowledge, to take care of quite another thing? What must a man do to take care of himself? Does he take care of himself when he takes care of the things that belong to him?

Alcib. * I think so.

Socrat. How! does a man take care of his feet, when he takes care of the things that belong to his feet?

Alcib. I do not understand you.

Socrat. Do you know nothing that properly belongs to hand? To what part of the body do the rings appertain? is it not to the fingers?

Alcib. Yes, doubtless.

Socrat. And in like manner, the shoes belong to the

Alcib. Very true.

Socrat. Do we then take care of our feet when we take of our shoes?

Alcib. Indeed, Socrates, I do not yet understand you.

Socrat. What do you mean then by taking care of a ? Is it not to make it better than it was? What art then that makes our shoes better?

Alcib. It is the shoemaker's art.

Socrat. † It is by the shoemaker's art then that we take of our shoes: is it by the same art too that we take of our feet, or is it by some other art that we make et better?

Alcib. Without doubt that is done by another art.

cibiades answers according to the principles that are almost ly received. Men think they take care of themselves, when ke care of the things that belong to them, but they are grossly n: and Socrates is going to confound this error with great . That which is mine, is not myself.
Greece the shoemakers mended shoes as well as made them.

Socrat. Do not we make our feet better by another art, which meliorates the whole body? And is not this the gymnastic art?

Alcib. Yes, certainly.

Socrat. It is then by the gymnastic art that we take care of our feet; and by the shoemaker's art that we take care of the things that belongs to our feet. It is by the gymnastic art we take care of our hands; and by the goldsmith's art that we take care of the things that belong to our hands. It is by the gymnastic art that we take care of our bodies; and by the weaver's art, and many other arts, that we take care of the things that appertain to our bodies.

Alcib. This is beyond all doubt.

Socrat. And consequently the art by which we take care of ourselves, is not the same with that whereby we take care of the things that belong to us.

Alcib. So it seems.

Socrat. Hence it follows, that when you take care of the things that belong to you, you do not take care of yourself.

Alcib. That is certain.

Socrat. For it is not by the same art that we take care of ourselves and of the things that belong to us.

Alcib. I acknowledge it.

Socrat. By what art is it then that we take care of our selves?

Alcib. I cannot tell.

Socrat. We are already agreed, that it is not that by which we can make any of those things that belong to us better; but that by which we can meliorate ourselves.

Alcib. It is true.

Socrat. Can we know the art of making shoes better, if we do not first know what a shoe is? or the art of taking care of rings, if we do not know first what a ring is?

Alcib. No, that cannot be.

Socrat. Can we then know what art it is that makes us better, if we do not first know what we ourselves are?

Alcib. It is absolutely impossible.

Socrat. But is it a very easy thing to know one's self? And was it some ignorant person that wrote that trivial precept on the gate of Apollo's temple at Delphos? Or is it, on the contrary, a thing of great difficulty, and which is not given to every man?

Alcib. For my part, Socrates, I have often thought it was given to all men; and yet it has often seemed to me to be a thing of very great difficulty.

Socrat. But, Alcibiades, let it be easy or difficult, it is still certain, that when once we know it, we immediately and easily know what care we ought to take of ourselves: whereas while we are ignorant of it, we shall never come to the knowledge of the nature of this care.

Alcib. That is beyond all doubt.

Socrat. Come on then: by what means shall we find out the * essence of things to speak universally? By this shall soon find what we are ourselves: and if we are ignorant of this essence, we shall always be ignorant of ourselves.

Alcib. You say right.

Socrat. Follow me close then, I conjure you in the name of God: With whom are you now discoursing? Is it with some other person, or with me?

Alcib. No, it is with you.

Socrat. And I in like manner discourse with none but : it is Socrates that now speaks, and Alcibiades that hears.

Alcib. True.

Socrat. It is by using words that Socrates speaks: for to speak, and to use words, is one and the same thing.

Alcib. It is so, without doubt.

---

this universal essence of things, αὐτοτοαυτὸ, is the divine intelligence, the eternal idea, the only cause of beings: and the singular, αὐτοἑκαστον, is the thing formed on this idea. So that there two ways of knowing one's self; the first is to know the Divine essence, and to descend from that to the soul, by following the which the all-wise Creator had in creating it: and the other ly to know the soul as a being different from the body, and to convinced that that alone is the man. The first is the most perfect however, Socrates leaves this at present, and applies himself the second, which is more easy: but he afterwards resumes from the knowledge of the soul raises Alcibiades to the contemplation of the Eternal Idea, in which alone, as in the true light, a may perfectly see his soul, and all that belongs to it. The whole of Socrates is worthy the most solid theology.

Socrat. Are not he who uses a thing, and the thing which he uses, different ?

Alcib. How do you say?

Socrat. For example, a shoemaker who uses knives, lasts, and other tools, cuts with his knife, and is different from the knife with which he cuts. A man that plays on the harp, is not the same thing with the harp on which he plays.

Alcib. That is certain.

Socrat. This is what I asked you just now; whether he that uses a thing, and the thing he uses, always seem to you two different things?

Alcib. So they seem to me.

Socrat. * But the shoemaker does not only use his tools, but his hands too.

Alcib. That is beyond all doubt.

Socrat. He also uses his eyes.

Alcib. That is certain.

Socrat. We are agreed that he who uses a thing, is always different from the thing he uses.

Alcib. That is agreed between us.

Socrat. So that the shoemaker and the harper are some other thing than the hands and eyes, which they both use.

Alcib. That is plain.

Socrat. Man uses his body.

Alcib. Who doubts it ?

Socrat. That which uses a thing, is different from the thing which is used.

Alcib. Yes.

Socrat. Man then is a different thing from his body ?

Alcib. I believe it.

Socrat. What is man then?

Alcib. Indeed, Socrates, I cannot tell.

Socrat. You can at least tell me that man is that which uses the body.

Alcib. That is true.

Socrat. Is there any thing that uses the body besides the soul?

Alcib. No, nothing else,

---

* He designs to prove, that the body is no less an instrument of the soul, than all the other remoter instruments which it uses.

Socrat. It is that that governs.

Alcib. Most certainly.

Socrat. I believe there is no man but is forced to confess——

Alcib. What?

Socrat. That man is one of these three things, either the soul, or the body, or the compound of them both. Now we are agreed that man is that which commands the body.

Alcib. That we are.

Socrat. What is man then? Does the body command itself? No. For we have said it is the man that commands that. So that the body is not the man.

Alcib. So it seems.

Socrat. Is it then the compound that commands the body? and shall this compound be the man?

Alcib. That may be.

Socrat. Nothing less. For since one of them does not command, as we have already said, * it is impossible they should command together.

Alcib. It is very true.

Socrat. Seeing then neither the body, nor the compound soul and body are the man; it is absolutely necessary either that man be nothing at all, or that the soul alone be man.

Alcib. Most certainly.

Socrat. Shall I demonstrate to you yet more clearly that soul alone is the man?

Alcib. No, I protest, this is sufficiently proved.

Socrat. We have not yet sounded this truth with all the accuracy it deserves; but it is sufficiently proved, and that may serve. We shall sound it farther, and penetrate it when we have found out what we just now quitted, since it required a longer investigation.

Alcib. What is that?

Socrat. It is what we said but now; that it is necessary we should first seek to know the very essence of things, to know universally; instead of which, we have stopped to

besides that this is a contradiction, seeing that which does not command would then command; there is not a third thing for the two to command together. If the soul and the body both command, what is it that is under their command?

examine and know the essence of a particular thing; and perhaps that is sufficient. For we can find nothing that is more properly and precisely ourselves, than our souls.

Alcib. That is very certain.

Socrat. So then this is a principle very well established, that when you and I converse together, by making use of discourse, it is my soul that converses with yours. And this is what we said just now, that Socrates speaks to Alcibiades, by addressing words not to the body which is exposed to my eyes, but to Alcibiades himself, whom I do not see, that is, to his soul.

Alcib. This is evident.

Socrat. He then who requires us to know ourselves, requires us to know our souls.

Alcib. I believe it.

Socrat. He who knows his body only, knows that which belongs to him, but does not know himself. Thus, a physician as a physician, does not know himself, nor a wrestling-master as a wrestling-master, nor a husband-man as a husband-man. All persons of these professions, and those of the like nature, are so far from knowing themselves,* that they do not know particularly what belongs to them: and their art makes them adhere to what is yet more foreign to them than that which properly belongs to them. For they know only those things that appertain to the body, and by which they cure, and preserve it in health.

Alcib. All this is very true.

Socrat. If, therefore, it be a piece of wisdom to know one's self, there is no man of any of these professions who is wise by his art.

Alcib. I am of the same mind.

Scrat. † And it is for this reason all these arts appear vile and sordid, and consequently unworthy of a good man.

---

* Physicians and masters of exercise indeed apply themselves to know the body; but they know it only to a certain degree. For as Hippocrates says in his Treatise of the Ancient Art of Medicine, they content themselves with knowing what man is, with respect to what he eats and drinks, and to the exercises he performs: and what may occur to him from any of these things. So that they only know some certain qualities of matter, but not the essence of it. It is more easy to know the essence of the soul, than that of the body.

† The only art truly worthy of a good man, is that of knowing, and labouring to perfectionate himself.

Alcib. It is very true.

Socrat. Well then, to return to our principle, every man hat takes care of his body, takes care of that which belongs to him, and not of himself.

Alcib. I grant it.

Socrat. Every man that loves riches loves neither himlf, nor that which belongs to him, but loves a thing uich is yet more foreign to him, and which only respects it which belongs to him.

Alcib. I think so.

Socrat. Then, according to this principle one may m, that he who employs his care to heap up riches, s not manage his affairs well.

Alcib. It is most certainly so.

Socrat. If any one has been in love with the body of biades, that person has not been in love with Alcibiades, with one of those things that appertain to him.

Alcib. I am convinced of it.

Socrat. That person who is in love with Alcibiades, be one that is in love with his soul.

Alcib. That is a necessary consequence of your principle.

Socrat. And this is the reason that that person who oves your body, retires when the beauty of this body s to decay.

Alcib. It is true.

Socrat. But one that loves your soul never retires e you make any progress in virtue, and every day yourself still a better man.

Alcib. That is very likely.

Socrat. And this likewise is the reason that I am the erson that does not leave you, but continue constant le flower of your beauty is faded, and all your admi- retired.

Alcib. You very much oblige me, Socrates; and I en- u not to abandon me.

Socrat. Labour then with all your might to become every e and more beautiful.†

----

is passage ought to be translated. The Latin interpreters e a mistake here, not remembering ἕως, has often the sig- of the present time.—*M. Le Fevre.*
:autiful he means virtuous.

Alcib. I will labour to become so.

Socrat. As matters stand with you, it is easy to judge that Alcibiades, the son of Clinias, never had, nor has yet, more than one friend, and this faithful friend is the * lovely Socrates, the son of Sophroniscus and Phenareta.

Alcib. It is very true.

Socrat. But did you not tell me when I met you, that I was before you but a moment, and that you had a design to speak to me, to know why I was the only person that had not left you?

Alcib. I told you so, and it is true.

Socrat. You now know the reason of it; it is because I always loved you, and others only loved what belongs to you. The beauty of that which belongs to you begins to decay, whereas your own beauty begins to flourish. And if you do not suffer yourself to be corrupted by the people, and become more deformed, I will not forsake you as long as I live. But I very much fear, since you are so much † in love with the applause of the people, that you will destroy yourself by this unhappy disposition, as it has been the lot of a great many of our best Athenians. For the people of the magnanimous ‡ Erectheus have a fair outside; but we ought to look into them, and remove that fair covering which hides them from us. Believe me then, Alcibiades, and take the precautions I give you.

Alcib. What precautions?

Socrat. To exercise yourself, and be instructed in what is necessary to be known, before you intermeddle with the affairs of the commonwealth; that you may be always fortified with an antidote; and that you may not perish in so contagious and fatal a conversation.

Alcib. All you say is very well, Socrates; but endeavour to explain to me, by what means we may be able to take care of ourselves.

Socrat. That is done already: for first of all we have

---

* He jokes on his own deformity and low birth, which he opposes to the beauty, fine air, and nobility of his rivals.

† He was so in love with the people, that he did not cease to bestow gifts on them, and to present them with shows and plays. Plutarch speaks of a distribution of money, which he made when he was very young, and carried quails in his bosom.

‡ Erectheus was one of the first kings of Athens.

roved what man is, and that with good reason; because
e feared, if that were not well known, we should take
ure of something quite different from ourselves, without
rceiving it. We afterwards agreed that we ought to take
re of our souls; that this is the only end we should pro-
se to ourselves; and that the care of the body, and of
at which appertains to it, as riches, should be left to others.

Alcib. Can any one deny this?

Socrat. How can we understand this truth * more
arly, and evidently? For when we have set it in its
e light, it is very certain that we shall know ourselves
fectly well. Let us then in the name of the gods en-
vour to understand well the precept of Delphos, of which
have already spoken. For we do not yet well compre-
d all its force.

lcib. What force? What do you mean?

crat. I am going to communicate to you what I take
e the meaning of that inscription, and the precept it
des. It is hardly possible to make you understand it
y other comparison than this, which is taken from
ight.

cib. How do you say?

rat. Observe well what I say. If this inscription
to the eye, as it speaks to the man, and should say
" Know thyself;" what should we think it required
Should we not think it required it to look upon
n something in which the eye might see itself?

ib. That is evident.

at. Let us then seek for this thing, in which, as
hold ourselves in it, we may see both it and our-

b. We may see ourselves in a looking-glass, and all
odies of the like kind.

ut. You say very well. Is not there likewise some
rt of the eye, which has the same effect as a look-
s ?

. Yes, certainly there is.

_____

e Fevre had reason to say, that ἐναργέστερα ought to be
ναργέστατα, and that it should be translated *more clearly.*
is now going to resume the proposition he had quitted,
s to know the universal essence of things; and all he is
ay on this subject is incomparably fine.

Socrat. You have observed then, that as often as you look into an eye, you see your own image, as in a glass, in that little part which is called by a name which signifies a * baby, because it is the image of him that looks on it.

Alcib. It is true.

Socrat. Then an eye, that it may see into another eye, ought to look into this part of it, which is the most beautiful, and which alone has the faculty of seeing.

Alcib. Who doubts it ?

Socrat. For if he should fix his looks on any other part of the body of man, or on any other object, unless it were like this part of the eye which sees, it would see nothing of itself.

Alcib. You are in the right.

Socrat. Therefore, an eye that would see itself, ought to look into another eye, and into that part of the eye in which all the virtue of it resides, that is, the sight.

Alcib. That is certain.

Socrat. My dear Alcibiades, is it not just so with the soul ? Ought it not to look into the soul to see itself, and into that part † of the soul in which all its virtues, that is to say, *wisdom*, is ingenerated? Or else ought it not to behold itself in some other thing yet more noble, which this part of the soul in some sort resembles ?

Alcib. So methinks, Socrates.

Socrat. But can we find any part of the soul which is more divine than that in which knowledge and wisdom reside?

* There is a fault in the Greek which I wonder to find left there; for what sense has κορυφὴν here, which signifies *the top of a thing*? It ought to be read κόρην, that is, the apple of the eye; κόρη, *pupilla*, a poppet or baby.

† That is, into our intellect or understanding. We ought strictly to remark with what wisdom Socrates here expresses himself. In speaking of the soul of man, he acknowledges, that wisdom is ingenerated in it; that is, that it comes to it from without, for it is not its own light; this is derived into it from God. And a few lines lower, as he speaks of the Divine Intelligence, he does not choose to say, in which knowledge and wisdom are Ingenerated; but says he, *in which they reside;* because it is wisdom itself, and the source of wisdom. The Latin interpreters, who did not pry into this accuracy of Socrates, have spoiled all the beauty of these passages by their translations. More attention and fidelity ought to have been used in handling theological truths.

Alcib. No, certainly.

Socrat. It is then in this soul, of which ours is but the image; it is in this divine soul we ought to behold ourselves, and to contemplate the whole Deity in it; that is to say, God, and Wisdom, if we would know ourselves perfectly.

Alcib. This seems very probable.

Socrat. To know one's self is wisdom, as we have both agreed.

Alcib. It is true.

Socrat. While we do not know ourselves, nor are wise with this wisdom, we cannot know either our goods or our ills; for it is not possible that he who knows not Alcibiades, should know that what belongs to Alcibiades does indeed appertain to him.

Alcib. It is impossible.

Socrat. It is only by knowing ourselves that we come to know that that which belongs to us, does indeed appertain to us: and if we know not what belongs to us, neither shall we know what has reference to the things that belong to us.

Alcib. I confess it.

Socrat. We therefore just now did ill to agree, that there are some persons, who though they do not know themselves, yet know that which belongs to them, without knowing the things that appertain to that which belongs to them. For these three knowledges, to know one's self, to know that which belongs to one, and to know the things that appertain to that which belongs to one, are linked together; they are the action of the same man, and the of one and the same art.

Alcib. It is very likely.

Socrat. Now, that man that knows not the things that belong to himself, neither will know those that belong to others.

Alcib. That is evident.

Socrat. And if he knows not what belongs to others, nor will he know what belongs to the city.

Alcib. That is a certain consequence.

Socrat. Therefore such a man can never be a good statesnay, he cannot be so much as a good master to a family; what do I say? he cannot so much as

E

govern himself, for he knows not what he does: and if he knows not what he does, it is impossible he should be free from faults.

Alcib. That is impossible indeed.

Socrat. And if he commits faults, does he not do ill both in private and public? If he does ill, is he not miserable? and as he is miserable, does he not involve those that obey him in his misfortunes?

Alcib. Who can deny it?

Socrat. Then it is not possible that he who is neither good nor wise, should be happy.

Alcib. No, certainly.

Socrat. Then all vicious persons are miserable.

Alcib. I acknowledge it.

Socrat. Then a man cannot deliver himself from his misery by riches, but by wisdom.

Alcib. That is certain.

Socrat. So that, my dear Alcibiades, cities have no need either of walls, or ships, or arsenals, or troops, or grandeur, to make them happy: the only thing they need is virtue. And if you would manage the affairs of the commonwealth well, you must give your citizens virtue.

Alcib. This is an evident truth.

Socrat. But can a man give that which he has not?

Alcib. How should he?

Socrat. Then you ought first of all to consider how to acquire virtue; and so must every man who desires to take care not only of himself, and the things that belong to him, but also of the city, and the things that belong to that.

Alcib. This is beyond all doubt.

Socrat. Therefore you ought not to consider how to acquire for yourself, or your city, a large extent of empire, and the absolute power of doing what you please, but only how to acquire wisdom and justice.

Alcib. I believe what you say.

Socrat. For if you and your city govern yourselves wisely and justly, you will please God.

Alcib. I am well convinced of that.

Socrat. And you will govern yourselves wisely and justly, if, as I just now told you, you behold yourselves always in the Deity; in that splendid light, which alone is capable of giving you the knowledge of the truth.

lcib. This seems very reasonable.

ocrat. For while you behold yourselves in this light, will see yourselves, and will see and know your true ds.

lcib. Without doubt.

ocrat. And so you will always do what is good.

lcib. Most certainly.

ocrat. If you always do what is good, I dare answer it, and warrant you, you shall be always happy.

lcib. Your warrant is very good in this case, Socrates.

ocrat. But if you govern yourselves unjustly, and in- l of beholding the Deity, and true light, you look into which is without God and full of darkness, you will othing but the works of darkness, and such as are full piety : and it cannot be otherwise, because you will know yourself.

cib. I am of the same mind.

crat. My dear Alcibiades, represent to yourself a per- hat has * power to do any thing he pleases, and yet o judgment; what is to be expected from him? and mischief is there that will not befall him? For ex- e, suppose a sick man has power to do whatever comes nis head, that he has no understanding in physic, is in e against every body, so that no person dare speak to or restrain him; what will be the event of this? He without doubt, destroy his body, and render himself able.

ib. It is very true.

rat. Suppose some person in a ship, who has not the ient and skill of a pilot, should yet have the liberty what he thinks fit; you yourself see what must cer- befall him, and those that abandon themselves to nduct.

ib. They must all necessarily perish.

rat. The case is the same with cities, republics, and tes; if destitute of virtue, their ruin is certain.

ib. It is impossible it should be otherwise.

rat. Consequently, my dear Alcibiades, if you would ppy, your business is not to acquire a large extent

hen **wisdom is wanting**, absolute power always transports men the limits of their duty, and induces them to trample reli- d **justice** under their feet.

of empire for yourself or your republic, but to acquire virtue.

Alcib. Very true.

Socrat. And before this virtue is acquired, it is better and more advantageous, I do not say for a child, but for a man, to obey him who is the most virtuous, than to command.

Alcib. I am of the same mind.

Socrat. And what is best is also most beautiful.

Alcib. Without doubt.

Socrat. That which is most beautiful is likewise most becoming, and suitable.

Alcib. That is beyond dispute.

Socrat. It is then becoming and suitable to a vicious person to be a slave, for that is best for him.

Alcib. Most certainly.

Socrat. Then vice is a vile thing, and suitable to a slave.

Alcib. So it seems.

Socrat. And virtue is a noble thing, and suits only with a free man.

Alcib. That cannot be contested.

Socrat. Then this vileness ought to be avoided, which only suits with slaves.

Alcib. Most certainly, Socrates.

Socrat. Well then, my dear Alcibiades, do you now perceive in what condition you are? Are you in this noble disposition of mind, so becoming a man of your birth; or ———

Alcib. Ah, Socrates, I perceive very well I am in the condition you speak of.*

Socrat. But do you know how to deliver yourself out of this condition, which I dare not name, when I speak of a man of your make?

Alcib. Yes, I do.

* After Socrates has confounded the pride of Alcibiades, he gives a finishing stroke to lay him low, in reducing him to pronounce this terrible sentence against himself, That he is only worthy to be a slave, because he has no virtue, since it is virtue alone that makes men free. It is upon this, without doubt, that Plutarch says, Alcibiades, struck with the victorious reasons of Socrates, was like a cock, that after a long fight hangs the wing, and yields himself conquered and that Socrates by his ingenious discourses touched him to the quick, and made him pour out a flood of tears.

Socrat. Well, how can you deliver yourself?

Alcib. I shall deliver myself, if Socrates pleases.

Socrat. You do not say well, Alcibiades.

Alcib. What should I say then?

Socrat. You should say, if God pleases.

Alcib. Well then, I say if God pleases; and I add, let us for the future change persons; you shall personate me, and I you: that is to say, I will now * make my court to you, as you have hitherto made yours to me.

Socrat. If so, my dear Alcibiades, what is reported of the stork, may be said of the love I have for you; for after it has hatched and nourished a little winged love in your bosom, this little love shall take his turn to cherish and nourish that in his old age.

Alcib. It shall be so; and from this day I will apply myself to righteousness.

Socrat. I desire you may, through the whole course of your life, persevere in this design; but I confess, I fear it very much. Not that I distrust your good temper: but the force of the examples that reign in this city, occasion these apprehensions. I tremble for fear they should be too strong both for you and me.

---

* This passage is corrupted in the text. It should be read ὡς ὑπὸ σοῦ ἐπαιδαγωγήθην, or ὡς σὺ ἐμε ἐπαιδαγώγησας, *I will be your pedagogue,* or schoolmaster, *as you have been mine.* We see Socrates has been constantly following Alcibiades as his schoolmaster; for the future, Alcibiades designs to follow Socrates in his turn; but it will be to learn of him, and not to teach him. In Greece they had schoolmasters for their children, because they went to public schools, and there were no private masters but for persons of the first quality; and they made use of them but rarely.—*M. Le Fevre.* In the translation it was requisite to put an equivalent term, because the word pedagogue, or schoolmaster, would not have sounded well.

THE SECOND ALCIBIADES;

OR,

OF PRAYER.

THE ARGUMENT.

PIETY is the only spring of our happiness, and it is prayer alone
that nourishes piety : by this we keep up a continual correspondence
with God, represent our necessities to him, and draw down his
favours upon us. So that the essence of religion consists in prayer.
For prayers are properly the sallies of a soul penetrated with piety,
discovering to God its misery, in order to request a remedy. But
our passions fill our minds with so much darkness, that we know
neither our goods nor our evils; but following our own desires every
day, offer such petitions to God, as would be fatal to us, and would
become real curses, if God should hearken to us. Therefore there is
nothing of so great importance as prayer; nothing that requires so
much prudence and attention, and yet we go about nothing with so
much temerity and negligence. Plato here vigorously opposes this
abuse; and teaches, that if we would pray well, we must learn to
know our goods and evils; that the knowledge of this is only taught
by God; and consequently, that it is God alone that can dissipate the
darkness of our souls, and teach us to pray. Till then we cannot
safely make any prayers of ourselves, without being exposed to great
dangers. But are we in the meantime to continue without prayer,
though we are in continual need of the Divine assistance? There
would be stupidity or pride in this kind of inaction. Certainly it
would be more eligible for the soul to continue in silence, than to
ask evils of God, when she desires to ask good; but God has given
her some help under this ignorance, in inspiring, even during the
time of darkness, a prayer which teaches us to abandon ourselves to
him, and to request of him, that he would do his own will in us, and
not ours. Of all the prayers men are capable of making, this is the
most agreeable to God, and this Socrates would have men continually
make. When God has once enlightened and instructed us, we shall
then ask of him what we think necessary; for seeing we shall speak
only by his Spirit, we shall request of him that which is truly good,
which he is always willing to grant; and will never fail to give it,
because he truly loves us. This is what Socrates designs to teach in

this Dialogue, which may be termed sacred; since it is full of maxims, worthy of Christianity itself, and very useful both for politics and religion. As when Socrates says, all the sciences in the world, without the knowledge of that which is very good, are pernicious, instead of being useful; when he teaches us, that God is not to be corrupted by bribes, and that he does not regard the sacrifices and offerings of the wicked, but the righteousness and holiness of those that invoke him; and when he assures us, that God is free, and has a sovereign power to hear or reject our supplications; whence it follows, that when he hears them, he shews us an act of grace, and not of strict justice. There are many other beauties which may be easily remarked, because they very sensibly and obviously offer themselves. This Dialogue is a kind of continuation of the preceding. As in the former, Alcibiades seemed to understand but little with respect to human affairs; in this he appears to be very ignorant in Divine things: for there is so great a connection between them, that those who are ignorant of the one, are necessarily ignorant of the other, as Socrates demonstrates, when he shews, that to know God, to know one's self, and to know what appertains to ourselves, and what to others, is the effect of one and the same art. We may observe, by the way, as we have done before, that this Dialogue is sustained, as all the rest are, by action. And this dramatic air is that which animates it, and is one of its greatest beauties.

All that is farther necessary to be known is, at what time Plato supposes it to be made. If we follow his interpreters, they make him fall into a very ridiculous inconveniency. For after he had said Archelaus, king of Macedonia, was killed, he speaks of Pericles as a person yet alive, contrary to what is certainly known, namely, that Archelaus survived Pericles, and was not assassinated till twenty years after his death; and contrary to what Plato himself says, in his Gorgias and Theages. We shall see in the notes what led Plato's interpreters into this mistake. In the meantime it may be maintained, that Socrates held these discourses with Alcibiades, the first year of the ninety-third Olympiad; for Perdiccas reigned thirteen years after the death of Pericles, who died the last year of the eighty-seventh Olympiad. Archelaus, who killed Perdiccas, reigned seven years, and then was killed the last year of the ninety-second Olympiad. This naturally leads us to the time of this Dialogue. They that make Archelaus to have reigned sixteen years, or Perdiccas twenty-three, make Archelaus survive Alcibiades and Socrates.

This Dialogue is of the same character with the preceding, μαιευτικὸς; that is, Socrates here makes Alcibiades find out the truths which he designs to teach him. It is also a moral Dialogue, as well as the former.

SOCRATES, ALCIBIADES.

Socrat. Alcibiades, are you going into this temple to say your prayers?

Alcib. Yes, Socrates, that is my design.

Socrat. Indeed you seem very thoughtful: I see your eyes are fixed on the ground, like a man that is thinking on some very serious matter.

Alcib. What should I think on, Socrates?

Socrat. What should you think on! on some very important thing, I suppose; for I beseech you, in the name of God, tell me, whether when we address our prayers to the Gods, either in public or private, do they not grant us some things, and refuse us others? Do they not hear some persons, and reject others?

Alcib. That is very true.

Socrat. Do not you think, then, that prayer requires a great deal of precaution and prudence, lest before we are aware we ask the Gods great evils, while we think we are requesting what is good; and lest they should be disposed to grant what is requested of them? as they granted Œdipus's petition, who prayed that his children might decide their rights by the sword. This unhappy father, who might have prayed to the Gods to remove from him the mischiefs that oppressed him, drew new miseries on himself by his horrible imprecations; for his petitions were heard, and this proved a source of terrible calamities to his family, the particulars of which I need not relate to you.

Alcib. But, Socrates, you tell me of a mad man; can you believe any man in his senses would have made such kind of prayers?

Socrat. Then to be mad, you think, is opposed to being wise.

Alcib. Most certainly.

Socrat. Do not you think that some men are fools, and others wise?

Alcib. Yes.

Socrat. Come, then, let us endeavour to know and distinguish them well; for you agree that there are some that are foolish, others that are wise, and others that are mad.

Alcib. I do so.

Socrat. Are not some people in health, and others sick

Alcib. That is certain.

Socrat. These are not the same persons.

Alcib. No, certainly.

Socrat. Is there a third sort, who are neither sick nor in health?

Alcib. No: that cannot be.

Socrat. For a man must necessarily be in health or sick. there is no medium.*

Alcib. So I think.

Socrat. But is it the same thing with respect to wisdom and folly, in your opinion?

Alcib. How do you say?

Socrat. I ask you, if a man must necessarily be either foolish or wise? or is there a certain medium which makes one become neither a wise man nor a fool?

Alcib. No: there is no medium.†

Socrat. Then we must necessarily be one or the other.

Alcib. So I think.

Socrat. Did you not just now grant, that madness is opposite to wisdom?

Alcib. Yes.

Socrat. And that there is no medium, or such a condition as to be neither wise nor foolish?

Alcib. I did grant it.

Socrat. But is it possible for the same thing to have two contraries opposed to it?

Alcib. By no means.

---

* If one were disposed to criticise, he might say, there is a third state, which is that of convalescence, in which men have not yet recovered health, neither are properly sick. But at bottom, this is not true; for one who is recovering is no longer under the power of sickness, but is in the way of health.

† To this it is objected, that there is a certain medium between virtue and vice, which is the state of such as are neither vicious nor virtuous, as Tacitus says of Galba, " *Magis extra vitia quam cum virtutibus.*" But it is easy to see, that this expression of Tacitus ' not true, but only in the common language of the world, which makes a superficial judgment, without penetrating deeply into things, and so calls none vicious but those who practise gross vices; and is false, when we speak with a philosophic accuracy. Wherever virtue is not, there vice must necessarily be. The same may be said of wisdom and folly. Every man who is not wise, can be no other than a fool.

Socrat. Then folly and madness will appear to be one and the same thing.

Alcib. So methinks.

Socrat. Then if we say all fools are mad, we shall say right.

Alcib. Certainly.

Socrat. Without going any farther: among all the men of your age, if there are any fools, as without doubt there are, and some of a longer standing, (for, I pray, do not you find wise men are very rare in this city, and fools very numerous) would you call these fools mad?

Alcib. Without any scruple.

Socrat. But do you think we should be very safe among so many mad men? and that we should not before now have borne the punishment of such conversation, in suffering from them whatever might be expected from mad men? Have a care what you say therefore, my dear Alcibiades, lest this matter be otherwise than you pretend.

Alcib. Well, then, how is it? for I perceive it may be otherwise than I say.

Socrat. I think so too; and we must examine the matter after this manner.

Alcib. After what manner?

Socrat. I am going to tell you. Some persons are sick, are they not?

Alcib. Who doubts it?

Socrat. Is it absolutely necessary, that every one that is sick, should have the gout, or fever, or sore eyes? and do not you think he may be free from all these distempers, and yet be sick of another disease? For there are divers kinds of diseases besides these.

Alcib. So I think.

Socrat. You believe every distemper of the eyes is a disease; but you do not think every disease is a distemper of the eyes.

Alcib. No certainly; but yet I do not see what that proves.

Socrat. But if you will follow me, I am persuaded we shall find that presently. You know that saying of the poet, " Two men that go together."*

* Plato often intermixes sentences of the poets in his Discourses, without giving any notice when he does it. To understand this

Alcib. I follow you with all my might, Socrates.

Socrat. Are we not agreed that every distemper of the eyes is a disease, and that every disease is not a distemper of the eyes?

Alcib. In that we are agreed.

Socrat. And that with good reason : for all that have a fever, are sick ; but all that are sick have not a fever, or the gout, or sore eyes. All these afflictions are diseases, but physicians assure us, that they are so many different diseases by their effects ; for they are not all alike, and they do not deal with them all after the same manner, but according to the nature and violence of them. Are there not a great many sorts of artificers? There are shoemakers, bricklayers, architects, carvers, painters, and a multitude of others, whom I need not name ; work is divided among them. They are all artificers, but they are not all carvers or architects.

Alcib. It is true.

Socrat. In like manner, folly is divided among men : those that have the greatest share of it we call mad, or distracted ; those that have a degree less, we call fools, and stupid. But while men seek to hide these vices under honourable and specious names, they call the former, men of magnanimity and courage ; and they call the others, men of simplicity ; or else they say they have no harm in them, but have little experience, and much youth. You will find a great many other names besides these, with which they palliate their weak side. But these are so many sorts of

---

passage well, and to know all its elegancy, it is necessary to remember the words Homer puts into Diomedes's mouth, when Nestor proposes to send spies into the Trojan camp. For he speaks thus : " My courage prompts me to go into the enemy's army ; but if any one would accompany me, I should go with greater boldness and confidence : for two men that go together take a better view of things ; one sees what the other does not observe. One man alone, though he want not prudence, yet has always less vigour and activity in his mind."—*Iliad*, K. ver. 224. So that here is a manifest allusion to this passage. Homer says, συντε δι' ερχομένω, " two men that go together ;" and Plato says, δύο σκοπτομένω, " two men that examine together." But because Homer is not now so well known as he was in Plato's time, I have elucidated the passage in the translation, by adding, " You know the saying of the poet ;" without which, the allusion would not have been perceivable. The Latin translators have slipt over it, without perceiving it.

folly, which differ only as one art does from another, and one disease from another. Do not you think so as well as I?

Alcib. I am of the same mind with you.

Socrat. To return then to our subject. Our first design was exactly to know and distinguish the foolish from the wise: for we agreed that some men are wise and others foolish, did we not?

Alcib. Yes, in that we agreed.

Socrat. Do not you call him wise who knows what he ought to say or do; and him foolish who knows neither one nor the other?

Alcib. Yes, certainly.

Socrat. Are they who know not what they ought to say or do, ignorant that they say and do what they ought not?

Alcib. I think so.

Socrat. I told you Œdipus was of that number: but you will yet find in our time a multitude of people, who, without being transported with an emotion of anger, like him, will request of God real evils, while they think they are asking real goods. For as to Œdipus, if he did not ask for what was good, neither did he think he asked it; whereas others every day do the quite contrary: and without going any farther, Alcibiades, if the God to whom you are going to pray, should appear suddenly to you, and before you have opened your lips, should ask you, if you would be content to be the tyrant of Athens, or (if that seem too little for you) of all Greece; or if you were not yet satisfied, should promise you all Europe together; and fully to gratify your ambition, should add, that that very day all the world should know that Alcibiades, the son of Clinias, is king: I am persuaded you would go out of the temple with abundance of joy, as one that has just received the greatest of all goods.

Alcib. And, Socrates, I verily believe there is no man but he would be transported with joy, if the same thing should happen to him.

Socrat. But you would not give your life for the empire of the Greeks, nor for that of the barbarians?

Alcib. No, certainly: to what purpose? for then I should not enjoy that empire.

Socrat. But suppose you could enjoy it, would you do so, if this enjoyment were to be fatal to you?

Alcib. No; neither would I do it on that condition.

Socrat. Then by this you see very well, that it is not safe to accept, or desire what one does not know; if it be true, that it may bring great mischief upon us, or even make us lose our lives: for I could name to you a great many of those ambitious men, who having passionately desired tyranny, and spared nothing to obtain it, as the greatest of all goods; yet have derived no other advantage from this great elevation, than to be exposed to the stratagems of their enemies, who have assassinated them on the throne. It is impossible but you must have heard of that tragical story that has lately happened. Archelaus, * king of Macedonia, had a favourite whom he loved with an unbounded passion: this favourite, who was yet more in love with the throne of Archelaus, than his prince was with him, killed him to fill up his place, flattering himself that he should be the happiest man in the world: but he had scarce enjoyed the tyranny three or four days, when he was cut off by others that were possessed with the same ambition. And among our Athenians, (for these are examples which come not to us by hearsay, but such as we have seen with our eyes) how many have there been, who, after they had ardently aspired to be generals of the army, and had obtained what they desired, have been put to death, or banished? How many others who have seemed more happy, have passed through innumerable dangers, and been exposed to continual fears, not only during the time of their being generals, but also after their return into their country, where they have all their lifetime had a more cruel siege to maintain against envious detractors, than all they sustained in war against the enemies of the state? So that the greatest part of them wished they had never been any more than private men, rather than to have had the command of armies at so dear a rate. If all these dangers and fatigues should produce a man any advantage in the end, there would be some reason for him to expose himself to them; but it is quite the contrary. What I say of honours, I say also of children: how many people

---

* Archelaus was the natural son of Perdiccas. He killed his father, his uncle Alcetas, and his son. He afterwards killed the legitimate son of Perdiccas; and after he had possessed the throne even years, was assassinated by his favourite Craterus.

have we seen, who, after they have importunately desired of God, that he would give them children, and have accordingly obtained them, have by this means precipitated themselves into terrible miseries and troubles? for some of them have spent their whole lives in sorrow and bitterness, because their children have proved wicked; and others who have had such as have proved good, have been no more happy than the former, because they have lost them for the most part in the flower of their age: so that they had much rather never have had them. Now though all these miseries, and many others, are very obvious, and common, yet there is scarce a man to be found, who would refuse these false goods, if God should give them him; or who would cease to importune him for them, if he were assured he should obtain them by his prayers. The generality of men would not refuse, either the supreme rule or the command of armies, or any other great honours, which yet are certainly much more pernicious than useful; but would even request them of God, if they did not spontaneously offer themselves to them. But wait a moment, and you will hear them sing a *palinodia*,* and offer petitions quite contrary to the former. For my part, I cannot choose but think, that men are really to blame in complaining of the Gods, and accusing them of being the cause of the miseries they suffer; for it is themselves, who, by their faults, or rather by their follies,

"In spite of fate draw mischiefs on themselves." †

And therefore, Alcibiades, that ancient poet seems to me to have had a great deal of sense and reason, who having (as I think) very imprudent friends, whom he saw every day going on in a course of asking of God such things as seemed good, and yet were very bad for them, composed for them this prayer: "Great God, give us the good things that are necessary for us, whether we ask them or not; and keep evil things from us, even when we ask them of thee." This seems to be a most excellent and very safe prayer. If you have anything to object against it, do not hide it from me.

Alcib. It is hard to contradict what is well spoken. The only reflection I make on it Socrates, is, how many

* A recantation.

† This is a passage of Homer, in the first book of his Odyssey, at the beginning.

evils are brought upon mankind by ignorance. For we do not so much as perceive that it is this that not only makes us every day do such things as are fatal to us; but (which is most deplorable) engages us to ask our own unhappiness of God: and this is what no man can tell how to imagine. There is no person but thinks himself capable of asking such things of God as are very useful for him; to desire such things as are pernicious to him, would not be a prayer, but a real imprecation.

Socrat. Hold a little, my dear Alcibiades; it is possible there may be found some person wiser than you and I, who might with good reason reprehend us, and tell us, we are very much in the wrong thus to blame ignorance, without adding what sort of ignorance it is that we condemn, and in what it consists. For if ignorance is bad in some things, it is good in others.

Alcib. How say you, Socrates? Is there anything of what kind soever, of which it is more useful to be ignorant, than to know it?

Socrat. So I think, and you think otherwise.

Alcib. That I do, I protest.

Socrat. Yet I shall never believe you capable of being irritated against your mother with the fury either of an Orestes, or an Alcmæon, or any the like parricides, if there have been any others who have committed the same crimes.

Alcib. Ah! Socrates, I entreat you in the name of God, alter your discourse.

Socrat. Alcibiades, you are to blame to desire that of me; of me, I say, who tell you, I do not think you capable of committing those crimes. You could do no more if I accused you of them. But since these actions appear so abominable to you, that one must not name them unless there be an absolute necessity of it; with all my heart, so let it be. I only ask you, do you think, if Orestes had been in his senses, and had known what was good and useful for him, he would have dared to do what he did?

Alcib. No, certainly.

Socrat. Neither he nor any body else would have done it.

Alcib. That is most certain.

Socrat. Then in my opinion this ignorance of what is good and useful, is a great evil.

Alcib. I am of the same mind.

Socrat. And that either in Orestes, or any other person.

Alcib. I am fully persuaded of that.

Socrat. Let us examine this matter yet a little farther. Suppose then it had formerly come into your head on a sudden, that it was a very good and laudable action for you to go and kill Pericles,* your tutor and friend ; and that you had taken a dagger, and gone directly to his door, to ask if he were at home, as having a design against him alone, and not any other ; and that you had been told he was within.   I do not mean by this, that you could ever have been capable of committing so horrible an action ; but I make this supposition, to show you, that there is nothing hinders, but a man who knows not what is comely and honourable, may be in a disposition of taking that for very good which is in itself very evil : do not you think so as well as I ?

Alcib. I am perfectly of the same mind.

Socrat. To go on then : supposing you had been told Pericles was at home, and you had gone in, and seen him, but not known him, and imagined that you saw somebody else ; would you have had the boldness to kill him ?   No, certainly, for your design would have been only against him ; and every time you had been at his house on the same design, and had mistaken him for another, you would not have done him the least injury.

* The Latin interpreters have translated this passage, as if Plato had said, " If it should come into your head of a sudden to go and kill Pericles. your tutor and friend ;" not considering that they make Plato fall into a very ridiculous fault.   For to speak thus, Pericles must have been still living.   And Plato had been saying, that Archelaus, king of Macedonia, had been assassinated ; and we know Pericles died twenty years before.   How, then, shall this contradiction be reconciled ? how shall we secure Plato from this fault of which he is not guilty, seeing he speaks the contrary in Gorgias and Theages ?   There is no great difficulty in the matter ; it is only to translate, as the Greek terms will bear, " If it had formerly come into your head on a sudden ;" that is, if while Pericles was living, &c.   By this means we not only prevent a great mistake, in regard of the time, but also escape a great fault against the rules of decency. For that Pericles should be yet alive when Socrates speaks thus to Alcibiades, is a hard and odious supposition : but supposing Pericles to be dead, it has not the same harshness in it.   Athenæus would not have forgot to improve this passage to strengthen his chicanery against Plato's Gorgias, if he had not very well understood it would bear another interpretation besides that given it by his translators.

Alcib. That is very certain.

Socrat. What then ? Do you think Orestes would have laid his parricidal hands on his mother, if he had mistaken her for another ?

Alcib. No, doubtless.

Socrat. For he did not design to kill the first woman he met, nor the mother of this or that person; but had a mind to kill his own mother.

Alci3. You say right.

Socrat. Then this sort of ignorance is very good for those that are in such a disposition of mind as his, and have such kind of fancies in their head.

Alcib. So I think.

Socrat. By this then you plainly see, that on some occasions, and in some persons whose minds are disposed after a certain manner, ignorance is a good, and not an evil, as you just now supposed.

Alcib. I perceive it very well.

Socrat. If you will take the pains to examine what I am now going to say, how strange soever it may at first seem to you, it may be you will be of the same mind with me.

Alcib. Well, Socrates, what is it?

Socrat. It is true, that possibly, all the sciences without the knowledge of that which is *very good*, are seldom of use to those that possess them; nay, most commonly are pernicious to them. Follow me a little in your thoughts, I intreat you. When we are about to say or do any thing, is it not altogether necessary either that we really know what we are going to do or say, or at least that we think we know it?

Alcib. Without doubt.

Socrat. According to this principle, the orators who every day advise the people, give them advice about what they know, or at least think they know. Some give them counsel about peace and war, others about the walls that ought to be built, about the fortifications, gates, and arsenals. In a word, all that the city does for itself, or against another city, is not done but by the advice of orators.

Alcib. It is true.

Socrat. Observe well what follows, and see if I can finish my proof. Do not you divide the people into wise men and fools?

Alcib. Yes.

Socrat. Do not you call the greatest number fools, and the least wise men?

Alcib. Yes.

Socrat. Is it not with reference to something that you call them so ?

Alcib. Most certainly.

Socrat. Do you then call him a wise man, who can give this counsel without knowing what is best, or in what time it is best?

Alcib. No, certainly.

Socrat. Nor do you call him wise, who can make war, but knows not when or how, nor how long it is best so to do ?

Alcib. No, not I.

Socrat. Neither do you call those magistrates wise, who know how to put to death, to fine, and to banish; and yet know not when or on what occasion these punishments are best and most just.

Alcib. No, indeed.

Socrat. Well, then, when any one knows well how to do all these things, and these sciences are accompanied with the knowledge of that which is *very good,* (and this is the same with the knowledge of that which is *very useful,* as you have granted) we call this man wise, and say he is very capable to advise and conduct himself, and govern the commonwealth. And we say directly the contrary of him who does not add the knowledge of that which is good to these sciences.

Alcib. This must be granted.

Socrat. When a man knows how to mount a horse,* to draw a bow, to wrestle, in a word to perform any of the l'ke exercises, or is well instructed in any other art ; how do you call him, when he knows perfectly well what is most conformable to the art he professes? Do not you call him an equery that employs himself in managing of horses, him a wrestler that makes it his business to wrestle, and him a musician who understands music, and so of the rest ? Do

---

* He is going to prove that to be skilful in the art a man professes, is not sufficient to merit the name of a wise man.

not you give them all such names as are derived from their art, and are suitable to it? or do you give them other appellations?

Alcib. We give them only such names as are taken from their art.

Socrat. Do you think it is of absolute necessity that he who well understands the art of which he makes profession, should also be a wise man; or shall we say he may be far from that character?

Alcib. He may be very far from it, Socrates.

Socrat. What will you say of a republic composed of wrestlers, pipers, archers, and other such kind of people, mingled with such persons as we have been speaking of, some of whom know how to make war, others to condemn to death; and with those statesmen, who are bloated with pride on account of their pretended capacity in politics?* Supposing all these people to have knowledge of what is very good, and that there is but one single man among them all who knows either on what occasion or with whom each of these different arts ought to be used?

Alcib. I should say, Socrates, that would be a very ill composed commonwealth.

Socrat. Much more would you say so, when you saw every one full of ambition, and striving to engross the greatest part of affairs to himself; that he might still exceed himself, and become every day more powerful in that part of the government which is the most noble: and if you should at the same time see every one making horrible mistakes against the knowledge of what is very good, both on his own account and that of the commonwealth; because he conducts himself by opinion without understanding. This being the state of the case, should we not have great reason to say that such a republic cannot choose but be full of disorder and injustice?

Alcib. This is manifestly true.

Socrat. Have we not agreed that it is absolutely necessary for us either to believe we know, or else really to know,

* This is a subtile satire against the republic of the Athenians, in which all arts and sciences were seen to flourish, but the knowledge of what is *very good* was not to be found there; and therefore nothing but confusion and disorder was to be seen among them.

what we are about to do or say without any farther deliberation ?

Alcib. That has been agreed between us.

Socrat. Have we not likewise acknowledged, that when
any man does that which he knows, or thinks he knows;
provided he possesses the knowledge of that which is very
good, great advantage hence accrues both to himself and
to the state?*

Alcib. Who can doubt that ?

Socrat. And that when it is otherwise, the contrary
ensues?

Alcib. That is evident.

Socrat. Do you still persist in the same sentiments?

Alcib. I do.

Socrat. Have you not said, that the greatest number
is that of fools, and that of wise men the least?

Alcib. Yes, and I say the same still.

Socrat. Did we not upon this say, that the greatest number keep at a distance from that which is good, because
they usually abandon themselves to opinion without understanding.

Alcib. Yes, so we said.

Socrat. Then it is useful for this great number to know
nothing, and to believe they know nothing, because what
they know, or believe they know, they will be willing to
put in execution; and in so doing, instead of gaining any
advantage, they will receive great prejudice.

Alcib. You say true.

Socrat. By this then you see very well, that I had reason
when I told you just now, that possibly all sciences, without the knowledge of what is very good, were seldom useful
to those that possessed them, but were most commonly very
pernicious to them. Were you not then sensible of this truth?

Alcib. I was not then sensible of it, Socrates, but now
I am.

Socrat. Then a city which would be well governed, and
a soul that would live well, applies itself only to this science;
as a sick man commits himself to his physician; and as a
sailor, that would arrive safe at his port, obeys his pilot.

---

* The knowledge of that which is *very good* conducts and directs
us not only in the things we know, but also in those we know not.

Without this, the greater fortune, men or states enjoy, the greater crimes will they commit,* either to acquire riches, or to augment their power, or satiate their passions. He that possesses all the arts and sciences, and is destitute of this, will be driven about and tossed by each of them, and be really battered with a furious tempest; and having neither helm nor pilot, it is impossible he should go very far, and his ruin must needs be near. Methinks what the poet speaks of one whom he would dispraise, may be applied to him: "He knew (says he) many things, but knew them all amiss."†

Alcib. How can one make such an application as this, Socrates? for my part I do not think there is any justness in it.

Socrat. On the contrary, I say there is a great deal of justness in it. For, my dear Alcibiades, it is a sort of enigma. Homer and the other poets are full of them. For all poesy is naturally enigmatic, but it is not given to every man to penetrate those obscurities: and if, besides its being enigmatic, it be handled by envious poets, who, instead of discovering their wisdom to us, only seek to hide it from us; it is then almost impossible to sound their thoughts. But you will never accuse Homer, the most wise and divine poet, of being ignorant that it is impossible

---

* This is one of the most difficult places in Plato; Marsilius Ficinus and De Serres have translated it very ill, and have rather obscured than interpreted it. However, Ficinus suspected that it was corrupted, though he could not correct it. I am of opinion, that we should read μέν for μὴ, and γε for γαρ. But that is not all, the principal fault in the text consists in the word ψυχῆς, which makes a very ill sense; we must therefore necessarily read τύχης, and take away the point. Plato's sense is, that without the knowledge of what is *very good*, the greater fortune a soul or a city enjoys, the greater crimes will they commit to satiate their passions. The corruption came from the word ψυχήν, which is three or four lines higher. But Plato speaks no more of the soul than he does of the city, and consequently could not repeat ψυχῆς. He certainly wrote τύχης, and this mode of speech ἐπουρίσῃ τὸ τῆς τύχης is very elegant, *quo magis fortuna afflaverit*, properly, *the more Fortune blows on their poop*. The beauty of this principle, and the truth which it contains, prove the necessity of restoring the sense after this manner: The greater fortune wicked men have, the greater sins do they commit.

† Or thus: To a great sum his knowledge did amount,
But all he knew turned to an ill account.

to know amiss what one knows; it is he that says of
Margites, that " He knew many things, but knew them all
amiss:"* and he speaks enigmatically, for he puts [he
knew] for his learning, and [amiss] for unhappy; which
terms could not well enter into the composition of his
verse : but what he certainly meant by it, is, that Margites
had a great deal of learning and knowledge, and that this
was an unhappy or unfortunate knowledge to him. If this
knowledge was unfortunate to him, he must needs have
been a poor worthless fellow.

Alcib. So I think, Socrates; I should scarce yield to the
most evident truths, if I should not grant that.

Socrat. You have reason. But, Alcibiades, I entreat
you, let us assure ourselves of the truth. You see how
many doubts and uncertainties present themselves. You
have your share of them, for you go sometimes to the
right, and sometimes to the left. That which seems true
to you this minute, you receive as such ; and the very next
moment it is quite another thing in your opinion. Let us
endeavour to know where to fix. And as I have already
said, if the God to whom you are going to pray, should
suddenly appear to you, and should ask you before you
have begun your prayers, if you would be satisfied that he
should grant you some one of those things we first spoke
of ; or rather supposing he should permit you to make
your request, which would you think most safe and advantageous to you, whether to receive what he should give you,
or to obtain what you should ask of him?

Alcib. I solemnly protest, Socrates, I know not how to
answer you : for nothing seems to me to be more foolish,
and more to be avoided with the greatest care, than to
run the risk of asking real evils of God, while one thinks
he is asking true goods of him, and thereby to expose
one's self, as you have very well said, to retract the next

---

* Homer made a poem against one Margites, who knew much,
and yet spent his life in idleness and debauchery; a certain sign
that he did not possess the knowledge of what is very good. This
poem, which was made up of a mixture of heroic and iambic
verses, is lost : in which Homer turned the pungent railleries of
those satirical pieces which were in vogue before him, into pleasant
stories and jests ; and by this means was the first that gave us any
strokes of comedy. See the fifth chapter of Aristotle of the Art of
Poetry.

moment, and make new requests quite contrary to the former.

Socrat. Is it not for this reason that that ancient poet I was speaking of in the beginning of our discourse, and who understood these things better than we, would have us end our prayers with these words; " And keep evil things from us, even when we ask them of thee?"

Alcib. So I suppose.

Socrat. In like manner the Lacedemonians, whether they imitate this poet, or have of themselves found out this truth, make both in public and private a prayer much like it. For they desire the Gods " to give them that which is comely with that which is good." They were never heard to make any other prayer; and yet they are as happy as any people in the world : and if they have sometimes seen an interruption in the course of their successes, still none can justly blame their prayer. For the Gods are free, and it depends on their will, whether they will grant what 'is desired of them, or give what is contrary to it. And on this occasion I will tell you another story, which I have often heard related by some ancient people. The Athenians being engaged formerly in a war with the Lacedemonians, it happened that they were always beat in every battle that was fought. Being deeply concerned at this misfortune, and seeking means to divert those miseries that impended, at last, after divers consultations, they thought it the best expedient to send to the oracle of Ammon, to enquire of him the reason of their misfortunes, and to pray him to tell them why the Gods granted victory rather to the Lacedemonians than to the Athenians, who every day offered them a great number of choicer sacrifices, who enriched their temples with nobler offerings, who annually made more magnificent and more devout processions in their honour; and, in a word, who themselves alone were at greater expence in their worship than all the rest of the Greeks together. Whereas (said they) the Lacedemonians have no regard to these ceremonies, they are so covetous in reference to the Gods, that they offer them mutilated victims, and are at much less charge in every thing that concerns religion than the Athenians, though they infinitely exceed them in riches. After they had thus presented their reasons, they asked how those miseries that pressed their city might be diverted. The prophet gave them no immediate answer, for doubtless the God would not permit him to give any. But after some time, recalling the ambassador, he told him, " This is the answer Ammon gives the Athenians ; he loves the benedictions of the Lacedemonians much more than all the sacrifices of the Greeks." This was all he said. By the benedictions of the Lacedemonians, I suppose he only meant their prayers, which indeed are more perfect than those of any other people. For as for the rest of the Greeks, some of them indeed offered bulls with gilded horns, and others consecrated rich oblations to the Gods ; but at the same time requested in their prayers whatever their passions suggested, without informing themselves, whether what they asked was good or evil. But the Gods, who hear their blasphemies, are not pleased with those magnificent processions, nor do they accept their costly sacrifices. Therefore nothing requires so much precaution and attention as prayer : to know what we ought to say, and what not. You will find many other things in Homer, which amount to the same thing with the story I have been telling you. For he says, " the Trojans, when they built a fort, offered whole hecatombs to the immortal Gods, that the winds carried a pleasant odour from earth to heaven ; and yet that the Gods refused to accept all this, but rejected it, because they had an aversion to the sacred city of Troy, for Priamus, and all his people." So that it was to no purpose for them to offer sacrifices, and make presents to the Gods that hated them ; for the Deity is not to be corrupted by bribes, like a covetous usurer. And we should be fools, if we should pretend by this means to render ourselves more agreeable to the Gods than the Lacedemonians. For it would be a very horrible and most unworthy thing, for the Gods to have more regard to our gifts and sacrifices, than to our souls, in distinguishing those that are truly holy and righteous. But they have regard only to our souls, and not at all to our processions, or sacrifices, upon which the most profligate persons, and those cities whose sins both against God and man arise to the greatest height, commonly value themselves more than good men. Nor do the Gods ever suffer themselves to be biassed by presents, but despise all those things, as the God himself, and his prophet, have assured us.

So that it seems plain, that nothing is so precious as wisdom and justice, both in the sight of Gods and men. And none are truly just and truly wise, but those who both in their words and actions know how to acquit themselves of their duty both to the Gods and to men. Therefore I would now willingly know what your sentiments are about what I have been saying.

Alcib. For my part, Socrates, I cannot choose but conform my sentiments in this matter to yours, and those of that God of whom we have been speaking. Would it be reasonable for me to go about to oppose my weak understanding to that of a God, and to contradict his oracles?

Socrat. Do not you remember you told me you were in great perplexity, for fear you should unawares pray for evil things while you designed only to ask for good?

Alcib. I remember it very well, Socrates.

Socrat. You see it is not at all safe for you to go and pray in the temple, in the condition you are in, lest the God hearing your blasphemies should reject your sacrifices; and to punish you, should give you what you would not have. I am therefore of the mind that it is much better for you to be silent, for I know you very well. Your pride, for that is the softest name I can give your imprudence; your pride, I say, probably will not permit you to use the prayer of the Lacedemonians.* Therefore it is altogether necessary you should wait for some person to teach you how you ought to behave yourself both towards the Gods and men.

Alcib. And when will that time come, Socrates? and who is he that will instruct me? With what pleasure should I look upon him!

Socrat. He will do it who takes a true care of you.† But methinks, as we read in Homer, that Minerva dissipated the mist that covered Diomedes' eyes, and hindered him from distinguishing God from man, so it is necessary he should in the first place scatter the darkness that covers your soul, and afterwards give you those remedies that are

---

* " Sovereign of Nature grant us what is good,
   Be it or not, the subject of our prayers:
   And from thy suppliants whate'er is ill;
   Though supplicating for it, still avert."

† That is God.

F

necessary to put you in a condition of discerning good and evil ; for at present you know not how to make a difference between them.

Alcib. Let him scatter then, let him destroy this darkness of mine, and whatever else he pleases ; I abandon myself to his conduct, and am very ready to obey all his commands, provided I may but be made better by them.

Socrat. Do not doubt of that. For this governor I tell you of, has a singular affection for you.

Alcib. I think I must defer my sacrifice to that time.

Socrat. You have reason, it is more safe so to do than to run so great a risk.

Alcib. Well then I will defer it, Socrates ; and to express my thankfulness for the good counsel you have given me, give me leave to place on your head this crown which I wear on mine. We will present other crowns to the Gods, and all the service we owe them, when I see that happy day ; it will not be long before that come, if they please.

Socrat. I receive this favour with very great pleasure ; and shall always kindly accept whatever comes from you. And as Creon, (in Euripides) seeing Tiresias approach him with a crown of gold, which was the first fruits of the spoils of the enemy, and with which the Athenians had honoured him for his art, said, " I take this crown, which is the sign of victory, for a good omen ; for you see we are also in a great storm of war :"* so I must say, I take the honour I receive at your hand for a happy presage ; for I am in no less a tempest than Creon, while I am endeavouring to gain the victory over all your admirers.

* It is in Euripides' Phœnicians.

THEAGES; OR, OF WISDOM.

THE ARGUMENT.

THE ancients cited this Dialogue under the title of Wisdom, or that of Philosophy, as may be seen in Diogenes Laertius. But how old soever these titles are, they were given by philosophers that were unacquainted with the design of Socrates, who here proposes only to treat of the education of children, which is the basis and foundation of philosophy. As plants do not thrive well, unless in ground that is well prepared, and which has been variously manured, and also receives the benign influences of the heavens; so virtues will not grow, unless in a soul well cultivated, and under the influences of the divine favour. On this good education, not only the happiness of families depends, but also that of cities, republics, and all states; this is what Socrates endeavours to maintain in this Dialogue. The young people of the best families of Athens, dazzled with the glory of Cimon, Themistocles, and Pericles; and full of vain ambition, thought of nothing but of adhering to the sophists, who promised to make them very great politicians, and to put them into a capacity of governing the Athenians and their allies. Their parents were tinctured with the same folly: the wisest of them were those that feared the consequences of this ambition, and only discovered the dangers to which their children were exposed by the corruption of those that instructed youth. Socrates here discourses with a father and a son of this character. The son aims only to make himself a good prince; and the father does not blame this ambition of his son, provided he avoided the corruption that reigned at that time. All the business is to find a good master. Socrates makes an admirable improvement of this disposition of theirs, to shew, that one man can never teach another true wisdom, which alone makes men govern well; but that the special favour of God is requisite to this purpose, without which all the endeavours of masters and scholars prove useless; and this he confirms by examples. This is the true subject of this Dialogue, in which we find divers surprising truths which shall be explained in their place. This conversation passed that year in which the Athenians were beat at Ephesus by Tisaphernes; which was the fourth year of the 92nd Olympiad, 407 years before the birth of Christ. Plato, being 20 years of age, was then the disciple of Socrates.

The character of this Dialogue is the same with that of the two former.

DEMODOCUS, SOCRATES, THEAGES.

Demod. SOCRATES, I have a great mind to discourse with you a little in private, if you are at leisure; and if you are not, I entreat you to take a little time for my sake, unless your business is very urgent.

Soc. I have always leisure, and more to serve you than any other person. If you have a mind to discourse with me, I am ready for you.

Dem. Shall we retire into the porch of the temple of Jupiter Eleutherius ?

Soc. As you please.

Dem. Let us go then, Socrates; methinks animals, and even man himself, are like plants: for we who manure the earth, know by experience that it is easy to prepare all things necessary, before we plant; but when that which we have planted is come up, the care and pains we must take about it is very great and troublesome.* It is the same with men; and I judge of others by myself. There is my son; ever since he has been born, his education will not suffer me to rest one moment, but keeps me in continual fear. Without entering into any particular account of all the occasions of fear I have concerning him, I will tell you one which has but very lately appeared; and that is, an ambition he has, which indeed is not dishonourable, but is a very nice and dangerous thing, and makes me afraid. He would fain fall upon the study of wisdom.† Probably some of his companions, and some young people of our town who frequent Athens, give him an account of some discourses they have heard, which have disturbed his brain. For he is so full of emulation, that he continually torments me with importunate entreaties, that I would give a piece of money to some sophist, to accomplish him. It is not the charge that I fear; but I see this passion of his will expose him to great danger. Hitherto I have re-

---

* In the original, Demodocus speaks like a good honest country-man, who is wholly taken up with husbandry: but I do not think it necessary to make my translation speak after that manner.

† Wisdom is a word that signifies divers things, as knowledge, skill, virtue. Plato, uses it for that science which teaches how to govern states.

strained him, by amusing him with good words; but now that I suppose I can be master of him no longer, I think the best course I can take, is to consent to let him take his own course, for fear the conversation he may have in secret, and without my knowledge, should corrupt him. Therefore I am now come to Athens, to put him under the tuition of some sophist : and it is very happy that I have met you; for you are the person whom above all others I should wish to consult upon this affair. If therefore you have any advice to give me, I entreat it of you, and you are too just to refuse me.

Soc. But have you not often heard, Demodocus, that advice is a sacred thing ? and if it is sacred in all other occasions of life, it is much more so in this; for of all things on which a man can ask advice, there is nothing more divine than that which respects the education of children. First then, let you and I agree what it is precisely that you desire, and about what we are to consult, lest I understand one thing, and you another, (as it may often happen) and so at the end of our discourse we both appear ridiculous to ourselves, for having talked so long without understanding one another.

Dem. You say right, Socrates.

Soc. I say right, ay certainly ———— And yet I do not say so right as I thought, but retract in part; for it comes into my mind, that this young man may have a desire very different from that which we think he has ; which would render us still more ridiculous for consulting about quite another thing than the object of his wishes. It is best therefore to begin with him, and ask him, what it is that he desires ?

Dem. Yes, certainly, that is the best way.

Soc. But I pray, what is this fine young man's name?

Dem. His name is Theages.

Soc. What an excellent and sacred name have you given him!* Well, then, Theages, you desire to become wise, and you urge your father to find you a man whose conversation may furnish you with that wisdom with which you are so much in love ?

* The Athenians were very careful to give fine names to their children; but all names are false, when they do not describe the character of those to whom they are given.

The. Yes.

Soc. Who are those persons you call wise? Are they such as are skilful in what they have learnt, or the ignorant?

The. Such as are skilful.

Soc. What! has not your father caused you to be instructed in every thing that the children of our best citizens learn; as to read, to play on musical instruments, to wrestle, and to perform all other exercises?

The. Yes, my father has caused me to be taught all this.

Soc. Well then; and do you think there is any other science in which your father is obliged to cause you to be instructed.

The. Yes, without doubt.

Soc. What science is that? Tell me, that I may render you some service in the matter.

The. My father very well knows it, for I have often told him of it; but he is pleased to speak after such a manner to you, as if he did not know what I desired. There is no day passes but he disputes with me, and still refuses to commit me to the care of some skilful man.

Soc. But all that you have hitherto said to him, has passed only between you two. Now therefore, take me for an arbitrator; and before me declare what science it is you have a mind to attain. For if you were willing to learn that science which teaches how to steer ships, and I should ask you, Theages, what science is it in which you complain your father is not willing to have you instructed; would you not immediately answer me, that it is the science of pilots?

The. Yes, doubtless.

Soc. And if you were willing to learn the art which teaches how to drive chariots, would you not in like manner tell me, it is that of charioteers?

The. I should tell you the very same thing.

Soc. Has that, of which you are so desirous, a name, or has it none?

The. I believe it has a name.

Soc. Do you know it then, without knowing the name of it?

The. I know it, and I know the name of it too.

Soc. Tell me what it is then.

The. What other name can it have than that of science?*

Soc. But is not the art of charioteers also a science? What! do you think it a piece of ignorance?

The. No, certainly.

Soc. Then it is a science: and what is the use of it? Does it not teach us to guide the horses that are fastened to a chariot?

The. Most certainly.

Soc. And is not the art of pilots also a science?

The. So I think.

Soc. Is it not that which teaches us how to guide ships?

The. The very same.

Soc. Well, what is that which you have a mind to learn? and what does that teach us to govern?

The. I think it teaches us to govern men.

Soc. What, sick men?

The. No.

Soc. For that belongs to the medicinal art, does it not?

The. It does.

Soc. Well then, does it teach us to regulate the choir of musicians?

The. Not at all.

Soc. For that properly appertains to music.

The. True.

Soc. But does it teach us to govern those who perform the exercises?

The. No more than the others.

Soc. For that belongs to the gymnastic art. What sort of men then does it teach us to govern? Explain yourself clearly, as I have done on the other sciences.

The. It teaches us to govern those who are in the city?

Soc. But are there not sick men too in the city?

The. Without doubt there are ; but I do not mean them : I speak of the other citizens.

Soc. Let us see if I understand well of what art you speak. I think you do not speak of that which teaches us to govern mowers, vine-dressers, ploughmen, sowers, and threshers : for that belongs to husbandry. Nor do you speak of that which teaches to govern those that handle

* This name is too general, and does not sufficiently explain the thing enquired after, as Socrates is going to shew.

the saw, the plane, and the lathe; for that belongs to the joiner's art. But you speak of the art that teaches to govern, not only these, but all other artificers, and all private persons, both men and women: perhaps this is the science you mean.

The. It is the very same: I had no design to speak of any other.

Soc. But I pray, answer me, did Ægisthus who killed Agamemnon at Argos, govern those sorts of people, artificers and private persons, both men and women, or others?

The. He governed only such as these: are there any other to be governed?

Soc. Did not Peleus, the son of Æacus, likewise govern these at Phthia? And did not Periander, the son of Cypselus, rule them at Corinth? Did not Archelaus, the son of Perdiccas, who some few years * since ascended the throne of Macedonia, also command these sorts of people? And did not Hippias, † the son of Pisistratus, who governs in this city, rule our citizens in like manner?

The. Who doubts it?

Soc. Tell me, what do you call Basis, ‡ the Sybil; and our Amphilytus, when you would denote their profession?

The. What should we call them but diviners?.

Soc. Very well. Answer me after the same manner about these: What do you call Hippias and Periander, when you would denote their profession by the dominion they exercise?

---

* It was five or six years before. He was killed at the end of this very year.

† Hippias, the son of Pisistratus, was tyrant of Athens four years; according to Thucydides, he succeeded his father, and not Hipparchus. After he had reigned four years, he was banished; and twenty years after his exile, was killed at the battle of Marathon, where he bore arms for the Persians.

‡ Basis was a prophet, who, long before Xerxes made a descent into Greece, predicted to the people all that should befall them. Herodotus relates some of his prophecies in his eighth book, and looks upon them to be so formal and plain, since their accomplishment, that he says he neither dares accuse these oracles of falsehood himself, nor suffer others so to do, or to refuse to give credit to them. Aristophanes speaks of this diviner in his comedy of Peace. As for Amphilytus, I know nothing of him.

The. Tyrants, I think; what other name can we give them?

Soc. Then every one who desires to command all the people in this city, desires to acquire a dominion like theirs, a tyrannical dominion, and to become a tyrant.

The. I think so.

Soc. This then is the science with which you are so much in love.

The. That is a natural consequence of what I have said.

Soc. You are a villain! Do you desire to become our tyrant; and have the boldness to complain that your father does not put you under the conduct of some person that may qualify you for tyranny? And you, Demodocus, who know your son's ambition,* and have wherewith to send him to be accomplished in this fine science which he desires; are you not ashamed to envy him this happiness, and not to provide him some great master? But since he now complains of you, as you see, in my presence; let us consider whither to send him, and if we know any one whose conversation may make him an accomplished tyrant.

Dem. Socrates, I beg of you for God's sake, let us consider it together.† For on such an occasion as this, we have need of good advice.

Soc. Hold a little, let us first know of him what he thinks of the matter.

Dem. You may ask him what you please.

Soc. Theages, if we had to do with Euripides, who somewhere says,

> Wise are the tyrants, who with the wise converse;

And should ask him, Euripides, in what do you say tyrants become wise by the conversation of wise men? If, instead of that, he should tell us,

> Wise are the ploughmen, who with the wise converse;

we should not fail to ask him, In what are the plough-

---

* This is an irony of Socrates, founded on what Demodocus said at the beginning of this discourse, viz.—that his son had an ambition that was not dishonourable. Marsilius Ficinus and De Serres were equally mistaken here; and not perceiving the irony, corrupted this passage by their translation.

† Demodocus takes this in earnest, which Socrates spoke ironically

men rendered wise? Do you think he would give us any other answer, than that they are rendered wise in that which belongs to husbandry?

The. No, he would give no other answer.

Soc. And if he should tell us,

Wise are the cooks, who with the wise converse;

and we should ask him wherein they are made wise: What do you think he would answer? Would he not say, they are made wise in the art of cookery?

The. Without doubt.

Soc. And if he should say,

Wise are the wrestlers, who with the wise converse:

Would he not upon the repetition of the same question give us the same reply, that they are made expert in the art of wrestling?

The. Yes, certainly.

Soc. This being so, since he tells us,

Wise are the tyrants, who with the wise converse;

if we should ask him, Euripides, in what are those tyrants rendered wise? What answer do you think he would make us? In what would he make this wisdom consist?

The. I protest I cannot tell.

Soc. Shall I tell you then?

The. With all my heart, if you please.

Soc. He would say they were made wise in that art, which Anacreon tells us, the wise Callicrete * knew perfectly well. Do not you remember his songs?

The. I do remember.

Soc. Well, then, do not you desire to be committed to the care of some man, who is of the same profession with this virgin of Cyane, and knows, like her, the art of forming tyrants, that you may become our tyrant, and that of the whole city?

The. Socrates, you have played and jested on me a great while.

Soc. How! Do not you say you desire to acquire that

---

* This was a virgin, who employed herself in teaching politics, as Aspasia, Diotima, and some others did after her. The verses which Anacreon made on her, are lost.

science which will teach you to govern all the citizens?
Can you govern them without becoming their tyrant?

The. I could heartily wish to become the tyrant of all
mankind, and if that be too much, at least of the greatest
part of them; and I believe, Socrates, you would have the
same ambition as well as other men. Nay, perhaps it would
so little content you to be a tyrant, that you would be a God; *
but I did not tell you that that was the thing I desired.

Soc. What is it you desire? Do not you say you desire to govern citizens?

The. Not to govern them by force as tyrants do; but
by their own consent, as those great men have done,
whom we have had in this city.

Soc. What! as Themistocles, Pericles, Cimon, and other
great politicians have done?

The. Yes.

Soc. Well, then, if you had a mind to become very expert
in the art of horsemanship, to what men do you think you
ought to apply yourself to become a good horseman?
Would you go to any other than equerries?

The. No, certainly.

Soc. Would you not make choice of the best equerries; those that have the greatest number of horses, and
such as ride not only their own horses, but those of other
men?

The. Without doubt, I should choose such.

Soc. And if you would become very expert at shoot-
ing, would you not address yourself to the best archers;
and to such as best know how to use all sorts of bows and
arrows?

The. Yes, certainly.

Soc. Tell me then, since you have a mind to become expert in politics, do you think you can acquire this skill in
addressing yourself to any beside politicians, who have a
depth of judgment in this science, and know how to conduct, not only their own city, but many others, as well of
the Greeks, as the barbarians? Or, do you think by conversing with any other sort of persons, to become as expert
as these great men?

---

* This is founded on what Socrates was wont to say, that men
should labour to make themselves like God.

The. Socrates, I have heard talk of some discourses of yours; which you made (as it is said) to shew, that the sons of these great politicians were no better than the sons of coblers; and as far as I can judge, it is an undeniable truth. I should therefore be a great fool to believe that any one of them could give me his wisdom, which he did not communicate to his own son, and which he ought to have bestowed on him much rather, if he were capable of doing it, than on a stranger. *

Soc. What would you do then, Theages, if you had a son that followed you so closely every day, telling you, he had a mind to be a great painter? And complained continually, that you who were his father, would not be at the least expense to satisfy his desire; while on the other side he despised the most excellent masters, and refused to go to school to them to learn their art? I say the same, if he had a mind to play on the flute, or to be an excellent harper: should you know any other way to gratify him, or any other people to send him to; when he should refuse such masters?

The. For my part, I know not what could be done.

Soc. This is exactly the same course that you take with your father. How then can you be surprised and complain, that he knows not what to do with you, nor where to send you to make you an accomplished man? For it lies wholly at your own door. If you desire, he will immediately put you under the conduct of our best masters, and such as are most expert in politics. You have nothing to do but to choose your teacher; they will ask nothing of you. So that you may save your money, and acquire with them more reputation among the people,† than you can obtain in the conversation of any other.

The. Well then, Socrates, are not you likewise one of those great men? If you will suffer me to attend you, it is enough, I will seek for no other master.

---

* All those great politicians could not teach their children to be wise; a sure sign that wisdom cannot be taught. There is nothing of it in man, but what God puts into him, as Socrates proves more at large in his *Menon.*

† For the common people are very ill judges, and may be easily deceived; they constantly take those men for the most wise and skilful, who are most bold and insolent.

Soc. What is that you say, Theages?

Dem. Ah, Socrates, my son has said very well, and you would do me a great kindness! No, I have no greater happiness than to see my son pleased with your company; and that you are so good as to permit him to take this liberty. I am ashamed to say how much I desire it: but I entreat you both, for God's sake, you, Socrates, to receive my son; and you, son, never to seek any other master than Socrates. By this means you will both deliver me from my greatest trouble and fears. For I am continually ready to die with fear, lest my son should fall into the hands of some person that will corrupt him.

The. Well, Sir, you may lay aside your fears on my account; if you are but happy enough to persuade Socrates, and engage him to be troubled with me.

Dem. Son, you have reason. I will now apply myself to none but you, Socrates; and not to amuse you with superfluous discourse, I am ready to give myself up to you, and all that I have in the world. You may entirely dispose of me, if you will love my Theages, and procure him all that good, you are capable of doing him.

Soc. I do not wonder, Demodocus, that you are so very importunate, if you believe your son may receive advantage from me; for I know nothing about which a wise father ought to be more earnest and careful, than about what concerns his son, and what may make him a good man. But that which surprises me, and which I cannot comprehend, is, how you came to think me capable of rendering you this great piece of service, and of forming him into a good citizen: and how he came to imagine me to be in a better condition of assisting him than his father? For in the first place, you have lived longer in the world than I; you have exercised the principal offices, and are the most considerable person in your town; and none is more honoured or esteemed than you, in all the rest of the city.* Neither you nor your son see any of these advantages in me. But if Theages despises the conversation of our politicians, and is looking after those persons, who promise to educate youth well; we have here Prodicus of Ceos, Gorgias the Leontine, Polus of Agrigentum, and divers others, who

* The city was composed of divers towns or boroughs.

---

are of so great ability, that as they go their rounds from city to city, they make a shift to persuade the young people of all the noblest and richest families, who might be instructed gratis by one of their own citizens, whom they would please to choose; they make a shift, I say, to persuade them to renounce those of their own city, and to adhere to them, though they must pay them great sums, and after all think themselves under great obligations to them. These are the men that you, and your son should choose, instead of thinking of me; * for I know none of those polite and happy sciences: I would indeed understand them with all my heart; but I have always professed to acknowledge, that I know nothing (as I may say) unless it be one little science which only respects love.† And I, for my part, dare boast of being more profound in this science, such as it is, than any of my predecessors, or those of the present age.

The. Sir, you see very well, Socrates will not trouble himself with me; if he would, I should very readily put myself under his conduct: but he jests, when he thus speaks of himself; for I know divers of my equals, and others of a more advanced age than mine, who, before they attended to him, had no great matter of merit; but since they have enjoyed his conversation, are in a little time become the finest men in the world; and far surpass those, to whom they were much inferior before.

Soc. Theages, do you know how this comes to pass?

The. Yes, truly, I know it very well; and if you were willing, I should soon be like those young men, and should have no occasion to envy them.

Soc. You are mistaken, my dear Theages, and are very far from the truth; which I am now going to inform you. I have had, by the favour of God, ‡ ever since I was born,

* This is an irony which Socrates uses to ridicule that excessive eagerness, with which the Athenians ran to these sophists, who were good for nothing but to corrupt their minds.

† Socrates means, that he was only fit to inspire men with the love of wisdom. Without this love all is dead. This is a principle of life, and, as he elsewhere says, the most speedy, most certain, and most efficacious help which God has given men to bring them to supreme happiness.

‡ I have had by the favour of God, the Greek says Θείᾳ μοίρᾳ, by a divine lot, that is, to speak properly, by predestination; and

a genius that always accompanies and governs me. This genius is a voice, which, whenever it speaks to me, always diverts me from what I have a mind to do, and never prompts me to it. When any one of my friends communicates any design to me, if I hear this voice, it is a certain sign that God does not approve of this design, but would divert him from it. I will name several persons to you, who are witnesses of what I say. You know the gallant Charmides, Glaucon's son: he came to me one day, to acquaint me with a design he had to go and contend at the Nemean games.* He had no sooner begun to communicate this matter to me, but I heard the voice ; therefore I endeavoured to dissuade him from it, and said thus to him : As soon as you began to open your mouth, I heard the voice of the genius that guides me, therefore I entreat you not to go. He replied, Perhaps this voice advertises you that I shall not be crowned : but if I do not obtain the victory, I shall, however, exercise myself; I shall engage with the rest, and that is enough. With these words he left me, and went to the afore-said exercises. You may know from his own mouth what befel him, and it well deserves your notice. And if you would ask Clitomacus, the brother of Timarchus, † what this latter told him when he was going to die, for having despised the admonition of my good genius ; and again, what was said to him by Evathlus, who was so famous for running races, and who entertained Timarchus when he fled; he would tell you, that Timarchus said to him in express terms——

The. What did he say to him, Socrates?

Soc. " I am going to die, because I would not believe Socrates." And if you are curious to know the story, I will tell it you. When Timarchus rose from table with Philemon, the son of Philemonides, to go and kill Nicias

consequently by the favour of God. μοῖρᾳ is here the same thing as κλῆρος in the writings of St. Paul ; as that learned and pious person, who has lately made a small extract of Plato, has observed before me.

* One of the four famous games of Greece, which were celebrated once in three years near the city of Nemea in Peloponnesus, in honour of Archemorus.

† I suppose this is Timarchus of Cheronea, who desired to be interred near one of Socrates' sons, who died a little before. I could never find any footstep of this history elsewhere.

the son of Heroscamander, for none but they two were in
the conspiracy; as he rose up, he said to me, What do
you say to me, Socrates? You have nothing to do, but to
stay all here, and drink together; I am obliged to be
gone, but will return in a moment, if I can. Upon this I
heard the voice, and immediately calling him back, said
to him, I beg you would not go out; my good genius has
given his wonted signal. Upon which he stayed: but some
time after rises up again, and says, Socrates, I am going.
The voice was repeated, and I stopped him again. In fine,
because he would escape me, he rose up the third time,
without saying any thing to me; and taking his opportunity,
when my thoughts were otherwise employed, he slipped
out, and did that which brought him to his end: this was
the reason he told his brother, he was going to die because
he would not believe me. You may also learn from many
of our citizens, what I told them about the expedition of
Sicily, and the shocks that our army would receive there;*
but not to mention things that are past, of which you may
be easily informed by those that know them perfectly well;
you may now make trial of this signal, which my good
genius commonly gives me, that you may see whether he
speaks true. For when the brave Sannion went for the
army, I heard this voice; and he is now going with Thrasyl-
lus† against Ephesus, and the other cities of Ionia: I am
persuaded he will die there, or some misfortune will befall
him; and I very much fear that enterprise will not succeed.‡ I have told you all this, to make you comprehend,
that even for those who are willing to adhere to me, all
depends on this good genius that governs me. For those
whom he opposes can never derive any advantage from
me: I cannot so much as have any conversation with them.
There are many, whom he does not hinder me from seeing; and yet these make no greater proficiency than the
former: but those, whose conversation with me is approved

* Under the government of Alcibiades and Nicias.
† Thrasyllus was chosen general with Thrasybulus, the fourth
year of the 92nd Olympiad.
‡ Indeed the Athenians were beaten and repulsed at Ephesus.
Xenoph. Book 1. Therefore Plutarch says in the Life of Alcibiades,
that Thrasyllus's army was terribly galled under the walls o
Ephesus; and that in memory of this defeat, the Ephesians erected
a trophy of brass, to the shame of the Athenians

and favoured by this good genius, are such as you told me
of just now, who, in a very little time, make a very great
progress ; in some this progress is stable and permanent,
and takes deep root; and in others it is but for a time:
that is, while they are with me, they advance after a surprising manner ; but they no sooner leave me, but they
return to their former condition, and do not at all differ
from the generality of men.* This is what happened to
Aristides, the son of Lysimachus, and grandson of Aristides:
while he was with me, he made a very strange progress in
a very short time ; but being obliged to go in some expedition, he embarked : at his return he found, that Thucydides,† the son of Melesias, and grandson of Thucydides,
had been willing to be acquainted with me; but it happened the day before, I know not how, that he fell out
with me for some words we had in disputing. Now
Aristides, coming to see me, after the first compliments;
Socrates, says he, I am just now told, that Thucydides is
angry with you, and acts with a great deal of haughtiness,
as if he were somewhat more than ordinary. It is true,
said I. Ha ! replied he, what, does he no longer remember what a slave he was before he saw you ?‡ It is very
likely he has forgotten it, said I. Truly, Socrates, added
he, a very ridiculous thing has happened to me. I presently asked him what it was. It is this, said he : before I went for the army, I was capable of discoursing with
men of the greatest sense ; and was not inferior to any
of them in conversation. I made as handsome a figure as
another; and always kept company with the best and most

* A remarkable passage. Here are four states of men. Some are
rejected of God for their wickedness, which cannot be hid from him
others are tolerated for a time : God gives them time to see, and
learn, but they are not attentive. Others are approved, but these
last succeed very differently : in some the good seed falling into good
ground, takes deep root, and in others it flourishes but for a time ;
as the Gospel says of those who receive the word in stony places, or
among thorns. This is the truth Socrates designs to teach in this
place.

† The grandson of Thucydides, who rivalled Pericles in the government.

‡ Men are no better than vile slaves, before they have attended
to philosophical discourses.

polite men I could find.* Whereas now it is quite contrary: I carefully avoid them, I am so much ashamed
of my ignorance. I asked him, if this faculty had left
him suddenly, or gradually. He answered me, that it left
him gradually. Well, how did you come by it? said I:
was it while you were learning something of me, or some
other way? I will tell you, Socrates, replied he, it is a
thing that will seem incredible, but yet it is very true:
I could never learn any thing of you, as you know very
well.† However, I made some proficiency, if I was but in
the same house where you were,‡ though not in the same
room; when I could be in the same room, I advanced
still more; and whenever you spoke, I sensibly found myself improve, yet more when I had my eyes upon you, than
when I looked another way: but this progress was incomparably greater, when I sat near you, and touched you,
whereas now all this habit is utterly vanished. You see,
then, Theages, said Socrates, what sort of conversation is to
be had with me. If it please God, you will advance consi-
derably, and in a very little time;§ otherwise your endeavours will be fruitless. Judge then, if it be not more advantageous, and safe for you, to apply yourself to one of those
masters, who are constantly successful with all their scholars,‖ than to follow me, with all the hazards you must run.

The. I will tell you, Socrates, what we ought to do, in
my opinion. When we begin to live together, let us try
this God that conducts us: if he approves our conversa-

---

* Those who spent their time in discoursing on solid and agreeable
subjects.

† He means, he learned nothing that had made a deep and lasting
impression on his mind; he had opinions only, and not science,
since he had been by himself; but was more knowing when he was
with Socrates.

‡ There are four degrees of light, according as you more or less
approach wise men. It is something to lodge in the same house, it
is a little more to be in the same room; it is yet a greater advantage to have one's eyes always upon them, that so one may lose none
of their words. Few persons are so confirmed in wisdom, that they
can lose sight of them with impunity, and without great damage.
These different degrees are still more remarkable in proportion to
the approach we make to the divine wisdom. I believe this is all
the mystery Socrates designs to teach here.

§ For all the good we either do, or receive, comes from God.

‖ A handsome banter of the sophists.

tion, I am at the top of my wishes : if he disapproves it, let us immediately consider what course to take, and whether I ought to seek another master, or should endeavour to appease this God by prayers, by sacrifices, or any other expiations,* which our diviners teach.

Dem. Do not oppose the young man's desires any longer. Theages speaks very well.

Soc. If you think it is best to do so; with all my heart. I agree with you.

* The ways men use to appease the anger of God are prayers, sacrifices, and purifications.

EUTYPHRON; OR, OF HOLINESS.

THE ARGUMENT.

In all times, and in all religions, there have been superstitious persons and hypocrites. Both these have offered almost the same injury to God, and equally hurt religion. Plato introduces one of these characters in this Dialogue; for it is not easy to determine whether Eutyphron acts superstitiously or hypocritically: the former is most probable. Eutyphron goes about to accuse his own father of murder; this is a very unnatural step: but on the other hand, it is the step of a man who consults not flesh and blood; when the question is about doing an action so agreeable to God, as that of bringing a criminal to punishment. The business in hand therefore here, is to examine this action, to know if it be just. And Plato renews this discourse to ridicule the false religions of the Pagans, and the plurality of Gods, together with the rest of their fables: and to shew, that they who then passed for most intelligent persons in matters of religion, had indeed no knowledge of it, and rendered God only false worship, which dishonoured him. This is a great design, and he executes it with marvellous address, to which purpose the person against whom Socrates had disputed, serves extremely well. For Eutyphron was no ordinary man; he was a diviner, and consequently clothed with the character, and trusted with the office of instructing others in religion. Nothing can be more ingenious and natural, than the beginning of this Dialogue, where Plato with great simplicity and modesty, and without the least appearance of affectation, discovers at first view not only the *character* of Eutyphron, and that of all superstitious persons, who by their religious mistakes are commonly carried to the commission of all sorts of injuries and crimes, but also that of Socrates, that of his persecutors, and in general, that of the Athenians. This Dialogue is full of excellent precepts of morality and religion. There is a great deal of ingenuity and subtilty in it. The lively descriptions, the frequent ironies, and satirical strokes admirably diversify it. Was there ever seen a more subtile piece of satire than that which Plato makes against Melitus? He is not content to mention his name, and in what part of the city he was born, but likewise draws his picture; and yet all these indications cannot make him known to Eutyphron. He that accuses Socrates, and thinks himself capable of reforming the commonwealth, by shewing what it is that corrupts youth, and overthrows religion, is neither known to him whom he accuses, nor to the ministers of that religion of which he pretends to be the great support. All the other like strokes will be easily observed in reading; and the beauty of the character of the superstitious man, who

believes a thing only because he believes it, and who is always near
the truth without ever attaining it, will be plainly discerned. The
reader will see with pleasure, that Eutyphron is a good honest man,
who has upright intentions, but is so full of respect for the fables that
have been taught him, that he receives them all as sacred, without
ever entertaining the least suspicion concerning them; he is so swelled
with pride, and full of that precipitant confidence, which superstition commonly inspires, that he publishes his visions as certain
truths, not to be contradicted by any man. And Socrates, who makes
as if he were willing to be instructed, receives his doctrine with refined ironies, and ambiguous railleries; and at length confutes it with
abundance of strength and solidity.

EUTYPHRON, SOCRATES.

Eut. WHAT news, Socrates? What! have you left the
company of Lyceus, to come hither into the King's Porch?*
You have no business to bring you hither, as I have.

Soc. It is somewhat worse than business, Eutyphron;
the Athenians call it an accusation.

Eut. How do you say? Then it is likely somebody
accuses you, for I can never believe you would accuse any
one.†

Soc. You are in the right.

Eut. Well, who is your accuser?

Soc. I do not know very well myself, I take him to be
a young man, who is not yet known; I think his name is
Melitus, he is of the town of Pittheus: if you remember
any one of that quarter of the city, who bears that name,
who has lank hair, a thin beard, and a crooked nose, that
is the man.

Eut. I do not remember any such person, Socrates;
but I pray what is the charge he brings against you?

Soc. What is the charge! Why, it is such a one as

---

* This King's Porch was a place on the right side of the Ceramique,
where one of the nine Archons, who was called the King, presided
for the space of a year, and took cognizance of the affairs of orphans
and of outrages that were committed against religion.

† This is very remarkable. Eutyphron, who is going to accuse
his own father, cannot believe that Socrates is capable of accusing
any man. Plato makes use of the precipitancy of this superstitious
man, or of the good opinion he has of himself, to insinuate that at
Athens honest men never drove the trade of accusers.

shews him to be no ordinary man. For it is no little
thing to be so knowing in such important and sublime
matters, at an age so little advanced as his. He says he
knows how our youth are corrupted, and who they are
that corrupt them. He seems to be some able man, who
has taken notice of my ignorance, and is come to accuse
me for having corrupted his companions; and to bring me
before the city, as our common mother. And it must be
confessed, he seems the only person that knows how to
lay the foundations of good policy. For it is reasonable
that a statesman should always begin with the education of
young people, to render them as virtuous as may be; as a
good gardener bestows his first labour and care on the young
plants, and then passes on to the other: Melitus, doubtless,
takes the same course, and begins by cutting us up who
hinder the young plants from sprouting and improving.
After this, without doubt, he will extend his beneficent
labours to those plants that are more advanced; and will
by this means do the greatest kindness imaginable to the
city. This is what may be expected from a person that
knows so well how to begin at the right end.

Eut. I should be glad to see it, Socrates; but I tremble
for fear of the contrary; for in attacking you, he seems
to me to attack the city in the most sacred part of it:* but
I pray tell me what he says you do, thus to corrupt young
people.

Soc. He says, I do such things, as at first hearing must
needs seem absurd and impossible; for he says, I am a
forger of Gods, that I introduce new Gods, and do not
believe the old ones. This is the charge he has against me.

Eut. I understand you; it is because you say, you have
a genius that daily guides you. Upon this he accuses you
of introducing new opinions in religion, and comes to
defame you in this court, well knowing, that the mob is
always ready to receive these sort of calumnies. What do
not I myself meet with, when in public assemblies I speak

---

* The Greek says, in injuring you, he labours to ruin the city,
and begins by the fire-side. It was a proverb in Greece, to begin
by the fire-side, when they spoke of beginning with what was most
excellent and sacred; for the fire-side contained the domestic Gods.
So that this was a great encomium of Socrates. Wise men are to
cities what domestic Gods are to families.

of divine things, and predict what shall come to pass? They all laugh at me as a fool; not that any one of the things I have foretold has failed of its accomplishment; but the business is this, they envy all such as we are. And what remains for us to do? The best way is never to trouble our heads about it; but to go on still in our own way.

Soc. My dear Eutyphron, is it so great an unhappiness to be laughed at? For at bottom I believe the Athenians do not much trouble their heads to examine whether a man has a great capacity or not, provided he does not go about to teach others what he knows. But I believe, if a man should make it his business to teach, they would be downright angry, either out of envy, as you intimate, or for some other reason that we do not know.

Eut. I have no mind to try to my cost, as you do, what sentiments they have of me.

Soc. That is another matter; it may be you are very reserved, and do not willingly communicate your wisdom to others;* whereas I am afraid they think the love I bear to all mankind engages me too freely to teach them all I know, not only without asking a reward, but even by soliciting and pressing them to hear me. But if they would content themselves with laughing at me, as you say they do at you, it would be no unpleasant thing to spend some hours in this court in laughing and divertisement; but if they take up the matter in earnest, none but your diviners know what will be the event of it.

Eut. Perhaps you may sustain no damage, but may come to a happy issue in your business, as well as I in mine.

Soc. Have you business here, then? Are you defendant or plaintiff?

Eut. I am plaintiff.

Soc. Whom do you prosecute?

Eut. If I should tell you, you would take me for a fool.

Soc. How! do you prosecute one that cannot be taken? Has he got wings?

* Socrates makes use of the confession which he has drawn out of Eutyphron, to shew by this diviner the character of those who were set up to teach religion: they neither taught nor refuted any thing but through fear left the people in superstition and ignorance.

Eut. The person I prosecute, instead of having wings, is so old that he can scarce walk.

Soc. Who is he?

Eut. It is my father.

Soc. Your father!

Eut. Yes, my father.

Soc. Of what do you accuse him?

Eut. Of murder.

Soc. Of murder, good God! That is an accusation indeed above the comprehension of the people, who will never conceive that it can be just; an ordinary man would have enough to do to give it any tolerable colour. This is a thing that belongs only to him who is arrived at the highest pitch of wisdom.*

Eut. You say true Socrates, it belongs only to such a person.

Soc. Is it any one of your relations that your father has killed? without doubt it must be so; for you would not prosecute your father in a court of justice for the sake of a stranger.

Eut. What an absurdity is that, Socrates, to think that in this respect there is any difference between a relation and a stranger! The thing is equal; that which ought chiefly to be considered, is to examine whether the person that has killed him, did it justly or unjustly. If it was justly, he ought not to be put to any trouble; but if unjustly, you are obliged to prosecute him, whatever friendship or relation there is between you. To have the least conversation with him, is to make yourself an accomplice of his crime; and so it is not to prosecute him, or bring him to punishment, which alone can purify and expiate you both.† But to apprize you of the fact: the deceased was one of our farmers, who rented a piece of land of us when we dwelt at Naxus: this man having one day drank too much, fell into a passion, and was so transported with rage against one of our slaves, that he killed him. My

---

* From this principle of Socrates, it follows by a just consequence, that it is only God's province to command and authorise such actions as appear severe and cruel to nature; which is a great truth.

† A false principle: for justice pushed too far, becomes injustice and impiety.

father ordered him to be cast into a deep pit with his hands and feet bound, and immediately sent hither to consult one of those who have the inspection of religious matters, and cases of conscience, to know what he should do with him;* and in the mean time neglected this poor prisoner, and left him without sustenance, as an assassin, whose life was of no consequence, so that he died : hunger, cold, and the weight of his chains, killed him, before the person, my father had sent, returned.—Now, our whole family fall upon me, because I, for the sake of an assassin accuse my father of murder, which they pretend he has not committed; and if he had, they maintain I ought not to prosecute him, because the deceased was a villain and a murderer; and besides, they say it is an impious action for a son to prefer a criminal process against his father : so blind are they about divine things, and so incapable of discerning what is profane and impious, from that which is just and holy.

Soc. But, I pray, Eutyphron, do you yourself think you so accurately understand all divine things, and that you can so precisely distinguish between what is holy and what is profane, that the state of the case being as you say, you can prosecute your father without fearing to commit an impious action ?

Eut. Certainly Eutyphron would scarce have any advantage above other men, if he did not understand all these things perfectly well.

Soc. O admirable Eutyphron, I see then the best course I can take is to become your disciple, and before the determination of my process, to let Melitus know : that I have hitherto looked upon it as the greatest advantage in the world, to have a good understanding in divine things, and to be well instructed in religion. But now, seeing he accuses me of falling into error, and of rashly introducing new opinions about the Deity, I have put myself into your school : so that, Melitus, I will say, if you acknowledge Eutyphron to be a person of ability in such matters, and that he has good notions, I declare to you, I have embraced

* In Greece, there were interpreters of divine things, who were public persons, to whom the people addressed themselves in all weighty cases. Those, who were any thing devout, would not undertake the least thing, without having first consulted them.

G

the same sentiments. Therefore forbear to prosecute me any farther. And if, on the contrary, you think Euty-phron is not orthodox, cause the master to be called in question before you meddle with the scholar : he is the cause of all this mischief; it is he that ruins both his father and me. He ruins me in teaching me a false reli-gion; and he ruins his father in prosecuting him by the principles of this same religion, and if he continues to prosecute me without any regard to my request, or leaves me to pursue you, you will not fail to make your appear-ance, and to speak the same thing which I shall have signified to him.

Eut. Upon my word, Socrates, if he is so impudent as to attack me, I shall soon find his weak side, and shall at least run but half the danger.

Soc. I know it very well, and that is the reason I am so desirous of being your disciple, being well assured, that no person is so bold as to dare look you in the face; no, not Melitus himself, who looks so intently, and who can see so well to the bottom of my soul, that he accuses me of impiety.

In the mean time, then, tell me, I beseech you, what you just now affirmed, and which you know so well, viz. what is holy and just, impious and unjust—in respect of *killing men*, for instance—and so in all other subjects that may offer themselves to us. Is not sanctity always like itself in all sorts of actions; and is not impiety, which is its contrary, always the same too? So that the same idea, the same character of impiety, is always found in every thing which is impious.

Eut. It is certainly so, Socrates.

Soc. What is it then that you call pious and holy, pro-fane and impious?

Eut. I call that pious and holy, for example, which I doing to-day, namely, to prosecute every man who mmits murder, sacrilege, and such other crimes, whether be father, mother, brother, or any other person. And call it an impious thing to suffer the criminal quietly to enjoy his crime. I pray, Socrates, mind well what I say; I will give you very certain proofs that my definition is conformable to the law.* I have already mentioned it to

* It is so indeed; but it is ill applied here, and is not true on all

many persons, and have made them confess, that there is
nothing more just, than not to spare a wicked man, let
him be who he will. All men are convinced that Jupiter
is the best and most just of all Gods; and all agree, that
he put his father in chains, because he, contrary to all
manner of justice, devoured his children. Saturn had
before treated his father with yet greater severity for some
other fault. And yet people cry out against me, when I
prosecute my father for an atrocious act of injustice; and
they fall into a manifest contradiction, in judging so differently of the actions of those Gods, and mine, in which
I had no other design than that of imitating them.*

Soc. Is this the thing, Eutyphron, which has brought
me to-day to this bar; because when I am told these
tales of the Gods, I cannot hear them without pain? Is
this the crime with which I am going to be charged? If
you, who are so able in matters of religion, agree with the
people in this, and believe these stories, it is absolutely
necessary that I should believe them too, who confess in-
genuously that I know nothing of these matters. Shall I
pretend to be wiser than my teachers, and make head
against them? Therefore, I beg of you, in the name of
that God who presides over friendship, do not deceive me:
Do you believe all these things you say?

Eut. I not only believe these, but others too that are
more surprising, of which the people are wholly ignorant.†

Soc. You seriously believe then that there are great
quarrels, animosities, and wars among the Gods? You
believe all those other passions that reign among them,
which are so surprising, and are represented by poets and
painters in their poems and pictures, which are exposed to
view in all parts of our temples; and are wrought with
various colours in that mysterious tapestry which is carried
in procession to the citadel every fifth year,‡ during the

occasions, as it is not on this. That which Eutyphron here calls the
law, is the law of nature, which teaches us to imitate God in all we
know of him.

* The imitation of those false Gods could only produce very ill
actions, as the poets themselves have acknowledged.

† Doubtless he means those mysteries which were known only to
those that were initiated.

‡ This tapestry was the sail of Minerva's ship, on which the principal actions of this Goddess were described in needle-work; which

Panathenea;* must we receive all these things as so many great truths, Eutyphron?

Eut. Not only these, Socrates, but a great many others besides, as I told you just now, which I will explain to you, if you please; and upon my word they will make you wonder.

Soc. No, they will not make me wonder much, but you may explain them to me another time when you are more at leisure. I pray now endeavour to explain to me what I asked you, a little more clearly, for you have not yet fully answered my question; you have not taught me what holiness is. You have only told me, that that is a holy thing which you do in accusing your father of murder.

Eut. And I have told you the truth.

Soc. It may be so: but are there not a great many other things which you call holy?

Eut. Without doubt there are.

Soc. I intreat you therefore to remember, that what I asked you was not to teach me one or two holy things among a great many others that are so too; but to give me a clear and distinct idea of the nature of holiness, and of that which causes all holy things to be holy. For you told me yourself, that there is only one and the same character which makes all holy things to be what they are; as there is one that makes wickedness to be always wickedness. Do not you remember it?

Eut. Oh yes, I remember it.

Soc. Then teach me to know what this character is, that I may have it always before my eyes, and may use it as the true model, and real original, that so I may be in a condition to affirm of every thing which I see you or others do, that that which resembles this model is holy, and that which does not resemble it is wicked.

Eut. If that is your desire, Socrates, I am ready to satisfy you.

Soc. Truly, that is what I would have.

---

after it had been exposed in the ship at the beginning of the feast, was carried in procession. The ship was rolled along on firm ground to the temple of Ceres at Eleusine, from whence it was brought back, and carried to the citadel; and the statue of the goddess was at last adorned with it.

* The feast of Minerva.

Eut. I say then, that holiness is that which is agreeable to the Gods, and wickedness is that which is disagreeable to them.

Soc. Very well, Eutyphron, you have at last answered me precisely according to my question. But I do not yet know whether you speak true. However, surely you will know how to convince me of the truth of what you advance.

Eut. I will answer you.

Soc. Come then, let us lay down what we say plainly. A holy thing, or a holy man, is a thing or a man that is agreeable to God; a wicked thing, or a wicked man, is a man or thing that is disagreeable to him. Thus what is holy and what is wicked are directly opposite, are they not?

Eut. That is beyond dispute.

Soc. I think this is very well laid down.

Eut. I think so too, Socrates.

Soc. But have we not also affirmed, that the Gods have frequent animosities and contentions among themselves, and are often embroiled and divided one against another?*

Eut. Yes, without doubt.

Soc. Therefore let us now examine what may be the occasion of that difference of sentiment which produces those quarrels and that enmity among them. If you and I should dispute about numbers, to know which was the greater, would this difference make us enemies, and carry us to all manner of excesses and violences? Should we not immediately set ourselves to reckon, that we might presently be of the same mind?

Eut. It is very true, we should so.

Soc. And if we should dispute about the different bigness of bodies, should we not presently go about measuring them? and would not that soon put an end to our dispute?

Eut. It would so.

Soc. And if we should contest about weight, would not our difference be soon determined by means of a pair of scales?

Eut. No doubt of it.

Soc. Well, then, what is there, about which if we should

* Socrates refutes this definition of holiness, by shewing that it cannot subsist with their theology,

come to dispute, without having a certain rule to which
we might recur, we should become irreconcileable enemies,
and fall into extravagant passion one against the other?
Perhaps none of these things at present occur to your
mind.   I will tell you some of them, and you shall judge
whether I am in the right.   Is it not what is just and unjust, comely and indecent, good and evil?   Are not these
the things about which we every day differ, and not finding
a sufficient rule to make us accord, we fall into the greatest
enmity? When I say *we*, I speak of all mankind in general.

Eut. That indeed is the true cause of all our law-suits,
and all our wars.

Soc. And if it be true, that the Gods are at variance
among themselves about any thing, must it not necessarily
be some one of these?

Eut. It must be so.

Soc. According to you then, excellent Eutyphron, the
Gods are divided about what is just and unjust, comely and
indecent, good and evil.* For if they did not contest about
these things, they would have no occasion of wrangling,
but would be always united, would they not?

Eut. You say very right.

Soc. And the things which each God takes to be comely,
good and just, are loved by him, and the contrary hated.

Eut. Most certainly.

Soc. According to you then, one and the same thing
seems just to some of them, and unjust to others, seeing
wars and seditions are stirred up among them by such disputes as these: is it not so?

Eut. It is so without doubt.

Soc. Hence it follows, that one and the same thing is
the object both of the love and hatred of the Gods, and is
at the same time pleasing and displeasing to them.

Eut. So it seems.

Soc. And consequently, according to you, what is holy
and profane, are the same thing.

Eut. I grant, this consequence may be just.

Soc. Then you have not answered my question, incomparable Eutyphron; for I did not ask you what it was that
at the same time was holy and profane, pleasing and dis-

---

* Socrates handsomely ridicules those Gods, who know not what
justice and injustice, vice and virtue, are.

pleasing to the Gods. So that I foresee it is possible, without a miracle, that the action you are about to-day, in prosecuting your father to bring him to punishment, may please Jupiter, and at the same time may displease Cœlum and Saturn; may be approved by Vulcan, and disapproved by Juno; and so of the rest of the Gods, who may be of different sentiments.

Eut. But, Socrates, I suppose there is no dispute about this among the Gods; nor does any one of them pretend, that he who has killed a man unjustly, should be suffered to go unpunished.

Soc. Neither is there any man that pretends to that: Did you ever see any one that dared put the matter in question, whether he that had wilfully murdered a man, or committed any other act of injustice, ought to be punished or not?

Eut. We every where hear and see scarce any thing else before the tribunals, but persons who have committed acts of injustice, saying and doing what they can to avoid punishment.

Soc. But do the persons of whom you speak, Eutyphron, confess that they have done those acts of injustice of which they are accused; and after this confession, maintain that they ought not to be punished?

Eut. They have no mind to confess so, Socrates.

Soc. Then they do not say and do all they can; for they dare neither maintain nor assert, that when their injustice is manifest, and sufficiently attested, they ought not to be chastised for it, Is it not so?

Eut. It is very true.

Soc. They do not put the matter in question, whether he that is guilty of injustice ought to be punished; nobody doubts that. But that about which they dispute, is the nature of injustice, to determine in what, how, and on what occasion it is committed.

Eut. That is certain.

Soc. And is it not the same in heaven, if it be true, as you have asserted, that the Gods are at variance about what is just and unjust? Do not some of them affirm that others of them are unjust? and do not the latter maintain the contrary? For there is not one among them, no more than among us, who dares advance such a notion as this That he that commits injustice ought not to be punished.

Eut. All you say is true, Socrates; at least, in general.

Soc. You may say in particular too: for it is about particular actions that both men and Gods dispute every day, if it be true that the Gods dispute about any thing. Do not some say such an action is just, and others that it is unjust?

Eut. Yes, doubtless.

Soc. Come, then, my dear Eutyphron, for my particular instruction, tell me what certain proof you have that the Gods all disapprove the death of your farmer, who, after he had so barbarously knocked his fellow-servant on the head, was laid in irons, and so perished before your father had received the answer which he expected from Athens. Demonstrate to me, that on this occasion it is a pious and just action for a son to accuse his father of murder, and to bring him to punishment for it; and see if you can fairly and evidently prove to me, that the action of such a son is pleasing to the Gods. If you do this, I shall never cease to admire and celebrate your capacity as long as I live.

Eut. It is somewhat difficult indeed, to prove it to you. For my part, I could prove it as evidently as ——

Soc. I understand you. That is to say, you think I have a duller head than any of your judges; for as to them, there is no difficulty in the case: you will make it appear to them that your farmer was unjustly killed, and that all the Gods disapprove your father's action.

Eut. I will make it appear to them as clear as the light, provided they will but hear me.

Soc. Oh! they will not fail to hear you, provided you make a fine speech to them.* But I will tell you what reflection I just now made, while I was hearkening to what you said. I said within myself, suppose it were possible for Eutyphron to persuade me that all the Gods are of the mind, that this farmer was unjustly killed; should I be ever the wiser? should I understand, better than I do, what is holy, and what is profane? The death of this farmer is displeasing to the Gods, as he pretends.—I will grant it: but this is not a definition of what is holy, and

---

* Socrates reproaches the Athenians, that they loved to hear such as could talk finely, and did not much trouble their heads about the truth of things. We learn from the Sacred History, that this was the character of the Athenians; they spent their time in hearing either novelists or orators.

its contrary, seeing the Gods are divided ; and that which is disagreeable to some of them, is agreeable to others. Very well, I pass that, Eutyphron: I am willing to suppose that all the Gods account your father's action unjust, and that they all abhor it. I pray then let us correct our definition a little, and say, "That which all the Gods condemn is profane, and that which all the Gods approve is holy; and that which is approved by some of them, and disapproved by others, is neither one nor the other, or rather is both together." Shall we stand by this definition of what is holy and what profane ?

Eut. What should hinder us, Socrates ?

Soc. For my part I will not hinder it : but do you see yourself if this suits your opinion, and if upon this principle you can instruct me better in what you have been endeavouring to teach me.

Eut. And for my part, I shall make no difficulty of asserting, that that is holy which all the Gods approve, and that profane which they all disapprove.

Soc. Examine this definition, to see if it be true : or shall we receive it without any ceremony? and shall we have that respect for ourselves and others, as to give our assent to all our imaginations and fancies ; so that for a man to tell us a thing is so, shall be sufficient to gain our belief; or is it necessary to examine what is said to us ?

Eut. Without doubt we should examine it ; and I am well assured, that what we have laid down is a good position.

Soc. That we shall see presently. Hear me a little. Is that which is holy beloved of the Gods, because it is holy, or is it holy because it is beloved of them ?*

* This thought is too high for Eutyphron, who, conceiving holiness as a thing distinct from God, could not tell how to comprehend that what is holy is at the same time loved of God, because it is holy ; and holy because loved of God ; for holiness comes from God, Sanctitas primitiva ; and the holiness of men is the effect of the divine communion, which Socrates understood, and of which he elsewhere speaks. So that Socrates here speaks with reference to the gross manner of conceiving the things of religion which was to be found in ignorant men, who judged of this as of all other things in which the relatives are very different, as that which is loved is different from that which loves; that which is moved is different from that which moves it, &c.

Eut. I do not well understand what you say, Socrates.

Soc. I will endeavour to explain myself. Do not we say, that a thing is carried, and that a thing carries? that a thing is seen, and that a thing sees? that a thing is moved, and that a thing moves it? and the like to infinity. Do you conceive that they are different? and do you understand in what they differ?

Eut. I think I do.

Soc. Is not the thing beloved different from that which loves?

Eut. A pretty question, indeed!

Soc. Tell me then, is the thing which is carried, carried because one carries it, or for some other reason?

Eut. Because one carries it, without doubt.

Soc. And the thing moved is moved because one moves it; and the thing seen because one sees it?

Eut. Most certainly.

Soc. Then it is not true that one sees a thing because it is seen; but, on the contrary, it is seen because one sees it. It is not true that one moves a thing because it is moved, but it is moved because one moves it. Nor is it true that one carries a thing because it is carried, but it is carried because one carries it. Do you understand me now? Is this plain enough? My meaning is, that one does not do a thing because it is done, but that it is done because one does it: that a being which suffers, does not suffer because it is passive, but is passive because it suffers. Is not this true?

Eut. Who doubts it?

Soc. Is not that which is loved something that is done, or that suffers?

Eut. Certainly.

Soc. Then it is with that which is loved as it is with all other things; it is not because it is loved that one loves it, but on the contrary it is because one loves it that it is loved.

Eut. That is as clear as the light.

Soc. What shall we say then of that which is holy, my dear Eutyphron? Shall we not say it is beloved of the Gods, as you have asserted?

Eut. Yes, certainly.

Soc. But is it beloved because it is holy, or is it for some other reason?

Eut. It is for no other reason.

Soc. Then it is beloved because it is holy; but it is not holy because it is beloved.

Eut. So I think.

Soc. But is it not beloved of the Gods because the Gods love it?

Eut. Who can deny it?

Soc. Then that which is beloved of God is not the same with that which is holy, nor that which is holy the same with that which is beloved, as you say : but they are very different.

Eut. How then, Socrates?

Soc. Because we are agreed that that which is holy is beloved because it is holy, and that it is not true that it is holy because it is beloved. Are we not agreed in that?

Eut. I confess it.

Soc. We are farther agreed, that that which is beloved of the Gods, is beloved of them only because they love it; and that it is not true, to say they love it because it is beloved.

Eut. That is right.

Soc. But, my dear Eutyphron, if that which is beloved of the Gods, and that which is holy,* were the same thing, seeing that which is holy is beloved only because it is holy ; it would follow, that the Gods should love that which they love, only because it is beloved of them. And on the other hand, if that which is beloved of the Gods, were loved only because they love it ; then it would be true likewise to say, that which is holy is holy, only because it is beloved of them. By this therefore you see that those two terms, *beloved of the Gods,* and *holy,* are very different. One is beloved because the Gods love him, and another is loved only because he deserves to be loved. Thus, my dear Eutyphron, when you should have given me an exact answer what it is to be holy, to be sure you

---

* For if these two terms *beloved* and *holy* were the same thing, one might be put for the other; whence all that absurdity would follow which Socrates represents here.

were not willing to explain to me wherein the essence of it consists, by an accurate definition; but were content to shew one of its qualities, which is that of being beloved of the Gods; but you have not given me an account of the nature of it. I conjure you, therefore, if you think fit, discover this great secret to me; and beginning with it from its very principle, teach me precisely to know what holiness is, without having respect to any thing that is adventitious: as whether it is beloved of the Gods or not. For we shall have no dispute about that. Come then, tell me freely, what is it to be holy, and what to be profane?

Eut. But, Socrates, I know not how to explain my thoughts to you on this subject; for all that we lay down vanishes from us, and does not continue fixed and stable in what condition soever we put it.

Soc. All the principles, Eutyphron, which you have established, are somewhat like the figures of Dædalus, one of my ancestors.* If I had asserted them, to be sure you would not have failed to jeer and reproach me, as if I had derived this pretty quality of making things that slip out of a man's hands, when he thinks he holds them fastest. But it unhappily falls out, that it is you that have asserted them. Therefore I must seek for some other turns of raillery; for it is certain your principles give us the slip, as you see very well.

Eut. For my part, Socrates, I need not seek any other turn of raillery; that suits you perfectly well: for it is not I that inspire our reasonings with this instability, which hinders them from fixing, but you are the Dædalus. If I were alone, I tell you they would continue firm and steady.

Soc. Then I am more expert in my art than Dædalus

---

* Dædalus was an excellent carver, who made statues that had springs within them, by means of which they would start out and go along as if they had been alive. There were two sorts of them, as appears by what is said in Menon. What Socrates says here of Dædalus, that he was one of his ancestors, is only in raillery. Dædalus descended from the kings of Athens; and Socrates was very far from having the vanity of pretending to be of that family. His meaning is only this, that he knew how to make himself wings, as Dædalus did, to fly towards heaven, and to raise his mind to the knowledge of divine things. This matter was spoken of in the first Alcibiades.

was; he could only give this mobility to his own works, whereas it seems I give it not only to my own, but also to those of other men: and that which is yet more strange, is, that I am thus expert against my will; for I should much rather choose to have my discourses continue fixed and immovable, than to have all the riches of Tantalus, together with all the skill of Dædalus, my progenitor. But enough of this jesting. Seeing you are afraid of the trouble, I will endeavour to ease you, and to open a shorter way to conduct myself to the knowledge of what is holy: and you shall see if it does not appear to be absolutely necessary, that whatever is holy is just.

Eut. It cannot be otherwise.

Soc. Do you think whatever is just is holy, or whatever is holy is just? Or do you suppose that that which is just is not always holy; but only that there are some just things that are holy, and others which are not so?

Eut. I cannot well comprehend what you mean, Socrates.

Soc. And yet you have two great advantages above me, having both more youth and more capacity than I. But, as I just now told you, swimming in the delicious abundance of your wisdom, you are afraid of putting yourself to much trouble. Shake off, I beseech you, this effeminate softness, and apply yourself a little to thinking. What I say, is not very hard to be understood. For I say just the contrary to what the poet asserts, who to excuse himself for not singing the praises of Jupiter, says,

Shame every where keeps company with fear.

I am not at all of his mind: shall I tell you in what?

Eut. You will oblige me in so doing.

Soc. I think it is not true that shame always accompanies fear; for I think we every day see people in fear of sickness and poverty, who yet are not at all ashamed of the things they fear. Do not you think so too?

Eut. I am of the same mind.

Soc. On the contrary, fear always follows shame: for is there any one who is ashamed, and put into confusion by any action, who does not at the same time fear the dishonour that is the consequence of it?

Eut. It cannot be otherwise, he must be afraid of it.

Soc. Then it is not true to say

Shame every where keeps company with fear.

But we should say

Fear every where keeps company with shame.

For it is false, that shame is continually found with fear, fear having more extent than shame : indeed shame is one part of fear, as the unequal is one part of number. Whenever you find a number, you do not necessarily find it unequal; but wherever it is unequal, there you necessarily find a number.   Do you understand me now ? .

Eut. Very well.

Soc. This is what I just now asked you ; namely, if wherever that which is just is to be found, there is also that which is holy ; and if wherever that which is holy is to be found, there is also that which is just ?   Now it appears that that which is holy is not always found with that which is just; for that which is holy is a part of that which is just.   Shall we then lay this down as a principle, or are you of a different sentiment ?

Eut. It is a principle that cannot be contested.

Soc. Now mind what follows : if that which is holy is a part of that which is just, we must find out what part of that which is just, is that which is holy.   As if you should ask me what part of number is that which is equal, and what number is that part ?   I should answer, that it is the Isosceles,* and not the Scalene.   Do not you think so as well as I ?

Eut. Yes, certainly.

Soc. Now do you in like manner, see if you can inform me what part of that which is just is that which is holy; that I may let Melitus know, that it is best for him to forbear to do me any farther injustice in accusing me of impiety; me, who I say, have been perfectly instructed by you what piety and holiness, and their contraries are.

Eut. For my part, Socrates, I think that holiness and piety is that part of what is just † which concerns the care

* The Isosceles signifies that which has two equal sides, for the even number divides itself into two equal parts. And the Scalene is that which has two unequal sides.

† This is true: but the Pagans had false ideas of it; because they did not understand that this care of God, which consists on

and worship of the Gods, and that all the rest of it is that which properly respects men.

Soc. Very well: yet there is some little matter still wanting. For I do not well understand what you mean by this word [care.] Is this care of the Gods the same with that which we take about all other things? For we every day say, that none but an equerry knows how to take care of a horse, and to look well after him, do we not?

Eut. Yes, doubtless.

Soc. Then the care of horses properly belongs to the equerry.

Eut. It does so.

Soc. All men are not fit to take care of dogs, and to look after them, but only the huntsman.

Eut. None but he.

Soc. Then the care of dogs properly belongs to the art of hunting.

Eut. Without doubt it does.

Soc. And it belongs to the grazier to take care of oxen.

Eut. True.

Soc. Now holiness and piety is the care of the Gods: Is not this what you say?

Eut. Yes, certainly.

Soc. Has not all care for its end, the good and advantage of that which is taken care of? Do not you every day see that the horses which an able equerry takes care of, become better, and more fit for service than others?

Eut. Yes, without doubt.

Soc. Does not the care which a good huntsman takes of dogs, and that which a good grazier takes of oxen, make both the one and the other better? and may not the like be said of all other cares? Or can you think that care tends to hurt and spoil that which is taken care of?

Eut. No, certainly.

Soc. Then it tends to make it better.

Eut. That is right.

Soc. Then holiness being the care we take of the Gods, tends to their advantage; and so the end of it must be

our part in obeying him, in conforming to his holy will, and in resigning ourselves to him, was preceded by his care of us, in creating us, and in enlightening our minds: and this is what Socrates teaches in other places.

to make them better. But would you dare to assert, when you do any holy action, that you make any one of the Gods better by it?*

Eut. I am far enough from uttering such horrid blasphemy.

Soc. Nor do I think you have any such thought; I am very far from such a supposition: and it is for this reason I asked you what this care of the Gods is, being persuaded that was not your meaning.

Eut. You have done me justice, Socrates.

Soc. So much for that: but tell me then, what sort of care of the Gods is holiness?

Eut. It is of the nature of that care which servants take of their masters.

Soc. I understand you; that is to say, holiness is a kind of servant to the Gods.

Eut. You have hit it.

Soc. Can you tell me what physicians effect by means of the art of medicine, which is their servant? Do they not restore health?

Eut. Yes.

Soc. What do the ship-carpenters, who are in ports, do? And what do our architects perform by the ministry of their servants? Do not the former build ships, and the latter houses?

Eut. Yes, certainly.

Sac. What then do the Gods perform by the ministry of their servants? For you must certainly know this, since you pretend to know religion better than any man in the world beside.†

Eut. And I have reason to make that pretence.

Soc. Tell me then, I beseech you, what wonderful work is it that the Gods perform by making use of our service?

Eut. They perform many very great and wonderful things.

---

* Men are incapable of doing any thing to the advantage of God.

† Socrates would hereby insinuate, what he elsewhere teaches, that God by the ministry of holiness works the conversion of souls: that this his conversion produces love, and that this love engages us to render him that which appertains to him, and which we cannot innocently refuse him.

Soc. The generals of our army perform many great things too; but yet there is always one thing which is the principal, and that is the victory they obtain in battle, is it not?

Eut. It is so.

Soc. And the graziers do many good things, but the principal is that of supplying mankind with food by their industry.

Eut. I grant it.

Soc. Well, then, of all those good things which the Gods operate by the ministry of holiness, what is the principal?

Eut. I just now told you, Socrates, that there needs more time and pains to arrive at an accurate knowledge of these things.. All that I can tell you in general, is, that to please the Gods by prayers and sacrifices, is that which we call holiness; and in this consists the welfare of families and cities: whereas to displease the Gods is impiety, which utterly ruins and subverts every thing.

Soc. Indeed, Eutyphron, you might have told me what I asked in fewer words, if you had pleased. It is easy to see you have a mind to instruct me; for when you seem to be just in the way to do it, you presently strike off again: if you had but answered me a word more, I had very well understood the nature of holiness. But now, (for he that asks must follow him who is asked) do not you say, holiness is the art of sacrificing and praying?

Eut. Yes, that I do.

Soc. To sacrifice, is to give to the Gods: to pray, is to ask of them.

Eut. It is right, Socrates.

Soc. It follows, then, from your discourses, that holiness is the science of giving to the Gods, and asking of them. *

Eut. Socrates, you perfectly comprehend my meaning.

Soc. It is because I am in love with your wisdom, and give myself up entirely to it. You need not fear that I shall let one of your words fall to the ground. Tell me

---

* This fourth definition is admirable. Socrates designs by it to shew that holiness leads us to ask of God, his spirit, his assistance and grace; and to ask even ourselves of him; for it is on him our very being depends; and that it also engages us to give ourselves to him. And this makes up the whole of religion.

then, what is this art of pleasing the Gods?   Do you say
it is to give to them, and to ask of them.

Eut. Most certainly.

Soc. To ask well, must we not ask such things as we
have need to receive of them?

Eut. And what then?

Soc. And to give well, must we not give them in exchange such things as they have need to receive of us?
For it would be a folly to give any one such things as he
does not want, but are entirely useless to him.

Eut. You say very well.

Soc. Holiness, my dear Eutyphron, is then a kind of
traffic betwixt the Gods and men.

Eut. Let it be so, if you will have it so.

Soc. I would not have it so, if it be not so : but tell me,
what advantage do the Gods receive from the presents
which we make them?   For the advantage we derive from
them is very evident, since we have not the least good but
what proceeds from their liberality.   Of what advantage
then are our offerings to the Gods?   Are we so crafty, as
to draw all the profit of this commerce to ourselves, while
they derive no advantage from it?

Eut. Socrates, do you think the Gods can ever draw any
advantage from the things they receive from us?

Soc. To what purpose then do all our offerings serve?

Eut. They serve to signify our veneration and respect
to them, and the desire we have to please them.

Soc. Then holiness does not profit, but please the Gods?

Eut. Yes, without doubt.

Soc. Then that which is holy, is only that which pleases
the Gods.

Eut. It is only that.

Soc. When you speak thus to me, do you wonder that
your discourse is not fixed and steady? and dare you accuse
me of being the Dædalus, that gives it this continual motion?   You, I say, who are a thousand times more ingenious than that great artist, and give your words a thousand
different turns?   Do not you find that your discourse
makes only a circle?   You remember very well, that that
which is holy, and that which is agreeable to the Gods,
were not counted the same thing by us just now, but

were acknowledged to be very different? Do not you remember this?

Eut. I do.

Soc. Well, and do not you consider that you now say, that which is holy is that which pleases the Gods? Is not what pleases them agreeable to them?

Eut. Most certainly.

Soc. Then one of these two things must be granted: either that we did not well distinguish just now; or, if we did, that we are now fallen into a false definition.

Eut. That is plain.

Soc. Then we must begin all again in our inquiry after holiness; for I shall not be weary nor discouraged till you have informed me what it is. I beg you would not despise me, but bend your mind with all the application you can, to teach me the truth; for you know it, if any man alive does: and I will not let you go, like another Proteus, till you have instructed me. For if you had not a perfect knowledge of what is holy and profane, doubtless you would never, for the sake of a wretched farmer, have undertaken to accuse your father of murder, when the good old man stoops under the burden of age, and has already one foot in the grave; but would have been seized with horror to see yourself about to commit, it may be, an impious act, and would have feared the Gods, and respected men. So that I cannot doubt but you think you know perfectly well what holiness and its contrary are. Inform me, therefore, most excellent Eutyphron, and do not hide your thoughts from me.

Eut. We will reserve it for another time,* for now I am a little in haste, and it is time for me to leave you.†

Soc. Alas, my dear Eutyphron, what do you intend to do! This hasty motion of yours ravishes from me the

* Observe the pride of this superstitious man; he is just confounded, and yet he always thinks himself capable of teaching what he does not know himself.

† The ancients inform us, that Eutyphron got some advantage by this conversation of Socrates; for he dropped his prosecution, and let his father alone. By which it is easy to see, that these Dialogues of Plato were not made upon feigned subjects, but had a very true and real foundation, as well as those which Xenophon has preserved to us.

greatest and sweetest of all my hopes : for I flattered myself, that after I had learned of you what holiness is and
its contrary, I should easily have got out of Melitus's
clutches, by making it plainly appear to him, that Eutyphron had perfectly instructed me in divine things, that
ignorance should never more prompt me to introduce of
my own head new opinions about the Deity; and that my
life should be more holy for the future.

INTRODUCTION TO CRITO.

SOCRATES, in his Apology, has furnished us with an admirable model of an honest man's defences, when unjustly arraigned. And in this Dialogue, which is entitled, "Of what is to be done," he gives us a yet more perfect plan of the conduct of a good man, and the obedience he owes to justice and the laws, even in dying when they require it, though at the same time it were easy for him to escape. While Socrates lay in prison, his friends being more concerned for his life than himself, had retained the gaoler. Every thing was in readiness for accomplishing his escape; and Crito goes into the prison before day, to tell him the good news, and persuade him not to slight the precious opportunity. Socrates hears him, and commends his zeal: but before he would comply, starts the question, whether it was just for him to depart the prison, without the consent of the Athenians. So that the point to be decided in this Dialogue, is, whether a man unjustly condemned to die, can innocently withdraw himself from the hand of justice and the law? Socrates was the only man of the age he lived in, that called that in question; and, which is yet more surprising, were he now alive, he would be the only man in this our age. All that we see before our eyes, or read of in our histories; in a word, all the instances of what men have done through the love of life, and the fear of death, have so debauched our judgments, that we are scarce able to judge of what true justice requires, and are apt to call every thing just, that is universally practised. Now there cannot be a more capital error. However, since the conduct of a heathen, that chose rather to die, than to break the course of justice, would seem to us the effect of folly, or strong prejudice; let us try if we can hit upon any solid rule, that may reclaim us by its authority, and convince us by its light.

The Christian religion affords a great many such : but·we shall confine ourselves to one, which in a sovereign degree is justly entitled to both these characters.   St. Paul, being in prison in Macedonia, one night the prison doors opened, and his chains dropped off, and he was so far from making his escape, that he hindered others to do it.   Peter being imprisoned by Herod, who had resolved to put him to death after the passover, made his escape the night before the day of execution.   But how did he do it ?   God did not content himself with unlocking his chains, and opening the prison-doors, but sent an angel, who pushed him on, and forced him to go along.   This was the conduct of the saints.   Though the prison be open, they do not offer to make their escape.   Nothing less than an angel can oblige them to depart the prison.   Socrates, who was no saint, but followed as ·close as possible the same light that guides and illuminates the saints, observes the same conduct.   They opened the prison and untied his chains, but his angel was silent, and he would not stir. He preferred an innocent death before a criminal life : but before he came to a resolution, he heard the reasons of his friend, who speaks with a great deal of force, and omits nothing that could move him ; and after that, with a divine eloquence, confronted him with incontestable maxims, grounded upon truth and justice, in which one may trace the rays of the evangelical doctrine, namely, that we ought to slight the opinions of men, and regard only the judgment of God ; that it is not living, but living well, that should be our wish ; that justice is the life, and injustice the death of the soul ; that we ought not to injure our enemies, or resent the injuries we receive ; that it is better to die, than to sin ; that we must obey the law of our country ; that the injustice of men cannot justify our disrespect to the laws ; and that the laws of this world have sister-laws in the other, which revenge the affronts put upon them here.

These were the principles that Socrates went upon. Those that take the pains to examine them, and weigh their consequences, will be fully satisfied, not only that Socrates acted the part of an honest man in refusing to make his escape, but likewise, that he could not be a good man if he did otherwise.   And it was with this view that

Quintilian said, This philosopher, by quitting the small remainder of his life, retrieved all the former part of his life, and likewise gained a life to all ages. It is such thoughts as these that our souls should always have in view, in order to keep out vice; for if once we relent, and allow the enemy to gain some ground, under a specious pretence, and a taking appearance, it will quickly master all, and overturn all the banks that should stop its course.

CRITO:

OR, OF WHAT WE OUGHT TO DO?

SOCRATES AND CRITO.

Soc. WHAT is the matter that you come here so soon, Crito? As I take it, it is very early.

Crit. It is true.

Soc. What time may it be then?

Crit. A little before the break of day.

Soc. I wonder the gaoler let you in.

Crit. He is one I know very well. I have been with him here often; and he is in some measure obliged to me.

Soc. Are you but just come? Or is it long since you came?

Crit. I have been here some time.

Soc. Why did you not awaken me then, when you came in?

Crit. Pray God forbid, Socrates. For my own part, I would gladly shake off the cares and anxiety that keep my eyes from closing. But when I entered this room, I wondered to find you so sound asleep, and was loth to awaken you, that I might not rob you of these happy minutes. Indeed, Socrates, ever since I knew you, I have been always charmed with your patience and calm temper; but in a distinguishing manner at this juncture, since in the circumstances you are in, your eye looks so easy and unconcerned.

Soc. Indeed, Crito, it would be a great indecency in one of my age to be apprehensive of death.

Crit. Ay! and how many do we see every day, under the like misfortunes, whom age does not exempt from those fears!

Soc. That is true. But after all, what brought you hither so early?

Crit. I came to tell you a troublesome piece of news, which though it may not seem to affect you, yet it overwhelms both me and your relations and friends with insufferable grief. In fine, I bring the most terrible news that ever could be brought.

Soc. What news? Is the ship arrived from Delos, upon the return of which I am to die?

Crit. It is not yet arrived; but without doubt it will be here this day, according to the intelligence we have from persons that came from Sunium, and left it there. For at that rate, it cannot fail of being there to-day, and so to-morrow you must unavoidably die.

Soc. Why not, Crito? Be it so, since it is the will of God. However, I do not believe the vessel will arrive this day.

Crit. What do you ground that conjecture upon?

Soc. I will tell you: I am not to die till the day after the arrival of the vessel.

Crit. At least those who are to execute the sentence say so.

Soc. The vessel will not arrive till to-morrow, as I conjecture from a certain dream I had this night, about a minute ago.* And it seems to me a happiness, that you did not awaken me.

Crit. Well, what is the dream?

Soc. I thought, I saw a very handsome comely woman, clad in white, come up to me, who, calling me by name, said, In three days thou shalt be in the fertile Phthia.†

---

* He speaks on this fashion, because the dreams of the morning were looked upon as more distinct and true. "Certiora et colatiora somniari affirmant sub extimis noctibus, quasi jam emergente animarum vigore, producto sopore." *Tertul. de Anima.*

† In the 9th Book of the Iliad, Achilles, threatening to retire, says to Ulysses, "After to-morrow you shall see the Hellespont covered with my ships, and if Neptune afford me a happy voyage, in three days I shall arrive at the fertile Phthia." It was this last verse that Socrates had from the mouth of the woman in his dream; for our dreams always bear a proportion to our genius, habits, and

Crit. That is a very strange dream, Socrates.

Soc. It is a very significant one, Crito.

Crit. Yes, without doubt. But for this time, pray Socrates, take my advice, and make your escape. For if you die, besides the irreparable loss of a friend, which I shall ever lament, I am afraid that a great many people, who are not well acquainted either with you or me, will believe that I have forsaken you, and not employed my interest for promoting your escape. Is there any thing more scandalous, than to lie under the disrepute of being wedded to my money more than my friend? For, in short, the people will never believe that you refused to go from hence, when we had enabled you to do so.

Soc. My dear Crito, why should we be so much concerned for the opinion of the people? Is it not enough, that the more sensible part, who are the only men we ought to regard, know how the case stands?

Crit. But you see, Socrates, there is a necessity of being concerned for the noise of the mob; for your example is a sufficient instance, that they are capable of doing, not only small, but the *greatest* of injuries, and display their passion in an outrageous manner, against those who are once run down by vulgar opinion.

Soc. Were the people capable of doing the greatest injuries, they would likewise be capable of doing the greatest good: that would be a great happiness. But neither the one nor the other is possible. For they cannot make either wise men or fools.*

Crit. I grant it. But pray answer me: is it not out of tenderness to me and your other friends, that you will not stir from hence? For fear, lest upon your escape we should

ways of thinking. Nothing can be a stronger evidence of the gentle and easy thoughts that Socrates had of death, than his application of this passage, by which he represents death as a fortunate voyage to one's own country. The grammarians, who are always tied up to the letter, were never able to point out the beauty and delicacy of this passage: for they only turned it into a coarse idea of death, upon the resemblance of the word Phthia with φθίνειν, to corrupt; as if a Grecian could ever have mistaken φθίη for φθίσις.—Phthia was Achilles's country.

* This is a noble principle of Socrates. None can do the greatest harm, but those that are able to do the greatest good. And this can only be attributed to God, not to men.

H

be troubled and charged with carrying you off; and by
that means be obliged to quit our possessions, or pay a
large sum of money, or suffer something more fatal than
either? If that be your fear, Socrates, in the name of the
Gods shake it off. Is it not highly reasonable that we
should purchase your escape at the rate of exposing ourselves to these dangers, and greater ones, if there be
occasion? Once more, my dear Socrates, believe me and
come away.

Soc. I own, Crito, that I have such thoughts, and several others besides in my view.

Crit. Fear nothing, I entreat you; for in the first place,
they require no great sum to let you out. And on the
other hand, you see what a pitiful condition those are in,
who probably might arraign us :* a small sum of money
will stop their mouths; my estate alone will serve for that.
If you scruple to accept my offer, here are a great number
of strangers, who desire nothing more than to furnish you
with what money you want. Simmias the Theban himself, has brought up very considerable sums. Cebes is capable of doing as much, and so are several others. Let
not your fears then stifle the desire of making your escape.
And as for what you told me the other day, in the court,
that if you made your escape, you should not know how
to live; pray let not that trouble you: wherever you go,
you will be beloved. If you will go to Thessaly, I have
friends there, who will honour you according to your
merit, and think themselves happy in supplying you with
what you want, and covering you from all occasions of
fear in their country. Besides, Socrates, without doubt
you are guilty of a very unjust thing in delivering up yourself, while it is in your power to make your escape, and
promoting what your enemies so passionately wish for.
For you not only betray yourself, but likewise your children, by abandoning them, when you might maintain
and educate them. You are not at all concerned at what
may befal them, though at the same time they are like
to be in as dismal a condition, as ever orphans were. A
man should either have no children, or else expose himself

* Those who made a trade of accusing at Athens, were a poor sort
of people, whose mouths were easily stopped with money.

to the care and trouble of bringing them up. You seem to me to act a soft and insensible part; whereas you ought to take resolution worthy of a generous soul;. above all, you, who boast that you have pursued nothing but virtue all the days of your life. I tell you, Socrates, I am ashamed upon the account of you and your relations, since the world will believe it was through our cowardliness, that you did not get off. In the first place, they will charge you with standing a trial that you might have avoided; then they will censure your conduct in making your defences; and at last, which is the most shameful of all, they will upbraid us with forsaking you through fear and cowardice, since we did not accomplish your escape. Pray consider of it, my dear Socrates; if you do not prevent the approaching evil, you will bear a part in the shame that will cover us all. Pray advise with yourself quickly. But now I think on it, there is no time for advising, there is no choice left, all must be put in execution the next night; for if we delay longer, all our measures will be broken. Believe me, I entreat you, and do as I bid you.

Soc. My dear Crito, your good will is very commendable, provided it agrees with right reason: but if it swerves from that, the stronger it is, the more is it blame-worthy. The first thing to be considered is, whether we ought to do as you say, or not? For you know it is not of yesterday that I have accustomed myself only to follow the reasons that appear most just, after a mature examination. Though fortune frowns upon me, yet I will never part with the principles I have all along professed. These principles appear always the same, and I esteem them equally at all times. So, if your advice be not backed by the strongest reasons, assure yourself I will never comply, not if all the people should arm against me, or offer to frighten me like a child, by laying on fresh chains, and threatening to deprive me of the greatest good, and oblige me to suffer the cruelest death. Now, how shall we manage this inquiry justly? To be sure, the fairest way is to resume what you have been saying of vulgar opinions; that is, to inquire, whether there are some reports that we ought to regard, and others that are to be slighted: or whether the doing so is only a groundless and childish proposition. I have a strong desire, upon this occasion, to try in your presence, whether this principle will appear to me in different colours from what it did while I was in other circumstances, or whether I shall always find it the same; in order to determine me to a compliance or refusal.

If I mistake not, it is certain, that several persons who thought themselves men of sense, have often maintained in this place,* that of all the opinions of men, some are to be regarded, and others to be slighted. In the name of the Gods, Crito, do not you think that was well said? In all human appearance, you are in no danger of dying to-morrow; and therefore it is presumed that the fear of the present danger cannot work any change upon you. Wherefore, pray consider it well: do not you think they spoke justly, who said, that all the opinions of men are not always to be regarded, but only some of them; and those not of all men, but only of some? What do you say? do not you think it is very true?

Crit. Very true.

Soc. At that rate then, ought not we to esteem the good opinions, and slight the bad ones?

Crit. Yes, doubtless.

Soc. Are not the good opinions then, those of wise-men, and the bad ones those of fools?

Crit. It cannot be otherwise.

Soc. Let us see then, how you will answer this. A man that makes his exercises, when he comes to have his lesson, whether shall he regard the commendation or censure of whoever comes first, or only of him that is either a physician or a master?†

Crit. Of the last to be sure.

Soc. Then he ought to fear the censure, and value the commendation of that man alone; and slight what comes from others.

Crit. Without doubt.

* This probably had been maintained in some of the former conferences in prison; for Socrates's friends met every day in the prison to keep him company.

† For they perform those exercises either for their health, or else to improve their dexterity and strength: for the first they followed the orders of a physician; and for the other, they were directed by a master.

Soc. For that reason, this young man must neither eat nor drink, nor do any thing, without the orders of that master, that man of sense; and he is not at all to govern himself by the caprices of others.

Crit. That is true.

Soc. But suppose he disobeys this master, and disregards his applause or censure; and suffers himself to be blinded by the caresses and applauses of the ignorant mob; will he not come to some harm by this means?

Crit. How is it possible it should be otherwise?

Soc. But what will be the nature of this harm that will accrue to him therefrom? where will it terminate? and what part of him will it affect?

Crit. His body, without doubt; for by that means he will ruin himself.

Soc. Very well; but is not the case the same all over? Upon the point of justice or injustice, honesty or dishonesty, good or evil, which at present are the subject of our dispute, shall we rather refer ourselves to the opinion of the people, than to that of an experienced wise man, who justly challenges more respect and deference from us, than all the world besides? And if we do not act conformably to the opinion of this one man, is it not certain that we shall ruin ourselves, and entirely lose that which only lives and gains new strength by justice, and perishes only through injustice? Or must we take all that for a thing of no account?

Crit. I am of your opinion.

Soc. Take heed, I entreat you; if by following the opinions of the ignorant we destroy that which is only preserved by health and wasted by sickness, can we survive the corruption of that, whether it be our body, or somewhat else?

Crit. That is certain.

Soc. Can one live then after the corruption and destruction of the body?

Crit. No, to be sure.

Soc. But can one survive the corruption of that which lives only by justice, and dies only through injustice? Or is this thing, whatever it be, that has justice or injustice for its object, to be less valued than the body?

Crit. Not at all.

Soc. What! is it much more valuable then?

Crit. A great deal more.

Soc. Then, my dear Crito, we ought not to be concerned at what the people say, but what that says, which knows what is just and what is unjust; and that alone is nothing else but truth. Thus you see, you establish false principles at first, in saying that we ought to pay a deference to the opinions of the people, upon what is just, good, honest, and its contraries. Some perhaps will object, that the people are able to put us to death.

Crit. To be sure, they will.

Soc. It is true. But that does not alter the nature of what we were saying; that is still the same. For you must remember, that it is not life, but a *good* life that we ought to court.

Crit. That is a certain truth.

Soc. But is it not likewise certain, that this good life consists in nothing else but honesty and justice.

Crit. Yes.

Soc. Now, before we go farther, let us examine upon the principles you have agreed to, whether my departure from hence without the permission of the Athenians, is just or unjust. If it be found just, we must do our utmost to bring it about; but if it is unjust, we must lay aside the design. For as to the considerations you alleged just now, of money, reputation, and family; these are only the thoughts of the baser mob, who put innocent persons to death, and would afterwards bring them to life, if it were possible. But as for us who bend our thoughts another way, all that we are to mind, is whether we do a just thing in giving money, and lying under an obligation to those who promote our escape; or whether both we and they do not commit injustice in so doing? If this be an unjust thing, we need not reason much upon the point, since it is better to abide here and die, than to undergo what is more terrible than death.

Crit. You are right in this particular, Socrates; let us proceed.

Soc. We will go hand in hand in the enquiry. If you have any thing of weight to answer, pray do it when I have spoken, that so I may comply; if not, pray forbear any farther to press me to go from hence without the consent of the Athenians. I shall be infinitely glad if you can persuade me to do it; but I cannot do it without being first convinced. Take notice then whether my way of pursuing this enquiry satisfies you, and do your utmost to make answer to my questions.

Crit. I will.

Soc. Is it true, that we ought not to do an unjust thing to any man? Or is it lawful in any measure to do it to one, when we are forbid to do it to another? Or is it not absolutely true, that every kind of injustice is neither good nor honest, as we were saying just now? In fine, are all those sentiments which we formerly entertained, vanished in a few days? And is it possible, Crito, that our most serious conferences, should resemble those of children, and we at the same time not be sensible that it is so? Ought we not rather to stand to what we have said, as being a certain truth, that all injustice is scandalous and fatal to the person that commits it?

Crit. That is certain.

Soc. Then we must avoid the least measure of injustice?

Crit. Most certainly.

Soc. Since we are to avoid the least degree of it, then we ought not to do it to those who are unjust to us, notwithstanding that this people thinks it lawful?

Crit. So I think.

Soc. But ought we to do evil or not?

Crit. Without doubt we ought not.

Soc. Is it justice to repay evil with evil, pursuant to the opinion of the people, or is it unjust?

Crit. It is unjust.

Soc. Then there is no difference between doing evil, and being unjust?

Crit. I own it.

Soc. Then we ought not to do the least evil or injustice to any man, let him do by us as he will. But take heed, Crito, that by this concession you do not speak against your own sentiments. For I know very well there are few that will go this length: and it is impossible for those who vary in their sentiments upon this point, to agree well together. Nay, on the contrary, the contempt of one another's opinions, leads them to a reciprocal contempt of one another's persons. Consider well then, if you are of the same opinion with me; and let us ground our reasonings upon this principle, that we ought not to do evil for evil, or treat those unjustly who are unjust to us. For my part, I never did, nor ever will entertain any other principle. Tell me then if you have changed your mind; if not, give ear to what follows.

Crit. I give ear.

Soc. Well: a man that has made a just promise, ought he to keep it, or to break it?

Crit. He ought to keep it.

Soc. If I go from hence without the consent of the Athenians, shall not I injure some people, and especially those who do not deserve it? Or shall we in this follow what we think equally just to every body?

Crit. I cannot answer you, for I do not understand you.

Soc. Pray take notice: when we put ourselves in a way of making our escape, or going from hence, or how you please to call it, suppose the law and the republic should present themselves in a body before us, and accost us in this manner: "Socrates, what are you going to do?—to put in execution what you now design, were wholly to ruin the laws and the state. Do you think a city can subsist when justice has not only lost its force, but is likewise perverted, overturned, and trampled under foot by private persons?" What answer could we make to such and many other questions? For what is it that an orator cannot say upon the overturning of that law, which provides that sentences once pronounced shall not be infringed? Shall we answer, that the republic has judged amiss, and passed an unjust sentence upon us? Shall that be our answer?

Crit. Without scruple, Socrates.

Soc. What will the laws say then? "Is it not true, Socrates, that you agreed with us to submit yourself to a public trial?" And if we should seem to be surprised at such language, they will continue perhaps; "Be not surprised, Socrates, but make answer, for you yourself used to insist upon question and answer. Tell then, what occasion you have to complain of the republic and of us, that you are so eager upon destroying it? Are not we the authors of your birth? Is it not by our means that your father married her who brought you forth?* What fault can you find with the laws we established as to marriage?" Nothing at all, should I answer. "As to the nourishing and bringing up of children, and the manner of your education, are not the laws just that we enacted upon that head, by which we obliged your father to bring you up to music and the exercises?" Very just, I would say. "Since then you were born, brought up, and educated under our influence, durst you maintain that you are not our nurse-child and subject, as well as your father? and if you are, do you think to have equal power with us, as if it were lawful for you to inflict upon us all we enjoin you to undergo? But since you cannot lay claim to any such right against your father or your master, so as to repay evil for evil, injury for injury, how can you think to obtain that privilege against your country and the laws, insomuch that if we endeavour to put you to death, you will counteract us, by endeavouring to prevent us, and to ruin your country and its laws? Can you call such an action just, you that are an inseparable follower of true virtue? Are you ignorant that your country is more considerable, and more worthy of respect and veneration before God and man than your father, mother, and all your relations together? That you ought to honour your country, yield to it, and humour it, more than an angry father? That you must either reclaim it by your counsel, or obey its injunctions, and suffer without a murmur all that it imposes upon you? If it orders you to be whipped, or laid in irons, if it sends you to the wars, there to spend your blood, you ought to do it without demurring; you must not shake off the yoke, or flinch or quit your post; but in the army, in prison, and every where else, ought equally to obey the orders of your country. For if offering violence to a father or a mother is a piece of grand impiety; to put a force upon one's country is a much

* This is an admirable way of making out the obligation of all men to obey the laws of their country, by virtue of the treaty made between them

greater." What shall we answer to all this, Crito? Shall we acknowledge the truth of what the laws advance?

Crit. How can we avoid it?

Soc. Do you see then, Socrates, (continue they) what reason we have to brand your enterprise against us, as unjust? Of us you hold your birth, your maintenance, your education; in fine, we have done you all the good we are capable of, as well as to all the other citizens. Indeed, we do not fail to make public proclamation, that it is lawful for every private man, if he does not find his account in the laws and customs of our republic, after a mature examination, to retire with all his effects whither he pleases. And if any of you cannot comply with our customs, and desires to remove and live elsewhere, not one of us shall hinder him, he may go where he pleases. But on the other hand, if any one of you continues to live here, after he has considered our way of administering justice, and the policy observed in the state, then, we say, he is in effect obliged to obey all our commands, and we maintain that his disobedience is unjust on a three-fold account; for not obeying those to whom he owes his birth; for trampling under foot those that educated him; and for violating his faith after he had engaged to obey us, and not taking the pains to make remonstrances to us, if we happen to do an unjust thing. For notwithstanding that we only propose things without using any violence to procure obedience, and give every man his choice either to obey us, or reclaim us by his counsel or remonstrances, yet he does neither the one nor the other. And we maintain, Socrates, that if you execute what you are now about, you will stand charged with all these crimes, and that in a much higher degree than if another private man had committed the same injustice. If I asked them the reason, without doubt they would stop my mouth by telling me, that I submitted myself in a distinguishing manner to all these conditions. And we, (continue they) have great evidence that you were always pleased with us and the republic; for if this city had not been more agreeable to you than any other, you had never continued in it, no more than any other Athenian. None of the shows could ever tempt you to go out of the city, except once, that you went to see the games at the Isthmus;* you never went any where else, excepting your military expeditions, and never undertook a voyage, as others are wont to do. You never had the curiosity to visit other cities, or enquire after other laws, as being contented with us and our republic. You always made a distinguishing choice of us, and on all occasions testified that you submitted with all your heart to live according to our maxims. Besides; your having had children in this city, is an infallible evidence that you liked it. In fine, in this very last juncture you might have been sentenced to banishment if you would, and might then have done, with the consent of the republic, what you now attempt without their permission. But you were so stately, so unconcerned at death, that in your own terms you preferred death to banishment. But now you have no regard to those fine words; you are not further concerned for the laws, since you are going to overturn them. You do just what a pitiful slave would offer to do, by endeavouring to make your escape contrary to the laws of the treaty you have signed, by which you obliged yourself to live according to our rules. Pray answer us :—did not we say right in affirming that you agreed to this treaty, and submitted yourself to these terms not only in words, but in deeds? What shall we say to all this, Crito? And what can we do else but acknowledge that it is so?

Crit. How can we avoid it, Socrates?

Soc. What else then, continue they, is this action of yours, but a violation of that treaty, and all its terms? That treaty you were not made to sign either by force or surprise, or without time to think on it; for you had the whole course of your seventy years to remove in, if you had been dissatisfied with us, or unconvinced of the justice of our proposals. You neither pitched upon Lacedemon or Crete, notwithstanding that you always cried up their laws; nor any of the other Grecian cities, or strange countries. You have been less out of Athens than the lame and the blind; which is an invincible proof

* These games were celebrated at the Isthmus of Corinth, to the honour of Neptune every three years, after they were received by Theseus.

that the city and its laws pleased you in a distinguishing manner, since a city can never be agreeable if its laws are not such. And yet at this time you counteract the treaty. But, if you will take our advice, Socrates, we would have you stand to your treaty, and not expose yourself to the ridicule of the citizens, by stealing out from hence. Pray consider what advantage can redound either to you or your friends, by persisting in that design: your friends will infallibly be either exposed to danger, or banished their country, or have their estates forfeited. And as for yourself, if you retire to any neighbouring city, such as Thebes or Megara, which are admirably well governed, you will there be looked upon as an enemy. All that have any love for their country, will look upon you as a corrupter of the laws: besides, you will fortify in them the good opinion they have of your judges, and move them to approve the sentence given against you: for a corrupter of the law will at any time pass for a debaucher of the youth, and of the vulgar people. What! will you keep out of these well-governed cities, and these assemblies of just men? or will you have the face to go and live with them? And pray, what will you say to them, Socrates? Will you preach to them, as you did here, that virtue, justice, the laws, and ordinances, ought to be reverenced by men? Do not you think that this will sound ridiculous in their ears? You ought to think so. But perhaps you will quickly leave these well-governed cities, and go to Thessaly to Crito's friends,* where there is less order, and more licentiousness; and doubtless in that country, they will take a singular pleasure in hearing you relate in what equipage you made your escape from this prison, that is, covered with some old rags, or a beast's skin, or disguised some other way, as fugitives are wont to be. Every body will say, This old fellow, that has scarce any time to live, had such a strong passion for living, that he did not stand to purchase his life by trampling under foot the most sacred laws. Such stories will be bandied about of you

* Thessaly was the country where licentiousness and debauchery reigned. And accordingly Xenophon observes, that it was there that Critias was ruined.

at a time when you offend no man; but upon the least occasion of complaint, they will assail you with a thousand reproaches. You will spend your time in sneaking and insinuating yourself into the favour of men, one after another, and owning an equal subjection to them all. For what can you do? Will you feast perpetually in Thessaly, as if the good cheer had drawn you thither? What then will become of all your fine discourses upon justice and virtue? Besides, if you design to preserve your life for the sake of your children, it cannot be in order to bring them up in Thessaly, as if you could do them no other service but make them strangers. Or if you design to leave them here, do you imagine that during your life they will be better brought up in your absence, under the care of your friends? But will not your friends take the same care of them after your death that they would do in your absence? You ought to be persuaded that all those who call themselves your friends, will at all times do them all the service they can. To conclude, Socrates, submit yourself to our reasons, follow the advice of those who brought you up, and do not put your children, your life, or anything whatever, in the balance with justice; to the end that when you arrive before the tribunal of Pluto, you may be able to clear yourself before your judges. For do not deceive yourself; if you perform what you now design, you will neither better your own cause, nor that of your party; you will neither enlarge its justice or sanctity, either here or in the regions below. But if you die bravely, you owe your death to the injustice, not of the laws, but of men: whereas if you make your escape by repulsing so shamefully the injustice of your enemies, by violating at once both your own faith and our treaty, and injuring so many innocent persons as yourself, your friends, and your country, together with us; we shall be your enemies, as long as you live: and when you are dead, our sisters, the laws in the other world, will certainly afford you no joyful reception, as knowing that you endeavoured to ruin us. Wherefore do not prefer Crito's counsel to ours.

Methinks, my dear Crito, I hear what I have now spoken, just as the priests of Cybele fancy they hear the cornets and flutes; and the sound of these words makes so strong an impression in my ears, that it stops me from hearing any thing else.*   These are the sentiments I like, and all you can say to divert me from them, will be to no purpose.   However, if you think to succeed, I do not hinder you from speaking.

Crit. I have nothing to say, Socrates.

Soc. Then be easy, and let us bravely run this course, since God calls and conducts us to it.

---

* Socrates means that all these truths make no slight impression upon him, but pierce him, and inspire him with an ardour, or rather a holy fury, that stops his ears from hearing any thing to the contrary.   The sound of the cornets and flutes of the priests of Cybele inspired the audience with fury; and why should the sound of divine truths fall short of the same virtue, and leave their hearers in a lukewarm indifferency?   This temper of Socrates unriddles and explains what Diogenes said of him: when somebody asked Diogenes what he thought of Socrates, he answered, "That he was a mad man;" for Socrates shewed an incredible warmth in pursuing whatever he took to be just.

THE

INTRODUCTION TO PHEDON.

SOCRATES, in his Apology, and in his Crito, teaches us how we ought to form our lives; and here he instructs us how to die, and what thoughts to entertain at the hour of death. By explaining his own views and designs, which were the springs of all his actions, he furnishes us with a proof of the most important of all truths, and of that which ought to regulate our life. For the immortality of the soul is a point of such importance, that it includes all the truths of religion, and all the motives that ought to excite and direct us. So that our first duty is to satisfy ourselves in this point: and self-love and mere human interest ought to spur us up to understand it; besides there is not a more fatal condition than to be ignorant of the nature of death: for, according to the notion we have of it, we may draw directly opposite consequences for managing the conduct of our lives.

Socrates spends the last day of his life in discoursing with his friends upon this great subject: he unfolds all the reasons that induce a belief of the immortality of the soul, and refutes all the objections moved to the contrary, which are the very same that are made use of at this day. He demonstrates the hope they ought to have of a happier life; and lays before them all that this blessed hope requires to make it solid and lasting, to prevent their being deluded by a vain hope, and after all, meeting with the punishment allotted to the wicked, instead of the rewards provided for the good.

This conference was occasioned by a truth that was casually started, viz. that a true philosopher ought to desire to die, and to endeavour it. This position taken literally, seemed to insinuate that a philosopher might lay violent hands on himself. But Socrates makes it out that there is nothing more unjust: and that as man is God's creature and property, he ought not to remove out of this life without his orders. What should it be then that made the philosopher have such a love of death? What is the ground of this hope?* Here we are presented with the grounds assigned by a heathen philosopher, viz. man is born to know the truth, but he can never attain to a perfect knowledge of it in this life, by reason that his body is an obstacle: perfect knowledge is reserved for the life to come. Then the soul must be immortal, since after death it operates and knows. As for man's being born for the knowledge of truth, that cannot be called in question, since he was born to know God.

From thence it follows, that a true philosopher hates and contemns this body, which stands in the way of his union to God; that he wishes to be rid of it, and looks upon death as a passage to a better life. This solid hope gives being to that true temperance and valour which is the lot of true philosophers; for other men are only valiant through fear, and temperate through intemperance: their virtue is only a slave to vice.

They object to Socrates, that the soul is nothing but a vapour that vanishes and disperses itself at death. Socrates combats that opinion with an argument that has a great deal of strength in his mouth, but becomes much stronger when supported by the true religion, which alone can set it in its full light. The argument is this: In nature, contraries produce their contraries. So that death being an operation of nature, ought to produce life, that being its contrary; and by consequence the dead must be born again: the soul then is not dead, since it must revive the body.

Before we proceed farther, it is fit to take notice of an error that is couched under this principle, which only the Christian religion can at once discover and refute. It is, that Socrates, and all other philosophers, are infinitely mistaken in making death a natural thing. There is nothing more false. Death is so far from being natural, that nature abhors it; and it was far from the design of God in

* It could be nothing but the hope of the good things he expected in another life.

the state in which man was first created. For he created him holy, innocent, and by consequence immortal; it was only sin that brought death into the world. But this fatal league betwixt sin and death could not triumph over the designs of God, who had created man for immortality. He knew how to snatch the victory out of their hands, by bringing man to life again, even in the shades and horrors of death itself. Thus shall the dead revive at the resurrection, pursuant to the doctrine of the Christians, which teaches that death must give up those whom it has swallowed down. So that the principle that Socrates did not fully comprehend, is an unshaken truth, which bears the marks of an ancient tradition that the heathens had altered and corrupted.

The third argument alleged by Socrates as a proof of the immortality of the soul, is that of remembrance; which likewise bears the marks of that ancient tradition corrupted by the heathens. To find out the truth couched under this argument, I advance the following conjectures.

That the philosophers grounded this opinion of remembrance upon some texts of the prophets, which they did not well understand; such as that of Jeremiah, "Before I formed thee in the belly, I knew thee." Our soul was created so as to be adorned with all manner of knowledge suitable to its nature; and now is sensible of its having been deprived of the same. The philosophers felt this misery, and were not admitted to know the true cause; in order to unriddle the mystery, they invented this creation of souls before the body, and a remembrance that is the consequence thereof. But we who are guided by a surer light, know, that if man were not degenerate, he would still enjoy the full knowledge of the truths he formerly knew; and if he had never been any other than corrupted, he would have had no ideas of these truths. This unties the knot. Man had knowledge before he was corrupted, and after his corruption forgot it. He can recover nothing but confused ideas, and stands in need of a new light to illuminate them. No human reason could have fathomed this. It faintly unravelled part of the mystery as well as it could, and the explication it gave discovers some footsteps of the ancient truth: for it points both to the first state of happi-

ness and knowledge, and to the second of misery and
obscurity. Thus may we make a useful application of
the doctrine of remembrance, and the errors of philosophers may oftentimes serve to establish the most incompre-
hensible truths of the Christian religion, and shew that the
heathens did not want traditions relating to them.

The fourth argument is taken from the nature of the
soul. Destruction reaches only compounded bodies: but
we may clearly perceive, that the soul is simple and immaterial, and bears a resemblance of something divine, immortal, and intelligent: for it embraces the pure essence
of things; it measures all by ideas which are eternal patterns, and unites itself to them when the body does not
hinder it : so that it is spiritual, indissoluble, and consequently immortal, as being not capable of dissolution by
any other means than the will of him who created it.

Notwithstanding the force of the proofs, and their tendency to keep up this hope in the soul, Socrates and his
friends own, that it is almost impossible to ward off doubts
and uncertainties: for our reason is too weak and degenerate to arrive at the full knowledge of truth in this world.
So that it is a wise man's business to choose from amongst
those arguments of the philosophers, for the immortality
of the soul, that which to him seems best, and most forcible, till he obtain a full assurance either of some promise, or by some divine revelation; for that is the only
vessel that is secure from danger. By this the most
refined Paganism pays homage to the Christian religion,
and all colour or excuse for incredulity is taken away,
for the Christian religion affords promises, revelations, and,
which is yet more considerable, the accomplishment of
them.

They moved two objections to Socrates: one, that the
soul is only the harmony resulting from the just proportion of the qualities of the body : the other, that though
the soul be more durable than the body, yet it dies at last,
after having made use of several bodies ; just as a man dies
after he has worn several suits of clothes.

Socrates, before he makes any answer, stops a little, and
deplores the misfortune of men, who by hearing the disputes of the ignorant, that contradict every thing, persuade

themselves that there is no such thing as clear, solid, and sensible reasons, but that every thing is uncertain. Like those who being cheated by men, become men-haters; so they being imposed upon by arguments, become haters of reason; that is, they take up an absolute hatred against all reason in general, and will not hear any argument. Socrates makes out the injustice of this procedure. He shews, that when two things are equally uncertain, wisdom directs us to choose that which is most advantageous with the least danger. Now, beyond all dispute, such is the immortality of the soul; and therefore it ought to be embraced. For if this opinion prove true after our death, are not we considerable gainers? And if it prove false, what do we lose?

Then he attacks that objection which represents the soul as a harmony, and refutes it by solid and convincing arguments, which at the same time prove the immortality of the soul.

His arguments are these: Harmony always depends upon the parts that conspire together, and is never opposite to them; but the soul has no dependence upon the body, and always stands on the opposite side. Harmony admits of less and more, but the soul does not: from whence it would follow, that all souls should be equal, that none of them are vicious, and that the souls of beasts are equally good, and of the same nature with those of men: which is contrary to all reason.

In music, the body commands the harmony; but in nature, the soul commands the body. In music, the harmony can never give a sound contrary to the particular sounds of the parts that bend or unbend, or move: but in nature the soul has a contrary sound to that of the body; it attacks all its passions and desires, it checks, curbs, and punishes the body. So that it must needs be of a very different and opposite nature; which proves its spirituality and divinity. For nothing but what is spiritual and divine can be wholly opposite to what is material and earthly.

The second objection was, that though the soul might outlive the body, yet that does not conclude its immortality; since we know nothing to the contrary, but that it dies at last, after having animated several bodies.

In answer to this objection, Socrates says we must trace the first original of the being and corruption of entities. If that be once agreed upon, we shall find no difficulty in determining what things are corruptible and what are not. But what path shall we follow in this inquiry ? Must it be that of physics ? These physics are so uncertain, that instead of being instructive, they only blind and mislead us. This he makes out from his own experience. So that there is a necessity of going beyond this science, and having recourse to metaphysics, which alone can afford us the certain knowledge of the reasons and causes of beings, and of that which constitutes their essences. For effects may be discovered by their causes ; but the causes can never be known by their effects. And upon this account we must have recourse to the divine knowledge, which Anaxagoras was so sensible of, that he ushered in his treatise of physics by this great principle: That "knowledge is the cause of being." But instead of keeping up to that principle, he fell in again with that of second causes, and by that means deceived the expectation of his hearers.

In order to make out the immortality of the soul, we must correct this order of Anaxagoras, and sound to the bottom the above-mentioned principle: which if we do, we shall be satisfied that God placed every thing in the most convenient state. Now this best and most suitable state must be the object of our inquiry. To which purpose we must know wherein the particular good of every particular thing consists, and what the general good of all things is. This discovery will prove the immortality of the soul.

In this view Socrates raises his thoughts to immaterial qualities, and eternal ideas: that is, he affirms that there is something that is in itself, good, fine, just, and great, which is the first cause ; and that all things in this world that are good, fine, just, or great, are only such by the communication of that first cause: since there is no other cause of the existence of things, but the participation of the essence proper to each subject.

This participation is so contrived, that contraries are

never found in the same subject. From which principle
it follows by a necessary consequence, that the soul, which
gives life to the body, not as an accidental form that adheres to it, but as a substantial form, subsisting in itself,
and living formally by itself, as the corporeal idea, and
effectually enlivening the body, can never be subject to
death, that being the opposite of life: and that the soul
being incapable of dying, cannot be injured by any attack
of this enemy; and is in effect imperishable, like the immaterial qualities, justice, fortitude, and temperance: but
with this difference, that these immaterial qualities subsist
independently and of themselves, as being the same thing
with God himself; whereas the soul is a created being,
that may be dissolved by the will of its Creator. In a word,
the soul stands in the same relation to the life of the body,
that the idea of God does to the soul.

The only objection they could invent upon this head,
was, that the greatness of the subject, and man's natural
infirmity, are the two sources of man's distrust and incredulity upon this head. Whereupon Socrates endeavours
to dry up those two sources.

He attacks their distrust, by shewing, that the opinion
of the soul's immortality, suits all the ideas of God. For,
by this mortality, virtue would be prejudicial to men of pro-
bity, and vice beneficial to the wicked; which cannot be
imagined. So that there is a necessity of another life for
rewarding the good and punishing the bad. And the soul
being immortal, carries along with it into the other world
its good and bad actions, its virtues and vices, which are
the occasion of its eternal happiness or misery. From
whence, by a necessary consequence, we may gather what
care we ought to have of it in this life.

To put a stop to the torrent of incredulity, he has recourse to two things, which naturally demand a great
deference from man, and cannot be denied without a visible authority. The first is, the ceremonies and sacrifices
of religion itself, which are only representations of what
would be put in execution in hell. The other is, the
authority of antiquity, which maintained the immortality
of the soul: in pursuit of which, he mentions some ancient
traditions, that point to the truth published by Moses and
the prophets, notwithstanding the fables that overwhelm

them. Thus we see, a Pagan supplies the want of proof, which is too natural to man, and silences the most obstinate prejudices, by having recourse to the oracles of God, which they were in some measure acquainted with; and by so doing, makes answer to Simmias, who had objected, that the doctrine of the immortality of the soul stood in need of some promise or divine revelation to procure its reception. Though some blinded Christians reject the authority of our Holy Writ, and refuse to submit to it; yet we see a Pagan had so much light as to make use of it to support his faith, if I may so speak, and to strengthen his sweet hope of a blessed eternity. He shews, that he knew how to distinguish the fabulous part of a tradition from the truth, and affirms nothing but what is conformable to the Scriptures, particularly the last judgment of the good and the bad; the eternal torments of those who committed mortal sins in this life; the pardon of sins after repentance; the happiness of those who during the whole course of their lives renounced the pleasures of the body, and only courted the pleasure of true knowledge, that is, the knowledge of God; and beautified their souls with proper ornaments, such as temperance, justice, fortitude, liberty and truth. He does not joke upon the groundless metempsychosis, or return of souls to animate bodies in this life; but speaks seriously, and shews that after death all is over, the wicked are thrown for ever into the bottomless abyss, and the righteous conveyed to mansions of bliss. Those who are neither righteous nor wicked, but committed sins in this life, which they always repented of, are committed to places of torment, till they be sufficiently purified.

When Socrates made an end of his discourse, his friends asked what orders he would give concerning his affairs. " The only orders I give," replied he, " is to take care of yourselves, and to make yourselves as like to God as possible." Then they asked him, how he would be interred? This question offended him. He would not have himself confounded with his corpse, which was only to be interred. And though the expression seems to import little, he shewed that such false expressions gave very dangerous wounds to the souls of men.

He goes and bathes. His wife and children are brought

to him. He talks to them a minute, and then dismisses
them. Upon his coming out of the bath, the cup is presented to him. He takes it, recollects his thoughts within
himself, prays, and drinks it off, with an admirable tranquillity of mind. Finding that he approached his end, he
gave them to know that he resigned his soul into the hands
of him who gave it, and of the true physician who was
coming to heal it. This was the exit of Socrates. Paganism never afforded such an admirable example. And
yet a modern author is so ignorant of its beauty, that he
places it infinitely below that of Petronius, the famous
disciple of Epicurus. " He did not employ the last hours
of his life," says that author, "in discoursing of the immortality of the soul, &c. but having chose a more plea-
surable and natural sort of death, imitated the sweetness
of the swans, and caused some agreeable and touching
verses to be recited to him." This was a fine imitation.
It seems Petronius sung what they read to him. But this
was not all. " Nevertheless," continues he, " he reserved
some minutes for thinking of his affairs, and distributed
rewards to some of his slaves, and punished others."

" Let them talk of Socrates," says he, " and boast of his
constancy and bravery in drinking up the poison! Petronius is not behind him; nay, he is justly entitled to a preference upon the score of his forsaking a life infinitely
more delightful than that of the sage Grecian, and that
too with the same tranquillity of mind and evenness of
temper."

We have no need of long comments to make out the vast
difference between the death of Socrates and that of this
Epicurean, whom Tacitus himself, notwithstanding his paganism, did not dare to applaud. On one side, we are pre-.
sented with the view of a man that spent his last minutes
in making his .friends better, recommending to them the
hope of a blessed eternity, and shewing what that hope
requires of them; a man that died with his eyes intent
upon God, praying to him, and blessing him, without any
reflections upon his enemies who condemned him so
unjustly. On the other side, we meet with a voluptuous
person, in whom all sentiments of virtue are quite extinguished; who, to be rid of his own fears, occasioned his
own death; and in his exit would admit of no other enter-

tainment but agreeable poems and pleasant verses; who
spent the last minutes of his time in rewarding those of his
slaves, who doubtless had been the ministers and accomplices of his sensualities, and seeing those punished who
perhaps had shewn an aversion to his vices.   A good death
ought to be ushered in by a good life.   Now, a life spent in
vice, effeminacy and debauchery, is far short of one entirely
taken up in the exercise of virtue, and the solid pleasures of
true knowledge, and adorned with the venerable ornaments
of temperance, justice, fortitude, liberty, and truth.   One
of Socrates's dying words was, that those who entertained
bad discourses upon death, wounded the soul very danger-
ously.   And what would not he have said of those who
scruple not to write them.

But it is probable our author did not foresee the consequence of this unjust preference.   He wrote like a man of
the world, that knew not Socrates.   Had he known him,
he had certainly formed a juster judgment.   And in like
manner, if he had known Seneca or Plutarch, he had never
equalled or preferred Petronius to them.   Had he made the
best use of his understanding, he would have seen reasons
to doubt, that the Petronius we now read, is not the Petronius
of Tacitus, whose death he so much admires; and would
have met with some such objections, which at least give
occasion to suspect its being suppositious.   But to return
to Socrates.

His doctrine of " death being no affliction, but, on the
contrary, a passage to a happier life," made a considerable
progress.   Some philosophers gave such lively and forcible
demonstrations of it in their lectures, that the greatest part
of their disciples laid violent hands on themselves, in order
to overtake that happier life.   Ptolemæus Philadelphus pro-
hibited Hegesias of Cyrene to teach it in his school, for
fear of dispeopling his countries.   And the poets of that
prince's court siding with their prince, as they commonly
do, used all means to decry that doctrine, and those who
were prevailed upon to embrace it.   It was their pernicious
complaisance that occasioned what we now read in Calli-
machus against the immortality of the soul; and above all,
that famous epigram which Cicero alleges to have been writ
against Cleombrotus of Ambracia, but was certainly œ-

signed likewise against Plato. It is to this purpose·
"Cleombrotus of Ambracia having paid his last compliment
to the sun, threw himself headlong from the top of a
tower into hell; not that he had done any thing worthy of
death, but only had read Plato's treatise of the immortality
of the soul."

But after all, it redounds to the glory of Socrates and
Plato, and the doctrine of the immortality of the soul, that
none but such enemies as these oppose it.

PHEDON:

OR,

A DIALOGUE OF THE IMMORTALITY OF THE SOUL.

ECHECRATES AND PHEDON.

Echec. PHEDON, were you by when Socrates drank the
poison? or did any body give you an account how he
behaved in that juncture?

Phed. I was present.

Echec. What were his last words then, and how died
he? You will oblige me much with the relation: for the
Phliasians* have but little correspondence with the
Athenians, and it is a great while since we had any stranger
from Athens to acquaint us how things went. We only
heard that he died after drinking the poison, but could not
understand any particulars relating to his death.

Phed. What! did not you hear how he was arraigned?

Echec. Yes, truly, somebody told us that; and we
thought it strange that his sentence was so long in being
put in execution after his trial.

Phed. That happened only by chance: † for the day

* The inhabitants of Phlius, a city in the Peloponnesus.
† Phedon's discourse implies that the time of the ship's departure
was uncertain: it was either anticipated or retarded, as the condition of the ship and other occurrences required. This uncertainty
occasions the difficulty of finding the true date of Socrates's death.

before his trial, the stern of the sacred ship which the Athenians send every year to Delos, was crowned for the voyage.

Echec. What is that sacred ship?

Phed. If you believe the Athenians, it is the same ship in which Theseus transported the fourteen young children to Crete, and brought them safe back again; and it is said the Athenians at that time vowed to Apollo, that if the children were preserved from the impending danger, they would send every year to Delos presents and victims aboard the same vessel; and this they do ever since. As soon as the ship is cleared, and ready to put to sea, they purify the city, and observe an inviolable law for putting none to death before the return of the ship. Now sometimes it stays long out, especially if the winds be contrary. This festival, which is properly called Theoria, commences when the priest of Apollo has crowned the stern of the ship. Now, as I told you, this happened on the day preceding Socrates's trial. And it was upon that account that he was kept so long in prison, after his commitment.

Echec. And during his imprisonment, what did he do? What said he? Who was with him? Did the judges order him to be kept from visits? And did he die deprived of the presence of his friends?

Phed. Not at all : several of his friends staid with him o the last minute.

Ethec. If you are at leisure, pray relate the whole story.

Phed. At present I have nothing to do, and so shall endeavour to satisfy your demands. Besides, I take the greatest pleasure in speaking or hearing others speak of Socrates.*

Ethec. Assure yourself, Phedon, you shall not take more pleasure in speaking, than I in hearing. Begin, pray, and above all, take care to omit nothing.

Phed. You will be surprised when you hear what a condition I was then in. I was so far from being sensibly touched with the misfortune of a friend whom I loved very

* Phedon had been infinitely obliged to Socrates; for being taken prisoner in war, and sold to a merchant that bought slaves, Socrates, who was mighty fond of his genius, obliged Alcibiades or Crito to ransom him, and received him into the number of his friends and disciples.

tenderly, and who died before my eyes, that I envied his circumstances, and could not forbear to admire the goodness, sweetness, and tranquillity, that appeared in all his discourses, and the bravery he shewed upon the approach of death.   Every thing that I saw, furnished me with a proof that he did not pass to the shades below without the assistance of some Deity, that took care to conduct him, and put him in possession of that transcendent felicity of the blessed.   But as, on the one hand, these thoughts stifled all the sentiments of compassion that might seem due at such a mortifying sight; so, on the other hand, they lessened the pleasure I was wont to have in hearing all his other discourses, and affected me with that sorrowful reflection, that in a very short time this divine man would leave us for ever.   Thus was my heart tossed with contrary emotions, that I can not define.   It was not properly either pleasure or grief, but a confused mixture of these two passions, which produced almost the same effect in all the by-standers.   One while we melted into tears, and another time gave surprising signs of real joy and sensible pleasure.   Above all, Apollodorus* distinguished himself upon this occasion; you know his humour.

Echec. Nobody knows it better.

Phed. In him was the difference of these emotions most observable.   As for me, and all the rest, our behaviour was not so remarkable, as being mixed with the trouble and confusion I spoke of just now.

Echec. Who was there then beside yourself?

Phed. There were no other Athenians, but Apollodorus, Critobulus, and his father Crito, Hermogenes, Epigenes, Æschines, Antisthenes, Ctesippus, Menexemus, and a few more.   Plato was sick.

Echec. Were there no strangers?

Phed. Yes; Simmias the Theban, with Cebes,† and Phedondes; and from Megara, Euclides and Terpsion.

* The same Apollodorus is spoken of in the Apology.
† The same Cebes, who made the table that we now have; which is an explication of an allegorical table, that he supposes to have been in the temple of Saturn at Thebes; and contains a very ingenious scheme of a man's whole life.   It hints at all the doctrine of Socrates, and the style resembles that of Plato.

Echec. What ! were not Aristippus and Cleombrotus there ?

Phed. No, sure; for it is said, they were at Ægina.*

Echec. Who was there besides ?

Phed. I believe I have named most of those that were present.

Echec. Let us hear then what his last discourses were.

Phed. I will endeavour to give you a full account. For we never missed one day in visiting Socrates. To this end, we met every morning in the place where he was tried, which joined to the prison ; and there we waited till the prison-doors were open; at which time we went straight to him, and there commonly passed the whole day. On the day of his execution, we came thither sooner than ordinary, having heard as we came out of the city, that the ship was returned from Delos. When we arrived, the gaoler that used to let us in, came out to us, and desired we should stay a little, and not go in till he came to conduct us. For, says he, the eleven magistrates† are now untying Socrates, and acquainting him that he must die, this day. When we came in, we found Socrates untied,‡ and his wife Xantippe (you know her) sitting by him with

---

* The delicacy and point of this satire, is thus explained by Demetrius Phalereus. Plato, says he, had a mind to suppress the scandal that Aristippus and Cleombrotus drew upon themselves, by feasting at Ægina, when Socrates, their friend and master, was in prison, without deigning to go to see him, or even to assist on the day of his death, though they were then at the entry of the Athenian harbour. Had he told the whole story, the invective had been too particular. But with an admirable decency and artfulness he introduces Phedon, giving a list of those who assisted at his death, and making answer to the question, (Whether they were there or not?) That they were at Ægina ; pointing at once to their debauchery and ingratitude. This stroke is the more biting, that the thing itself paints out the horror of the action, and not he that speaks. Plato might securely have attacked Aristippus and Cleombrotus ; but he chose rather to make use of this figure, which in effect gives the greater blow. This is a notable piece of delicate satire. Athenæus, by charging Plato with slander upon this score, prejudiced himself more than Plato, who will always be cried up for having this zeal for his master.

† These magistrates were the overseers of the prison and prisoners, and executed the sentences of the judges.

‡ At Athens, after the sentence was pronounced to the criminal, they untied him, as being a victim to death, which it was not lawful to keep in chains.

one of his children in her arms; and as soon as she spied
us, she fell a crying and making a noise, as you know women generally do on such occasions. "Socrates," said
she, "this is the last time your friends shall see you."
Upon which, Socrates, turning to Crito, says, "Crito, pray
send this woman home." Accordingly it was done. Crito's
folks carried Xantippe off, who beat her face and cried bitterly. In the mean time, Socrates, sitting upon the bed,
softly strokes the place of his leg where the chain had
been tied, and says, "To my mind what men call pleasure, is a pretty odd sort of a thing, which agrees admirably well with pain; though people believe it is quite
contrary, because they cannot meet in one and the same
subject. For, whoever enjoys the one, must unavoidably
be possessed of the other, as if they were naturally joined.
Had Æsop been aware of this truth, perhaps he had
made a fable of it, and had told us, that God designing to
reconcile these two enemies, and not being able to compass
his end, contented himself with tying them to one chain,
so that ever since the one follows the other, according to
my experience at this minute; for the pain occasioned by
my chain, is now followed with a great deal of pleasure."

I am infinitely glad, replies Cebes, interrupting him,
that you have mentioned Æsop. For by so doing, you have
put it in my head to ask you a question, that many have
asked me of late, especially Evenus.* The question relates to your poems, in turning the fables of Æsop into
verse, and making a hymn to Apollo. They want to know
what moved you, that never made verses before, to turn
poet since you came into the prison? If Evenus asks
the same question of me again, as I know he will, what
would you have me say?

You have nothing to do, says Socrates, but to tell him
the plain matter of fact as it stands, viz. that I did not at
all mean to rival him in poetry, for I knew such an attempt was above my reach, but only to trace the meaning
of some dreams, and put myself in a capacity of obeying,
in case poetry happened to be the music that they allotted

* Evenus of Paros, an elegiac poet, the first that said, Habit was a
second nature.

for my exercise. For you must know, that all my life-
time I have had dreams, which always recommended the
same thing to me, sometimes in one form, and sometimes
in another. Socrates, said they, apply yourself to music.
This I always took for a simple exhortation, like that commonly given to those who run races, ordering me to pursue my wonted course of life, and carry on the study of
wisdom, that I made my whole business, which is the most
perfect music. But since my trial, the festival of Apollo
having retarded the execution of my sentence, I fancied
these dreams might have ordered me to apply myself to
that vulgar and common sort of music: and since I was
departing this world, I thought it safer to sanctify myself
by obeying the Gods, and essaying to make verses, than
to disobey them. Pursuant to this thought, my first essay
was a hymn to the God, whose festival was then celebrated.
After that, I considered, that a true poet ought not only to
make discourses in verse, but likewise fables. Now finding myself not disposed to invent new fables, I applied
myself to those of Æsop, and turned those into verse that
came first into my mind.

This, my dear Cebes, is the answer you are to give
Evenus; assuring him, that I wish him all happiness;
and tell him, that if he be wise he will follow me; for in
all appearance I am to make my exit this day, since the
Athenians have given orders to that effect.

What sort of counsel is that you give to Evenus? replies Simmias; I have seen that man often: and by what
I know of him, I can promise you, he will never willingly
follow you.

What, says Socrates, is not Evenus a philosopher?

I think so, says Simmias.

Then, replies Socrates, he and all others that are worthy
of that profession, will be willing to follow me. I know
he will not kill himself, for that, they say, is not lawful.
Having spoken these words, he drew his legs off the bed,
and sat down upon the ground, in which posture he entertained us the whole remaining part of the day.

Cebes put the first question to him, which was this:
How do you reconcile this, Socrates, that it is not lawful
to kill one's self, and at the same time that a philosopher
ought to follow you?

What, replies Socrates, did neither you, nor Simmias ever hear your friend Philolaus* discourse that point?

No, replied they, he never explained himself clearly upon that point.

As for me, replies Socrates, I know nothing but what I have heard, and shall not grudge to communicate all that I have learned. Besides, there is no exercise so suitable for a man upon the point of death, as that of examining and endeavouring thoroughly to know what voyage this is that we must all make, and making known his own opinion upon it.

What is the ground of that assertion, says Cebes, that it is not lawful for a man to kill himself? I have often heard Philolaus, and others say, that it was an ill action, but I never heard them say more.

Have patience, says Socrates, you shall know more presently, and perhaps you will be surprised to find it an eternal truth that never changes; whereas most other things in this world alter according to their circumstances: this is still the same, even in the case of those to whom death would be more agreeable than life. Is it not a surprising thing, that such men are not allowed to possess themselves of the good they want, but are obliged to wait for another deliverer?

Jupiter only knows that, replies Cebes smiling.

This may seem unreasonable to you, says Socrates, but after all, it is not so. The discourses we are entertained with every day in our ceremonies and mysteries, viz. "that God has put us in this life, as in a post which we cannot quit without his leave," &c. These, I say, and such like expressions, may seem hard, and surpass our understanding. But nothing is easier to be understood, or better said, than this: "That the Gods take care of men, and that men are one of the possessions that belong to the Gods." Is not this true?

Very true, replies Cebes.

Would not you yourself, continues Socrates, be angry if

---

* Philolaus was a Pythagorean philosopher, who could not fail to assert his master's doctrine, of the unlawfulness of self-murder. He wrote only one volume, which Plato purchased at 400 crowns.

one, of your slaves killed himself without your order, and would not you punish him severely if you could?

Yes, doubtless, replies Cebes.

By the same reason, says Socrates, a man should not kill himself, but should wait for an express order from God, for making his exit, like this sent to me now.

That stands to reason, says Cebes; but your saying, that a philosopher ought nevertheless to desire to die, is what I think strange, and I cannot reconcile these two opinions; especially, if it be true, which you said just now, that the Gods take care of men as being their property; for that a philosopher should not be troubled to be without the Gods for his guardians, and to quit a life where such perfect beings, (the better governors of the world,) take care of him, seems very unreasonable to me. Do they imagine, they will be more capable to govern themselves, when left to themselves? I can easily conceive that a fool may think it his duty to flee from a good master at any rate; and will not be convinced that he ought to stick to what is good, and never lose sight of it: but I affirm, that a wise man will never desire to quit a dependence upon one more perfect than himself. From whence I infer the contrary of what you advanced, and conclude, that the wise are sorry to die, and that fools are fond of death.

Socrates seemed to be pleased with Cebes's wit; and turning to us, told us, that Cebes had always something to object, and takes care not to assent at first to what is told him.

Indeed, replies Simmias, I must say, I find a great deal of reason in what Cebes advances. What can the sages pretend to gain, by quitting better masters than themselves, and willingly depriving themselves of their aid? Do you mind that: it is you alone that he addresses himself to, meaning to reprove you for your insensibility, in being so willing to part with us, and quit the Gods, who, according to your own words, are such good and wise governors.

You are in the right of it, says Socrates: I see you mean to oblige me to make formal defences, such as I gave in at my trial.

That is the very thing, replies Simmias.

Then, says Socrates, you must satisfy yourselves, so that this my last apology may have more influence upon you, than my former upon my judges. For my part, continues he, if I thought I should not find in the other world Gods as good and as wise, and men infinitely better than we are here, it would be a piece of injustice in me not to be troubled at death. But, be it known to you Simmias, and to you Cebes, that I hope to arrive at the assembly of the just. Indeed in this point, I may flatter myself, but as for finding masters infinitely good and wise, that I can assure you of, as much as things of that nature will bear; and therefore it is, that death is no trouble to me, hoping that there is something reserved for the dead, after this life; and that the good meet with better treatment in the world to come, than the bad.

How, replies Simmias, would you have quitted this life, without communicating those sentiments to us? This, methinks, will be a common good; and if you convince us of all that you believe, with reference to this point, you have made a sufficient apology.

That is what I design to try, says Socrates, but I would first hear what Crito has to say: I thought he had a mind to offer something a good while ago.

I have nothing to say, replies Crito, but what your executioner has been pushing me on to tell you this great while, that you ought to speak as little as you can, for fear of overheating yourself, since nothing is more contrary to the operation of poison; insomuch, that if you continue to speak so, you will be obliged to take two or three doses.*

Let him do his office, says Socrates, let him make ready two doses of poison, or three if he will.

I knew you would give me that answer, replies Crito; but still he importunes me to speak to you.

Pray let that alone, says Socrates, and suffer me to explain before you, who are my judges, for what reasons, a man

---

* Probably the executioner meant by this advice to keep fair with Socrates, and save his money; for he was to furnish the hemlock, of which a pound (the common dose) cost 12 drachms, *i. e.* 3 livres and 12*d*. See Plutarch upon the death of Phocion, who was obliged to pay his executioner for a dose of poison.

enlightened by philosophy, ought to die with courage and a firm hope, that in the other world he shall enjoy a felicity beyond any thing in this. Pray do you, Simmias and Cebes, listen to my arguments.

True philosophers make it the whole business of their life-time to learn to die. Now it is extremely ridiculous for them, after they run out a whole course incessantly, in order to compass that one end, to flinch and be afraid when it comes up to them, when they are just in a capacity of obtaining it after a long and painful search.

Whereupon Simmias laughed, and said, In earnest, Socrates, you make me laugh, notwithstanding the small occasion I have to laugh in this juncture. For I am certain the greatest part of those who hear you talk so, will say you talk much better of the philosophers than you believe. Above all, the Athenians would be glad that all the philosophers should learn that lesson so well, as to die in effect; and they will be ready to tell you, Death is the only thing they are worthy of.*

Simmias, replies Socrates, our Athenians would so speak the truth, but without knowing it to be such: for they are ignorant in what manner philosophers desire to die, or how they are worthy of it. But let us leave the Athenians to themselves, and talk of things within our own company: Does death appear to be any thing to you?

Yes, without doubt, replies Simmias.

Is it not, continues Socrates, the separation of soul and body, so that the body has one separate being, and the soul another?

Just so, says Simmias.

Let us try then, my dear Simmias, if your thoughts and mine agree: by that means we shall set the object of our present enquiry in a clearer light. Do you think a philosopher courts what the world calls pleasure, as that of eating, drinking, &c.

Not at all, Socrates.

Nor that of love?

By no means.

* A satirical rub upon the Athenians, who could not abide philosophers.

Do you think they pursue or mind the other pleasures relating to the body, such as good clothes, handsome shoes, and the other ornaments of the body? Whether do you think they value or slight those things, when necessity does not enforce their use?

In my mind, replies Simmias, a true philosopher must needs contemn them.

Then you believe, continues Socrates, that the body is not at all the object of the care and business of a philosopher, but on the contrary, that his whole business is to separate himself from it, and mind only the concerns of his soul.

Most certainly.

Thus, continues Socrates, it is plain upon the whole, that a philosopher labours in a more distinguishing manner than other men, to purchase the freedom of his soul, and cut off all commerce between it and the body. I am likewise of the opinion, Simmias, that most men will grant, that whoever avoids these corporeal things, and takes no pleasure in them,* is not worthy to live; and that he who does not use the pleasures of the body, is near to death.

You speak truth, Socrates.

But what shall we say of the acquiring of prudence? Is the body an obstacle or not, when employed in that work? I will explain my meaning by an example: Have seeing and hearing any thing of truth in them, and is their testimony faithful? Or, are the poets in the right in singing, that we neither see nor hear things truly? For, if these two senses of seeing and hearing are not true and trusty, the others, which are much weaker, will be far less such. Do not you think so?

Yes, without doubt, replies Simmias.

When does the soul then, continues Socrates, find out the truth? We see, that while the body is joined in the enquiry, this body plainly cheats and seduces it.

That is true, says Simmias.

Is it not by reasoning that the soul embraces truths?

* It is a truth acknowledged by almost all the world, that he who does not enjoy the pleasures of the body, is not worthy to live. So that it is a true saying, that a philosopher is worthy of nothing but death.

And does it not reason better than before, when it is not encumbered by seeing or hearing, by pain or pleasure? When shut up within itself, it bids adieu to the body, and entertains as little correspondence with it as possible: and pursues the knowledge of things without touching them.

That is incomparably well spoken.

Is it not, especially upon this occasion, that the soul of a philosopher despises and avoids the body, and wants to be by itself?

I think so.

What shall we say then, my dear Simmias, of all the objects of the soul? For instance, shall we call JUSTICE something or nothing?

We must certainly give it the title of *something*.

Shall we not likewise call it good and fine?

Ay, doubtless.

But did you ever see these objects with the eyes of your body?

No, to be sure.

Or with any other sense? Did you ever touch any of those things, such as magnitude, health, fortitude, and, in a word, the essence of all other things? Is the truth of them discovered by the body? Or is it not certain, that whoever puts himself in a condition to examine them more narrowly, and trace them to the bottom, will better compass the end, and know more of them?

That is very true.

Now the simplest and purest way of examining things, is to pursue every particular by thought alone, without offering to support our meditation by seeing, or backing our reasonings by any other corporal sense; by employing the naked thought without any mixture, and so endeavouring to trace the pure and genuine essence of things without the ministry of the eyes or ears: the soul being, if I may so speak, entirely disengaged from the whole mass of body, which only cumbers the soul, and cramps it in the quest of wisdom and truth, as often as it is admitted to the least correspondence with it. If the essence of things be ever known, must it not be in the manner above mentioned!

Right, Socrates; you have spoken admirably well.

Is it not then, continues Socrates, a necessary consequence from this principle, that true philosophers should have such language among themselves? This life is a road that is apt to mislead us and our reason in all our inquiries ; because while we have a body, and our soul is drowned in so much corruption, we shall never attain the object of our wishes, i. e. truth. The body throws in a thousand obstacles and crosses in our way, by demanding necessary food; and then the diseases that ensue, do quite disorder our inquiry : besides it fills us with love, desires, fears, and a thousand foolish imaginations, insomuch that there is nothing truer than the common saying, that "the body will never conduct us to wisdom." What is it that gives rise to wars, and occasions sedition and duelling? Is it not the body and its desires ? In effect, all wars arise from the desire of riches, which we are forced to heap up for the sake of our body, in order to supply its wants, and serve it like slaves ; it is this that cramps our application to philosophy. And the greatest of all our evils is, that when it has given us some respite, and we are set upon meditation, it steals in and interrupts our thoughts all of a sudden. It cumbers, troubles, and surprises us in such a manner, that it hinders us from descrying the truth. Now we have shown that in order to trace the purity and truth of any thing, we should lay aside the body, and only employ the soul to examine the objects we pursue. So that we can never arrive at the wisdom we court, till after death. Reason is on our side. For if it is impossible to know any thing purely while we are in the body, one of these two things must be true: either the truth is never known, or it is known after death; because at that time the soul will be left to itself, and freed of its burden, and not before. And while we are in this life, we can only approach to the truth in proportion to our removing from the body, and renouncing all correspondence with it, that is not of mere necessity, and keeping ourselves clear from the contagion of its natural corruption, and all its filth, till God himself comes to deliver us. Then indeed being freed from all bodily infirmity, we shall converse in all probability with men that enjoy the same liberty, and shall know within ourselves the pure essence of things, which perhaps is nothing else but truth. But he who is not pure, is not allowed to approach to purity itself.   This, my dear Simmias, as I take it, should be the thought and language of true philosophers.   Are not you of the same mind?

Most certainly, Socrates.

Then, my dear Simmias, whoever shall arrive where I am now going, has great reason to hope, that he will there be possessed of what we look for here with so much care and anxiety; so that the voyage I am now sent upon, fills me with a sweet and agreeable hope.   And it will have the same effect upon all who are persuaded that the soul must be purged before it knows the truth.   Now the purgation of the soul, as we were saying just now, is only its separation from the body, its accustoming itself to retire and lock itself up, renouncing all commerce with it as much as possible, and living by itself, whether in this or the other world, without being chained to the body.*

All that is true, Socrates.

Well! as to what we call *death*, is not that the disengagement and separation of the body from the soul?

Most certainly.

Are not the true philosophers the only men that seek after this disengagement? and is not that separation and deliverance their whole business?

So I think, Socrates.

Is it not a ridiculous fancy, that a man that has lived in the expectation of death, and during his whole life has been preparing to die, upon his arrival at the point of desired death, should think to retire, and be afraid of it? Would not that be a very scandalous apostacy?

How should it be otherwise?

It is certain then, Simmias, that death is so far from being terrible to true philosophers, that their whole business is to die; which may be easily inferred thus: if they slight and contemn their body, and passionately desire to enjoy their soul by itself, is it not a ridiculous way of

* The obstacles raised in the pursuit of wisdom, inspired the true philosophers with such an aversion to the body, that they pleased themselves with the fancy that after death they should be rid of it for ever. They knew no better: and though they had some idea of the resurrection, yet they were absolutely ignorant that the body will be likewise purged and glorified, that this corruptible body would put on incorruptibility, and the mortal part be invested with immortality.

belying themselves, to be afraid and troubled when Death comes? And is it not a piece of extravagance to decline going to that place, where those who get to it, hope to obtain the good things they have wished for all their lives? For they desired wisdom, and a deliverance from the body, as being their burden, and the object of their hatred and contempt. Do not many, upon the loss of their wives, children, or friends, willingly cut the thread of life, and convey themselves into the other world, merely upon the hope of meeting there, and conversing with the persons they love? * And shall a true lover of wisdom, and one that firmly hopes to attain the perfection of it in the other world, be startled by death, and unwilling to go to the place that will furnish him with what his soul loves? Doubtless, my dear Simmias, if he be a true philosopher, he will go with a great deal of pleasure; as being persuaded that there is no place in the regions below that cannot furnish him with that pure wisdom that he is in quest of. Now, if things stand thus, would it not be a piece of extravagance in such a man to fear death?

To be sure, says Simmias, it would be so.

And consequently, continues Socrates, when a man shrinks and retires at the point of death, it is a certain evidence that he loves not wisdom, but his own body, or honour, or riches, or perhaps all these together.

It is so, Socrates.

Then, Simmias, does not that we call fortitude belong in a peculiar manner to philosophers? And does not temperance, or that sort of wisdom that consists in controlling our desires, and living soberly and modestly, suit admirably well with those who contemn their bodies and live philosophically?

That is certain, Socrates.

Were you to inspect the fortitude and temperance of other men, you would find them very ridiculous.

---

* The greater part, though scarce convinced of the immortality of the soul, used to kill themselves upon the loss of what they loved, hoping to retrieve it in the other world: and is it not reasonable that the true philosophers, who are fully convinced of that truth, and fully persuaded that true wisdom is to be enjoyed in another world, should give death a welcome reception?

How so, Socrates?

You know, says he, all other men look upon death as the greatest affliction.

That is true, replies Simmias.

When those you call stout-hearted suffer death with some courage, they do it only for fear of some greater evil.

That I grant.

And by consequence, all men, excepting the philosophers, are only stout and valiant through fear. And is it not ridiculous to believe a man to be brave and valiant, that is only influenced by fear and timorousness?

You are in the right, Socrates.

Is not the case the same with your temperate persons? It is intemperance alone that makes them such. Though at first view this may seem impossible, yet it is no more than what daily experience proves. For such persons disclaim one pleasure, only for fear of being robbed of other pleasures that they covet, and which have an ascendant over them. They will cry out to you as long as you will, that intemperance consists in being ruled and governed by our passions; but at the same time that they give you this fine definition, it is only their subjection to some predominant pleasures, that makes them discard others. Now this is what I just said, that they are only temperate through intemperance.

That is clear, Socrates.

Let us not be imposed upon, my dear Simmias: the straight road to virtue does not lie in shifting pleasures for pleasures, fears for fears, or one melancholy thought for another, and imitating those who change a large piece of money for many small ones. WISDOM is the only true and unalloyed coin, for which all others must be given in exchange. With that piece of money we purchase fortitude, temperance, justice. In a word, that virtue is always true which accompanies WISDOM without any dependance upon pleasure, grief, fear, or any other passion. Whereas all other virtues stript of wisdom, which run upon a perpetual change, are only shadows of virtue. True virtue is really and in effect a purgation from all these sorts of passion. Temperance, justice, fortitude, and prudence or wisdom itself, are not exchanged for passions, but cleanse us of them. And it is pretty evident, that those

who instituted the purifications, called by us Teletes, i. e.
Perfect Expiations, were persons of no contemptible
rank, men of great genius,* who in the first ages meant
by such riddles to give us to know that whoever enters
the other world without being initiated and purified, shall
be hurled headlong into the vast abyss; and that whoever
arrives there after due purgation and expiation, shall be
lodged in the apartment of the Gods.† For, as the dis-
pensers of those expiations say, "There are many who bear
the Thyrsus, ‡ but few that are possessed by the spirit of
God." Now those who are thus possessed, as I take it,
are the true philosophers. I have tried all means to be
listed in that number, and have made it the business of my
whole life to compass that end. If it please God I hope
shortly to know that my efforts have not been ineffectual,
and that success has crowned my endeavours. This, my
dear Simmias, and my dear Cebes, is the apology with
which I offer to justify my not being troubled or afflicted
for parting with you, and quitting my governors in this
life; hoping to find good friends and rulers there, as well
as here. This the vulgar cannot digest. However, I shall
be satisfied if my defences take better with you than they
did with my judges.

Socrates having thus spoke, Cebes took up the discourse
to this purpose. Socrates, I subscribe to the truth of all
you have said. There is only one thing that men look upon
as incredible, viz. what you advanced of the soul. For
almost everybody fancies, that when the soul parts from
the body, it dies with it and is no more; that in the very
minute of parting, it vanishes like a vapour or smoke,
which flies off, and disperses, and has no existence.§ If

* Such as Orpheus, Musæus, &c.
† There is a passage to this purpose in the second book of his
Republic: they say, that by virtue of these purifications and sacrifices, we are delivered from the torments of hell; but if we neglect
them, we shall be liable to all the horrors of the same.
‡ The Thyrsus was a spear wrapt in vines or ivy, carried by tle
followers of Bacchus.
§ This was the imagination of those who denied the immortality
of the soul. The author of the Book of Wisdom has set them in their
true colours. " Our life," says he, " is but a breath; after death it
vanishes like a vapour, and passes like a cloud, or a mist dispersed by

it subsisted by itself, were gathered and retired into itself, and freed from all the above-mentioned evils; there were a fair and promising prospect. But, that the soul does really live after the death of a man, that it is sensible, that it acts and thinks; that, I say, needs solid proofs to make it go down.

You say right, Cebes, replies Socrates ; but how shall we manage this affair ? Shall we in this interview examine whether that is probable or not ?

I shall be glad, says Cebes, to hear your thoughts upon the matter.

At least, says Socrates, I cannot think that any man, hearing us, though he were a comedian,* would upbraid me with raillery, and charge me with not speaking of such things as concern us very much. If you have a mind that we should trace this affair to the bottom, my opinion is, that we should proceed in the following method, in order to know whether the souls of the dead have a being in the other world or not.

It is a very ancient opinion,† that souls quitting this world repair to the infernal regions, and return after that to live in this world. If it be so, that men return to life after death, it follows necessarily, that during that interval, their souls are lodged in the lower regions : for if they had not a being, they could not return to this world. And this will be a sufficient proof of what we affirm, if we be convinced that the living spring from the dead ;‡ if otherwise, then we must look out for other proofs.

the rays of the sun." Then he tells us, that those who entertain themselves with such language, " were not acquainted with the secrets of God, for God created man incorruptible, after his own image, and the hope of the righteous is full of immortality." Now this is just Socrates's doctrine.

* A satirical touch upon Aristophanes, who, in his Comedy of the Clouds had charged Socrates with amusing himself only with trifles.

† The first argument is grounded on the opinion of the Metempsychosis; which Socrates only makes use of to shew that it supposed the future existence of souls as a certain truth.

‡ Since all things take rise from their contraries, life cannot swerve from the common rule. Now, if life come from death, then the soul has a being. This is a certain truth, but can only be made out by the resurrection. Wherefore, St. Paul tells the opposers of

That is certain, says Cebes.

But to assure ourselves of this truth, replies Socrates, it is not sufficient to examine the point upon the comparison with men; but likewise upon that with other animals, plants, and whatever has a vegetable principle. By that means, we shall be convinced that all things are born after the same manner; that is, whatever has a *contrary*, owes its first rise to its contrary. For instance, handsome is the *contrary* to ugly, and just to unjust. And the same is the case of an infinite number of other things. Now, let us see if it be absolutely necessary that whatever has a contrary, should spring from that contrary. As when a thing becomes bigger, of necessity it must formerly have been lesser, before it acquired that magnitude. And when it dwindles into a lesser form, it must needs have been greater before its diminution. In like manner, the strongest arises from the weakest, and the swiftest from the slowest.

That is a plain truth, says Cebes.

And pray, continues Socrates, when a thing becomes worse, was it not formerly better? and when it grows just, is it not because it was formerly unjust?

Yes, surely, Socrates.

Then it is sufficiently proved, that every thing is generated by its contrary.

Sufficiently, Socrates.

But, is not there always a certain medium between these two contraries? There are two births, or two processions, one of *this* from *that*, and another of *that* from *this*. The medium between a greater and a lesser thing, is increase and diminution.* The same is the case of what we call mixing, separating, heating, cooling, and all other things *in infinitum*. For though it sometimes falls out,

that truth, "Thou fool, that which thou sowest is not quickened except it die."—1 Cor. xv. 36. Socrates goes upon the same principle, but it is only the Christian religion that can explain it. Plato and Socrates had some idea of the resurrection; but they spoiled t by mingling it with the gross doctrine of Pythagoras.

* Between two contraries there is always a medium which we may call the point of their generation.

that we have not terms to express those changes and mediums, yet experience shews, that by an absolute necessity, things take rise from one another, and pass reciprocally from one to another through a medium.

There is no doubt of that.

And, continues Socrates, has not life likewise its contrary, as awaking has to sleeping?

Without doubt, says Cebes.

What is that contrary?

Death.

Since these two things are contrary, do not they take rise one from the other? And between these two, are there not two generations, or two processions?

Why not?

But, says Socrates, I am about to tell you how the now-mentioned combination stands, and to shew you the original and progress of each of these two things which make up the compound. Pray tell me how awaking and sleeping are related? Does not sleep beget watchfulness, and watchfulness sleep? And is not the generation of sleep, the falling asleep; and that of watching, the awakening?

All very clear.

Now, pray view the combination of life and death. Is not death the contrary of life?

Yes.

And does not one breed the other?

Yes.

What is it that life breeds?

Death.

What is it that death breeds?

It must certainly be life.

Then, says Socrates, all living things, and men, are bred from death.

So I think, says Cebes.

And by consequence, continues Socrates, our souls are lodged in the infernal world after our death.

The consequence seems just.

But of these two generations, the one, viz. death, is very palpable; it discovers itself to the eye, and is touched by the hand.

Most certainly.

Shall not we then attribute to death the virtue of producing its contrary, as well as to life?   Or, shall we say, that nature is lame and maimed on that score?

There is an absolute necessity, replies Cebes, of ascribing to death the generation of its contrary.

What is that contrary?

Reviving, or returning to life.

If there is such a thing as returning to life, it is nothing else but the birth of the dead returning to life.   And thus · we agree, that the living are as much the product of the dead, as the dead are of the living.   Which is an incontestable proof, that the souls of the dead must remain in some place or other, from whence they return to life.

That, as I take it, says Cebes, is a necessary consequence from the principles we have agreed on.

And as I take it, Cebes, these principles are well grounded : consider them yourself.   If all these contraries had not their productions and generations in their turns, which make a circle ; and if there were nothing but one birth, and one direct production from one to the other contrary, without the return of the last contrary to the first that produced it ; were it not so, all things would terminate in the same figure, and be affected in the same manner, and at last cease to be born.*

How do you say, Socrates?

There is no difficulty in conceiving what I now say. If there were nothing but sleep, and if sleep did not produce watching, it is plain that every thing would be an emblem of the fable of Endymion,† and nothing would be seen anywhere, because the same thing must happen to them that happened to Endymion, viz. they must always sleep.   If every thing were mingled, without any subsequent separation, we should quickly see Anaxagoras's doctrine fulfilled, and all things jumbled together.‡   At the same rate, my dear Cebes, if all living things died, and

* If death did not give rise to life, as life does to death, all things would quickly be at an end.

† Whom the moon lulled eternally to sleep, according to the fable.

‡ That is to say, all things would quickly tumble into their primitive chaos.

being dead, continued such without reviving, would not
all things unavoidably come to an end at last, insomuch
that there would not be a living thing left in being?   For,
if living things did not arise from dead ones, when the
living ones die; of necessity all things must at last be
swallowed up by death, and entirely annihilated.*

It is necessarily so, replies Cebes; all that you have
said seems to be incontestable.

As I take it, Cebes, there is no objection made against
these truths, neither are we mistaken in receiving them :
for it is certain there is a return to life; it is certain that
the living rise out of the dead; that the souls departed
have a being, and upon their return to life, the good
souls are in a better, and the bad ones in a worse condition.

What you now advance, says Cebes, interrupting
Socrates, is only a necessary consequence of another principle,† that I have often heard you lay down, viz. That all
our acquired knowledge is only remembrance.   For, if
that principle be true, we must necessarily have learnt at
another time what we call to mind in this.   Now that is
impossible, unless our soul had a being before it became
invested with this human form.   So that this same principle concludes the immortality of the soul.

But, Cebes, says Simmias, interrupting him, what demonstration have we of that principle ?   Pray refresh my
memory with it, for at present it is out of my head.

There is a very pretty demonstration for it, replies
Cebes.   All men being duly interrogated, find out all
things of themselves ; which they could never do without knowledge and right reason.   Put them unawares
upon the figures of geometry, and other things of that
nature, they presently perceive that it is, as it is said.

Simmias, says Socrates, if you will not rely upon this

* I have corrected this passage, by reading μὴ γίνοιτο ; for without μὴ it was not sense.

† Socrates made use of that principle, as being established to his
hand, and a necessary consequence of the creation of souls before
the body.   But he did not teach it for a certainty, as we shall see
of Menon.

experience, pray try whether the same method will not bring you over to our sentiments. Do you find great difficulty in believing that learning is only remembering.

I do not find very much, replies Simmias, but I would gladly understand that remembrance you speak of. By what Cebes has said, I begin to believe it; but that will not hinder me from hearing with pleasure the arguments you shall offer.

I argue thus, replies Socrates : We all agree, that in order to remember, a man must have known before, what he then calls to mind.

Most certainly.

And let us likewise agree upon this, that knowledge coming in a certain manner is remembrance. I say, in a certain manner; for instance, when a man by seeing, hearing, or perceiving a thing by any of the senses, knows what it is that thus strikes the senses; and at the same time imagines to himself another thing, independent of that knowledge, by virtue of a quite different knowledge ; do not we justly say, that the man remembers the thing that comes thus into his mind ?*

How do you say, replies Simmias ?

I say, replies Socrates, for example, that we know a man by one sort of knowledge, and a harp by another.

That is certain, quoth Simmias.

Well then, continues Socrates, do not you know what happens to lovers, when they see the harp, dress, or any other thing that their friends or mistresses formerly made use of? As I said but now. Upon seeing and knowing the harp, they form in their thoughts the image of the person to whom the harp belongs. This is remembrance. Thus it often falls out, that one seeing Simmias, thinks of Cebes.† I could cite a thousand other instances. This then is remembrance, especially when the things called to mind are such as had been forgot through length of time, or being out of sight.

That is very certain, quoth Simmias.

* Socrates's proofs only conclude a remembrance of things once known, and afterwards forgot in this life; not of things learnt in the other world.

† By reason of their intimacy, which occasioned their being always together.

But, continues Socrates, upon seeing the picture of a horse or a harp, may not one call to mind the man? And upon seeing the picture of Simmias, may not one think of Cebes?

Sure enough, says Simmias.

Much more, continues Socrates, upon seeing the picture of Simmias, will he call to mind Simmias himself?

Yes, with ease.

From all these instances we infer, that remembrance is occasioned sometimes by things that are like the thing remembered, and sometimes by things that are unlike. But when one remembers a thing by virtue of a likeness, does it not necessarily come to pass, that the mind at first view discovers whether the picture does resemble the thing designed, lamely or perfectly?

It must needs be so, replies Simmias.

Then pray mind whether your thoughts of what I am about to say, agree with mine. Is not there something that we call equality?* I do not speak of the equality between one tree and another, one stone and another, and several other things that are alike: I speak of the abstracted equality of things. Shall we call that something or nothing?

Surely, we should call it something; but that will only come to pass when we mean to speak philosophically, and of marvellous things.

But then do we know this equality?

Without doubt.

From whence do we derive that knowledge? Is it not from the things we mentioned just now?† It is upon seeing equal trees, equal stones, that we form the idea of that equality, which is not either the trees or the stones, but something abstracted from all subjects. Do not you find

---

* He speaks of an intelligible, not a sensible equality.

† Socrates is wrong in thinking to prove that the knowledge of intelligible qualities was acquired in the other world.; such knowledge is rather the effect of the light with which God illuminates the soul, or primitive impressions that are not quite defaced by sin : it is the remainder of the knowledge we have lost, and of the perfection we have forfeited. So that if *the other life* be taken in Socrates's sense, the proposition is false : if in ours, for the state of the soul before sin. it is true.

it such? Pray take notice. The stones and the trees are always the same, and yet do not they sometimes appear unequal?

They do.

What! Do equal things appear unequal? Or, does *equality* take up the form of *inequality*?

By no means, Socrates.

Then equality, and the thing which is equal, are two different things.

Most certainly.

But after all, these equal things, which are different from equality, furnish us with the idea and knowledge of that abstracted equality.

That is true, replies Simmias.

The case is the same, whether this equality bear a resemblance to the things that occasioned its idea, or not.

Most certainly.

When, upon seeing one thing, you call to mind another, whether it be like it or not; still it is *remembrance*.

Without doubt.

But what shall we say to this, continues Socrates; when we behold trees or other things that are equal, are they equal according to the equality of which we have the idea, or not?

Very far from it.

Then we agree upon this: when a man sees a thing before him, and thinks it would be equal to another thing, but at the same time is far from being so perfectly equal, as the equality of which he has the idea; then I say, who thinks thus, must necessarily have known beforehand this intellectual being which the thing resembles, but imperfectly.

There is an absolute necessity for that.

And is not the case the same, when we compare things equal with the equality?

Surely, Socrates.

Then of necessity we must have known that equality before the time, in which we first saw the equal things, and thereupon thought, that they all tended to be equal as equality itself, but could not reach it.

That is certain.

K

But we likewise agree upon this, that the thought can be derived from nothing else but one of our senses, from seeing, touching, or feeling one way or another: and the same conclusion will hold of all beings, whether intellectual or sensible.

All things will equally conclude the same.

Then, it is from the senses themselves that we derive this thought; that all the objects of our senses have a tendency towards this intellectual equality, but come short of it: is it not so?

Yes, without doubt, Socrates.

In effect, Simmias, before we began to see, feel, or use our senses, we must have had the knowledge of the intellectual equality; else we could not be able to compare it with the sensible things, and perceive that they have all the tendency towards it, but fall short of its perfection.*

That is a necessary consequence from the premises.

But is it not certain, that immediately after our birth, we saw, we heard, and made use of our other senses?

Very true.

Then it follows, that before that time we had the knowledge of that equality?

Without doubt. And by consequence we were possessed of it before we were born.

So I think.

If we possessed it before we were born, then we knew things before we were born; and immediately after our birth knew not only what is equal, what great, what small, but all other things of that nature. For what we now advance of equality, is equally applicable to goodness, justice, sanctity, and, in a word, to all other things that have a real existence. So that of necessity we must

* One might have answered, that we had not that knowledge before we were born, but received it afterwards by the gradual communication of light from God into the soul. But as the soul was created full of light and perfection, so this truth was known to the Pagans, and upon that account, Socrates's friends were obliged to assent to what he said. If by the first life of the soul, we understand the very instant of creation, or the state of the soul before the fall, the proposition is true.

have known all these things before we came into this world.*

It seems so.

And being possessed of that knowledge, if we did not forget every day, we should not only be born with it, but retain it all our life-time. For to know, is only to preserve the knowledge we have received, and not to lose it. And to forget, is to lose the knowledge we enjoyed before.

That is certain, Socrates.

Now if, after having possessed that knowledge before we were born, and having lost it since, we come to retrieve it by the ministry of our senses, which we call learning, shall we not justly entitle it *remembrance?*

With a great deal of reason, Socrates.

For we have agreed upon this ;† that it is very possible that a man seeing, hearing, or perceiving one thing, by any of his senses, should frame to himself the imagination of another thing that he had forgotten ; to which the thing perceived by the senses has some relation, whether it resembles the other, or not. So that one of two things must necessarily follow: either we were born with that knowledge, and preserved it all along; or else retrieved it afterwards by way of remembrance. Which of these two do you prefer, Simmias? are we born with that knowledge; or do we call it to mind after having had it, and forgot it?

Indeed, Socrates, I know not which.

But mind what I am about to say to you, and then let us see which you will choose. A man that knows any thing, can he give a reason of his knowledge or not ?

Doubtless he can, Socrates.

And you think all men can give a reason for what we have been speaking of?

---

* The Greek exposition is very remarkable; it turns thus, ' Things upon which we have put this stamp, that it is so." That s, to distinguish things that have a true existence, from sensible hings that have no true existence.

† It was agreed before, that upon seeing one thing, we call to iind another unseen : as upon seeing a lute we think of a mistress; pon seeing equal trees, we call to mind equality

I wish they could, replies Simmias: but I am afraid that to-morrow we shall have none here that is capable of doing it.

Then you think all men have not this knowledge?

Certainly not.

Do they call to mind then, the things they have known ?*

That may be.

At what time did our souls learn that knowledge? It cannot be since we were men.

No surely.

Then it must be some time before that?

Yes, without doubt. And by consequence, Simmias, our souls had a being before that time; that is to say, before they were invested with a human form, while they were without the body, they thought, they knew, and understood.

Unless Socrates, you will allow, that we learned it in the minute of our birth; there is no other time left.

Be it so, my dear Simmias, but at what other time did we lose it ?† For we did not bring it into the world with us, as we concluded but now. Did we lose it in the same minute that we obtained it ? Or, can you assign any other time?

No, Socrates ; I did not perceive that what I said was to no purpose.

Then, Simmias, this must be a standing truth:‡ that if the objects of our daily conversation, have a real existence;

---

* If they are not born with that knowledge, then they must have forgot it, and recovered it again by way of remembrance. A false consequence.

† All the heathen philosophers are at a loss to find out the time of this forgetting. They were sensible that God created the soul full of light and understanding, but did not perceive that the first man lost that light and knowledge by his rebellion; and that if he had continued innocent, he had transmitted to us those valuable qualities together with his innocence; as well as that now he is fallen, he has transmitted to us obscurity and sin.

‡ Socrates means to prove, that as goodness, justice, and all those intelligible beings, which are the patterns of the sensible and real beings, subsist intelligibly in God from all eternity; so our soul exists by itself, and has an eternal being in the idea of God; and from this idea it derives all its knowledge.

mean, if justice, goodness, and all that essence with
ich we compare the objects of our senses, and which
ring an existence before us, proves to be of the same
ure with our own essence, and is the standard by which
measure all things ; I say, if all these things have a
l existence, our soul is likewise entitled to exist-
e, and that before we were born ; and if these
ngs have no being, then all our discourses are useless.
t not a standing truth, and withal a just and necessary
sequence, that the existence of our souls before our
h, stands or falls with that of those things ?

That consequence, replies Simmias, seems to me to
equally just and wonderful : And the result of the
le discourse affords something very glorious and
rable on our behalf, since it concludes, that before we
e born, our souls had an existence, as well as that
lligible essence you mentioned but now. For my part,
link there is nothing more evident, and more sensi-
than the existence of all these things, goodness,
ice, &c. and you have sufficiently proved it.

ow for Cebes, says Socrates; for Cebes must like-
be convinced.

believe, replies Simmias, though he is not easily
by arguments, that he will admit your proof to
very convincing. In the mean time though I am
ciently convinced that our souls had a being before
were born, I have not yet heard sufficient proof
its continuing after our death. For that popular
ion, which Cebes mentioned, still remains in all
orce, viz. That after the death of man, the soul
erses and ceases to be. And indeed I cannot see
the soul should not be born, or proceed from
part or other, and have a being before it animates
ody in this life, and when it removes from the body,
to be, and make its exit as well as the body.

u speak well, Simmias, says Cebes; to my mind, So-
s has only made good one half of what he proposed.
true, he has proved that the soul has a being
e the body; but to complete his demonstration, he
ld have shown that our soul has an existence after
, as well as before this life.

t I have demonstrated it to you both, replies Socrates; and you will be sensible of it, if you join this last proof with what you acknowledged before, viz. That the living take rise from the dead.*   For if it is true, that our soul was in being before we were born, then of necessity, when it comes to life, it proceeds, so to speak, from the bosom of death: and why should it not lie under the same necessity of being after death, since it must return to life ? Thus what you speak of is made good. But I perceive both of you desire to sound this matter to the bottom ; and are apprehensive, like children, that when the soul departs the body, the winds run away with it, and disperse it, especially when a man dies in an open country in a place exposed to the winds.

Whereupon, Cebes, smiling, replied, Pray then, Socrates, try to convince us, discuss our fears, as if we feared nothing : though indeed there be some among us, who lie under those childish apprehensions.   Persuade us then not to fear death, as being a vain phantom.

As for that, says Socrates, you must employ spells and exorcisms every day, till you be cured.

But pray, Socrates, where shall we meet with that excellent conjurer, since you are going to leave us ?

Greece is large enough, replies Socrates, and well stored with learned men.   Besides, there are a great many barbarous nations,† which you must scour in order to find out the conjurer, without sparing either labour or charges : for you cannot employ your money in a better cause. You must likewise look for one among yourselves ; for it is possible there may be none found more able to perform those enchantments.

We shall obey your orders, Socrates, in looking out for one: but in the mean while if you please, let us resume our former discourse.

With all my heart, Cebes.

Well said, Socrates.

* Though our soul has no being before our coming into the world, yet it continues after death, since it must return to life by the resurrection, and the living take rise from the dead.   The defeat of death is the triumph of life.   This proof of the necessary rise of the living from the dead, is an admirable support for our Christian hope.

† It was from those nations whom he calls barbarous, that he derived the rays of that truth, that the soul is immortal.

* The first question we ought to ask ourselves, says So-
ates, is, What sort of things they are that are apt to be
ssipated; what things are liable to that accident, and
lat *part* of those things? Then we must enquire into
e nature of soul, and form our fears or our hopes accord-
gly.

That is very true.

Is it not certain, that only compounded things, or such
are of a compoundable nature, admit of being dissipated
the same rate that they were compounded? If there
any uncompounded beings, they alone are free from
is accident, and naturally incapable of dissipation.

That I think is very clear, replies Cebes.

Is it not very likely, that things which are always the
ne, and in the same condition, are not at all compounded?

I am of your mind, Socrates.

Let us betake ourselves to the things we were speaking
but now, † the existence whereof is never contested
doubted; are these always the same, or do they some-
les change? Equality, beauty, goodness, and every
gular thing, *i. e.* the essence itself; do these receive the
st alteration, or are they so pure and simple, that
y continue always the same, without undergoing the
st change?

Of necessity, replies Cebes, they must continue still the
ne, without alteration.

And all these fine things, says Socrates, such as men,
rses, habits, moveables, and a great many other things of
same nature, are they entirely opposite to the former,
it they never continue in the same condition, either with
'erence to themselves, or to others; but are subject to
rpetual alterations?

They never continue in the same condition, replies
bes.

Now these are the things that are visible, touchable, or

---

* Hitherto Socrates has endeavoured to make good the existence
louls before their bodies, as being a point of the received theology.
d forasmuch as the principle is false, it was impossible for him
give better proof, since error does not admit of demonstration.
t now he is about to make good the future existence and immor-
ity of the soul, which he does by solid unshaken arguments.

† Intellectual beings.

perceptible by some other sense; whereas the former, which continue unchangeable, can only be reached by thought, as being immaterial and invisible.

That is true, Socrates.

If you please, continues Socrates, I will instance two things, one visible, the other invisible; one still the same, and the other betraying continual alterations.

With all my heart, says Cebes.

Let us see then. Are we not compounded of a body and a soul? or is there any other ingredient in our composition?

Surely not.

Which of the two kinds of things does our body most resemble?

All men own that it is most conformable to the visible.

And pray, my dear Cebes, is our soul visible or invisible?

It is invisible, at least to men.

But when we speak of visible or invisible things, we mean with reference to men, without minding any other nature. Once more then; is the soul visible or not?

It is not visible.

Then it is immaterial and invisible?

Yes.

And by consequence the soul is more conformable than the body to the invisible kind of things; and the body suits better with the visible?

This is absolutely necessary.

When the soul makes use of the body. in considering any thing, by seeing, hearing, or any other sense (it being the sole function of the body, to consider things by the senses) should not we then say that the body draws the soul upon mutable things? In this condition it strays, frets, staggers, and is giddy like a man in drink, by reason of its being engaged in matter. Whereas when it pursues things by itself, without calling in the body, it betakes itself to what is pure, immortal, immutable; and, as being of the same nature, dwells constantly upon it while it is master of itself, then its errors are at an end, and it is always the same, as being united to that which never changes; and this passion of the soul is what we call wisdom.

That is admirably well spoken, Socrates, and a very great truth.

After all then, which sort of things does the soul seem to resemble most ?

To my mind, Socrates, there is no man so stupid and obstinate, as not to be obliged to acknowledge by your method of arguing, that the soul bears a greater resemblance and conformity to the immutable Being, than to that which is always upon the change.

And as for the body ?

It bears a greater resemblance to the other.

Let us try yet another way. During the conjunction of body and soul, nature orders the one to obey and be a slave, and the other to command and hold the empire. Which of these two characters is most suitable to the Divine Being; and which to *that* that is mortal ? Are you not sensible, that the divine principle is only capable of commanding and ruling; and what is mortal is only worthy of obedience and slavery ?

Surely I am.

Which of these two then agrees best with the soul ?

It is evident, Socrates, that our soul resembles what is divine, and our body that which is mortal.

You see then, my dear Cebes, the necessary result of all, that our soul bears a strict resemblance to what is divine, immortal, intellectual, simple, indissolvable ; and is always the same, and always like it : and that our body does perfectly resemble what is human, mortal, sensible, compounded, dissolvable, always changing, and never like itself. Can any thing be alleged to destroy that consequence, or to make out the contrary ?

Certainly not, Socrates.

Does it not then suit with the body to be quickly dissolved, and with the soul to be always indissolvable, or something very near it ?

That is an evident truth.

Accordingly you see every day,* when a man dies,

Socrates is about to shew the ridiculousness of the opinion of soul's dissipation after death. What! shall the body, a compounded being, subsist a while after death, and the soul a simple thing, be immediately dissipated ? After what has been said, the ridiculousness of the supposition is very plain.

his visible body, that continues exposed to our view, and which we call the corpse; that alone admits of dissolution, alteration, and dissipation; this I say, does not immediately undergo any of these accidents, but continues for some time in its entire form, or in its bloom, if I may so speak, especially in this season.* Bodies embalmed after the manner of those in Egypt, remain entire for an infinity of years : and even in those that corrupt, there are always some parts, such as the bones, nerves, or the like, that continue in a manner immortal. Is not this true ?

Very true.

Now as for the soul, which is an invisible being, that goes to a place like itself, marvellous, pure, and invisible, in the infernal world; and returns to a God full of goodness and wisdom; which I hope will soon be the fate of my soul, if it please God. Shall a soul of this nature, and created with all these advantages, be dissipated and annihilated, as soon as it parts from the body, as most men believe ? No such thing, my dear Simmias, and my dear Cebes. I will tell you what will rather come to pass, and what we ought to believe steadily. If the soul retains its purity without any mixture of filth from the body, as having entertained no voluntary correspondence with it; but, on the contrary, having always avoided it, and collected itself within itself in continual meditations; that is, in studying the true philosophy, and effectually learning to die; for philosophy is a preparation for death : I say, if the

---

* This passage is enough to stun the critics, who make a great bustle to find out the precise time of Socrates's death ; and after straining hard in demonstrating the Attic Calendar, and computing its months, assure us he died in the month of July. Here, to their great misfortune, Socrates himself says he died in the season in which corpses keep best. The month of July is not entitled to that character, especially in Greece. So that they must make a new computation. But how came this passage to escape their view ? The reason is plain : Most of them do not read the originals. When they look for any thing, they content themselves with running over a translation. Now, the translation of this passage is very faulty. Neither Marcilius Ficinus, nor de Cerres understood it. They took ὥρα for the good condition and entireness of the parts ; whereas it signifies the season. Upon which mistake the one renders ἐν τοιαύτῃ ὥρα, cum quadam moderatione ; and the other, corpore perbelle affecto.

soul depart in this condition, it repairs to a being like
itself, a being that is divine, immortal, and full of wisdom;
in which it enjoys an inexpressible felicity, as being freed
from its errors, its ignorance, its fears, its passions, that
tyrannized over it, and all the other evils pertaining to
human nature: and as it is said of those who have been
initiated into holy mysteries, it truly passes a whole course
of eternity with the Gods.*   Ought not this to be the matter of our belief?

Surely, Socrates.

But if the soul depart full of uncleanness and impurity,
as having been all along mingled with the body, always
employed in its service, always possessed by the love
of it, and charmed by its pleasures and lusts; insomuch that it believed there was nothing real or true beyond what is corporeal; what may be seen, touched,
drank, or eaten, or what is the object of carnal pleasure;
that it hated, dreaded and avoided what the eyes of the
body could not descry, and all that is intellectual, and can
only be enjoyed by philosophy: Do you think, I say, that
a soul in this condition can depart pure and simple from
the body?

No, Socrates, that is impossible.

On the contrary, it departs stained with corporeal pollution, which was rendered natural to it, by its continual
commerce and too intimate union with the body at a time
when it was its constant companion, and still was employed
n serving and gratifying it.

Most certainly.

This pollution, my dear Cebes, is a gross, heavy, earthy,
nd visible mass; and the soul loaded with such a weight,
s dragged into that visible place, not only by its weight,
ut by its own dread of the light and the invisible
lace and as we commonly say, wanders in cemeteries,†,

---

* The initiation into mysteries was only a shadow of what was to
: completed in the other world.

† Socrates speaks here of the impure spirits that dwelt among the
mbs in church-yards, such as are mentioned in the Gospel, *Matt.*
i. 28. *Mark* v. 2. *Luke* viii. 26, which wandered night and
y round the tombs and upon the mountains. He alleges that they
re corrupt and polluted souls, which bore the pollution they had
ttracted by sin, in plunging themselves too deep in matter.

among the tombs, where dark phantoms and apparitions
are often seen; like to those souls that did not depart
the body in purity or simplicity, but polluted with that
earthly and visible matter which makes them degenerate
into a visible form.

That is very likely, Socrates.

Yes, without doubt, Cebes; and it is also likely that it is
not the good, but the bad souls, that are forced to wander
in those places of impurity ; where they suffer for their
former ill life, and still continue, till through the love
they have to this corporeal mass, which always follows
them, they again enter a new body, and in all probability plunge themselves into the same manners and
passions, as were the occupation of their first life.*

How do you say, Socrates ?

I say, Cebes, for instance, that those who made their
belly their God, and loved nothing but indolence and impurity without any shame, and without any reserve ;
these enter into the bodies of asses, or such like creatures.† Do not you think this very probable ?

Yes, surely.

And those souls who loved only injustice, tyranny, and
rapine, are employed to animate the bodies of wolves,
hawks, and falcons. Where else should souls of that
sort go ?

No where else, Socrates.

The case of all the rest is much the same. They go to
animate the bodies of beasts of different species, according
as they resemble their former dispositions.

According to these principles, it cannot be otherwise.

---

* An error derived from Pythagoras's Metempsychosis, taken in
a gross sense.

† I shall only remark, that by Socrates's way of expressing
himself, one would believe that this imaginary transmigration
of souls was grounded upon those impure spirits that entered
into men and beasts : we are not to doubt, but that in those times
of obscurity, under the real empire of the devil, there were a great
many people possessed in that manner; and that was a sufficient
ground for forming the idea of the transmigration of souls; that
being most apt to frighten them. They fancied, that these impure spirits took to themselves bodies in the sepulchres where they
dwelt

The happiest of all these men, are those who have made a profession of popular and civil virtues, such as TEMPERANCE and JUSTICE ; to which they have brought themselves only by habit and exercise, without any assistance from philosophy and the mind.

How can they be so happy then ?

It is probable that after their death, their souls are joined to the bodies of politic and meek animals, such as bees, wasps, and ants; or else return to human bodies, and become temperate and wise men. But as for approaching to the nature of God, that is not at all allowed to those who did not live philosophically, and whose souls did not depart with all their purity. That great privilege is reserved for the lovers of true wisdom. And it is upon this consideration, my dear Simmias, and my dear Cebes, that the true philosophers renounce the desires of the body, and keep themselves apart, from its lusts; they are not apprehensive of the ruin of their families, or of poverty, as the vulgar are, and those who are wedded to their riches : they fear neither ignominy nor reproach, as those do who court only dignities and honours. In a word, they renounce all things, and even themselves.*

It would not be suitable for them to do otherwise, replied Cebes.

No, continues Socrates. In like manner, all those who value their souls, and do not live for the body, depart from all such lusts, and follow a different course from those insensible creatures that do not know where they go. They are persuaded that they ought not to do any thing contrary to philosophy, or harbour any thing that destroys its purification, and retards their liberty ; and accordingly resign themselves to its conduct, and follow it whithersoever it leads them.

How do you say, Socrates ?

I will explain it to you. The philosophers finding their soul tied and chained to the body, and by that means obliged to employ the body in the pursuit of objects which it cannot follow alone, so that it still floats in an abyss of

* A fine character of true philosophers. They fear neither poverty, ignominy, nor death : they renounce themselves, and all things beside.

ignorance; are very sensible that the force of this bond lies
in its own desires, insomuch that the prisoner itself helps
to lock up the chains.   They are sensible that philosophy
coming to seize upon the soul in this condition, gently instructs and comforts it, and endeavours to disengage it, by
giving it to know, that the eye of the body is full of illu-
sion and deceit, as well as all its other senses: by advertising
it not to use the body further than necessity requires ;   and
advising it to recollect and shut itself up within itself, to
receive no disposition but its own, after it has examined
within itself the intrinsic nature of every thing, and stript
it of the covering that conceals it from our eyes, and to
continue fully persuaded, that whatever is tried by all its
other senses, being different from the former discovery, is
certainly false.   Now, whatever is tried by the corporeal
senses, is visible and sensible.   And what it views by itself
without the ministry of the body, is invisible and intelligible.   So that the soul of a true philosopher, being convinced that it should not oppose its own liberty; disclaims
as far as possible, the pleasures, lusts, fears, and sorrows
of the body : for it knows that when one has enjoyed
many pleasures, or given way to extreme grief or timorousness, or abandoned himself to his desires ; he not only is
afflicted by the sensible evils known to all the world, such
as loss of health or estate, but is doomed to the last and
greatest of evils ; an evil that is so much the more dangerous and terrible, because it is not obvious to our senses.

What evil is that, Socrates ?

It is this ; that the soul being forced to rejoice or be
afflicted upon any occasion, is persuaded that what causes
its pleasure or grief, is a real and true thing, though at
the same time it is not : and such is the nature of all sensible and visible things that are able to occasion joy or
grief.

That is certain, Socrates.

Are not these passions then the chief instruments that
particularly imprison the soul within the body ?

How is that, Socrates !

Every pleasure, every melancholy thought, being armed
with a strong and keen point, nails the soul to the body
with such force, that it becomes material or corporeal, and

fancies there are no real and true objects, but such as the body accounts so: for as it entertains the same opinions, and pursues the same pleasures with the body, so it is obliged to the same actions and habits. For which reason it cannot descend in purity to the lower world, but is daubed over with the pollution of the body it left, and quickly re-enters another body, where it takes root as if it had been sown, and puts a period to all commerce with the pure, simple, and divine essence.

That is very true, Socrates.

These are the motives that oblige philosophers to make it their business to acquire temperance and fortitude, and not such motives as the vulgar think of. Are not you of my opinion, Cebes?

Certainly I am.

All true philosophers will still be of that mind. Their soul will never entertain such a thought, as that philosophy should only disengage it, to the end that when it is freed, it should follow its pleasures, and give way to its fears and sorrows; that it should put on its chains again, and always want to begin anew, like Penelope's web. On the contrary, it continues in a perfect tranquillity and freedom from passion, and always follows reason for its guide; it incessantly contemplates what is true, divine, immutable, and above opinion, being nourished by this pure truth: it is convinced that it ought to follow the same course of life while it is united to the body; and hopes that after death, surrendered to the immortal being as its source, it will be freed from all the afflictions of human nature. After such a life, and upon such principles, my dear Simmias and Cebes, what should the soul be afraid of? Shall it fear, that upon its departure from the body, the winds will dissipate it, and run away with it, and that annihilation will be its fate?

Socrates having thus spoken, stopped for a while, seeming to be altogether intent upon what he had said. Most of us were in the same condition: and Cebes and Simmias had a short conference together. At last, Socrates perceiving their conference, asked them what they were speaking of? Do you think, says he, that my arguments are lame? I think indeed there is room left for a great many doubts and objections, if any will take the pains to mention them. If you are speaking of any thing else, I have nothing to say. But though you have no doubts, pray, tell me freely whether you think of any better demonstration, and make me a companion in your enquiry, if you think I can assist you to compass your end.

I will tell you, says Simmias, the naked truth. Sometime since, Cebes and I had harassing doubts; and being desirous to have them resolved, pushed on one another to propose them to you. But we were both afraid to importune you, and suggest disagreeable questions in the unseasonable hour of your present misfortune.

O! my dear Simmias,* replies Socrates smiling, certainly I should have great difficulty in persuading other men that I find no misfortune in my present circumstances, since I cannot get you to believe it. You think that upon the score of foreknowledge and divining, I am infinitely inferior to the swans.† When they perceive death approaching, they sing more merrily than before, because of the joy they have in going to the God they serve.‡ But men, through fear of death, reproach the swans, in saying that they lament their death, and tune their grief in sorrowful notes. They forget to make this reflection, that no bird sings when it is hungry, cold, or sad; nay, not the nightingale, the swallow, or the lapwing, whose music they say is a true lamentation, and the effect of grief. But, after all, these birds do not sing from grief: and far less the swans, which by reason of their belonging to Apollo, are diviners,. and sing more joyfully on the day of their death than before, as foreseeing the good that awaits them in the other world. And for my part, I think I serve Apollo as well as they; I am consecrated to that God as

* Socrates is angry with his friends for reckoning his present condition as an unfortunate one.

† He could not take a better method to shew that he reckoned no misfortune in death, than this of rallying upon the Pythagorean and vulgar religion.

‡ As if their fowls were admitted to the mansions of the blessed. Socrates ridicules that opinion. We shall see afterwards, that they admitted beasts to the land of the just; of which they had a very confused idea. But that is to another purpose.

well as they; I have received from our common master
the art of divining as well as they; and I am as little concerned at making my exit as they are.   So that you may
freely propose what doubts you please, and put questions
to me as long as the eleven magistrates suffer me to
live.

You say well, Socrates, replies Simmias; since it is so,
I will propose my doubts first, and then Cebes shall give
in his.   I agree with you, that it is impossible, or at least
very difficult to know the truth in this life; and that it is
the property of a lazy and a dull head, not to weigh exactly what is proposed to his consideration, or to supersede
the examination before he has made all his efforts, and is
obliged to give over by insurmountable difficulties.   For one
of these two things must be done: we must either learn the
truth from others, or find it out ourselves.   If both ways fail
us, amidst all human reasons, we must fix upon the
strongest and most forcible, and trust to that as to a ship,
while we pass through this stormy sea, and endeavour to
avoid its tempests, until we find out one more firm and
sure, such as a promise or revelation, upon which we
may happily accomplish the voyage of this life, as in
a vessel that fears no danger.*   I shall therefore not be
ashamed to put questions to you, now that you allow
me; and avoid the reproach I might one day cast upon
myself, of not having told you my thoughts upon this
occasion.   When I survey what you spoke to me and to
Cebes, I must own I do not think your proofs sufficient.

Perhaps you have reason, my dear Simmias, but where
does their insufficiency appear?

In this: that the same things might be asserted of the

---

* This is a very remarkable passage. Here the philosophers acknowledge that we should endeavour to make out the immortality of
the soul by our own reason; and that as this reason is very weak
and narrow, so it will be always assaulted by doubt and uncertainty; that nothing but a divine promise or revelation can disperse
the clouds of ignorance and infidelity. Now the Christian religion
the only thing that furnishes us, not only with divine promises
and revelations, but likewise with the accomplishment of them by
the resurrection of Christ, *who became the first-fruits of them that
slept*, 1 Cor. xv. 20. And thus according to the philosophers themselves, the church is the only vessel that fears no dangers, in which
we may happily accomplish the voyage of this life.

harmony of a harp.   For one may reasonably say, that the harmony of a harp well stringed and well tuned, is invisible, immaterial, excellent and divine; and that the instrument and its strings are the body, the compounded earthy and mortal matter.   Now suppose the instrument were cut in pieces, or its strings broken, might not one with equal reason affirm, that this harmony remains after the breaking of the harp, and has no end?   For, since it is evident that the harp remains after the strings are broken, or that the strings, which are likewise mortal, continue after the harp is broken or dismounted; it must needs be impossible, one might say, that this immortal and divine harmony should perish before that which is mortal and earthy; nay, it is necessary that this harmony should continue to be without the least damage, when the body of the harp and its strings are gone to nothing.   For, without doubt, Socrates, you are sensible that we hold the soul to be something that resembles a harmony; and that as our body is a being composed of hot and cold, dry and moist, so our soul is nothing else but the harmony resulting from the just proportion of these mixed qualities.   Now, if our soul is only a sort of harmony, it is evident, that when our body is over-stretched, or unbended by diseases, or any other disorder, of necessity our soul with all its divinity, must come to an end, as well as the other harmonies which consist in sounds, or are the effect of instruments; and that the remains of every body continue for a considerable time, till they be burnt or mouldered away. This, you see, Socrates, might be alleged in opposition to your arguments, that if the soul be only a mixture of the qualities of our body, it perishes first in what we call death.

Then Socrates looked upon us all, one after another, as he did often, and began to smile. Simmias speaks with reason, says he, his question is well put; and if any one of you has greater dexterity in answering his objections than I have, why do you not do it? For he seems thoroughly to understand both my arguments, and the exceptions they are liable to. But before we answer him, it is proper to hear what Cebes has to object, that while he speaks, we may have time to think upon what we are to say; and after we have heard them both, that we may

yield if their reasons are uniform and valid; and if otherwise, may stand by our principles to the utmost.   Tell us
then, Cebes, what it is that hinders you from agreeing
with what I have laid down.

I will tell you, says Cebes: Your demonstration seems
to be lame and imperfect; it is faulty upon the same head
that we took notice of before.   That the soul has a being
before its entrance into the body, is admirably well said;
and, I think, sufficiently proved: but I can never be
persuaded that it has likewise an existence after death.
At the same time, I cannot subscribe to Simmias's allegation, that the soul is neither stronger nor more durable
than the body; for it appears to me to be infinitely more
excellent.   But why then, it may be objected, do you refuse to believe it?   Since you see with your eyes, that
when a man is dead, his weakest part remains still : is it
not therefore absolutely necessary that the more durable
part should last longest?   Pray take notice, if I answer this objection right.   For to let you into my meaning, I must use resemblance or comparison, as well as
Simmias.   Your allegation, to my mind, is just the same,
as if upon the death of a tailor, one should say, this
tailor is not dead, he has a being still somewhere or other,
and for proof of that, here are the garments he wore,
which he made for himself, so that he is still in being.   If
any one should not be convinced by this proof, he would
not fail to ask him, whether the man or the garments he
wears is the most durable?   To which, of necessity, he
must answer, that the man is :   And upon this your philosopher would pretend to demonstrate, that since the less
durable possession of the tailor is still in being, by a
stronger consequence, he himself is so too.   Now,
the parallel is not just; pray hear what I have to answer
it.

It is evident at first view, that the objection is ridiculous.
For the tailor, having used several garments died only
before the last, which he had not time to wear; and though
his last survived the man, if I may so speak, yet we cannot
the man is weaker, or less durable than his garments.
This simile is near enough, for as the man is, to his garments,
as the soul, to the body; and whoever applies to the soul

and body what is said of the man and his garments, will speak to the purpose. For he will make the soul more durable, and the body a weaker being, and less able to hold out for a long time. He will add, that every soul wears several bodies, especially if it lives several years. For the body wastes while the man is yet alive, and the soul still forms to itself a new habit of body, out of the former that decays; but when the last comes to die, it has then its last habit on, and dies before its consumption: and when the soul is dead, the body quickly betrays the weakness of its nature, since it soon corrupts and moulders away. So that we cannot put such confidence in your demonstration, as to hold it for a certain truth, that our souls continue in being after death. For supposing it were granted, that our soul has not only a being antecedent to our birth, but that, for any thing we know, the souls of some continue in being after death; and that it is very possible they may return again to the world, and be born again, so to speak, several times, and die at last; for the strength and advantage of the soul beyond the body, consists in this, that it can undergo several births, and wear several bodies one after another, as a man does his clothing: supposing, I say, that all this were granted, still it cannot be denied, but that in all those repeated births, it decays and wastes, and at last comes to an end in one of these deaths. However, it is impossible for any man to discern in which of the deaths it is totally sunk: since things stand thus, whoever does not fear death, must be senseless; unless he can demonstrate that the soul is immortal and incorruptible. For otherwise every dying man must of necessity fear for his soul, lest the body it is quitting should be its last, and it perish without any hope of return.

Having heard them propose these objections, we were very much troubled, as we afterwards told them, that at a time when we were just convinced by Socrates's arguments, they should come to perplex us with their objections, and throw us into a state of doubt and uncertainty, not only of all that had been said to us by Socrates, but likewise of what he might say afterwards; for we might always be apt to believe, that either we were not proper judges of the points in debate, or else that his arguments were fallacious.

Echec. Indeed, Phedon, I can easily pardon your trouble upon that account. For I myself, while I heard you relate the matter, was saying to myself, what shall we believe hereafter, since Socrates's arguments, which seemed so valid and convincing, are become doubtful and uncertain? In effect, that objection of Simmias's, that the soul is only a harmony, moves me wonderfully. It awakes in me the memory of my having been formerly of the same opinion. So that my belief is unhinged; and I want new proofs to convince me, that the soul does not die with the body. Wherefore, pray tell me, Phedon, in the name of God, how Socrates came off; whether he seemed to be as much piqued as yourselves; or, if he maintained his opinion with his wonted temper, and, in fine, whether his demonstration gave you full satisfaction, or seemed chargeable with imperfections. Pray tell me the whole story, without omitting the minutest cirumstance.

Phed. I protest to you, Echecrates, I admired Socrates all my life-time, and upon this occasion admired him more than ever. That such a man as he, had his answers in readiness, is no great surprise; but my greatest admiration was, to see in the first place with what calmness, patience, and good humour, he received these objections; and then how dexterously he perceived the impression they had made upon us, and set about to remove them. He rallied us like men put to flight after a defeat, and inspired us with fresh ardour to turn our heads, and renew the charge.

Echec. How was that?

Phed. I am about to tell you. As I sat at his right-hand upon a little stool lower than his, he drew his hand over my head, and taking hold of my hair that hung down upon my shoulders, as he was wont to do for his diversion; Phedon, says he, will not you cut this very pretty hair to-morrow? It is probable I shall, said I. If you take my advice, said he, you will not stay so long. How do you mean? said I. Both you and I, continued he, ought to cut our hair, if this our opinion be so far dead that we cannot raise it again.* Were I in your place, and defeated, I would make a vow, as the men of Argos did,† never to wear my hair till I conquered these arguments of Simmias and Cebes. But said I, Socrates, you have forgotten the old proverb, that Hercules himself is not able to engage two. And why, says he, do not you call on me to assist you as your Iolas, while it is yet time? And accordingly I do call on you, said I, not as Hercules did on Iolas, but as Iolas did Hercules. It is no matter for that, says he, it is all one. Above all, let us be cautious to avoid one great fault. What fault? said I. That, said he, of being reason-haters ; for such there are, as well as man-haters. The former is the greatest evil in the world, and arises from the same source with the hatred of man. For the latter comes from one man's plighting his faith for another man, without any· precaution or enquiry, whom he always took for a true-hearted, solid, and trusty man, but finds him at last to be false and faithless: And thus being cheated in several such instances, by those whom he looked upon as his best friends, and at last weary of being so often betrayed, he equally hates all men, and is convinced there is not one that is not wicked and perfidious. Are not you sensible, that this man-hating is formed at this rate, and by degrees? Certainly, said I. Is it not a great scandal then, continued he, and a superlative crime, to converse with men, without being acquainted with the art of trying and knowing them? For if one were acquainted with this art, he would see how things stand, and would find that the good and the wicked are very rare; but those in the middle region swarm in infinite numbers.

How do you say, Socrates?

I say, Phedon, the case of the good and bad is much

---

* It was a custom among the Greeks to cut off their hair at the death of their friends, and throw it into the tombs. The belief of the immortality of the soul is so good a friend, that we ought to cut off our hair when it dies.

† The Argives being routed by the Spartans, with whom they waged war for seizing the city of Thyre, cut their hair, and swore solemnly never to suffer it to grow, till they had retaken the town that belonged to them: which happened in the 57th Olympiad, when Crœsus was besieged at Sardis. Herodot. lib. I.

the same with that of very large or very little men. Do
not you see that there is nothing more uncommon than a
very big or a very little man ?   The case is the same with
reference to dogs, horses, and all other things ; and may
likewise be applied to swiftness and slowness, handsome-
ness and deformity, whiteness and blackness.   Are not
you convinced, that in all these matters the two extremes
are very uncommon, whilst the medium is very common?

I perceive it very plainly, Socrates.

If a match were proposed for wickedness, would not
there be very few that could pretend to the first rank ?

That is very likely, Socrates.

It is certainly so, replies he.   But upon this score, the
case of reason, and men, is not exactly the same.   I will
follow you step by step.   The only resemblance of the two
lies in this, that when a man unskilled in the art of examination, entertains a reason as true, and afterwards finds it
to be false, whether it be so in itself or not ; and when the
same thing happens to him often, as indeed it does to
those who amuse themselves by disputing with the sophists
that contradict every thing ;* he at last believes himself to be extremely well skilled, and fancies he is the
only man that has perceived there is nothing true or certain, either in things or reasons; but that all is like Eury-
pus, in a continual flux and reflux, and that nothing continues so much as one moment in the same state.

That is the truth, Socrates.

Is it not then a very deplorable misfortune, my dear
Phedon, that while there are true, certain, and very com-
prehensible reasons, there should be men found, who after
they have suffered them to pass, call them again in question, upon hearing these frivolous disputes, where sometimes truth and sometimes falsehood come uppermost ;
and instead of charging themselves with these doubts, or
blaming their want of art, cast the blame at last upon the
reasons themselves; and being of a sour temper, pass their
life in hating and calumniating all reason, and by that
means rob themselves both of truth and knowledge ?

* Those who fancy that Socrates and Plato taught no positive
truths, but reckoned every thing uncertain, may undeceive themselves by reading this passage.

That is certainly a most deplorable thing, said I.

We ought to be very cautious, continues he, that this misfortune be not our lot; and that we are not prepossessed by this thought, that there is nothing solid or true in all arguments whatever. We should rather be persuaded, that it is ourselves who are wanting in stability and truth; and use our utmost efforts to recover that solidity and justness of thought. This is a duty incumbent upon you, who have time yet to live; and likewise upon me who am about to die.* And I am much afraid, that upon this occasion I have been so far from acting the part of a true philosopher, that I have rather behaved myself like a disputant overborne with prejudice; like all those ignorant dogmatists, who in their disputes mind not the perception of truth so much, as to draw their hearers over to their opinions. The only difference between them and me, is, that the convincing my audience of the truth of what I advance is not my only aim: I shall be infinitely glad if that come to pass; but my chief concern is to persuade myself of the truth of these things.

If my propositions prove true, it is well done to believe them;† and if after my death they be found false, I still reap the advantage in this life, of having been less affected by the evils which commonly accompany it. But I shall not remain long under this ignorance. If I were to do so, I should consider it a great misfortune: But happily, it will quickly be dispelled. Fortified by these thoughts, my dear Simmias and Cebes, I proceed to answer your objections; and if you take my advice, you will rely less upon the authority of Socrates, than that of truth. If what I am about to advance appear true, embrace it; otherwise, attack it with all your force. Thus I

---

* The belief of the immortality of the soul is useful, both for living and for dying well.

† If these are true, I am a great gainer with little trouble; if false, I lose nothing: On the contrary, I have gained a great deal: For besides the hope that supported me through my afflictions, infirmities and weaknesses, I have been faithful, honest, humble, thankful, charitable, sincere and true, and have only quitted false and contagious pleasures in exchange for real and solid ones. Mr. Pascal in his Art. 7, has enlarged upon this truth, and backed it with a demonstration of infinite force.

shall neither deceive myself, nor impose upon you by the influence of zeal and good-will, nor quit you like a wasp that leaves its sting in the wound it has made.

To begin then, pray see if I remember rightly what was objected. Simmias, as I take it rejects our belief, only because he fears our souls, notwithstanding their being divine and more excellent, will die before our bodies, as being only a sort of harmony. And Cebes, if I mistake not, granted that the soul is more durable than the body, but thinks it possible that the soul, after having used several bodies, may die when it quits the last body, and that this death of the soul is a true death. Are not these the two points I am to examine, my dear Simmias and Cebes?

When they had all agreed that the objections were justly summed up, he continued thus· Do you absolutely reject all that I have said, or do you acknowledge part of it to be true? They answered, that they did not reject the whole. What then, says he, is your opinion of that which I told you? viz. That LEARNING is only REMEMBRANCE, and that by a necessary consequence the soul must have an existence before its conjunction with the body.

As for me, replies Cebes, I perceived the evidence of it at first view; and do not know any principles of more cer· tainty and truth. I am of the same mind, says Simmias, and should think it very strange, if ever I changed my opinion.

But, my dear Theban, continues Socrates, you must needs change it, if you retain your opinion that harmony is compounded, and that the soul is only a sort of harmony, arising from the due union of the qualities of the body : for it is presumed you would not believe yourself, if you said that harmony has a being before those things of which it is composed.

Surely, replies Simmias, I would not believe myself if I did.

Do you not then see, continues Socrates, that you are not consistent with yourself, when you say that the soul had a being before it came to animate the body, and at the same time that it is compounded of things that had not then an existence? Do not you compare the soul to a harmony? And is it not evident that the harp, the strings, and the very discordant sounds, exist before the harmony, which is an effect that results from all these things, and perishes sooner than they? Does this latter part of your discourse correspond with the first?

Not at all, replies Simmias.

And yet, continues Socrates, if ever there should be agreement in a discourse, it ought to be such when harmony is its subject..

That is right, says Simmias.

But yours is not so, continues Socrates. Let us hear then which of these two opinions you side with. Whether learning is only remembrance, or the soul is a sort of harmony?

I side with the first, replies Simmias.

And that opinion I have explained to you, without having recourse to any demonstrations full of similes and examples, which are rather colours of the truth, and therefore please the people best ;* but as for me, I am of opinion, that all discourses proving their point by similes, are full of vanity, and apt to seduce and deceive, unless one be very cautious, whether it relate to geometry, or any other science: whereas the discourse I made, proving that knowledge is remembrance, is grounded upon a very creditable hypothesis; for I told you that the soul exists as well as its essence before it comes to animate the body. By essence I mean the principle from which it derives its being, which has no other name, but *that which is.* And this proof I take to be good and sufficient.

---

* Marsilius Ficinus and De Serres have strangely misunderstood this passage, not only in making Simmias speak all this: but what is more considerable, in putting a favourable construction on those words, μετὰ εἰκότος τινὸς ὴ πεὐρεπεὶας, which the one renders, " verisimilis tantum venustique exempli indicatione ;" and the other, " ex verisimili quadum convenientia :" and in separating the words ἀνευ ἀποδείξεως, whereas they are joined ; for Socrates says, " I made this discourse without having recourse to demonstrations crammed with similes and colours, that take so much with the people." In effect, Socrates did not so much as make use of one comparison in making good the opinion of remembrance: whereas Simmias had brought in the comparison of a harp to prove that the soul is a harmony. Now there is nothing misleads the ignorant more than similitudes, for the imagination is so seduced by the representation, that it blindly embraces all that presents itself to it. And by that means this opinion of Simmias did always meet with a favourable reception, and does to this day among the ignorant. This is a very important passage, and deserved a larger explication.

By that reason, says Simmias, I must not listen either
to myself or others, who assert the soul to be a sort of
harmony.

In earnest, Simmias, replies Socrates, do you think that
a harmony, or any other composure, can be any thing different from the parts of which it is compounded?

By no means, Socrates.

Or, can it do or suffer, what those parts do not? Simmias answered, It could not. Then, says Socrates, a harmony does not precede, but follow the things it is composed of: and it cannot have sounds, motions, or any
thing else contrary to its parts.

Surely not, replies Simmias. What! continues Socrates,
is not all harmony only such in proportion to the concord
of its parts?

I no not understand you, says Simmias.

I mean, according as the parts have more or less of
concord, the harmony is more or less a harmony: is it
not?

Yes, certainly.

Can we say of the soul, after the same manner, that a
small difference makes a soul to be more or less a soul?

No, surely, Socrates?

How is it then, in the name of God? Do not we say,
for example, that such a soul endowed with understanding
and virtue, is good; and another filled with folly and mischief is wicked. Is not this right?

Yes, quoth Simmias.

But those who hold the soul to be a harmony, what will
they call these qualities of the soul, vice, and virtue?
Will they say, the one is harmony, and the other discord?
That a virtuous and good soul, being harmony in its nature, is entitled to another harmony; and that a vicious
and wicked soul wants that additional harmony?

I cannot be positive, replies Simmias; but indeed it is
very probable that the patrons of that opinion may advance
some such thing.

But we concluded, that one soul is not more or less a
soul than another; that is, that it is not more or less a
harmony, than another harmony,

I admit it, says Simmias.

And since it is not more or less a harmony, then it has not more or less concord. Is it not so ?

Yes, surely, Socrates.

And since it has not more or less of concord, can one have more harmony than another, or must the harmony of them all be equal ?

Doubtless it must be equal.

Since one soul cannot be more or less a soul than another, by the same reason it cannot have more or less concord than another.

That is true.

Than it follows necessarily, that one soul cannot have either more harmony or discord than another.

I agree to it.

And by consequence, since the soul is of that nature, it cannot have more virtue or vice than another; if so be that vice is discord, and virtue harmony. ?

That is true, Simmias.

Or, would not right reason rather say that vice could find no place in the soul, if so be the soul is harmony; for harmony, continuing in its perfect nature, is not capable of discord ?

There is no question of that.

In like manner, the soul while perfectly a soul, is not capable of vice.

According to the principles we agreed upon, I cannot see how it should.

From the same principles it will follow, that the souls of all animals are equally good, since they are equally souls.

So I think, says Simmias.

But do you think that agreeable to reason, if the hypothesis of the soul's harmony be true ?

No, Socrates.

Then I ask you, Simmias, if of all the parts of man, the soul is not best entitled to command, especially when it is prudent and wise ?

There is no other part that can pretend to it.

Does it command by giving way to the passions of the body, or by resisting them ? As for example, when the body is seized with thirst in the cold fit of a fever, does not the soul restrain it from drinking? or, when it is hungry, does it not restrain it from eating? As well as in a thousand other instances, which manifestly shew, that the soul curbs the passions of the body.   Is it not so?

Without doubt.

But we agreed before that the soul being a sort of harmony, can never be contrary to the sound of those things which raise, or lower, or move it; nor can have other passions different from those of its parts; and that it is necessarily obliged to follow, being incapable of guiding them.

It is certain we agreed upon that, says Simmias: how could we avoid it?

But, says Socrates, is it not evident that the conduct of the soul is the reverse of this! That it governs and rules those very things which are alleged for ingredients in its composition; that it continually thwarts and attacks them; that it is every way their mistress, punishing and repressing some by the harder measures of school-exercises, and pain; and treating others more gently, as contenting itself with threatening or insulting over its lusts. In a word, we see the soul speaks to the body as something of a different nature from itself; which Homer was sensible of, when, in his Odyssies, he tells us, that " Ulysses, beating his breast, rebuked his heart, and said to it, Support thyself, thou hast stood out against harder and more difficult things than these."

Do you think the poet spoke that under the apprehension of the soul's being a harmony to be managed and conducted by the body! Or, do you not rather believe that he knew it was the soul's part to command, and that it is of a more divine nature than harmony?

Yes, Socrates; I am persuaded Homer knew that truth.*

And by consequence, my dear Simmias, continues Socrates, there is not the least colour of reason for the soul's being a harmony: should we assert it to be such, we

---

* Homer knew that the nature of the soul is different from that of the body, as manifestly appears from the beginning of the 19th book of his Odyssey.

should contradict both Homer, that divine poet, and likewise ourselves.   Simmias yielded; and Socrates proceeded thus:

I think we have sufficiently tempered and moderated this Theban harmony,* so that it will do us no harm. But, Cebes, how shall we do to appease and disarm this Cadmus?†   How shall we hit on a discourse duly qualified with persuasive force?

If you will be at the pains, Socrates, you can easily find such an argument. The last you urged against the harmony of the soul moved me mightily, and indeed beyond my expectation; for when Simmias proposed his doubts, I thought nothing short of a prodigy or miracle could solve them: and I was mightily surprised when I saw he could not stand the first attack. So that now it will be no surprise to me to see Cadmus undergo the same fate.

My dear Cebes, replies Socrates, do not you speak too big upon the matter, lest envy should overturn all I have said, and render it useless and ineffectual. But that is in the hands of God. As for us, let us approach one another, as Homer says, and try our strength and arms. What you want comes all to this point: you would have the immortality and incorruptibility of the soul demonstrated, to the end that a philosopher who dies bravely in the hopes of being infinitely more happy in the other world than in this, may not hope in vain. You say, the soul's being a durable and divine substance, existing before its joining with the body, does not conclude its immortality; and the only inference that it will bear, is, that it lasts a great while longer. The soul, say you, was in being many ages before us, during which it knew and did several things, but without immortality: for on the contrary, the first minute of its descent into the body, is the commencement of its death,

* He calls Simmias's opinion a Theban harmony, alluding to the fable of Amphion, who by the harmony of his harp built the walls of Thebes. In like manner, Simmias, with his pretended harmony, proposed to construct the human being.
† He calls Cebes another Cadmus, because as Cadmus by sowing the teeth of the dragon he had killed, fetched out of the bosom of the earth a race of fierce men that lived but one minute; so Cebes, by the opinion of the mortality of the soul, a thing more poisonous than the teeth of a dragon, made men base and earthy, and left them but a short and miserable existence.

or, as it were, a gradually consuming disease; for it passes this life in anguish and trouble, and at last is quite swallowed up and annihilated by what we call Death. You add, that it is the same thing, whether it animates a body only once, or returns to it several times, since that does not alter the occasion of our fears, forasmuch as all wise men ought still to fear death, while they are uncertain of the immortality of their souls. This, I believe, is the sum of what you said; and I repeat it so often, on purpose that nothing may escape my view, and that you may have the opportunity of adding or impairing as you please.

At present, says Cebes, I have nothing to alter; that is the sum of what I have yet said.

Socrates was silent a while, as being drowned in profound meditation. At last, Cebes, says he, it is truly not a small matter that you demand; for in order to a just satisfaction, there is a necessity of making a narrow enquiry into the cause of generation and corruption. If you please I will tell you what happened to me upon this very matter; and if what I say seem useful to you, you will be at liberty to make use of it to support your sentiments.

With all my heart, says Simmias.

Pray give ear then, says Socrates : In my youth I had an insatiable desire to learn that science which is called Natural History; for I thought it was something great and divine to know the causes of every thing, of their generation, existence, and death. And I spared no pains, nor omitted any means for trying, in the first place, if a certain corruption of heat and cold will, as some pretend, give nourishment to animals; if the blood makes the thought; if air or fire, or the brain alone is the cause of our senses, of seeing, hearing, smelling, &c; if memory and opinion take their rise from these senses, and if knowledge be the result of memory and opinion.* Then I wanted to know the causes of their corruption, and extended my curiosity both to the heavens and the cavities of the earth, and would fain have known the cause of all the

---

* Socrates said he was ignorant of all these things, because he knew nothing but second causes. Now to know them justly, one ought to know God, and the virtue he displays in nature.

phenomena we meet with. At last, after a great deal of trouble, I found myself strangely unqualified for such inquiries; and of this I am about to give you a sensible proof.* This fine study made me so blind in the things I knew more evidently before, according to my own and other persons' thoughts, that I quite forgot all that I had known upon several subjects. I thought it was evident to the whole world, that a man grows only by eating and drinking: for flesh being added to flesh, bones to bones, and all the other parts joined to their similar parts by nourishment, make a small bulk to swell and grow, so that a little man becomes large. This was my thought : Do you not think it was just ?

Yes, surely, replied Cebes.

Mind what follows, says Socrates. I thought likewise that I knew the reason why one man is taller than another, and one horse higher than another : and with reference to plainer and more sensible things, I thought, for instance, that ten was more than eight, because two was added to it; that two cubits were larger than one, because they contained one half more.

And what are your present thoughts of those things, says Cebes ?

† I am so far, replies Socrates, from thinking that I know the causes of all these things, that when one is added to one, I do not believe I can tell whether it is that very one to which the other is added that becomes two, or whether the one added, and the one to which the addition was made, make two together ? For in their separate state, each of them was one, and not two; and after their being placed one by the other, they became two. Neither can I

---

* The utmost reach of physical investigation amounts to no more than an imperfect knowledge of second causes. Now these second causes do not lead us into the knowledge of the essence of things. A man is so far from improving his knowledge by them, that he must needs own his ignorance of the things he pretends to know. All philosophers at this day know, that nourishment by the means of heat is the cause of the growth of any animal. But they are all at a loss to know by what virtue it grows, or ceases to grow, and what are the limits of its growth. What misfortune is it for a man to plot and contrive all his life for the knowing of nothing !

† He afterwards gives the reason of these doubts.

tell how, upon the division of any thing, that which was
formerly one becomes two, from the very moment of division; for the cause is quite contrary to that which makes
one and one become two: As in this; one and one became
two by reason of their being placed near, and added the
one to the other; but in that; one thing becomes two by
reason of its division and separation. Far less do I pretend
to know whence this one thing comes, and by this method,
(i. e. by physical reasons) I cannot find out how the least
thing takes rise or perishes, or how it exists. But without
so much ceremony, I join another method of my own with
it, for by this I can learn nothing: having one day heard
somebody reading a book of Anaxagoras's, who said the
divine intellect was the cause of all beings, and drew them
up in their proper ranks and classes,* I was ravished with
joy. I perceived there was nothing more certain than this
principle: that intellect is the cause of all beings. For I
justly thought that this intellect having methodized all
things, and ranked them in their classes,† planted every
thing in the place and condition that was best and most
useful for it, in which it could best do and suffer whatever
the supreme intelligence had allotted to it; and I appre-
hended that the result of this principle was, that the only
thing a man ought to look for, either for himself or others,
is this better and more useful thing: for having once found
what is best and most useful, he will necessarily know
what is worst; since there is but one knowledge for both.

* Anaxagoras was the first that said the intellect or spirit of God
arranged the parts of matter and put them in motion. And it was
that principle that ushered in his physics. This fair exordium gave
Socrates occasion to think that he would explain all the secrets of
nature, by unfolding the divine virtue displayed upon it, and assign
all the reasons why every thing was so and so. But that philosopher did not keep up to his first principle; for he left the first
cause, and insisted only on second causes, and by so doing frustrated
the expectation of his readers.

† Here Socrates recals us to the first truth, that God created all
things good, and in their best state; according to Moses, who says,
"God saw all things that he had made, and behold they were very
good." Now in order to know why things are thus good, we must
inquire into the nature of this original goodness, and survey the state
they were created in: what a sorry thing is physics then, that knows
nothing but second causes, or rather, that does not certainly know
these second causes?

Upon this score I was infinitely glad that I had found such a master as Anaxagoras, who I hoped would give a satisfactory account of the cause of all things; and would not only tell me, for instance, that the earth is flat or round, but likewise assign the necessary cause of its being so : who would point out to me what is best, and at the same time give me to understand why it was so. In like manner, if he affirmed the seat of the earth to be in the centre of the universe, I expected he would give me a reason why it was so: and after I should have received sufficient instruction from him, I designed not to admit of any other cause as a principle.

I prepared some questions to be put to him concerning the sun, moon, and the stars, in order to know the reason of their motions, revolutions, and other accidents, and why that which each of them does is always the best : for I could not imagine, that after he had told me, that intellect arranged them, and drew them up in order, he could give me no other reason of that order than this, *that it was best*. And I flattered myself with hopes, that after he had assigned both the general and particular cause, he would inform me wherein the particular good of every individual thing, as well as the common good of all things, consists. I would not have parted with these hopes for all the treasures of the world.

So I bought his books with a great deal of impatience, and made it my business to peruse them as soon as possible, in order to acquire a speedy knowledge of the good and evil of all things; but I found myself frustrated in my mighty hopes: for as soon as I had made a small progress in the perusal, I found the author made no use of this *intellect*, and assigned no other cause of that fine order and disposition, than the air, whirlwinds, the waters, and other things equally absurd.

His whole performance seemed to reach no farther, than if a man should say, that Socrates does all by intellect; and after that proposing to give a reason for all my actions, should say, I am sttting upon my bed, for instance, to-day, because my body is composed of bones and nerves; the bones being hard and solid, are separated by joints; and the nerves* being able to bend and unbend themselves,

* Under the notion of nerves he comprehends muscles.

tie the bones to the flesh and the skin, which receives and includes both the one and the other; that the bones being disengaged at the joints, the nerves, which bend and unbend, enable me to fold my legs as you see; and that forsooth is the reason that I sit in this posture.   Or if a man pretending to assign the cause of my present conference with you, should insist only upon second causes, the voice, air, hearing, and such other things, and should take no notice of the true cause, viz. that the Athenians thought fit to condemn me, and that by the same reason I thought it best to be here, and patiently await the execution of my sentence; for I can safely* swear that these nerves and bones should long ere now have been translated to Megara, or Bœotia, if that had been fitter for me, and if I had not been still persuaded that it was better to endure the punishment I am doomed to by my country, than to flee like a slave or a banished person. As I take it, it is highly ridiculous to assign such causes upon such an occasion, and to rest satisfied in them.

If it be replied, that without bones and nerves, and such other things, I could not do what I mean to do; the allegation is true. But it savours of the greatest absurdity to suppose that these bones or nerves should be the cause of actions, rather than the choice of what is best, for that were to sink the difference between the cause and the thing; without which the cause could not be such.   And yet the vulgar, who take things by hearsay, and see by other people's eyes, as if they walked in thick darkness, take the true cause of things to be of that nature.   Pursuant to this notion, some surround the earth with a vortex that revolves eternally, and suppose it to be fixed in the centre of the universe:† others conceive it to be a broad and large trough, which has the air for its base and foundation. And

---

* In the Greek it runs, "For I swear by the dog." Lactantius checks him for this oath.   But St. Augustin in Lib. IV. On true Religion, justifies him; as if Socrates meant to give the Athenians to know, that even a dog, being the workmanship of God, deserved more honour than all the idols they swore by. It may likewise be alleged that Socrates swore by a dog, a goose, &c. in order to accustom men to forbear taking the name of God so often in vain.

† The former was the opinion of Anaximenes, Anaxagoras, and Democritus.

as for the power which orders and disposes every thing to
its best advantage, that is left entirely out of their consideration.   They fancy they know of a stronger and more
immortal Atlas, one more capable of supporting all things.*
And that great, good, and immortal tie, which is alone able
to unite and comprehend all things, they take for a
chimera.

Now I am of their mind who would willingly list themselves disciples to any that could tell this cause, let it be
what it may.   But since I could not compass the knowledge of it, either by myself or others, I will, if you please,
give you an account of a second trial I made in order to
discover it.

I am very desirous to hear it, observes Cebes.

After I had wearied myself in examining all things, I
thought it my duty to avoid what happens to those who
contemplate an eclipse of the sun ; for they lose the sight
of it, unless they view its reflection in water or some
other medium.   A thought much like that occurred to me,
and I feared I should lose my mental eyes, if I viewed
objects with corporeal ones, or employed any of my senses
in endeavouring to know them.   I thought it best to have
recourse to reason, and contemplate the truth of all things
as reflected from it.   It is possible the simile I use in explaining myself is not exact ; for I myself cannot affirm,
that he who beholds things in the glass of reason, sees
them more by reflection and similitude than he who beholds them in their operations.   However, the way I proceeded was this : From that time forward I grounded all
upon the reason that seemed best, and took all for truth
that I found conformable to it, whether in things or causes.
And what was not conformable, I rejected, as being false.
I will explain my meaning more distinctly ; for I fancy
you do not yet comprehend me.

Indeed, says Cebes, I do not clearly understand you.

But, after all, says Socrates, I advance no new thing.
This is no more than what I have said before, and particularly in the foregoing discourse : for all that I aim
at, is to demonstrate what sort of cause this is that I

* This Atlas is their own judgment, overrun with obscurity and
weakness.

so carefully sought after.   I begin with its qualities, which
are so much talked of, and which I take for the foundation.   I say, then, there is *something* that is GOOD, FINE,
JUST, and GREAT, of itself.   If you grant me this principle,
I hope by it to demonstrate the cause, and make out the
immortality of the soul.

I grant it, says Cebes ; you cannot be too quick in per-
fecting your demonstration.

Mind what follows, and see if you agree to it as I understand it.   If there is anything fine, besides fineness itself,
it must be such by partaking of that first good ; and so of
all the other qualities.   Are you of this opinion ?

I am. ·

I protest, continues Socrates, I cannot well understand
all the other learned causes that are commonly assigned.
But if any man ask me what makes a thing fine, whether
the liveliness of its colours, or the just proportion of its
parts, and the like; I waive all these plausible reasons,
which serve only to confound, and, without ceremony or
art, make answer, and perhaps too simply, that its fineness is only owing to the presence, or approach, or communication of the original fine Being, whatever be the way
of that communication; for I am not yet certain in what
manner it is : I only know certainly that all these fine
things are rendered such by the presence of this fine Being.
While I stand by this principle, I suppose I cannot be
deceived; and am persuaded, that I may safely make
answer to all questions whatever, that all fine things owe
their fineness to the presence of this Being.   Are not you
of the same mind ?

Yes, Socrates.

Are not great and small things rendered such in like manner ?   If one told you, that such a thing is larger than
another by the head;* would not you think the expression far from being exact ? and would not you make answer,
that whatever is larger, is rendered such by magnitude
itself, and what is smaller owes its littleness to littleness
itself ?   For if you said, that such a thing is greater or
smaller than another by the head, I fancy you would fear

---

* Socrates does not condemn the received expressions, but means
to shew that they do not reach the nature and essence of things.

being censured, for making both the greater and lesser
thing to be such by the same cause; and besides, for using
such an expression as seems to imply, that the head, which
is a small part, makes the largeness of the greater, which,
in effect, is an absurdity; for what can be more absurd
than to say, that a small matter makes a thing large?
Would not you fear such objections?

Yes, replies Cebes, smiling.

By the same reason, would not you hesitate to say,
that ten is more than eight, and surpasses it by two?
And would not you rather say, that ten are more than
eight by quantity?   In like manner, of two cubits; would
you say, they are larger than one by magnitude, rather
than by the half?   For still the same cause of objection
remains.

You say well.

But when one is added to one, or a thing is divided
into halves, would not you avoid saying, that in the former
case addition makes one and one two; and in the latter, division makes one thing become two? And would not you protest that you know no other cause of the existence of things,
than the participation of the essence that is peculiar to every
subject, and consequently no other reason why one and one
makes two, but the participation of duality, as one is one by
the participation of unity? Would not you discard these ad-
ditions, divisions, and all the other nice distinctions, and
leave them to those who know more than you do? And, for
fear of your own shadow, as the proverb goes, or rather
of your ignorance, would not you confine yourself to
this principle?   And if any one attacked it, would not
you let it stand without deigning him a reply, until you
had considered all the consequences?   And if afterwards
you should be obliged to give a reason for them, would not
you do it by having recourse to some of these other hypo-
theses, that should appear to be the best, and so proceed
from hypothesis to hypothesis, till you lighted upon something that satisfied you, as being a sure and standing truth?
At the same time, you would be unwilling to perplex and
confound all things, as those disputants do, who question
every thing.   It is true, these disputants perhaps are not
much concerned for the truth; and, by thus mingling and
perplexing all things by an effect of their profound know-

ledge, care only to please themselves. But as for you, if you are true philosophers, you will do as I say.

Simmias and Cebes jointly replied, that he said well.

Echec. Indeed, Phedon, I think it no wonder; for to my mind, Socrates has explained his principles with wonderful clearness, sufficient to make an impression upon any man of common sense.

Phed. All the audience thought the same.

Echec. Even we, who have it only at second hand, find it so. But what was said next?

Phed. If I remember right, after they had granted, that the species* of things have a real subsistence, and that the things participating of their nature take their denomination from them; then, I say, Socrates interrogated Cebes as follows:

If your principle be true, when you say Simmias is larger than Socrates, and smaller than Phedon, do not you imply that both greatness and littleness are lodged at the same time in Simmias?

Yes, replies Cebes.

But do not you admit that the proposition, *Simmias is bigger than Socrates,* is not absolutely and in itself true? For Simmias is not bigger because he is Simmias, but because he is possessed of magnitude. Neither is he bigger than Socrates because Socrates is Socrates, but because Socrates has littleness in comparison with Simmias's magnitude. Neither is Simmias less than Phedon because Phedon is Phedon, but because Phedon is big when compared to Simmias who is little.

That is true.

Thus, continues Socrates; Simmias is called both big and little, as being between two: by partaking of bigness he is bigger than Socrates, and by partaking also of littleness he is smaller than Phedon. Then he smiled, and said, methinks I have insisted too long on these things; but I should not have amused myself with these large strokes, had it not been to convince you more effectually of the truth of my principle: for, as I take it, not only magnitude itself cannot be at the same time big and small;

* By species, he means the eternal ideas of things, which subsist really in the mind of God.

but besides, the magnitude that is in us does not admit of littleness, and has no mind to be surpassed: for either the magnitude flees and yields it place when it sees its enemy approaching, or else it vanishes and perishes entirely; and, when once it has received it, it desires to continue as it is. As I, for instance, having received littleness, while I am as you see me, cannot but be little : for that which is big does never attempt to be little. And in like manner little-ness never encroaches upon magnitude. In one word, any of the contraries, while it is what it is, is never to be found with its contrary; but either disappears or perishes when the other comes in.

Cebes agreed to it : but one of the company, I forget who, addressed himself to Socrates thus : In the name of all the Gods, did you not say contrary to what you now advance ? Did not you conclude upon this, that greater things take rise from the lesser, and the lesser from the greater ; and, in a word, that contraries do still produce their contraries ? Whereas now, as I take it, you say that cannot be.

Whereupon Socrates put his head further out of the bed, and, having heard the objection, said to him: Indeed you do well to put us in mind of what we said; but you do not perceive the difference between the former and the latter. In the former we asserted, that every contrary owes its being to its contrary : and in the latter we teach, that a contrary is never contrary to itself, neither in us, nor in the course of nature.* There we spoke of things that had contraries, meaning to call every one of them by their proper names; but here we speak of such things as give a denomination to their subjects, which we told you, could never admit of their contraries. Then, turning to Cebes, did not this objection, says he, likewise give you some trouble ?

No, indeed, Socrates, replies Cebes ; I can assure you, that few things are capable of troubling me at present.

* That is, he spoke there of sensible things which have contraries, and are capable of receiving these contraries reciprocally, as a little thing becomes big, and a big thing little. But here he speaks of the things themselves, the intelligible contraries, such as cold and heat, which give name to the subjects they are lodged in, by their own name, and are never capable of receiving their contraries; for cold can never become heat, nor heat cold : they are always what they are.

Then we are agreed upon this simple proposition, says Socrates, that a contrary can never be contrary to itself.

That is true, says Cebes.

But what do you say to this? Is cold and heat any thing?

Yes, certainly.

What! is it like snow and fire?

No, Socrates.

Then you admit, that heat is different from fire, and cold from snow.

Without question, Socrates.

I believe you will likewise admit, that when the snow receives heat, it is no more what it was, but either gives way, or disappears when the heat approaches. In like manner the fire will either yield or be extinguished when the cold prevails upon it; for then it cannot be fire and cold together.

It is so, says Cebes.

There are also some contraries, that not only give name to their species; but likewise impart it to other things different from it, which preserve its figure and form while they have a being. For instance, must not an odd thing have always the same name?

Yes, surely.

Is that the only thing that is so called? Or, is not there some other thing different from it, which must needs be called by the same name, by reason that it belongs to its nature never to be without odds? For instance, must not the ternary number be called not only by its own name, but likewise by the name of an odd number;* though at the same time to be odd and to be three are two different things? Now such is the nature of the number three, five, and all other odd numbers; each of them is always odd, and yet their nature is not the same with the nature of the odd. In like manner, even numbers, such as two, four, eight, are all of them even, though at the same time their nature is not that of even. Do you not acknowledge this?

How can I do otherwise, says Cebes?

Pray mind what I infer from thence. It is, that not only those contraries, which are incapable of receiving their

---

* For the ternary number partakes of the odd.

contraries, but all other things which are not opposite to one another, and yet have always their contraries; all these things, I say, are incapable of receiving a form opposite to their own; and either disappear or perish upon the appearance of the opposite form. For instance: The number three will sink a thousand times rather than become an even number, while it continues to be three. Is it not so?

Yes, replies Cebes.

But, after all, says Socrates, two are not contrary to three.

No, certainly.

Then the contrary species are not the only things that refuse admission to their contraries; since, as you see, other things that are not contrary cannot abide the approach of that which has the least shadow of contrariety.

That is certain.

Do you desire then that I should define them as near as possible?

With all my heart, Socrates.

Must not contraries be such things as give such a form to that in which they are lodged, that it is not capable of giving admission to another thing that is contrary to them?

What do you say?

I say, as I said before: Wherever the idea or form of three is lodged, that thing must of necessity continue, not only to be three, but to be odd.

Who doubts that?

And, by consequence, it is impossible for the idea or form that is contrary to its constituent form, ever to approach.

That is a plain case.

Well, is not the constituent form an odd?

Yes.

Is not *even* the form that is contrary to the odd?

Yes.

Then the form of even is never lodged in three?

Certainly not.

Then three is incapable of being even?

Most certainly.

And that, because three is odd?

Just so.

Now this is the conclusoin that I would come to,—that

some things, that are not contrary to one another, are as
incapable of that other thing, as if it were truly a contrary; as for instance, though three is not contrary to an
even number, yet it can never admit of it. For two brings
always something contrary to an odd number, like fire to
cold, and several other things. Would not you agree,
then, to this definition, that a contrary does not only
refuse admission to its contrary, but likewise to that which,
being not contrary, brings upon it something of a contrary nature, which by that sort of contrariety destroys its
form?

I pray you let me hear that again, says Cebes; for it is
worth the while to hear it more than once.

I say, number five will never be an even number; just
as ten, which is its double, will never be odd; no more
than three-fourths, or a third part, or any other part of a
whole, will admit of the form and idea of the whole. Do
you not understand me, and agree with what I say?

I apprehend you perfectly, and fully agree with you.

Since you understand me, says Socrates, pray answer
me as I do you; that is, answer not what I ask, but something else, according to the idea and example I have given
you; I mean, that besides the true and certain way of answering, spoken of already, I have yet another in my view
that springs from it, which is equally certain. For instance, if you ask me what it is, that being in the body,
makes it hot, I would not give you this ignorant though
sure answer, that it is heat; but would draw a more particular answer from what we have been speaking of, and
would tell you that it is fire. And if you should ask what
it is that makes the body sick, I would not say, it was the
disease, but the fever. If you ask me what makes a
number odd, I would not tell you that it is the oddness,
but unity; and so of the rest.

Do you understand what I mean?

I understand you perfectly, replies Cebes.

Answer me, then, continues Socrates; what makes the
body live?

The soul.

Is the soul always the same?

How should it be otherwise?

Does the soul, then, carry life along with it into all the bodies it enters?

Most certainly.

Is there any thing that is contrary to life, or is there nothing?

Yes, death is the contrary of life.

Then the soul will never receive that which is contrary to what it carries in its bosom? That is a necessary consequence from our principles.

It is a plain consequence, says Cebes.

But what name do we give to that which refuses admission to the idea and form of evenness?

It is the odd number.

What do we call that which never receives justice, and that which never receives good?

The one is called injustice, and the other evil.

And what do we call that which never admits of death? Immortal.

Does the soul admit of death?

No.

Then the soul is immortal?*

Most certainly.

Is that fully demonstrated, or was the demonstration imperfect?

It is fully made good, Socrates.

If an odd number of necessity were incorruptible, would not three be so too?†

Who doubts it?

If whatever is without heat were necessarily incorruptible, would not snow, when put to the fire, withdraw itself safe from the danger? For, since it cannot perish, it will never receive the heat, notwithstanding its being held to the fire.

What you say is true.

In like manner, if that which is not susceptible of cold, were by a natural necessity exempted from perishing,

* His meaning is, that the soul is as far from dying as good from giving admission to evil, or justice to injustice, or odd to even. And that the soul is immortal, as necessarily as three is odd.

† If the soul be immortal, it is incorruptible; i. e. it resists and triumphs over all the assaults of death.

though a whole river were thrown upon the fire, it would never go out, but, on the contrary, would remain in its full force.

That is certain, says Cebes.

Then of necessity we must say the same of what is immortal. If that which is immortal is incorruptible, though death approach the soul, it shall never fall in the attack; for, as we said, the soul will not receive death, and consequently never dies; just as three, or any odd number, will never be even; and as fire will never be cold, or its heat turned into coldness.

Perhaps some may answer, that it is true, the odd can never become even, by the accession of what is even, while it continues odd; but what should hinder the even from taking up the room of the odd, when the latter has perished? To this objection, it cannot be answered that the odd does not perish, for that it is not incorruptible. Had we established its incorruptibility, we should justly have maintained, that notwithstanding the attacks of the even, the odd of three would still come off without loss. And we should have asserted the same of fire, heat, and such other things; should we not?

Most certainly, says Cebes.

And, by consequence, if we agree in this, that every immortal thing is incorruptible, it will necessarily follow, not only that the soul is immortal, but that it is incorruptible. And if we cannot agree upon that, we must look out for another proof.

There is no occasion for that, Socrates, replies Cebes; for what should avoid corruption and death, if an immortal and eternal being be liable to them?

All the world will agree, says Socrates, that God, and life itself, and whatever is immortal, cannot perish.

At least, says Cebes, all men profess to do so. The consequence seems necessary.* Hence, continues Socrates, when a man dies, his mortal and corruptible part suffers

---

* Cebes means, that men will be forced to say so, because, perhaps, they have not light enough to answer these reasons, even though they were none of the best. Socrates, discerning this to be the import of Cebes's words, on that view makes this incomparable reply,—That the Gods will yet more agree to it. Meaning to say, that truth is more true in the intellect of God than in the mind of man, which is always too weak to comprehend it.

dissolution; but the immortal part escapes unhurt, and triumphs over death.

That is plain and evident.

Then, my dear Cebes, if there be any such thing as an immortal and incorruptible being, such a being is the soul; consequently our souls shall live hereafter.

I have nothing to object, says Cebes; and cannot but yield to your arguments. But if Simmias, or any of the company has any thing to offer, they will do well not to stifle it; for when will they find another opportunity of discoursing and satisfying themselves upon these important subjects?

For my part, says Simmias, I cannot but subscribe to what Socrates has said; but I own, that the greatness of the subject, and the natural weakness of man, occasion within me a sort of distrust and incredulity.

You have not only spoken well, says Socrates; but, notwithstanding the apparent certainty of our first hypothesis, it is needful you should resume the discourse, in order to a more leisurely view, and to convince yourself more clearly and effectually. When you thoroughly understand it, you will need no other proof.

That is well said, replies Cebes.

There is one thing more, my friends, that is a very just thought, viz. that if the soul is immortal, it stands in need of cultivation and improvement, not only in the time that we call this life; but for the future; or what we call eternity.* For if you think justly upon this point, you will find it very dangerous to neglect the soul. Were death the dissolution of the whole man, it would be a great advantage to the wicked after death, to be rid at once of their body, their soul, and their vices also. But forasmuch as the soul is immortal, the only way to avoid those evils and obtain salvation, is to become good and wise; for it carries nothing along with it, but its good or bad qualities, its virtues or vices, which are the cause of its eternal happiness or misery, commencing from the first moment of its arrival in the other world. And it is said, that after

---

* It is not enough that the understanding be convinced of the immortality of the soul; the affections must likewise be moved. To which end he dwells upon the consequences of that important truth, and all that it requires

the death of every individual, the demon or genius, that was partner with it, and conducted it during life, leads it to a certain place, where all the dead are obliged to appear in order to be judged, and from thence are conducted by a guide to the world below. And, after they have there received their good or bad deserts, and continued their appointed time, another conductor brings them back to this life, after several revolutions of ages. Now this road is not a plain and straight one, else there would be no occasion for guides, and nobody would miss their way. But there are several by-ways and cross-ways, as I conjecture from the method of our sacrifices and religious ceremonies. So that a temperate wise soul follows its guide, and is not ignorant of what happens to it. But the soul, that is nailed to its body, that is inflamed with the love of it, and has been long its slave, after much struggling and suffering in this visible world, is at last dragged along against its will by the demon allotted for its guide. And when it arrives at that fatal rendezvous of all souls, if it has been guilty of any impurity, or polluted with murder, or has committed any of those atrocious crimes, that desperate and lost souls are commonly guilty of, the other souls abhor it and avoid its company. It finds neither companion nor guide, but wanders in a fearful solitude and horrible desert; till after a certain time necessity drags it into the mansions it deserves : whereas the temperate and pure soul, has the Gods themselves for its guides and conductors, and goes to converse with them in the happy mansions prepared for it. For, my friends, there are several marvellous places in the earth; and it is not at all such as the describers of it are wont to make it,* as I was taught by one who well knew it.

What do you say, Socrates, says Simmias, interrupting him? I have likewise heard several things of the earth, but not what you have heard. Wherefore I wish you would be pleased to tell us what you know.

To recount that to you, my dear Simmias, I do not be-

---

* Socrates does not mention who taught him this doctrine of the pure faith; but it is no hard matter to find out the author. Proclus himself acknowledges, that Socrates and Plato owed this idea to the sacred tradition of the Egyptians, that is, to the Hebrews, ὁ καὶ ἡ τῶν Αἰγυπτίων ἱερὰ φήμη παραδίδοσι. In Tim. lib. L.

lieve we have any occasion, for you know Glaucus's art.[*]
But to make out the truth of it, is a more difficult matter,
and I question if all Glaucus's art can reach it.   Such an
attempt is not only above my reach; but supposing it
were not, the short time I have left me, will not suffer me
to embark in so long a discourse.   All that I can do is, to
give you a general idea of this earth, and the places it
contains.

That will be enough, says Simmias.

In the first place, continues Socrates, I am persuaded,
that if the earth is placed in the air, in the middle of heaven, as they say it is, it stands in no need of air, or any
other support to prevent its fall; its own *equilibrium* is sufficient to keep it up.   For whatever is equally poised in
the middle of a thing, that presses equally upon it, cannot
incline to either side, and consequently stands firm and
immovable.   This I am convinced of.

Doubtless you have reason, replies Simmias.

I am farther persuaded, that the earth is very large and
spacious, and that we only inhabit that part of it which
reaches from the river Phasis to the Straits of Gibraltar,
upon which we are scattered like so many ants dwelling in
holes, or like frogs that reside in some marsh near the sea.
There are several other nations that inhabit its other parts
that are unknown to us; for, all over the earth there are
holes of all sizes and figures, always filled with gross air,
and covered with thick clouds, and overflown by the waters
that rush in on all sides.

There is another pure earth[†] above the pure heaven
where the stars are, which is commonly called Æther.

---

* When they meant to imply the difficulty of a thing, they were
wont to say, by way of proverb, that they stood in need of Glaucus's
art, who, from a man, became a sea-god.   But those who comment
upon this proverb, allege that it was made upon another Glaucus,
who invented the forging of iron.   But I am induced to believe the
contrary by this, that the fable of Glaucus, the sea-god, was founded
upon his being an excellent diver ; to which it is probable, Socrates
alluded : seriously, if one would visit the earth he speaks of, of
which ours is only a sediment, he must be a better diver than Glaucus, in order to pass the currents and seas that divide them.   He
must raise his thoughts above all earthly or material things.

† The idea of this pure earth is taken from the writings of the
prophets, from whence the Egyptians derived it.

The earth we inhabit is properly nothing else but the sedi ment of the other, and its grosser part which flows continually into those holes. We are immured in these cells, though we are not sensible of it, and fancy we inhabit the upper part of the pure earth: much after the same manner, as if one living in the deeps of the sea, should fancy his habitation to be above the waters; and when he sees the sun and other stars through the waters, should fancy the sea to be the heavens; and by reason of his heaviness and weakness, having never put forth his head or raised himself above the waters, should never know that the place we inhabit is purer and better than his, and should never meet with any person to inform him. This is just our condition; we are mewed up within some hole of the earth, and fancy we live at the top of all: we take the air for the true heavens, in which the stars run their rounds; and the cause of our mistake, is our heaviness and weakness, that keep us from surmounting this thick and muddy air. If any could mount up with wings to the upper surface, he would no sooner put his head out of this gross air, than he would behold what is transacted in those blessed mansions; just as the fishes skipping above the surface of the waters, see what is done in the air which we breathe. And if he were a man fit for long contemplation, he would find it to be the true heaven and the true light; in a word, to be the true earth.* In order to make you conceive the beauty of this pure earth situated in the heavens, I will tell you, if you please, a story that is worth your hearing.

We shall hear it, says Simmias, with a great deal of pleasure.

First of all, my dear Simmias, continues Socrates, if we look upon this perfect earth from a high place, they say, it looks like one of our packs covered with twelve welts of different colours.† For it is varied with a greater number of different colours, of which those made use of by our painters are but imperfect patterns. For the colours of this earth are infinitely more clear and lively. One is

* The true heavens and the true light cannot be known any other way but by long and continual meditation.
† This description of the beauty of this pure earth, the mansion of the blessed, is grounded on the 54th chapter of Isaiah, and the 18th of Ezekiel.

M

an admirable purple; another a colour of gold, more spark-
ling than gold itself; a third a white, more lively than the
snow; and so on of all the rest, the beauty whereof leaves all
our colours far behind it.   The chinks of this earth are
filled with water and air, which make up an infinity of
admirable shadows, wonderfully diversified by that infinite variety of colours.

In this so perfect an earth, every thing has a perfection
answerable to its qualities.   The trees, flowers, fruits, and
mountains are charmingly beautiful; they produce all
sorts of precious stones of an incomparable perfection,
clearness and splendour; those we esteem so much here,
as jasper, emeralds, and sapphire, are not comparable to
them.   There is *not one* in that blessed earth that is not
infinitely superior to any of ours.

Besides the beauties now mentioned, this earth is
encircled with gold and silver, which being scattered all
over in great abundance, casts forth a charming splendour
on all sides.   A sight of this earth is a view of the blessed.
It is inhabited by all sorts of animals,* and by men, some
of whom are cast into the centre of the earth, and others
are scattered about the air, as we are about the sea.
There are some also that inhabit the isles, formed by the
air near the continent.†   For there the air is the same
thing that water and the sea are here; and the æther
does them the same service that the air does to us.   Their
seasons are so admirably well tempered, that their life is
much longer than ours, and always free from diseases:
and as for their sight, hearing, and all their other senses,
and even their intellect itself, they surpass us as far as the
æther they breathe exceeds our gross air in simplicity and
purity.   They have sacred groves, and temples actually
inhabited by the Gods, who give evidence of their presence
by oracles, divinations, inspirations, and all other sensible

* The notion of these animals seems to be taken from the vision
of Ezekiel.

† In this description we may perceive most of the marks given
by Moses of the terrestrial paradise, which was a type of this
land of the just, the true paradise.   And, what I take to be very remarkable, we may plainly see that these philosophers held this pure
earth to be actually in being at the same time with this our impure
and grosser earth.

signs; and also personally converse with them.   They see the sun and moon, without an intervening medium, and view the stars as they are in themselves; and all the other branches of their felicity are proportional to these.

This is the situation of that earth, and this is the matter that surrounds it.   About it are several abysses, some of which are deeper and more open than the country we inhabit; others are deeper, but not so open; and some again have a more extensive breadth, but lesser depth. All these abysses are perforated in several parts, and have pipes communicating one with another, through which there runs, just as in the caves of Mount Ætna, very large and deep rivers, springs of cold and hot water, fountains, and rivers of fire.*

These abysses are filled with waters falling out of one into another.   All these sources move both downwards and upwards, like a vessel hung above the earth; which vessel is naturally one, and indeed the greatest of these abysses.   It goes across the whole earth, and is open on two sides.   Homer speaks of it,† when he says, I will throw it into obscure Tartarus, a great way from hence,‡ the deepest abyss under the earth.   Homer is not the only author that called this place by the name of Tartarus; most of the other poets did the same.

All the rivers run into this abyss, and flow from thence again.   Each of these rivers is tinctured with the nature of the earth through which it runs.   And the reason of their not stagnating in this abyss, is, that they find no resting-place, but roll and throw their waters upside down. The air and wind that surround them, does the same, for it follows them, both when they rise above they earth, and when they descend towards us.   And just as in the respiration of animals, there is an incessant ingress and egress

* Plato borrowed from the writings of the prophets those rivers of fire prepared for the punishment of the wicked after their judgment; and particularly had read the 8th chapter of Daniel.   *Theodoret.*

† In the beginning of the 8th book of his Iliads.

‡ The prophet Ezekiel calls this Tartarus " the nether part of the earth." He speaks of the rivers and waters in the pit, ch. xxxi. 14, 13. and xxxii. 18. But long before Ezekiel, Homer had the same ideas from the tradition of the Egyptians.

of air, so the air that is mingled with the waters, accompanies them, and raises raging winds.

When these waters fall into this lower abyss, they diffuse themselves into all the channels of springs and rivers, and fill them; just as if one were drawing up water with two pails, one of which fills as the other empties. For the waters flowing from thence, fill up all our channels, from whence diffusing themselves, they make our seas, rivers, lakes, and fountains. After that they disappear, and diving into the earth, some with a large compass, and others by small windings, repair to Tartarus, where they enter by other and lower passages than those they came out by. Some re-enter on the same side, and others on the opposite side to that of their egress; and some again enter on all sides, after they have made one or several turns round the earth; like serpents folding their bodies into several rolls; and having gained entrance, rise up to the middle of the abyss, but cannot reach farther, by reason that the other half is higher than that level. They form several very great and large currents; but there are four principal ones,* the greatest of which is the outermost of all, and is called the ocean.

Opposite to that is Acheron, which runs through the desert places, and diving through the earth, falls into the marsh, which from it is called the Acherusian Lake, where all souls repair upon their departure from the body; and having remained there the time appointed, some a shorter, some a longer time, are sent back to the world to animate beasts.

Between Acheron and the ocean, there runs a third river, which retires again not far from its source, and falls into a vast space full of fire: there it forms a lake greater than our sea, in which the water mixed with earth, boils and setting out from thence black and muddy, runs along the earth to the end of the Acherusian Lake, without mixing with its waters; and having made several turnings

* These four rivers, which have their course in the places appointed for the punishment of the wicked, might easily have been imagined from the four rivers of the terrestrial paradise. As the apartment of the just was watered by four rivers, which increase its delightfulness, it was proper that the apartment of the wicked should likewise be watered by four rivers of a contrary nature, which might add to the horror of that place of darkness and sorrow.

throws itself underneath Tartarus: this is the flaming river called Phlegeton, the streams whereof are seen to ascend up to the earth in several places.

Opposite to this is the fourth river, which falls first into a horrible place, of a bluish colour, called by the name of Stygian, where it makes the formidable Lake of Styx: and after it has imbibed the most horrible qualities from the waters of that lake, descends into the earth, where after making several windings, it directs its course towards Phlegeton, at last meets it in the Lake of Acheron, where it does not mingle its waters with those of the other rivers; but after it has made its circuit round the earth, throws itself into Tartarus by a passage opposite to that of Phlegeton. This fourth river is called by the poets Cocytus. Nature having thus disposed of these things, when the dead arrive at the place where their demon leads them, they are all tried and judged, both those that lived a holy and just life, and those who wallowed in injustice and impiety.

As for those who are found to have lived neither entirely a criminal, nor absolutely an innocent life,—these are sent to Acheron, where they embark in boats, and are transported to the Acherusian Lake. Here they dwell, and suffer punishments proportionable to their crimes; till at last, being purged and cleansed from their sins, and set at liberty, they receive the recompence of their good actions.

Those whose sins are incurable, who have been guilty of sacrilege, murder, or such other crimes, are, by a just and fatal destiny, thrown headlong into Tartarus, where they are kept prisoners for ever.

But those who are found guilty of curable sins, though very great ones,—such as offering violence to their father or mother in a passion, or murder, and afterwards repenting of it,—these must of necessity be likewise cast into Tartarus; but after a year's abode there, the tide throws the homicides back into Cocytus, and the parricides into Phlegeton, which draws them into the Acherusian Lake. There they cry out bitterly, and invoke those whom they have killed or offered violence to, to forgive them, and to suffer them to pass the lake. If they are prevailed with, they pass the lake, and are delivered from their misery; if not, they are thrown back again into those rivers; and this continues to be repeated, till they have satisfied the injured persons. For such is the sentence pronounced against them.

But those who have distinguished themselves by a holy life, are released from these earthly places, these horrible prisons, and are received above into that pure earth, where they dwell; and those of them who are sufficiently purged by philosophy, live for ever without their bodies,* and are received into yet more admirable and delicious mansions, which I cannot easily describe; neither do the narrow limits of my time allow me to launch into that subject.

What I have said, my dear Simmias, ought sufficiently to shew, that we should labour all our lives to acquire virtue and wisdom, since we have so great a reward proposed to us, and so bright a prospect before us.

No man of sense would pretend to assert that all these things are exactly as you have heard; but all thinking men will agree that the state of the soul, and the place of its abode after death, is either such as I represent it to be, or very near like it, provided the soul be immortal; and will certainly find it worth while to run the risk, for what was ever more inviting? One cannot but be charmed with that blessed hope. And for this reason I have produced the fable just now related.

Every one who, during his life-time, has renounced the pleasures of the body; has pursued only the pleasures of true knowledge; and beautified his soul, not with foreign ornaments, but with ornaments suitable to its nature, such as temperance, justice, fortitude, liberty, and truth. Such a one, being firmly confident of the happiness of his soul, ought to wait peacefully for the hour of his removal, as being always ready for the voyage, whenever his fate calls him.

As for you, my dear Simmias and Cebes, and all you of this company, you will all follow me shortly. My hour is come; and, as a tragic poet would say, the surly pilot calls me aboard; wherefore it is time I should go to the bath, for I think it better, before I drink the poison, to be washed, in order to save the women that trouble after I am dead.

* This was a great error among the heathens. They did not believe that the body could be glorified.

Socrates having spoken, Crito thus addressed him:
Alas, then! in God's name be it so.   But what orders do
you give us with reference to your children, or your affairs,
that, by putting them in execution, we may at least have
the comfort of serving you?

What I now recommend to you, replies Socrates, is
what I always recommended, viz. to take care of yourselves.   You cannot do me a greater service, nor oblige me
and my family more,* than by promising me at this time
to do so.   Whereas, if you neglect yourselves, and refuse
to conform your lives to the model† I always proposed to
you, and follow it as it were by the footsteps; your pro-
testations and offers of service will be altogether useless.

We shall do our utmost, Socrates, replies Crito, to obey
you.   But how will you be buried?

Just as you please, says Socrates, if I do not slip from
you.   At the same time, looking upon us with a gentle
smile, I cannot, says he, attain my end, in persuading
Crito that this is Socrates who discourses with you, and
methodizes all the parts of this discourse; and still he
fancies that Socrates is the thing that shall shortly see
death.   He confounds me with my corpse; and in that
view asks how I will be buried?   And all this after the
long discourse that I made to you lately, in order to shew
that as soon as I shall have taken the poison, I shall stay
no longer with you, but shall part from hence, and go to
enjoy the felicity of the blessed; in a word, all that I
have said for your consolation and mine, is to no purpose,
but is all lost with reference to him.   I beg that you
will be bail for me to Crito, but after a contrary manner to that in which he offered to bail me to my judges;

* There is a great deal of sense in what Socrates here tells his
friends. He desires them only to take care of themselves, because
if they take care of themselves, they will prove good men; and, being such, will do all good offices to his family, though they did not
promise it: for good men are honest, they love their neighbours,
and take pleasure in doing good. Whereas, if they neglect themselves, notwithstanding all their fair promises, they would not be
able to do any one good. None but good men can do us service.
How great is this truth!

† This mode. is God; for he still told them that they should render themselves conformable to God, as much as human weakness
would bear.

for he engaged that I would not be gone. Pray engage for me, that I shall no sooner be dead, than I shall be gone, to the end that poor Crito may bear my death more steadily, and that, when he sees my body burnt or interred, he may not despair, as if I suffered great misery, and say at my funeral that Socrates is laid out; Socrates is carried out; Socrates is interred. For you must know, my dear Crito, says he, turning to him, that speaking amiss of death is not only a fault in the way of discourse, but likewise wounds the soul. You should have known that my body is to be buried; and that you are at liberty to inter it as you please, and in the manner that is most conformable to our laws and customs.

Having spoken thus, he went into the next room to bathe. Crito followed him, and he desired we should attend. Accordingly we all attended him, entertaining ourselves at one time with repeating and farther examining what he had said; at another time in speaking of the miserable prospect that was before us. For we all looked upon ourselves as persons deprived of our good father, and doomed to pass the rest of our lives in an orphan state.

After he came out of the bath, they brought his children to him; for he had three, two young ones, and one that was older: and all the women of his family went to him. He spoke to them for some time in the presence of Crito, gave them their orders, obliged them to retire with his children, and then came back to us. It was then towards sun-setting, for he had been a long while in the little room.

When he came in, he sat down upon his bed, without saying much: for about the same time the officer of the eleven magistrates came in, and drawing near to him, Socrates, says he, I have no occasion to make the complaint of you, that I have every day of those in the same condition; for as soon as I come to acquaint them, by orders from the magistrates, that they must drink the poison, they are incensed against me and curse me: but as for you, since you came here, I have found you to be the calmest and best man that ever entered this prison; and I am confident that at present you are not angry with me: doubtless you are angry with none, but those who are the cause of your misfortune. You know them without naming. Socrates, you know what I come to tell you; farewell, endeavour to bear this necessity with a constant mind. Having thus spoken, he began to weep, and turning his back upon us, retired a little. Farewell, my friend, says Socrates, looking upon him, I will follow the counsel thou givest me. Observe, says he, what honesty is in that fellow! During my imprisonment he has come often to see me, and discourse with me: observe how he weeps for me. My dear Crito, if the poison be prepared, bring it; if not, let him prepare it himself.

But, methinks, Socrates, says Crito, the sun shines upon the mountains, and is not yet set; and I know that several in your circumstances did not drink the poison till a long time after the order was given; they supped first, and enjoyed any thing they had a mind to: wherefore I conjure you not to press so hard; you have yet time enough.

Those who do as you say, Crito, says Socrates, have their own reasons; they think it is just as much time gained: and I have likewise my reasons for not doing so; for the only advantage I can have for drinking it later, is to make myself ridiculous to myself, in being so foolishly fond of life, as to pretend to husband it in the last minute, when there is no more to come.* Go then, my dear Crito, and do as I bid you, and trouble me no longer.

Whereupon Crito gave the sign to the slave that waited just by. The slave went out, and after he had spent some time in preparing the poison, returned, accompanied by him that was to give it, and brought it all together in one cup. Socrates seeing him come in, said, That is well my friend; but what must I do? For you know best, and it is your business to direct me.

You have nothing else to do, says he, but whenever you have drank it, to walk until you find your legs stiff, and then to lie down upon your bed. This is all you have to do. And at the same time he gave him the cup: Socrates took it, not only without any commotion, or change of colour or countenance, but with joy; and looking upon the fellow with a bold and lively eye, as he was wont to do, What do you say of this mixture, says he, is it allowable

---

* He alludes to a verse of Hesiod, who says, " it is an unlucky sparing when one is come to the bottom."

to make a drink-offering of it? Socrates, replied the man, we never make more at once than serves for a dose.

I understand you, says Socrates: but at least it is lawful for me to pray to the Gods. This I beg of them with all my soul, that they would bless the voyage, and render it happy. Having said that, he drank it off, with an admirable tranquillity and an inexpressible calmness.

Hitherto we had, almost all of us, the power to refrain from tears; but when we saw him drink it off, we were no longer masters of ourselves. Notwithstanding all my efforts, I was obliged to cover my face with my mantle, that I might freely give utterance to my feelings, for it was not alone Socrates's misfortune, but my own, that I deplored, in reflecting what a friend I was losing. Crito, likewise, could not abstain from weeping; and Apollodorus, who had scarce ceased to shed tears during the whole conference, did then howl and cry aloud, so as to move every one with his lamentations. Socrates himself alone remained unmoved: on the contrary, he reproved them. What are you doing, my friends? says he. What! such fine men as you are! O where is virtue? Was it not for that, I sent off those women? I have always heard it said that a man ought to die in tranquillity, and blessing God? Be easy then; and shew more constancy and courage. These words filled us with confusion, and forced us to suppress our sorrows.

In the mean time, he continued to walk, and when he felt his legs stiff, he lay down on his back, as the man had ordered him. At this time, the same person who gave him the poison, came up to him, and after looking upon his legs and feet, bound up his feet with all his force, and asked him if he felt it? He said, No. Then he bound up his legs; and having carried his hands higher, gave us the signal that he was quite cold. Socrates likewise felt himself with his hand, and told us, that when the cold came up to his heart, he should leave us. And then uncovering himself, for he was covered, Crito, says he, these were his last words, "We owe a cock to Æsculapius, discharge this vow for me, and do not forget it."* It shall

---

* Those who have not dived into the true meaning of Socrates, charge him with idolatry and superstition, upon the score of this cock that he had vowed to Æsculapius. But these words should not be taken

be done, says Crito; but see if you have any thing else to say to us. He made no answer, and after a little space of time, departed. The man, who was still by him, having uncovered him, received his last looks, which continued fixed upon him. Crito, seeing that, came up and closed his mouth and eyes.

This, Echecrates, was the exit of our friend; a man, who, beyond all dispute, was the wisest and the best of all our acquaintance.*

literally; they are enigmatical, as many of Plato's words are; and can never be understood, unless we have recourse to figures and allegories. The cock here is the symbol of life, and Æsculapius the emblem of physic. Socrates's meaning is, that he resigns his soul into the hands of the true physician, who comes to purify and heal him. This explication suits admirably well with the doctrine taught by Socrates in this same treatise, where he shews that religious sacrifices were only figures. Theodoret had a juster notion of this passage than Lactantius and Tertullian; for he not only did not condemn it, but insinuated that it was figurative, in his 7th Discourse of the Opinions of the Pagans. "I am persuaded," says he, "that Socrates ordered a cock to be sacrificed to Æsculapius, to shew the injustice of his condemnation." For he was condemned for owning no God, but he did acknowledge a God, and shewed that his God stood in no need of our sacrifices or homage, and required nothing else from us but piety and sanctity.

* Xenophon, that faithful historian of the actions and memorable sayings of Socrates, gives him the same encomium; and having said, that he was the best man in the world, and the greatest favourite with God, concludes in these words: "If any man be of another mind, pray let him compare his manners and actions with those of other men, and then let him judge." In fact, that is the true way of judging men. Nothing but true religion did ever form a more wonderful and divine man.

THE

INTRODUCTION TO LACHES.

THE education of children is a thing of such importance, that the welfare of families and the good of estates depend wholly upon it. It is no wonder then, that Socrates, who so passionately loved his country, was so watchful in preventing the Athenians from adopting false measures in reference to that point, and made it his business to correct their notions. The most erroneous, and perhaps the most pernicious to the republic, was that which they entertained of valour. The wars they were then engaged in, together with those that threatened them afar off, had inspired them with such a martial ardour, that they thought of nothing but training up their children to the exercise of arms; as being persuaded that that was the only way to render them serviceable to their country. Besides, a circumstance had occurred which tended to increase this predilection; for not long before, a fencing-master had come to Athens, who talked wonders of his art, pretending to teach valour, and to put his scholars in a condition to resist by themselves a greater number of enemies. The people crowded to his school, and the youth neglected every thing to apply themselves to this exercise. Socrates, foreseeing the dangerous consequence of this their application, labours to prevent it : and that is the subject of this conference. As this dialogue recommends itself by its imposing title, so the character of its actors excites our curiosity. Lysimachus, son of the great Aristides, and Melesias, son of the great Thucydides, dissatisfied with their own education, and resolving to take more care of their children than their fathers had taken of them, went to Nicias and Laches, who already made a considerable figure in the republic, and carried them to see this fencing-master.

After the show was over, they asked the advice of these two friends, whether they approved of that exercise, and whether they would have their children learn? So that valour became the subject of discourse; and it was very probable that no persons could speak better upon that subject, than those who had given proof of their valour on several occasions. But, after all, they do not think themselves able to decide so difficult a question, without help : therefore they call in Socrates to assist them, as being one who made the interest of youth his peculiar study; and, besides, had given proof of heroic courage at the siege of Potidæa, and the battle of Delium. Nicias is of opinion, that the exercise is very proper for youth, and admirably well calculated for rendering them brave and expert ; and considers it as a means leading to a good end, namely, the art of war. Laches attacks this opinion, and makes out the uselessness of that exercise by the insignificancy of its teachers, who never did a good action in their whole lives ; and as for valour, had never gained the least reputation in the army. Socrates is called in to decide the controversy. At first he pleads incapacity as an excuse : but afterwards insinuates that there is a necessity of knowing men, before one can be acquainted with valour. He shews the falsity of the notion that great men had entertained of this virtue, and which is still kept up to the present day. And though he does not reveal his mind plainly to those who call every thing in question ; yet one may easily perceive his opinion to be this: That valour is a virtue that reaches through all the actions of life, and includes all other virtues. For a valiant man is one that is always accompanied by prudence, and judges equally of things past, present, and to come ; who being acquainted with the good and evil, that has been, or is to come, is in a condition to arm himself against the one, and omits nothing to compass the other. So that to be valiant, one must be good; and to educate youth aright, they must be taught wisely to avoid all evil, and pursue all the good they can attain, not only from men, but which is more important, from God himself ; and to spare neither labour nor life in the pursuit. This is Socrates's doctrine. And Plato has made the world a good present, in preserving this excellent conference : for we ought not to look on it as a trial of skill, but as a solid and instructive discourse. Pursuant to this doctrine of Socrates, we plainly see that the martyrs were the most valorous of men; for their valour was accompanied by true prudence, which taught them to distinguish that which is truly terrible, from that which is not; to know past, present, and future happiness or misery; and this moved them to avoid the one, and pursue the other, even at the expence of their lives.

It seems Aristotle did not perceive the full force and solidity of these principles of Socrates, when he arraigned him for saying that valour was a science. Doubtless, it is a science, but a divine one, that cannot be learned from men.

The solidity of this dialogue is enlivened by a variety of agreeable and interesting matter: for whether we regard the beauty of his characters, the liveliness of the narrative, the spirit of the dialogue, or the satirical strokes it is full of, we find nothing more perfect in its kind. His satire upon those mighty politicians who employ all their care on affairs of state, and neglect their children, suffering them to be overrun with vice, is very natural. Socrates means by it to shew that these men do more harm to the commonwealth, by this unhappy negligence, than good by all the services they have done. His satire against fencing-masters is likewise very ingenious, in which the character of our modern pretenders is admirably drawn. Those who have taken notice of Nicias in Thucydides, haranguing in the Athenian council against the Sicilian expedition, will here find an exact transcript of his true character. And that which above all deserves to be remarked, is Plato's dexterity in extolling Socrates, and setting his merit in a true light.

This Dialogue is supposed to have been composed soon after the defeat of the Athenians at Delium, which happened in the first year of the 89th Olympiad.

LACHES; OR, OF VALOUR.

LYSIMACHUS, *Son of Aristides the Just.*
MELESIAS, *Son of Thucydides.*
ARISTIDES, *Son of Lysimachus,* } *Both of them*
THUCYDIDES, *Son of Melesias,* } *very young.*
NICIAS, *General of the Athenians.*
LACHES, *another Athenian General.*
SOCRATES.

Lysim. Well, Nicias and Laches, you have seen this man parry in armour :* When Melesias and I desired you to come and see this display, we did not tell you the reasons that induced us to it; but now we will tell you, being persuaded that we may speak with entire confidence. Now each of us has a son here: That youth, the son of Melesias, is called Thucydides, his grandfather's name : and this, which is mine, is called Aristides, after my father. We are resolved to take a singular care of their education, and not act as most fathers do, who, when their children become young men, suffer them to live according to their fancy. We design to keep them still in awe, and educate them to the best advantage. And forasmuch as you have likewise children, doubtless you have thought as much as any man upon the method of making them virtuous: or if you have not yet considered of it, by reason of their tender age, we presume you will not take it ill that we put you in mind, that this is an indispensable duty; and call upon you to deliberate with us, what education all of us should give our children. This was the reason of our coming to see you.

Though the discourse may seem long, yet you will have the goodness to hear it. You know, Melesias and I have but one table, and these children eat with us: we shall conceal nothing from you, and, as I told you

---

* I use the same terms as are now in use, because the exercise this man taught was much the same with what is now taught in our fencing-schools. He taught them to fence in armour with sword and buckler, and to resist several combatants at once, by parrying and striking. It is very remarkable, that these sort of fencing-masters were not known at Athens till after the defeat at Delium.

at first, shall speak to you with an entire confidence.
Both he and I have entertained our children with thou-
sands of brave actions done by our fathers both in peace
and war, while they headed the Athenians and their allies:
but to our great misfortune, we can tell them no such thing
of ourselves.   This covers us with shame : we blush for it
before our children, and are forced to cast the blame upon
our fathers; who, after we grew up, suffered us to live in
effeminacy and luxury ; while they were employing all
their care for the interest of the public.   This we incessantly impress upon our children, telling them, that if they
neglect themselves, and disobey us, it will prove a discredit
to them ; whereas, if they will take pains, they may quickly
approve themselves, to be worthy of the name they bear.
They answer, that they will obey us; and upon that account we desired to know what they should be taught, and
what education we should give them, in order to their
greatest improvement.   Some one told us, there was nothing more proper for a young gentleman than fencing; and
extolled to the very heavens this man, who just now performed his exercise before us, and pressed us to come and
see him again.   Accordingly, we thought it convenient
to take you along with us; not only that you might partake of the pleasure, but likewise that you might communicate to us your knowledge; and that we might all consult together upon the care we ought to have of our children.   And this is all I had to say to you.   Now it is your
turn to aid us with your counsel, in telling us, whether
you approve or condemn the exercise of arms; and in advising us, what occupation, and what kind of instruction
we should give our children;—in a word, what method
you propose for the education of your own children.

Nic. Lysimachus, I commend your proposal: I am very
ready to join with you in this deliberation : and will engage that Laches will be as glad as I am to act a part in
the conference.

Lac. You may be sure of that, Nicias. In my judgment,
all that Lysimachus has said against his father and the father
of Melesias, is admirably well said; not only against them,
but against us and all those who embark in the government of a state ; for, as he has remarked, we too often
neglect the education of our children and our domestic
affairs, and regard them no more than if we had neither

house nor family. Lysimachus, you have spoken well; but I am surprised that you should call us to consult with you upon that subject, and not Socrates, our fellow-citizen, who bends all his thoughts to the education of children: pursuing the sciences that are most useful to them, and finding out for them the most suitable occupations.

Lys. What do you say, Laches? Would Socrates direct us in the instruction of youth?

Lac. I assure you he would, Lysimachus.

Nic. And I assure you of the same: for it is not four days since he gave me a music-master for my son, one Damon, brought up by Agathocles; who, besides the excellences of his art, is possessed of all the other qualities that can be desired in a tutor.

Lys. Indeed, Socrates, and you Nicias and Laches, must pardon this ignorance in me and others of my age; we are not acquainted with young people, for we seldom stir abroad, by reason of our old age. But, Socrates, if you have any good counsel to give me, who am your countryman, pray do it: I can say that it is your duty, for you are a friend of our family. Your father Sophroniscus and I were comrades from our infancy; and our friendship lasted till his very death, without interruption. At present, it occurs to me, that I have often heard these children mention the name of Socrates, of whom they speak much good, in their interviews among themselves, but I never thought of asking them if they spoke of Socrates the son of Sophroniscus. And now, pray tell me, children, is this the Socrates I have heard you speak of so often?

Aristides and *Thucydides*, both together. Yes, father, the same.

Lys. I am infinitely glad of that. My dear Socrates, you keep up the reputation of your deceased father admirably well, who was not only very well skilled in his art,* but likewise a very good man. You and I must renew our ancient friendship, and henceforward your interest shall be mine, and mine yours.

Lac. You do well, Lysimachus; do not let him go: for I have seen occasions in which he maintained not only the

* He was an engraver.

reputation of his father, but that of his country. At the defeat of Delium,* he retired along with me : and I can assure you, if all the rest had done their duty as he did, our city would have been admirably well supported, instead of meeting with so great a shock.

Lys. This is a high encomium, Socrates; and by whom is it given ? By persons that are worthy to be credited in all things, especially upon that point for which they applaud you. I assure you, nobody can hear your praises with more pleasure than I do. I am infinitely glad that you have purchased such a reputation, and I enlist myself in the number of your greatest well-wishers. And therefore pray come, without ceremony, to see us, and live with us : since you are of our family, you ought to do it. Let this day be the renewing of our ancient friendship; and from henceforward be familiar with us and these children, to the end that you and they may keep our friendship as a paternal pledge. We hope you will make that use of it; and for our parts we will not suffer you to forget it. But to return to our subject : what do you say ? What think you of this exercise of arms? Does it deserve to be learned by young men ?

Soc. Upon that point, Lysimachus, I shall endeavour to give you the best counsel I am able; and shall not fail to put all your orders in execution. But since I am the youngest, and least experienced of any of you, it is but just that you should speak first; that so, after I have heard you, I may give in my sentiments if I differ from you, and back them with forcible reasons. Let us hear you speak then, Nicias? It is your turn to speak first.

Nic. I will not refuse to give my opinion. In my mind, that exercise is very proper for young people, and merits their application : for besides that it diverts them from the amusements which when unemployed they commonly pursue, it also inures them to labour, and of necessity renders them more strong and vigorous. There is no better exercise; none that requires more strength and dexterity : there is none more suitable to a person of quality than this, and riding the great horse; especially to those of our

* In this battle, Socrates saved Xenophon's life, whose horse was killed under him; and Socrates being on foot, took him upon his back, and carried him away.

profession: In regard to the wars we are already engaged in, and which are likely to come upon us, we must reckon those only true and good exercises, that are performed with the arms used in war; for they are of admirable use, whether in set battles in rank and file, or single combat after the ranks are broken; whether we pursue an enemy that rallies from time to time, or upon a retreat in order to get clear of an obstinate enemy, that pursues us with sword in hand. He who is acquainted with these exercises, will never be afraid of one man, or several together, but will still stand his ground, or get off clear. Besides, these exercises have this advantage, that they inspire their votaries with a passion for another and a higher pursuit: for I suppose all those who give themselves to fencing, think of nothing but the end they proposed in going to be taught, namely, battles and fights; and when engaged in these, are so full of ambition, and so fond of glory, that they carefully instruct themselves in all that belongs to the art of war; and make it their business to rise by degrees to the highest posts in the army. It is manifest, that nothing is more desirable, and more worthy the care of a good man, than these different posts of honour, and all the functions of war, to which this exercise leads. To all these advantages we shall add one more, which is not a small one, it is, that this art of fencing makes men more valiant and more adventurous in engagements; and if we reckon up every thing; there is another advantage that is not to be despised, viz. that it gives men a good appearance and a graceful carriage. So that I am fully of opinion, Lysimachus, that children should learn those exercises; and have now given my reasons for thinking so. If Laches is of another mind, I shall be glad to hear him.

Lac. Indeed, Nicias, he must be a bold man, who says that any science whatever is not worthy to be learned: for it is very commendable to know every thing; and if this exercise of arms is a science, as its teachers allege, and as Nicias says; I admit that it ought to be taught. But if it is not a science, if the fencing-masters impose upon us their bravados, or if it is only an inconsiderable science, to what purpose should we amuse ourselves with it? I mention this, because I am persuaded, that if it were a very considerable science, it would never have escaped the Lacedemonians, who spend their whole lives in inquiring after such

things as may render them superior to their enemies in war.
Nay, supposing it had hitherto escaped the Lacedemonians, *
these fencing-masters could not have been ignorant that of
all the Grecians, the Lacedemonians are the most curious
in what relates to arms; and that masters of any reputation would have made their fortune there much better than
elsewhere, just as tragic poets of any note do here.   For
every one that has a genius for writing tragedies comes
straightly here with them, and does not travel from city to
city to publish his performances.†   Whereas those valiant
champions who teach fencing, look upon Lacedemon as an
inaccessible temple that they dare not approach;‡ and ram-
ble round about it, teaching their art to others, particularly
to those who confess themselves inferior to all their neighbours in whatever relates to war.   In a word, Lysimachus,
I have seen a great many of those masters engaged in hot
actions, and I know perfectly what their humour is, upon
which it is easy to form a just estimate of their merit : It
seems Providence has purposely so ordered it, that none of
that profession ever acquired the least reputation in war.
We see several of other professions, not only successful
in the way of their business, but likewise famous in war.
But these men are unfortunate by a peculiar sort of fata-
lity : for this same Stesilius, who exposed himself before
this crowd of spectators, and spoke so magnificently of
himself ; I say, I have seen this same man make a different display, against his will, upon a better occasion :
When the ship he was in attacked a merchant-man, he fought
with a pike-headed scythe, and all the prowess he shewed
scarcely merits a relation ; but the success of this warlike stratagem, in fixing a scythe on the head of a pike,
is worthy of attention.   While the fellow was fencing with
his new arms, they were unhappily entangled in the tackling of the enemy's ship, and stuck there.   He pulled with
all his force to get it clear, but could not obtain his end.

* They were the most warlike people of all the Grecians, and yet
had no fencing-masters.

† A satirical rub upon Athens, which was as fond of tragedies as
Lacedemon was of arms.

‡ He compares Lacedemon to the temple of the Furies, which
none durst approach; for they had such a terrible impression of
these goddesses, that they durst not either name them, or look upon
them, or offer their addresses to them.   These fencing-masters were
equally afraid of Lacedemon.   A noble eulogy.

While his ship kept close to the other, he followed it, and kept his hold; but when the enemy's ship steered off, and was going to haul him in, he suffered his pike to slip by degrees through his hands, till he had only hold of it by the small end. The enemy's crew made huzzas, upon the pleasant accident; at length, somebody having thrown a stone that just fell at his feet, he quitted his beloved arms, and the enemy redoubled their shouts, when they saw the armed sickle hanging upon the tackling of their ship like a trophy. It is possible that, as Nicias says, it may be a very considerable and useful science; but I tell you what I have seen: so that, as I said in the beginning, if it is a science, it is a useless one; and if it is none, and we are only inveigled by its fine name, then it does not deserve our regard. In a word, those who apply themselves to that art, are either cowards or brave men; if cowards, they are the more insolent, and their cowardice is only the more exposed : if brave, all the world has their eyes upon them; and if they happen to be guilty of a false step, they must bear a thousand jests and railleries : for this is not an indifferent profession; it exposes them to perpetual envy; and if the man that follows it, does not highly distinguish himself by his courage, he will be ridiculed, and has no possibility of avoiding it. These are my thoughts of that exercise : it remains that you request Socrates to give us his opinion.

Lys. Pray do so, Socrates; for we want an umpire to decide the difference. Had Nicias and Laches been of one opinion, we should have spared you the trouble: but you see they are directly opposite. So that now our business is to hear your judgment, and see which of the two you agree with.

Soc. What! Lysimachus, are you for following the greatest number then?

Lys. How can one do better ?

Soc. And you, Melesias? Were you to choose exercises to be learned by your son, would you rather be directed by a great number, than by one man that has been well educated himself, and has had excellent masters?

Mel. For my part, Socrates, I would be directed by the latter.

Soc. You would be more influenced by his opinion, than by that of us all?

Mel. Perhaps I might.

Soc. Because a wise judgment ought to be formed from knowledge, and not from the multitude?

Mel. Without doubt.

Soc. The first thing then that we are to enquire into, is, whether any of us is expert in the thing we consult about, or not? If any one is, we must refer ourselves to him, and leave the others; if not, we must see for some such man elsewhere: for do you, Melesias and Lysimachus, imagine that this is a business of small consequence, and that you run but an ordinary risk? Do not deceive yourselves! the matter in hand relates to the greatest imaginable good. All the happiness of families depend upon the education of children: and houses rise or sink according as their children are virtuous or vicious.

Mel. You say well.

Soc. So that one cannot be too cautious and prudent upon this occasion.

Mel. Most certainly.

Soc. How then should we know which of us is most expert and best skilled in the exercises? Should not we presently pitch upon him who learned them best, and followed them most, and had the best masters?

Mel. So I think.

Soc. And before that, should we not endeavour to know the thing itself that we would have our children learn?

Mel. What do you mean?

Soc. Perhaps you will understand me better in this manner: we did not at first agree upon the nature of the thing we are consulting about, in order to know which of us is most dexterous at it, and was taught by the greatest master.

Nic. Are not we, Socrates, considering of fencing, in order to know whether our children ought to learn it, or not?

Soc. I do not say otherwise: but when a man advises about a remedy for the eyes, and wants to know whether he should apply it, or not; do you think this consultation relates more to the remedy than to the eyes, to which it is to be applied?

Nic. It relates most to the eyes.

Soc. And when a man consults what bit he should put upon his horse, does not the question relate more to the horse than to the bit?

Nic. Yes, surely.

Soc. In a word, as often as a man advises about a thing with reference to another, the direct object of the consultation is the thing referred to,* and not that which is only regarded for the sake of the other.

Nic. It is necessarily so.

Soc. Then we ought to examine well whether the man we advise with, is expert and skilled in the thing about which we advise.

Nic. That is certain.

Soc. At present we are consulting what our children should learn; so that the question turns upon the children, and the knowledge of their mental powers is our first concern.

Nic. Just so.

Soc. And by consequence the question is, whether there is any of us experienced in the culture of the mind? who knows how to direct it, and has been taught that art by the best masters?

Lac. Did you, Socrates, never know any persons that have become greater proficients in some sciences and arts without a master, than others with all the masters that could be obtained for them?

Soc. Yes, Laches, I have known some: but though any of that sort of men should be proud of telling you that they are very skilful, you would never trust the least affair to them, unless you had seen them make, I will not say one, but several elaborate and skilful exhibitions?

Nic. Right, Socrates.

Soc. Since Lysimachus and Melesias have called us to give our advice of the education of their children; we are obliged, O Nicias and Laches, if we pretend to be endowed

* For instance, when we think of purging a sick person, we consider of the patient before we think of the dose: and having first discovered the state of the patient, then we think of a proper medicine.

with the capacity that is necessary for it, to tell them what masters we had, that they were very good men, and that, having instructed several scholars, they had formed and disposed their minds to virtue. And if any of us pretends to have had no master, he must produce his performances, and instance in some either among the Athenians, or among foreigners, who have been benefited by his precepts. If we can neither name our master, nor shew our works, we must send our friends for advice elsewhere, and not expose ourselves to just reproach upon a point of so much importance. For my part, Lysimachus and Melesias, I acknowledge I never had a master for that science, notwithstanding that from my youth I was passionately in love with it: but I had not money enough to reach the high fees of those sophists, who boasted they were the only men that could benefit me; and by my own ingenuity I have not yet been able to find out the art. If Nicias and Laches have compassed it by themselves, or have learned it of masters, I shall not be surprised, for being richer than I am, they could afford to have masters; and being older, they may have learned it of themselves: and upon that account I consider them admirably well qualified for instructing a· young gentleman. And besides, if they had not been very well assured of their own capacity, they would never have been so positive in determining what exercises are useful, and what useless to youth: so that I submit to them in all things. But what surprises me, is, that they are of two different opinions: however, since Laches entreated you to detain me, and oblige me to speak, pray let me implore you, in my turn, not to suffer Laches and Nicias to go, but press them to answer, by telling them that Socrates knows nothing of these matters, and is unable to determine which of them is right: That he had no masters, and could not find out the art by himself. Wherefore, Nicias and Laches, pray tell us if ever you knew any excellent man for the education of youth? Did you learn this art from any one, or did you find it out of yourselves? If you learned it, pray tell us who was your master, and who they are that follow the same profession; to the end that, if the public affairs do not afford you so much leisure, we may go to them, and by presents and caresses engage them to take care of our children and yours, to prevent their reflecting dishonour upon their ancestors by their vices. If you found out this art by your own ingenuity, pray name those you have instructed; who, being vicious before coming to you, became virtuous under your care. If you are but yet beginning to teach; take care that you do not make your first essay upon base souls; but upon your own children, and those of your best friends. Tell us then what you can do, and what not. This, Lysimachus, is what I would have you ask of them: do not let them go without giving you an answer.

Lys. In my mind, Socrates speaks admirably well. Wherefore, my friends, consider of answering all these questions; for you may assure yourselves that in so doing, you will oblige me and Melesias very much. I told you before, that the reason we called for your advice, was, that since you, as well as ourselves, have children that will quickly be of that age which requires a wise education, you might ere now have thought maturely upon it. If, then, you are at leisure, pray discuss the matter with Socrates; for, as he has well said, this is the most important affair of our lives.

Nic. It seems, Lysimachus, you have no knowledge of Socrates, otherwise than by his father, and that you have never frequented his company. You never saw him, surely, but in his infancy, in the temples or public assemblies, or when his father brought him to your house.

Lys. What ground have you for that supposition, Nicias?

Nic. That I perceive you are ignorant that Socrates looks upon everybody as his neighbour; and that he is as much obliged to every one who converses with him, as if he were his relation. Though at first he speaks only of indifferent things, yet at last he who converses with him is obliged, by the thread of his discourse, to give him an account of the conduct of his life, and to tell him how he lives, and has lived. And when Socrates has once brought him thus far, he does not part with him till he has sounded him to the bottom, and got an account of all his good and evil actions. I know it by experience. There is a necessity of passing that

N

ordeal: I find that I myself cannot get off, and I am very glad of it; for I always take a singular pleasure in discoursing with him. It is no great harm for a man to be informed of his faults, and after that he will become more wise and prudent, if he attend to and love the admonition, and, according to Solon's maxim, is willing to be instructed, whatever his age, and is not foolishly persuaded that old age necessarily brings wisdom along with it. So that it shall neither seem new nor disagreeable to me, if Socrates puts me to a trial. And, indeed I was aware from the beginning, that since he was here, it would not be our children, but ourselves that would be examined. For my part, I submit to him with all my heart. It remains that Laches should tell his sentiments.

Lac. My sentiments are various. Sometimes I am in one humour, and sometimes in another. Sometimes I love nothing so much as discoursing, and at other times I cannot endure it. When I meet with a man that speaks well of virtue or any science, and find him a man of veracity, and worthy of his profession, I am charmed with him, and take an inexpressible pleasure in observing the harmony of his words and actions. Such a man is to me the only excellent musician that produces a perfect concord, not with the harp or musical instruments, but with the sum total of his life. For all his actions suit with his words, not according to the Lydian, Phrygian, or Ionian tones, but according to the Dorian; which is the only one that deserves the name of Grecian harmony.* When such a man speaks, I am overjoyed and charmed; and drink in his words so greedily, that everybody perceives me to be fond of his discourses. But a man that acts the contrary, mortifies me most cruelly; and the more he seems to

* The Grecians had four measures or tones which they called Harmonies, and multiplied by joining them with others. The Lydian was doleful, and proper for lamentation; the Phrygian was vehement, and fit to raise the passions; the Ionian effeminate and soft; the Dorick was masculine, and so preferred by Socrates to all the rest. Accordingly, Aristotle, in the last chapter of his Politics, says, That all the world agreed that the Dorick was most manly and smooth, and a sort of medium between the others: upon which account it was more proper and suitable for children. Plato absolutely condemns the Lydian and Ionian in the Third Book of his Republic.

speak well, the more aversion I have to him. I am not yet acquainted with Socrates by his words, but by his actions I am; and think him worthy to discourse with all freedom upon any subject. I am therefore willing to enter into a conference with him, and shall be very glad if he will take the pains to examine me. I shall never be unwilling to learn; for I am of Solon's opinion, that we ought to be learning all our lives. I would only add a word to his maxim, which I wish he had added, viz. That we should learn of good men. In earnest, you must grant me this, That a teacher ought to be a good man, that I may not learn of him with reluctancy, and that my disrelish may not pass for stupidity and indocility. For it matters not to me if my master be younger than myself, and has not yet gained a reputation. So, Socrates, if you will examine and instruct me, you shall find me very docile and submissive. I have always had a good opinion of you since the day that you and I escaped a considerable danger, and you gave such proof of your virtue. Tell me, then, what you please; and let not my age be any hindrance.

Soc. At least we cannot complain that you are not very ready to ask good counsel and follow it.

Lys. This is our business; I call it ours, because it is upon our account that you are engaged in it. Wherefore, I beseech you for the love of these children, see, in my stead, what we ought to ask of Nicias and Laches, and join your thoughts in conference with theirs. As for me, my memory is almost gone, by reason of my old age. I forget most of the questions I designed to ask, and a great part of what was said. I remember nothing of the matter, when the principal question is crossed by fresh incidents. Discuss this matter among yourselves; I and Melesias will hear you; and after that, shall do as you direct us.

Soc. Nicias and Laches, we must obey Lysimachus and Melesias. Perhaps it will not be improper to discuss the question we before proposed, viz. Whether we had masters in this art, or if we have formed any scholars, and rendered them better men than they were? But there may be a shorter way of compassing our end, and at the same time of going nearer to the source; for if we have a certain knowledge of anything, that being communicated to another, will render him better, and have likewise the secret of communicating it to him; it is plain, not only that we know the thing itself, but that we know what means are to be employed in acquiring it.* Perhaps you do not understand me; but an example will illustrate my meaning. If we know certainly that sight communicated to the eyes, renders them better, and are able to communicate it; it is certain we know what the sight is, and all that is to be done for procuring it. Whereas, if we do not know what seeing or hearing is, our advice will be to no purpose; we cannot pretend to be good physicians, either for the eyes or ears, or to furnish them with the means of seeing or hearing.

Lys. You say well, Socrates.

Soc. Have not your two friends called you, Laches, to advise with us, how virtue may be best implanted in the minds of their children?

Lac. They have.

Soc. Is it not necessary then, that, in the first place, we should know what virtue is? for if we are ignorant of that, how should we be capable of prescribing means for acquiring it?

Lac. By no means, Socrates.

Soc. Then it is presumed you know what it is?

Lac. Without doubt.

Soc. But when we know a thing, cannot we tell what it is?

Lac. Yes, surely.

Soc. At present we shall not enter upon the enquiry, what virtue is in general: that would be too long, and too perplexed a task: let us content ourselves with tracing one of its branches, and try if we have all that is necessary for knowing that well. This will be a shorter and easier enquiry.

Lac. If you are of that mind, I am satisfied.

Soc. But what branch of virtue shall we select? shall

---

* This is an important and very useful principle. Socrates's scope is, to make them sensible, that men may well know the vices and faults of one another, and the virtues they all want to make them perfect, but do not know how to communicate it. God alone knows our weakness and misery, and he alone can heal it.

it be that which seems to be the only end of FENCING; for the people allege, that this exercise tends directly to VALOUR?

Lac. Yes, that is the point.

Soc. Let us endeavour, Laches, in the first place to give an exact definition of valour; and then we shall pursue the means of communicating it to these children, as much as possible, both by habit and by study. Say then, what is valour? -

Lac. Indeed, Socrates, that is not a very difficult question. A valorous man is one who maintains his post in battle, who never turns his back, and who repulses the enemy.

Soc. Very well, Laches; but perhaps it is my faulty expression that occasioned your giving an answer remote from my question.

Lac. What do you mean, Socrates?

Soc. I will tell you, if I can. A valiant man is one that keeps his post, and bravely attacks the enemy.

Lac. That is what I say.

Soc. So I say too. But as to him that fights the enemy upon a flight, and without keeping his post?

Lac. How, upon a flight?

Soc. In fleeing; as the Scythians, for instance; who fight as fiercely upon a retreat, as upon a pursuit: and as Homer says in commendation of Æneas's horses, they were swifter than the wind, in the field of battle, and knew how to escape and how to pursue an enemy. And does not he commend Æneas for his skill in the art of fleeing, when he calls them expert in retreat?

Lac. That is very true, Socrates; for Homer in that place speaks of chariots. And as for the Scythians, you know they had troops of cavalry; for that was their way to engage with horse: but our Grecian infantry fight by standing their ground.

Soc. Perhaps you will except the Lacedemonians; for I have heard, in the battle of Platea, when the Lacedemonians were engaged with the Gerrophori, who had made a bulwark of their bucklers, and killed many of their men with their arrows; that the Lacedemonians, on this occasion, thought it not proper to keep their post, but fled: and when the Persian ranks were disordered in the pursuit, rallied and attacked the cavalry you speak of, and by that means gained a noble victory.

Lac. You say true.

Soc. And for that reason, as I told you, I occasioned your faulty answer by putting the question amiss. For I want to know what valour is in a man, that is valiant not only in cavalry, but in infantry, and all other sorts of war; that is, not only valiant in war, but in dangers at sea; in diseases, in poverty, in the management of public affairs; not only valorous in grief, sorrow, and fears, but likewise in his desires and pleasures; a man that knows how to make head against his passions, whether by standing his ground, or fleeing. For valour extends to all these things.

Lac. That is certain.

Soc. Then all these men are valiant. One displays his courage by opposing his pleasures, another by restraining his sorrow: one controuls his desires, and another his fears: and upon all these occasions a man may be cowardly and mean-spirited.

Lac. Without doubt.

Soc. So I wanted to know of you, what each of these contraries, valour and cowardice is. To begin with valour: tell me, if you can, what is this quality that is always the same, upon all those different occasions? Do you understand me now?

Lac. Not perfectly.

Soc. What I would say, is this. For instance, if I asked you what that swiftness is, which extends itself to running, playing upon instruments, speaking, learning, and a thousand other things. For we apply swiftness to the actions of the hands, feet, tongue, and mind: these are the principal subjects. Is it not so?

Lac. Yes.

Soc. If any one asked me, what this swiftness is, that extends to all these different things? I would answer, it is a faculty that does much in a little space of time. For this definition agrees to the voice, to running, and all the other things that the word can be applied to.

Lac. Right, Socrates; the definition is very good.

Soc. Define valour then after the same manner. Tell me what faculty this is, that is always the same in pleasures, in affliction, and in all the above mentioned cases; and that never changes either its name or its nature.

Lac. Since I must give a definition, including all the different species of that virtue; it seems to me to be a disposition of the soul always ready to suffer any thing.

Soc. To answer my question fully, your definition must certainly be such. But this definition seems also defective: for, I suppose, you do not take all the patience of the soul to be valour. I see plainly you place valour in the number of fine things.

Lac. Yes, without doubt; and indeed the finest that is.

Soc. Accordingly this patience of the soul, when accompanied with wisdom, is good and fine?

Lac. Most certainly.

Soc. And when imprudence is its companion, is it not quite the contrary? Is it not then bad and pernicious?

Lac. Without question.

Soc. Do you call a pernicious thing fine?

Lac. God forbid, Socrates!

Soc. Then you will never call that sort of patience by the name of valour, since it is not fine; and valour is somewhat that is very fine.

Lac. You say right.

Soc. Then, according to you, a wise and prudent patience is wisdom?

Lac. So I think.

Soc. Let us see whether this patience is only prudent in some things, or in every thing, whether small or great? For instance: a man spends his estate very patiently and prudently, with a firm certainty, that his spending will one day procure him great riches: would you call this man valiant and stout?

Lac. I would be very loath to do that, Socrates.

Soc. But a physician has a son or some other patient lying ill of an inflammation in the breast. This son teazes him for something to eat. The physician is so far from yielding to his importunity, that he patiently bears his complaints and his anger: Would you call this physician valiant?

Lac. No more than the other.

Soc. But as for war. Here is a man of that disposition of soul we now speak of. He has a mind to fight; and his prudence supporting his courage, tells him he will quickly be relieved, and that his enemies are the weaker party, and that he has the advantage of the ground. This brave man, that is thus prudent, will you make him more valiant and courageous than his enemy, who stands his ground, notwithstanding the disadvantages he lies under, and that too without these considerations ?

Lac. No, surely; the last is the bravest.*

Soc. And, after all, the courage of the last is far less prudent than that of the former.

Lac. That is true.

Soc. Then it follows from your principle, that a good horseman, who in an engagement behaves himself bravely, and trusts to his dexterity of managing a horse, is less courageous than he who wants that advantage.

Lac. Yes.

Soc. You will say the same of an archer, a slinger, and all the other orders of soldiery ?

Lac. Without doubt.

Soc. And those, who, without being acquainted with the art of diving, have the courage to dive, and are the first who throw their heads into the waters, are, according to you, more bold and courageous than the expert divers ?

Lac. Yes, certainly.

Soc. According to your principle it must be so.

Lac. These are my principles.

Soc. But, after all: those artless and inexperienced men encounter danger much more imprudently than those who expose themselves with the advantage of art.

Lac. Yes, certainly.

Soc. But we concluded just now, that indiscreet bold- ness and imprudent patience, are very scandalous and per- nicious.

Lac. That is true.

Soc. And we looked upon valour to be a good and a fine thing.

Lac. I grant it.

Soc. And do you think it is well done ?

Lac. I am not so foolish, Socrates.

Soc. Thus, Laches, by your own principles, you and I

* Socrates makes Laches fall into the common prejudice, that an imprudent and indiscreet temerity is valour.

are not upon the foot of the Dorick tone; for our actions
do not agree with our words. If one took a view of our
actions, I presume he would say we are men of courage.
But if he heard our words, he would quickly change his
sentiments.

Lac. You say right, Socrates.

Soc. But do you think it fit that we should continue in
this condition?

Lac. No, certainly.

Soc. Are you willing we should for a minute act conformably to the definition we gave just now?

Lac. What definition is that?

Soc. That true courage or true valour is patience. If
you please, then, let us shew our patience in carrying on
our enquiry, that so valour may not laugh at us for pursuing her without courage; since, according to our principles, patience is courage.

Lac. I am willing, Socrates, and shall not at all
flinch, though I am a novice in such disputes. But I
must own I am out of humour and vexed that I cannot explain my thoughts; for I think I conceive perfectly
what valour is. But the idea so baffles me, that I cannot
explain it.

Soc. But, Laches, a good huntsman ought to follow the
animal he pursues, and not weary himself in running after
every thing he sees.

Lac. I admit it

Soc. Are you willing we should call Nicias to hunt with
us, to try if he will have any better fortune?

Lac. With all my heart, Socrates.

Soc. Come then, Nicias, and help your friends. You see
the condition we are in, and how impossible it is for us to
get clear of it. Pray rescue us, by shewing what valour is,
and proving it.

Nic. I thought all along that you defined this virtue
amiss. How comes it to pass, Socrates, that you do not
upon this occasion make use of what I have heard you
speak so often and so well?

Soc. What is that, Nicias?

Nic. I have often heard you say, that a man is dextrous
at the things he knows, but very unhappy at what he does
not know.

Soc. That is very true.

Nic. And by consequence, if a valiant man be good at anything, he is good at what he knows.

Soc. Do you hear him, Laches?

Lac. Yes, I hear him; but I do not well understand what he means.

Soc. But methinks I perceive his meaning. As I take it, he means that valour is a science.

Lac. What science, Socrates?

Soc. Why do you not ask him?

Lac. I desire the same favour of him.

Soc. Nicias, answer Laches a little, and tell him what science valour is in your opinion; for it is neither the science of playing upon the flute, nor that of playing upon the harp.

Nic. No, surely.

Soc. What is it then?

Lac. You ask him well, Socrates; let him tell us, then, what science it is.

Nic. I say, Laches, that it is the science of things that are terrible, and of those that do not surpass our strength, and in which one may show a steadfastness, whether it be in war, or in other contingencies of life.*

Lac. A strange definition, Socrates!

Soc. Why do you think it so strange?

Lac. Why, because science and valour are two very different things.

Soc. Nicias pretends they are not.

Lac. Yes, he pretends it, which is foolish.

Soc. Then let us endeavour to instruct him; reproaches are not reasons.

Nic. He has no design to abuse me, but he wishes that what I have said may be of no weight, because he himself has been deceived all along.

* Nicias himself knew not all the strength of this definition; he understood only, that valour was the effect of experience and custom. For example, men who have run through many dangers, are commonly more valiant than those who have never seen any; for, as they have already escaped those dangers, they believe that they may likewise overcome all others. This is the sentiment of Nicias; but it is not that of Socrates, who, from his definition, draws a principle far more excellent, as will be seen by what follows.

Lac. It is very true, and I shall die of grief, or make it appear that you have not spoken better than myself. Without going any further, do not the physicians know what there is that is dangerous in diseases ? Do the most valiant men know it better ? Or do you call the physicians valiant men ?

Nic. No, surely.

Lac. Neither do you give that name to labourers; yet they know what it is that is most to be feared in their labours. It is the same with all other tradesmen : they all know very well what is most terrible in their profession, and what it is that may give them assurance and confidence : but they are not the more valiant for that.

Soc. What say you, Nicias, of that criticism of Laches? For my part, I think there is something in it.

Nic. It certainly has something in it, but nothing of truth.

Soc. How so ?

Nic. Because he thinks that physicians know more of diseases, than to say that a thing is healthful or unhealthful. It is very certain that they know nothing more of it : for, in good earnest, Laches, do you imagine that the physician knows whether his patient has more reason to be afraid of health or of sickness? And do not you think that there are abundance of sick to whom it would be more advantageous not to be cured, than to be cured ? Dare you say that it is always good to live, and that there are not abundance of people to whom it would be more advantageous to die.

Lac. I am persuaded that there are some people who would be more happy to die.

Nic. And do you think that the things that seem terrible to those who would willingly live, appear the same to those who had rather die.

Lac. No, doubtless.

Nic. And who will you be judged by on these occasions? The physicians. They do not in the least see into it. People of other professions know nothing of the matter. It belongs then only to those who are skilful in the science of terrible things; and it is those whom I call valiant.

Soc. Laches, do you understand what Nicias says ?

Lac. Yes, I understand that according to his reckoning there is none valiant but prophets : for who else but a prophet can know if it be more advantageous to die than to live ? And I would ask you, Nicias, Are you a prophet?* If you are not, farewell to your valour.

Nic. How then ? Do you think it is the business of a prophet to know himself in things that are terrible, and in those wherein he can shew steadfastness ?

Lac. Without doubt, and whose business is it else ?

Nic. Whose ! His of whom I speak, the valiant man ; for the business of a prophet is only to know the signs of things that are to happen, as of deaths, diseases, losses, defeats, and victories, whether it be in war or in other combats; and do you think, that it is more proper for him, than for another man, to judge which of all those accidents are more or less advantageous to this man or that ? Never had any prophet the least thought of such a thing.

Lac. Truly, Socrates, I cannot comprehend his meaning; for according to his account, there is neither prophet, nor physician, nor any other sort of men, to whom the name of valiant can be applicable. This valiant person, of whom he has an idea, must then be God. But to tell you my thoughts : Nicias has not the courage to confess, that he knows not what he says; he only quibbles and shifts to conceal his confusion. You and I could have done as much, if we had had nothing else in view but to hide the contradictions we fall into. If we were before a judge, this conduct might perhaps be reasonable ; it is a piece of cunning to entangle a bad cause ; but in conversations like ours, to what purpose is it to endeavour to triumph by vain discourse ?

Soc. Certainly that is a very ill thing : but let us see if Nicias does not pretend to say something to the purpose, and whether you do not injure him by accusing him of talking merely for talking's sake. Let us desire him to explain his thoughts to us more fully; and if we find that he has reason on his side, we will be of his mind; if not, we will endeavour to speak better.

---

* Laches jeers Nicias here in obscure terms, because of his respect to the diviners; for he was a very religious man, he had a great respect for all diviners, and kept one always in his house.

Lac. Ask him yourself, Socrates, if you please; I have asked questions enough of him.

Soc. I will do it: I will argue with him both for you and me.

Lac. If you please.

Soc. Tell me, I pray you, Nicias, or rather tell us, for I speak also for Laches, do you maintain that valour is the knowledge of things that are terrible, and of things in which one may testify some assurance and confidence?

Nic. Yes, I do maintain it.

Soc. You maintain also, that this knowledge is not given to all sorts of people, seeing it is not known either to the physicians, or to the prophets, and yet that nobody can be valiant without this knowledge. Is not this what you said?

Nic. Yes, doubtless.

Soc. Then we may apply the proverb in this case: "That it is not the same of every wild sow; every wild sow is not valiant and courageous."

Nic. No, surely.

Soc. It is evident from this, Nicias, that you are fully persuaded, that the wild sow of Crommion* was not courageous, whatever the ancients have said of her. I do not tell you this in jest, but in good earnest: he who speaks as you do, must not of necessity admit of any courage in beasts, or grant, that the lions, leopards, and boars, know many things which most men are ignorant of. Besides, he who maintains that valour is what you say it is, must also maintain, that lions, bulls, harts, foxes, are born equally valiant with one another.

Lac. By all that is sacred, Socrates, you speak to admiration. Tell us truly then, Nicias, do you believe that beasts, which are generally reckoned full of courage, are more understanding than we? or dare you go against the common opinion, and maintain that they have not courage?

Nic. I tell you in a word, Laches, that I do not call either beast or man, or any thing whatever, that through

---

* The aim of Socrates is to try Nicias, and to shake him in his opinion, by making him fear that his principle would hurt their religion: for if the wild sow of Crommion had not been valiant and courageous, Theseus is not so great a hero for having overcome her, nor Hercules for having defeated the lion of Nemea.

imprudence or ignorance fears not the things that are terrible, valiant and courageous; but I call them fearless and senseless. Alas! do you think that I call all children, who through imprudence, fear no danger, valiant and courageous? In my opinion, to be without fear, and to be valiant, are two very different things: there is nothing more rare than valour accompanied with prudence; and nothing more common than boldness, audaciousness, and intrepidity, accompanied with imprudence; for it is the property of most men and women, and of all beasts and children. In a word, those whom you and most people call valiant, I call rash and fool-hardy; and I give the name of valiant only to those who are prudent and wise: these only are the persons I mean.

Lac. Do you see, Socrates,* how he offers incense to himself, as if he were the only valiant man; for he strives to rob all those, who pass for such, of that glory.

Nic. That is none of my design, Laches; do not you fret yourself, I know that you and Lamachus,† are prudent and wise, if you be valiant. I say the same of many of our Athenians.

Lac. Though I could answer you in your own way, yet I will not, lest you should accuse me of being ill-natured and detracting.‡

Soc. Do not say so, Laches, I see plainly you do not perceive that Nicias hath learned these fine things of our friend Damon, and that Damon is the intimate friend of Prodicus, the ablest of all the sophists for those kind of distinctions.

Lac. Oh, Socrates, it becomes a sophist very well to make ostentation of his vain subtilties; but for a man

---

* Wisdom and prudence were the true character of Nicias, who undertook nothing but where he saw at least an apparent safety, and who, by waiting for opportunities to act safely, did often let them slip; which procured him the character of a cowardly man, although he undertook and executed things well, performing his part always in an admirable manner.

† It is that Lamachus who was general of the Athenians with Nicias and Alcibiades in the expedition of Sicily, where he was killed.

‡ The Greek copy says, " lest you should take me for a man of the tribe of Axionides:" for the people of that tribe were much cried down for their railing temper and ill-nature.

like Nicias, whom the Athenians have chosen to sit at the helm of the republic—

Soc. My dear Laches, it well becomes a man who hath so great affairs upon his hands, to study to be more learned and more wise than others; wherefore I think that Nicias deserves to be heard, and that we ought at least to enquire into his reasons why he defines valour thus.

Lac. Enquire then as much as you please, Socrates.

Soc. It is what I am about to do; but do not think that I acquit you of it, and that you shall not assist me in some things. Listen a little then, and take heed to what I am going to say.

Lac. I shall do so, since it pleases you.

Soc. That is so far well: now come on, Nicias; pray tell us, in resuming the matter from the beginning, is it not true, that at first we considered valour as a part of virtue?*

Nic. It is true.

Soc. Did you not answer, that valour was certainly but one part, and that there were other parts, which all together were called by the name VIRTUE?

Nic. How could I say otherwise?

Soc. You say then as I do: for, besides valour, I acknowledge there are other parts of virtue, as temperance, justice, and many others; do not you also acknowledge them?

Nic. Doubtless I do.

Soc. That is good; we are agreed upon this point; let us go then to those things which we call terrible, and wherein you say a man may shew some assurance and confidence; let us examine them well, lest it happen that you understand them one way, and we another; we are going to tell you what we think of them. If you do not agree with us, you will correct us. We believe the things which you call terrible, are such as inspire people with fear and terror; and that those wherein you say we may shew some assurance, are such as do not inspire us with that fear. Now those that cause fear, are neither things that have already happened, nor things that actually happen, but such as we expect: for fear is only the

* Socrates would prove, that virtue being one, he, who has not all the parts that compose it, cannot boast of being virtuous.

expectation of an evil to come.   Are you not of this opinion, Laches?

Lac. Yes, perfectly.

Soc. This then is our opinion, Nicias. By those things that are terrible, we understand the evils to come; and by the things wherein one may shew some assurance, we understand those things which are also to come, and which appear good, or at least do not appear ill. Do you admit our definition, or not?

Nic. Yes, I admit it.

Soc. Then the knowledge of those things, is what you call valour?

Nic. Yes, it is.

Soc. Let us go to a third point, and see if we can agree upon that also.

Nic. What is that?

Soc. You shall hear presently. We say, (that is, Laches and I) that in all things science never differs from itself;* it is not one thing, as things past, to know how they passed; another, as to the things present, to know how they are, and how they happen; and another upon the things to come, to know how they will be; but it is always the same: for example, as to health, let the time be what it will, Physic never differs from itself, it is always the same art that judges of it, and that sees what has been, what is, and what will be healthful or unhealthful. Husbandry in the same manner judges of what has come, of what is now come, and of what will come. And as to war, you can very well testify, and will be believed, that the art of a General extends itself to all, to what is past, what is present, and what is to come; that he has no occasion for the art of Divination, but that on the contrary has it at command, as knowing what

---

* Socrates would make Nicias understand, that in defining valour to be the knowledge of things that are terrible, that is to say, of evils to come, he has not been large enough in his definition; for knowledge extending itself to what is past, what is present, and what is to come, valour must have all that extent, if it be truly a science. Then we must say, that it is the knowledge of all the evil and of all the good that hath been, that is, and that shall be; for valour ought no less to judge of what has been, and of what is, than of what will be. But of what use is all this: that Socrates will make plain by and by.

happens, and what ought to happen. Is not the law
itself express in that? For it commands not that the
diviner shall command the general, but that the general
shall command the diviner.* Is not this what we say,
Laches?

Lac. Yes certainly, Socrates.

Soc. And you, Nicias, do you also say as we do, and do
you agree, that knowledge, being always the same, judges
equally of what is past, present, and to come?

Nic. I say as you say; for I think it cannot be otherwise.

Soc. You admit then, most excellent Nicias, that valour
is the knowledge of things that are terrible, and of those
that are not so? Is not that what you say?

Nic. Yes.

Soc. Have we not agreed, that those things that are
terrible, are evils to come, and those things that are not
terrible, and in which we can shew some assurance, is some
good that we expect.

Nic. We are agreed upon it.

Soc. And that knowledge, does not extend itself only to
what is to come, but also to things present, and to what
is past.

Nic. I agree to it.

Soc. Then it is not true, that valour is only the knowledge of things that are terrible, and of those that are not
terrible; for it does not only know the good and the evil
that is to come, but its jurisdiction extends as far as that
of other sciences, and it also judges of what is past, and
of what is present, and, in a word, of all things, whether
they be near at hand, or at a distance.

Nic. That seems to be true.

Soc. Then you have only defined to us the third part of
valour, but we desired you to give us a full definition of
it: at present it seems to me, that, according to your principle, it is the knowledge not only of things that are
terrible and not terrible,† but also of almost all the good

* If the diviner commanded the general, he would then be general himself.

† Socrates will have us understand, that valour puts us in a condition to attract the good, and to avoid the evil that may happen to
us, on the part of man and on the part of God; for it may serve to

and all the evil, at what distance soever they be from us, before or after. Have you then changed your opinion, Nicias? what do you say?

Nic. It appears to me, that valour has all the extent you claim for it?

Soc. That being granted, do you think that a valiant man wants any part of virtue, if he knows all the good and all the evils that have been, that are, and that may be? and do you believe, that such a man can want temperance, justice, and sanctity? he to whom alone it belongs to use a prudent precaution against all the evils that may happen to him on the part of God, and to put himself in a condition to draw from thence all the good that can be expected, seeing he knows how he ought to behave himself both towards man and towards God.

Nic. What you say, Socrates, seems to have something in it.

Soc. Valour then is not a part of virtue, but is virtue in all its parts?

Nic. So it seems.

Soc. Yet we said, that it was but a part of it.

Nic. We did so.

Soc. And what we said then does not now appear to be true.

Nic. I admit it.

Soc. And consequently, Nicias, we have not yet found out what valour is.

Nic. It seems so, Socrates.*

Lac. Yet I should have thought, my dear Nicias, by the contempt you showed me, when I was answering Socrates, that you would have found it out better than

---

correct what is past, to dispose well of what is present, and to use wise precautions against what is to come. It is so solid a principle, that nothing can shake it.

* Nicias does not comprehend that which Socrates makes him almost touch with his finger, that virtue cannot be divided, and that each of its parts is virtue entire. Valour is not without temperance, sanctity, and justice, and there is not one of these without valour. But how comes it that Nicias and Laches do not understand this language? It is because they were used to the unhappy distinctions of sophists, who had filled their minds with their false notions, and who had ruined virtue, by dividing and cutting it in pieces. This will be explained more at large in the following dialogue.

another: and I had great hopes that, with the assistance of Damon's high wisdom, you would have accomplished it very well.

Nic. Cheer up, Laches, that is admirable. You think it nothing that you appeared very ignorant of what relates to valour, provided I appear as ignorant as yourself; you regard nothing but that; and you believe yourself no way blameable, when you have me for a companion in the ignorance which is so scandalous to men of quality: but that is the humour of men, they never look to themselves, but always to others. For my part, I think I am answered indifferently well. If I am deceived in any thing, I do not pretend to be infallible, I shall undeceive myself, by taking instruction, whether it be from Damon, whom you would so willingly ridicule, or from any others: and when I am well instructed, I will communicate my knowledge to you; for I am not envious, and you seem to me to have great need of instruction.

Lac. And for you, Nicias, if we may believe you, you will suddenly be the eighth wise man: In the mean time, for all this fine reasoning, I advise Lysimachus and Melesias to get rid of us and our good counsels for the education of their children, and fix only upon Socrates; as for my part, if my children were old enough, I should at once do so.

Nic. Oh! as for that I agree with you. If Socrates will take care of our children, we need not look out for another master, and I am ready to give him my son, if he will be so good as to take charge of him: but always, when I speak to him of it, he recommends me to other masters, and refuses me his assistance. Try then, Lysimachus, if you can have any more power over him, and if he will have so much complaisance for you.

Lys. It would be an act of justice. For my part, I could entrust to him what I would not do to many others.* What do you say then, Socrates? will you suffer yourself to be prevailed upon, and will you take charge of these children to make them virtuous?

* This passage must not be translated as Des Serres translated it. "I would give him more." Lysimachus had no thoughts of speaking of a salary; that would have offended Socrates, who did not teach for money; nor does the Greek expression bear more than I have said

Soc. He must be a very strange and cruel man that will not contribute to make children as honest as they can be. For my part, if in the conversation we have now had together, I had appeared more learned, and the rest more ignorant, I would have thought you had reason to choose me preferably to others: but you see very well, that we labour all under the same uncertainty and perplexity. Then why should I be preferred? I think that neither one nor the other of us deserves preference: and, if it be so, consider if I am not about to give you good advice: I am of opinion, that we should all seek the best master, first for ourselves, and then for these children, and for that end should spare no expense, nor any thing else in the world: for I shall never advise our remaining in the state wherein we now are. If any body derides us for going still to school at these years, we will defend ourselves by the authority of Homer, who says, that it is very bad for the poor to be shame-faced.* And thus, by laughing at all they can say, we shall take care, not only of ourselves, but of these children.

Lys. That counsel, Socrates, pleases me infinitely well; and for my part, the older I am, the more desire I shall have to instruct myself at the same time with our children. Do then as you have said, come to-morrow morning early to my house; do not fail therein, I pray you, that we may advise how to put in practice what we have resolved upon; it is time that this conversation should end.

Soc. I will not fail therein, Lysimachus; I will be with you to-morrow morning very early, if it please God.

* In the 17th book of his Odyss.

THE

ARGUMENT OF THE RIVALS.

THIS dialogue is entitled, THE RIVALS; for the ancients quote it by this name. It is moral, and treats of Philosophy. Socrates disputes here against two errors prevalent among the young people of his time: some misunderstanding a passage of Solon, fancied that philosophy consisted in knowing all the sciences. And others believed that to deserve the name of Philosopher, a superficial knowledge of arts and sciences was sufficient. All that they desired, was to acquire the reputation of universal scholars who could judge of every thing. Socrates argues very solidly against those two principles. He overthrows the latter, in making it appear that there is nothing more ridiculous than to fancy the philosopher to be a superficial man, inferior to masters in each science, and consequently fit for none. And he refutes the first, by insinuating that as too much food hurts the body, so too great a heap of science and knowledge hurts the soul; whose health, like that of the body, proceeds from a just measure of food that is given it. The most skilful is not always he who knows most, but he who knows well the things that are necessary. Which puts me in mind of a fine saying of one of the most learned men of this age, and whose works are universally known and admired: he said, * *That he should have been as ignorant as many others, if he had read as much as they.*

There are millions of things useless to lead us to true philosophy, and which instead of advancing, retard our progress. Philosophy is something greater than arts, and more admirable than that which is commonly called the sciences; for nothing less than the knowledge of things divine and human, can dispose us to submit to the first,

* Mr. Le Fevre.

and to guide and govern others by the rules of prudence
and justice ; so that we may be useful to our neighbours
and to ourselves, in opposing vice, and making virtue to
grow and flourish.   It is by this that one friend gives good
advice to another ; by this a magistrate executes justice ;
by this the master of a family governs his house : and, in
a word, by this a king governs his people.   These are the
truths that Socrates teaches in this short conversation,
which is very valuable.   One would say, that he is Solo-
mon's disciple, and that he had heard what wisdom spoke
from his mouth : "To me belong counsel, equity, prudence,
and strength ; it is by me that kings reign, and that law-
givers establish laws ; it is by me that princes command,
and that the powers of the earth decree justice."

THE RIVALS.

SOCRATES.   I went the other day into the school of
Denis, who teacheth learning.   I found there some of the
handsomest young people, and of the best families of the
city.   Above all, I observed two of them disputing together, but could not understand the subject of their dispute ; it seemed to me to be upon some points óf the
doctrine of Anaxagoras or Oenopidas, for they were stooping, drawing circles, and marking out certain turnings and
motions of the heavens with wonderful attention; curious to
know what it was, I addressed myself to a young man who
sat by me, a friend of one of those who were disputing
together, and asked him what occasioned this great attention ?   Is the subject of the discourse so great, said I, as
to require such a serious application.

Yes, answered he.   They are talking of heavenly things,
but with all their philosophy they only speak folly.

Surprised at the answer, How, said I, my friend, do you
think it a foolish thing to be a philosopher ?   How comes
it that you speak so harshly ?   Another young man that
was seated by him, and had heard my question, said to me,
In truth, Socrates, you will not find your account in applying yourself to that man ; and in asking his opinion of

philosophy : do not you know that he has spent all his life in eating, sleeping, and in bodily exercises? Can you expect any other answer from him, unless it were, that there is nothing more shameful nor more foolish than philosophy? He who spoke to me thus, had always applied himself to sciences ; whereas the other had applied himself wholly to exercises.

I thought it convenient to let alone that champion who had neglected the mind, only to exercise the body, and to keep to his rival, who pretended to be more able. And that I might the better draw from him what I desired, I said, What I asked at first, I asked of you both in common. But if you think you are better able to answer me than he, I will apply myself only to you. Say then, do you think that it is a fine thing to be a philosopher? or do you believe the contrary? The two disputants, who were near us, gave over their dispute, and drawing nearer seemed resolved to hear us with a deep silence.

He to whom I spoke did not fail to answer me, and with some sort of assurance. For my part, Socrates, if I thought it was a shame to be a philosopher, I should not think myself a man, and whosoever has that thought, I have altogether as bad an opinion of him.

Then it is a fine thing, answered I, to be a philosopher? Yes, assuredly, said he. But, answered I, do you think it possible for one to decide whether a thing be handsome or ugly, unless he knows it before? Do you know what it is to be a philosopher? Without doubt, said he, I know it. Then I asked him, what it was?

It is nothing else, answered he, than what Solon said : " In making myself old, I learn an infinity of things." For he who would be a philosopher ought to learn something every day of his life, both in his youth and in his old age, to the end that he may know all that can be known.

At first I considered that he had said something, but having paused a little upon it, I asked him if he held that philosophy was nothing else but Polymathy, that is to say, a heap or confused mass of all sciences? He told me, it was nothing more. But, said I, do you think that philosophy is only a fine thing, or do you believe it also a good thing? I believe it to be very good,

answered he. Do you think that good is particular to
philosophy, continued I, or do you find it in other
things? For example, do you think the love of exercises
is as good, as it is fine, or are you of opinion that it is
neither fine nor good. In my opinion, answered he,
jesting merrily; for you, the love of exercise is very fine
and very good; but as for him, speaking of his rival, it is
neither the one nor the other. And do you believe, said
I, that the love of exercise consists in having a mind to
do all exercises? Without doubt, said he; as the love of
wisdom, that is to say, philosophy, consists in having a
mind to know all things. But, I asked him, do you
think that those who apply themselves to exercise have
any other aim than that of the health of their body? No,
without doubt, said he, they propose to themselves no
other end. And consequently, said I, is it not the *great
number* of exercises that makes people enjoy health?

Would it be possible, answered he, that one could
be in good health by applying himself only to a few exercises?

Upon that I thought of stirring up my champion a
little, that he might come to my assistance with the experience he had in exercises: then directing my discourse
to him, why are you silent, said I, when you hear your
rival speak of your art? Do you also believe that it is the
great number of exercises that cause health? Or, on the
other hand, do you think that it is caused by the use of
such of them as you shall think fit, and by neither exer-
cising yourself too much nor too little?

For my part, Socrates, he answered, I am still persuaded, as I have always been, that there is nothing more
true than what the common proverb says, that moderate
exercise causes good health : is not this a fine proof of it?
That poor man with his application to study, and his desire to know every thing, see how he is; he has lost his
appetite and does not sleep: he is as stiff as a stake and
as dry as a match.

At these words the two young men began to laugh,
and our philosopher blushed.

Seeing his confusion, I turned towards him:What do
you pretend to then, said I? Do not you confess that it
is neither the great nor the small number of exercises,

that cause health; but moderate exercise, and keeping directly in the middle way? Will you resist this?

If I had to do with him only, said he, I would make my part good, and I find myself strong enough to prove to him what I have advanced, even though much less probable; he is far from being a dangerous enemy. But with you, Socrates, I will not dispute against my opinion. I confess then, that it is not the great number of exercises, but moderate exercise that causes health.

Is it not the same with food, said I? He agreed to it; and I made him confess the same, as to all other things that relate to the body: that it was the just medium that was useful, and in no wise the too much, or too little. And as to what relates to the soul, said I, is it the quantity of food that is given it which is useful, or is it only a just measure?

It is the just measure, said he.

But, continued I, are not sciences of the number of those foods of the soul? He acknowledged it. And consequently, said I, it is not the great number of sciences that nourish the soul, but the just measure, which is equally distant from too much and too little?

He acquiesced in it.

To whom then should we reasonably address ourselves, continued I, to know exactly what is the just measure of food and exercise that is useful for the body? We all agreed that it must be to a physician, or to a master of exercises. And as to sowing of seed, to whom should we apply ourselves to know that just measure? To a husbandman without doubt. And as to other sciences, I added, whom shall we consult to know the just medium that must be kept in sowing or planting them in the soul? Upon that, we found ourselves all three equally full of doubts and uncertainties. Seeing we cannot overcome this difficulty, I said smiling, shall we call those two studious youths to our assistance, or shall we be ashamed to call them, as Homer says of Penelope's lovers, *

* In the 21st Book of the Odyss. v. 285. the lovers of Penelope openly testify the fear they were in that the beggar, who was not yet known to be Ulysses, should bend the bow, whereof Penelope was to be the reward.

o

who not being able to bend the bow, would not allow
that any other should do it?

When I saw that they despaired of finding what we
sought for, I took another method. What sciences, said
I, shall we fix upon that a philosopher ought to learn?
For we have agreed that he ought not to learn them all,
nor even the greater part.

Our learned man, answering, said they ought to be the
finest, the most agreeable, and those that could do him
the greatest honour; and that nothing could do him more
honour than to seem to understand all the arts, or at
least the most considerable; and that thus a philosopher
ought to learn all the arts that were worthy of an honest
man's knowledge; not only those that depend upon the
understanding, but those also that depend upon handi-
craft.

You mean, continued I, for example, the joiner's trade:
one may have a very able joiner for five or six marks.
That is a trade that depends upon manual labour. And
the art of architecture depends on the understanding.
But you cannot have an architect for ten thousand
drachms,* for there are few among the Greeks. Are not
these the sort of arts you mean? When he had answered me; I asked him, if he did not think it impossible
that a man could learn two arts perfectly; and much more
learn a great number, and those the most difficult?

Upon that, he answered: do not you understand me,
Socrates? It is not my meaning that a philosopher
should know those arts as perfectly as the masters, who
practise them; it is sufficient that he knows them like a
gentleman, so as to understand what those masters say
better than the vulgar sort of men; and also be able to
give his opinion, to the end that he may make it appear,
that he has a very fine and delicate taste of all that is said
or done in relation to those arts.

And I, still doubting what his meaning was, said, see
I pray you, if I apprehend your idea of a philosopher;
you pretend that a philosopher should be the same as the
Pentathle or champion, who does five sorts of exercises in
the academy with the runner or the wrestler; for he is over-

* For 100 crowns. Architects were very scarce in Greece in Socrates's time.

come by all those champions in the exercises that are proper to each, and holds but the second rank after them; whilst he is above all the other champions who enter the list against him. Perhaps that is the effect which you pretend philosophy produces upon those who follow it; they are truly below masters in the knowledge of every art, but they are superior to all other men who pretend to judge of them; so that, according to you, we must conceive a philosopher, as a man who in every thing is below the master that professes that thing. This, I believe, is the idea you would give of a philosopher.

Very well, Socrates, said he, you have admirably well comprehended my meaning, and there is nothing more just than your comparison; for the philosopher is a man who does not keep to one thing only like a slave, so as to neglect all others: as tradesmen do, in order to carry it to the last perfection, but he applies himself indifferently to all.

After this answer, as if I still desired to know his meaning more clearly, I asked him if he believed that able men were useful or useless.

I believe them to be very useful, Socrates, answered he.

If the able are very useful, replied I, the unable are very useless.

He agreed to that.

But, said I, are the philosophers useful or not?

They are very useful, answered he.

Let us see then, replied I, if you say true, and let us examine how it can be that those philosophers, who hold only the second rank in any thing whatever, should be so useful; for by what you just now said, it is clear that the philosopher is inferior to tradesmen in all the arts which they profess.

He agrees to it.

Now, said I, let us see, if you or any of your friends were sick; tell me, I pray you, would you call a philosopher, that inferior man, or would you send for a physician to recover your health, or that of your friend?

For my part, I would send for both, answered he.

Ah! do not tell me that, answered I, you must choose which of them you would rather call.

If you take it that way, said he, I think no one would hesitate, but would much rather call the physician.

And if you were in the middle of the sea, tossed with a furious tempest, to whom would you abandon the conduct of your ship, to the philosopher, or to the pilot?

To the pilot, without doubt, said he.

Thus then, both in storm and in sickness, and in all other things, while the artist or the master of every one of those things is present, is not the philosopher very useless? Would he not be, as it were, a dumb person?

So it seems, answered he.

And consequently, replied I, the philosopher is a very useless man: for we have artists in every thing, and we have agreed that the able are only useful, and that others are not so. He was óbliged to agree to it. Shall I presume to ask you some other things, said I, and will not you think me rude to ask so many questions?

Ask me what you think fit, said he.

I want nothing more than that we should settle what we have already agreed on. Have we not agreed on the one side, that philosophy is a fine thing; that *there are* philosophers; that philosophers are able men; that able men are useful; and that unable men are useless; and on the other hand, we have agreed that philosophers are useless, when we have people at hand that are masters of every particular profession. Is not that what we have agreed to?

It is so, answered he.

And consequently, seeing philosophy, according to you, is only the knowledge of *all arts*. Whilst arts shall flourish among men, the philosophers will not have any lustre among them; on the contrary, they will be altogether useless. But, believe me, the philosophers are not what we have fancied; and to be a philosopher is not to meddle with all arts, and to spend one's life in shops stooping and working like a slave. Neither is it to learn many things: it is something more sublime and noble. For such an application is shameful, and those who take it upon them are only called mechanics and mean tradesmen. The better to see, if I speak true, answer me further I pray you; who are those that can discipline a horse well?   Are not they such as can make him better?

Yes.

And is it not the same with dogs?

Yes.

Thus one and the same art makes them both better?

Yes.

But that art which disciplines them, and makes them better, is it the same by which we know those that are bad?   Or is it another?

No, said he, it is the same.

Will you say the same thing of men, replied I?   The art which makes them better, is it the same with that which reclaims them, and which knows those that are good, and those that are bad?

It is the same, said he.

Does the art which judges of many, judge also of one, and that which judges of one, does it also judge of many?

Yes.

Is it the same, said I, of horses, and of all other animals?   He agrees to it.   But, say I, what do you call that science or art which chastises and reclaims the wicked that are in cities, and who violate the laws?   Is it not judicature?   And is not this art that which you call justice?

Without doubt, answered he.

Thus, said I, that art which serves the judges to correct the wicked, serves also to make them know who are wicked and who are good?

Assuredly.

And the judge who knows one of them, may also know more; and he who cannot know many of them, cannot know one?   Is it not so?

I confess it, said he.

Is it not also true, said I, that a horse which knows not the other horses that are good or bad, does not know what he is himself? and I say as much of all other animals.

He agreed to it.

Then, added I, a man who knows not men, whether they be good or bad, is he not also ignorant of himself, though he be a man?

It is most true, said he.

Now not to know one's self, is it to be wise, or to be foolish?

To be foolish.

And consequently, continued I, to know one's self is to be wise. Thus the precept that is written upon the gate of the temple of Delphos, *Know thyself*, exhorts us to apply ourselves to wisdom and justice. It is the same art that teacheth us to chastise and reform the wicked: By the rules of wisdom we learn to know them, and ourselves also.

That seems very true, said he.

And consequently, say I, justice and wisdom are but the same thing. And that which makes cities well governed, is the just punishment of the wicked. Is not that the occasion of good government?

He agreed to it.

When a man, say I, governs a state well, what name is given to that man? Is he not called king?

Without doubt.

Then he governs by the royal art, by the art of kings; and is not that the same with those we just spoke of?

So it would seem.

When a private man governs his house well, what name is given to him? Is he not called a good steward, or good master?

Yes.

By what art does he govern his house well? Is it not by the art of justice?

Certainly.

Then it follows that king, politician, steward, master, just, and wise, are but one and the same thing; and that royalty, policy, economy, wisdom and justice, are but one and the same art?

He agreed to it.

What then, continued I, shall a philosopher be ashamed when a physician shall speak before him of distempers, or others shall speak of their arts; I say, shall he be ashamed that he does not understand what they say, and that he cannot give his advice? So also when a king, a magistrate, a politician, an economist, shall speak of their art, he should not be ashamed that he cannot understand them, nor say any thing of his own head.

But would it not oe shameful, Socrates, said he to me, not to be able to say any thing upon such great and important things ?

I continued, Shall we then agree, that upon these same things the philosopher should be as the Pentathle, whom we just now spoke of, that is to say, always below the masters ; so that he will always be useless when those masters are present? Or shall we rather say, that he ought to be master himself, that he may not be of the second rank, and may not give his house to the conduct of another, but that he may manage it himself in the rules of wisdom and justice ?

He agreed with me.

In fine, said I : If his friends should abandon themselves to his conduct, or his city call him to the office of the magistracy, or should order him to be arbitrator upon public or private affairs, would it not be a shame for him to be only of the second or third rank, instead of being the head ?

So I think, said he.

Then indeed ! my dear philosophy wants much of being a love of all sciences, or an application to all arts. At these words, our learned man being confounded, knew not what to answer, and his rival, the master of exercises, assured me that I was right. All the rest likewise submitted to the same proofs.

INTRODUCTION TO PROTAGORAS.

AFTER Plato had, in a foregoing dialogue, given a specimen of the false notions that prevailed in his time, and that had infected the chief persons of the Republic, he here discovers their authors, and attacks them with great force. He introduces Socrates disputing with Protagoras, who was the most considerable of all the sophists, and who, by the art of poisoning men's minds, had acquired great reputation and much wealth.

At first he shews, with a natural simplicity, the veneration men had throughout Greece for those impostors. They were followed wherever they went, and they no sooner arrived in a city, than the news of it was everywhere spread abroad; people flocked to them with all possible eagerness, and their houses were filled betimes in the morning. Men that were so followed, could not be without some sort of merit, and particularly in so discerning an age. It is also evident, that Protagoras was a man of great wit, and expressed himself with wonderful ease. What could not such qualities do, especially when supported by much presumption, which rarely fails to accompany them? Instances of it are seen daily, so that it is needless to cite them. Who is it that goes to examine whether such persons advance false maxims? Who is it that is able to distinguish the false gloss of opinion from the true light of knowledge? They speak agreeably; they flatter our passions and prejudices; they promise us knowledge and virtue, and fill us with a high opinion of ourselves. What needs there more to make them popular?

This was the profession of the sophists. As nothing is more opposite to that spirit of error than true philosophy, Socrates was ever opposed to those false teachers; and Plato, who trod in his footsteps, could not mortify them more than by preserving the memory of all the disputes

which that wise man had with them, and of all the rail.
lery put upon them. This is what he does in several
Dialogues.

I have placed the present Dialogue after Laches, because
it is a natural continuation of it; for here is examined
that famous question, if virtue can be taught? and what
valour is, properly speaking?

Nothing is more natural than the plan of this Dialogue,
and nothing more solid than the manner in which it is
performed.

A young man an admirer of the Sophists, goes to Socrates before the break of day, to request him to conduct
him to Protagoras, who was just arrived at Athens. Socrates agrees. They go to the house of Callias, where he
lodged; and Callias was one of the chiefs of the Republic.

They find Protagoras walking in the midst of a crowd
of Athenians and foreigners, who listened to him as an
oracle. Prodicus of Ceos and Hippias of Elis, two of the
greatest Sophists of the age, were also there. And therefore the victory which Socrates obtains in this famous
dispute, ought to be looked upon as the defeat of the
whole body of Sophists, who assisted therein by their
leaders.

At first, Protagoras seems to be an admirable man; to
prove that virtue can be taught, he tells a very ingenious
story, and it must be confessed, that he gives this opinion
the most specious colours that could be, he omits nothing
that can be said, and what he says is now every day repeated by people who are far from thinking themselves
sophists.

Socrates confutes him with a dexterity that cannot be
sufficiently praised; and by his way of treating them, he
teaches us, that at all times, when one has to do with that
sort of people, the true secret to get the depth of them,
is not to suffer them to speak so much as they would, in
order to build up their chimerical systems; for thus they
.ude all your arguments, and escape from you at last by
their long discourses. You must then oblige them to
answer positively, and without rambling, to all you ask
them: with this precaution the dispute will soon be
at an end. The man, who when suffered to harangue,

has many times confounded every body: seems to be weakness itself, when he is confined to the limits of a regular dispute.   In short, it is seen that Protagoras had nothing but confused notions, such as he had collected by desultory reading, and that instead of knowledge, he had nothing but a monstrous heap of opinions, which when compared, contradict and destroy one another.

The aim of Socrates, in this dialogue, is not to confound and triumph over the Sophists, he has a nobler object in view ; he would divert the Athenians from the admiration of such learned trifling, and teach them important truths, the ignorance of which is the only source of all the evils that happen to men.

I shall not enter upon the particular beauties of this Dialogue, which consist in the variety, and in the liveliness of the characters ; in the mirth and in the pleasant humour of Socrates, in the simplicity and nobleness of the narratives, and in the knowledge of antiquity therein discovered : these beauties are perceptible enough.

But I cannot but relate a passage here which seems to me very remarkable, and which Socrates only touches cursorily, without insisting upon it, as finding it too sublime for those with whom he conversed.   It is when he says, That even though the pleasures of the world were not attended with any kind of evil in this life, yet they would be no less bad, because they cause men to rejoice ; and to rejoice in vice, is the most deplorable of all conditions.

We must not finish this argument without speaking of the date of this Dialogue, with respect to which Athenæus accuses Plato of having committed very considerable faults in chronology.   The whole strength of his criticism consists in this.   Plato tells us, that this dispute of Socrates with Protagoras happened the year after the poet Pherecrates's play, called *the Savages*, was acted. This play was acted in the time of the Archon Aristion, in the 4th year of the 89th Olympiad.   The true time then of this Dialogue, according to Plato, is in the year following ; that is to say, the first year of the 90th Olympiad, in the time of the Archon Astyphilus.   Yet there are two things that contradict this date.

The first is, that from a passage in a play of Eupolis's

which was acted a year before that of Pherecrates, it appears that Protagoras was then at Athens : now Plato says positively, that in the time of this Dialogue, that is to say, the first year of the 90th Olympiad, Protagoras arrived at Athens but three days before.

The second is, that Hippias of Elis was present at that dispute : which could not be ; for the truce which the Athenians had concluded with the Lacedemonians, being expired, no Peloponnesian could be at Athens at that time.

I should not have revived this accusation, if that wise and judicious critic, Casaubon, had not been so struck with it as to say, that he could not see what should be said in justification of Plato. It will, however, quickly appear, that the objections of Athenæus serve only to confirm the date of this Dialogue as fixed by Plato.

We certainly know that the Athenians made peace with the Lacedemonians for fifty years, in the time of the Archon Alcæus, in the third year of the 89th Olympiad.* It is true, that this treaty was not faithfully observed on either side ; but it is also true, that this ill-cemented peace lasted six years and ten months, without coming to an open rupture. Then Hippias of Elis might have been at Athens in the second year of this treaty. So much for the last objection.

The first is no better founded : let us see what Eupolis says. *"Protagoras of Teos is within there."* He says nothing more ; and it may be observed at first sight, that he is deceived as to the country of Protagoras : he assures us, that he is of Teos; but he was of Abdera. This remark will be of use to us.

I say then, that Athenæus, instead of employing this verse of Eupolis to contradict Plato, ought rather to have made use of the passage of Plato to understand Eupolis. The poet and the philosopher are both right, and Athenæus is the only person that is wrong. Protagoras had made two journeys to Athens. Plato speaks of the second, and the verse of Eupolis must be understood of the first : for though Protagoras was not at Athens when the play was acted in the time of the Archon Alcæus, it

* Thucyd. L. 5.

was enough that he had been there : Poets have the privilege of bringing the times nearer, and of noticing things that are past, as if they were present ; besides, he might be there when the poet composed it. Thus the verse of Eupolis serves on the one hand for a commentary to what Hippocrates says in this dialogue : "Socrates, I come to pray you to speak for me to Protagoras ; for, besides being too young, I never saw, nor knew him, I was but a child when he made his first journey."

And, on the other hand, this passage of Plato serves to excuse the ignorance of Eupolis about the country of Protagoras ; for Eupolis might very well be ignorant of it at his first journey, that sophist not being then very well known, whereas it would not have been pardonable in him to have been ignorant of it at the second.

This fault of Athenæus is less surprising than that of Casaubon, who followed him, and who in explaining his reasons commits another more considerable mistake, in assuring us that Thucydides does not speak of the one years truce that was made between the Athenians and the Lacedemonians under the Archon Isarchus, in the first year of the 89th Olympiad, at the end of the eighth year of the war, and two years before the treaty of peace that has been spoken of ; for it is expressly set down in the fourth book, and the treaty is there related at length, with the date of the year, of the month, of the day, and of the season.*

The wranglings of Athenæus serve only to vindicate Plato's exactness, and to make it appear that this Dialogue is beyond all criticism ; for if his censurer had found any other thing to find fault with, the envy with which he was animated against this philosopher would not have suffered him to have forgotten it.

According to Diogenes Laertius, this dialogue is ἐνδεικτικὸς, a dialogue of accusation, a satiric dialogue. One may say, that it is also ἀνατρεπτιχὸς, destructive. But such names mark only the turn and the manner of the Dialogue. Its true character is logical and moral.

* He sets the end of the eighth year of war, the 14th day of the month Esaphebollon (February) and the beginning of the Spring.

PROTAGORAS:

OR,

THE SOPHISTS.

A FRIEND OF SOCRATES.

SOCRATES.

*Socrat: Friend.** From whence come you, Socrates? But we need not ask; you come from Alcibiades: you are highly in favour with that promising youth!

Soc. This very day, he said a thousand things in my favour, and always took my part: I have but just parted from him. And I will tell you a thing that may seem very strange to you, which is, that whilst he was present, I saw him not, and did not so much as think of him.

Soc. Fr. What happened to you then, that you neither saw nor thought of him? Is it possible that you have

---

* Enquiry is made why Plato does not name this Friend of Socrates, and it is what will never be found out: It can only be guessed at. Perhaps Plato was afraid of exposing the friend of Socrates to the resentment of the sophists, who were in great credit at Athens, and revengeful; or, that the part which this friend here acts, not being considerable, it was not worth while to name him.

met with a more promising young man in the city than Alcibiades? I cannot believe it.

Soc. It is even so.

Soc. Fr. In earnest? Is he an Athenian, or a stranger?

Soc. He is a stranger.

Soc. Fr. Whence comes he then?

Soc. From Abdera.

Soc. Fr. And was he so fine, as to efface the comeliness of Alcibiades?

Soc. The greatest comeliness is not to be laid in the balance with great wisdom.

Soc. Fr. Then you have just come from a wise man?

Soc. Yes, a wise man; nay, a very wise man, at least if you look upon Protagoras to be the wisest of men now living.

Soc. Fr. What do you tell me? Is Protagoras in this city?

Soc. Yes: he has been here these three days.

Soc. Fr. And you have just parted from him?

Soc. Yes, I have, after a very long conversation.

Soc. Fr. If you are at leisure, will you relate that conversation to us.

Soc. I will willingly do it; and shall be obliged if you will give ear to it.

Soc. Fr. We shall be much more obliged to you.

Soc. The obligation then will be reciprocal. Your business is only to hear me. This morning while it was yet dark, Hippocrates, the son of Apollodorus, and Phason's brother, knocked very hard at my gate; it was no sooner opened, than he came directly to my chamber, calling with a loud voice, Socrates, are you asleep? Knowing his voice, I said, what! Hippocrates! what news do you bring me? Very good news, says he. God grant it, replied I. What is it then, that you come so early? Protagoras is in town, says he. I replied, he has been here these two days. Did you not hear of it till now? I heard it but this night: and having said this, he drew near my bed, and feeling with his cane, sat down at my feet, and went on in this manner. I returned last night very late from the village of Doinoe, where I went to take my slave Satyrus, who had run away : I was resolved to come and tell you that I was in search of him, but some other thing put it out of my thoughts. After I returned, had supped, and was going to bed, my brother came to tell me, that Protagoras had arrived : at first I thought of coming at once to acquaint you with this good news ; but considering that the night was already too far advanced, I went to my bed, and after a short slumber, which refreshed me a little, I arose and came to you. I, who knew Hippocrates to be a man of courage, perceiving him thus excited, asked him what was the matter? Has Protagoras, said I, done you any injury? Yes, certainly, answered he, laughing ; he has done me an injury that I will not forgive, that is, that he is wise, and does not make me so. Oh! said I, if you will pay him liberally and induce him to receive you as his disciple, he will doubtless make you wise also.

I wish to God, says he, that were all; I would not leave myself a half-penny, and I would even drain the purses of my friends. It is this only that brings me here ; I come to entreat you to speak to him for me ; for besides being too young, I never saw him nor knew him : I was but a child, when he first came, but I hear every body speak well of him, and they assure me, that he is the most eloquent of men. Let us visit him, before he goes abroad. I am told he lodges with Callias, son of Hipponicus.* Let us go, I conjure you. It is too early, said I, but let us walk in our court, where we will argue till day-light, then we will go ; I assure you we shall not miss him, for he seldom goes abroad. Then we went down into the court, and while we were walking, I had a wish to find out what Hippocrates's design was. To this end, I said to him: Well, Hippocrates, you are going to Protagoras to offer him money, that he may teach you something ; what sort of a person do you think him to be, and what would you have him to teach you? If you should go to the great physician of Cos, who is your name-sake, and a descendant of Æsculapius, and should offer him money ; if

---

* Callias was one of the first citizens of Athens. His father Hipponicus had been general of the Athenians with Nicias at the battle of Tanagre.

any one should ask you, to what sort of man you propose
to give that money, and what would you become by means
of it ; what would you answer ?—I would answer, that I
give it to a physician, in order to be made a physician.

And if you should go to Polycletus of Argos, or to
Phidias, to give them money to learn something of them,
and any one should ask you the question, to whom and
for what purpose did you give your money, what would
you answer ?

I would answer, says he, that I give it to a statuary, in
order to be made a statuary.

That is very well. Now then we are going, you and I,
to Protagoras, with a disposition to give him all that he
shall ask for your instruction, if all that we have will
satisfy him, or is enough to tempt him ; and if it be not
enough, we are also ready to make use of the credit of
our friends. If any person perceiving our extraordinary
eagerness, should ask us to inform him why we give so
much money to Protagoras, and what sort of a man we
suppose him to be ; what should we answer him : What
other denomination has Protagoras? We know that
Phidias has that of statuary, and Homer that of poet :
what shall we call Protagoras, to describe him by his proper profession ?

Protagoras is called a sophist, Socrates.

Well then, said I, we are going to give our money to a
sophist.

Yes, certainly.

And if the same person should continue to ask you,
what do you design through Protagoras, to become ?

At these words my friend blushing, for it was then light
enough to let me see the alteration in his countenance :
if we will follow our principle, says he, it is evident that I
would become a sophist.

By all that is good, said I ! would you not be
ashamed to proclaim yourself a sophist among the
Greeks ?

I swear to you, Socrates, seeing I must tell you the
truth, I should be ashamed of it.

Ha ! I understand you, my dear Hippocrates ; your
design then is to go to the school of Protagoras, as you
went to that of a grammarian, music-master, or master of

exercises : to whom you went not to learn the depth of
their art, and to make profession thereof; but only to
exercise yourself, and to learn that which a gentleman
and a man who would live in the world, ought necessarily
to know.

You are in the right, said he; that is exactly the use
that I would make of Protagoras.

But, said I, do you know what you are going to do?

In what respect?

You are going to trust a sophist with your understanding; and I dare assert, that you do not know what a
sophist is; and, since it is so, you know not with whom
you are about to trust that which is most valuable to
you, and you know not whether you put it into good or
bad hands.

Why, I believe I know what a sophist is.

Tell me then, what is it?

A sophist, as his name denotes, is a learned man, who
knows abundance of good things.

We say the same thing of a painter, or an architect:
They are also learned men, who know a great many good
things : but if any body should ask us, wherein are they
learned? we should certainly answer them, that it is in
what regards drawing of pictures and building of houses.
If any one should ask us in like manner, wherein is
a sophist learned? What should we answer? What is
the art positively that he makes profession of? And
what should we say it is?

We should say, that his profession is to make men
eloquent.

Perhaps we might speak true in so saying; that is
something, but it is not all : your answer occasions another question, to wit, in what is it that a sophist renders
a man eloquent? For does not a player upon the lute
also render his disciple eloquent in that which regards the
lute?

That is certain.

In what is it then, that a sophist renders a man eloquent? is it not in that which he knows?

Without doubt.

What is it that he knows, and teaches others?

In truth, Socrates, I cannot tell.

How then, said I, taking advantage of this confession : Alas ! do not you perceive to what frightful dangers you are about to expose yourself? If you had occasion to put your body into the hands of a physician whom you know not, and who might as well destroy it as cure it, would you not look to it more than once? Would you not call your friends and relations to consult with them? And would you not take time to resolve on the matter? You esteem your soul infinitely above your body, and you are persuaded that on it depends your happiness or unhappiness, according as it is well or ill-disposed ; and notwithstanding that its welfare is now at stake, you neither ask advice of your father, nor brother, nor of any of us who are your friends : you do not take so much as one moment to deliberate whether you ought to entrust it with this stranger who is just arrived ; but having heard of his arrival very late at night, you come the next morning, before break of day, to put it into his hands, and are ready not only to employ all your own riches for that purpose, but also those of your friends. You have resolved that you must deliver up yourself to Protagoras, whom you know not, as you yourself confess, and with whom you have not even spoken ; you call him a sophist, and, without knowing what a sophist is, you throw yourself into his hands.

All that you say, Socrates, is very true ; you are in the right.

Do not you find, Hippocrates, that the sophist is but a merchant, and a retailer of those things wherewith the soul is nourished?

So it seems, Socrates ; but what are the things wherewith the soul is nourished?

SCIENCE, I answered. But, my dear friend, we must be very careful that the sophist, by boasting too much of his merchandise, does not deceive us, as those people do, who sell what is necessary to the nourishment of the body: for these, without knowing whether the provisions which they sell be good or bad, ca mend them excessively, that they may sell them the better; and those who buy them know them no better unless it be some physician, or master of exercises.* It is the same with those merchants who go into the cities to sell sciences to those who have a mind to them; they praise indifferently all that they sell; it may be, that most of them know not if what they sell is good or bad for the soul: but all those who buy any thing of them are certainly ignorant as to that matter, unless they meet with some person who is a good physician for the soul. If you are skilled in that matter, and know what is good or bad, you may certainly buy science of Protagoras and of all the other sophists; but if you are not skilled in it, have a care, my dear Hippocrates, that when you go there, you do not make a very bad market, and hazard that which, of all things in the world, is dearest to you, for the risk we run in buying sciences, is far greater than that which we run in buying provisions, after we have bought the last, they may be carried home in vessels which they cannot spoil; and before using them we have time to consult and to call to our assistance those who know what we ought to eat and drink, and what not; the quantity we may take, and the time when; insomuch that the danger is not very great. But it is not the same with sciences, we cannot put them into any other vessel than the mind; as soon as the bargain is made, it must of necessity be carried away, and that too in the soul itself; and we must withdraw with it, being either enriched or ruined for the rest of our days. Let us therefore consult people of greater age and experience than ourselves upon the subject; for we

* In Hippocrates's time, and a little before; the physicians, having neglected the study of diet, which requires an exact knowledge of every thing in nature, the masters of exercises laid hold on it as on a deserted estate, and took upon themselves to order their disciples such diet as was agreeable to them in regard to their temperament and exercises. Hippocrates began to put himself again in possession of it, and by degrees the physicians regained the places of exercise. There were but few masters of exercise who kept it up in the time of Plato. Most of them had hired physicians.

are too young to determine such an important affair ; but
let us go on, however, since we are in the way ; we shall
hear what Protagoras will say ; and after having heard
him, we will communicate with others.   Doubtless Protagoras will not be there alone, we shall find Hippias of
Elis with him, and I believe we shall also find Prodicus of
Ceos, and many others, all of them wise men, and of great
experience.

This resolution being taken, we went on.   When we
came to the gate, we stopped to conclude a small dispute
we had by the way ; this continued a short time.   I believe the porter, who is an old eunuch, heard us ; and
that the number of sophists who came there constantly,
had put him in an ill-humour against all those who came
to the house.   We had no sooner knocked, but opening
the gate and seeing us, " Ah, ah, (said he) here are more
of our sophists, he is not at leisure."   And taking the
gate with both his hands, he shut it in our face with
all his force.   We knocked again, and he answered us
through the door, " Did you not understand me ?
Have not I already told you, that my master will see no
one ?"

My friend, said I, we do not come here to interrupt
Callias ; you may open without fear: we come to see
Protagoras.   Notwithstanding this, it was with much difficulty that we obtained admission.   When we entered, we
found Protagoras walking before the portal, and with him
on the one side Callias, the son of Hipponicus, and his
brother by the mother ; Paralus, the son of Pericles ; and
Charmides, the son of Glaucon ; and on the other, were
Xanthippus, the other son of Pericles ; Philippides, the
son of Philomelus, and Antimoerus of Sicily the most
famous disciple of Protagoras, and who aspires to be a
sophist.   After them marched a troop of people, most of
whom seemed to be strangers that Protagoras had brought
with him from all the cities through which he passed,
and whom he attracts by the sweetness of his voice, like
another Orpheus :   there were also some Athenians
amongst them.   When I perceived this fine troop, I took
great pleasure to see with what discretion and respect

hey marched always behind, being very careful not to be before Protagoras. As soon as Protagoras turned with his company, this troop opened to the right and left, with a religious silence to make way for him to pass through, and after he had passed, began again to follow him.

I perceived Hippias of Elis was seated upon the other side of the portal, on an elevated seat; and near him, upon the steps, I observed Eryximachus, the son of Acumenus, Phedras of Myrrhinuse,* Andron the son of Androtion, and some strangers of Elis mixed with them. They seemed to propose some questions of physic and astronomy to Hippias, who answered all their doubts. I also saw Tantalus there; Prodicus of Ceos was also there, but in a little chamber, which was usually Hipponicus's office, and which Callias, because of the number of people that came to his house, had given to those strangers, after having fitted it up for them. Prodicus was still in bed, wrapped up in skins and coverings, and Pausanias of Cerame† was seated by his bed-side, and with him a young man, who seemed to be of noble birth, and the comeliest person in the world. I think I heard Pausanias call him Agathon. There were also the two Adimantes, the one the son of Cephis, and the other the son of Leucolophides, and some other young people. Being without, I could not hear the subject of their discourse, although I wished passionately to hear Prodicus, for he appears to me to be a very wise, indeed a divine man: but he has so loud a voice, that it caused a sort of echo in the chamber, which hindered me from understanding distinctly what he said. We had been there but a moment, when Alcibiades came in, and Critias the son of Calaischrus.

After we had been there a short time, and considered a little what passed, we went out to join Protagoras. In accosting him: Protagoras, said I, Hippocrates and myself are come to see you.

Would you speak to me in private, said he, or in public?

* Myrrhinuse, a town of Attica.
† Ceramis, or Cerame, a borough of Attica.

When I have told you what brings us here, said I, you yourself shall judge which will be most convenient.

What is it then, said he, that has brought you?

Hippocrates, whom you see there, replied I, is the son of Apollodorus, of one of the greatest and richest families of Athens, and as nobly born as any young man of his age; he designs to acquire reputation and to make himself illustrious in his country; and he is persuaded that to succeed therein, he has need of your help. Will you then, rather entertain us upon this subject in private or public?

That is very well done, Socrates, to use this precaution towards me; for a stranger who goes to the greatest cities, and persuades young persons of the highest rank to leave their fellow-citizens, parents, or others, and only to adhere to him, in order to become more able men by his conversation, cannot make use of too much precaution : for it is a very nice art, much exposed to the darts of envy, and which attracts much hatred and many snares. For my part, I maintain, that the art of sophistry is very ancient ; but those who professed it at first, to hide what is odious or suspected in it, sought to cover it, some with the veil of poetry, as Homer, Hesiod, and Simonides ; others with purifications and prophecies, as Orpheus and Museus : some disguised it under the name gymnastic, as Iccus of Tarentum, Herodicus of Selymbra in Thrace, originally from Megara : and others concealed it under the specious pretext of music, as your Agathocles, a great sophist, if ever there was one, Pythoclides of Ceos, and an infinite number of others.

All those people, I tell you, to shelter themselves from envy, have sought after sally-ports to withdraw themselves out of trouble in time of need. In that I am no way of their opinion, being persuaded that they have not effected what they proposed. For it is impossible that they can hide themselves long from the eyes of those who have the chief authority in cities ; they will at last discover your subtilties. It is true, that the people do not usually perceive them, but that does not save you ; for they are always of the opinion of their superiors, and speak only by their mouth. Besides, there is nothing more ridiculous than to be surprised, like a fool, when one

would hide himself; as that but increases the number of
your enemies, and renders you more suspected; for then
you are considered to be a dissembler, and crafty in all
things. For my part, I take the opposite way; I have no
disguise, I make an open profession of teaching men,
and I declare myself a sophist. The best cunning of all,
is to have none : I would rather show myself than be discovered. With this frankness, I fail not to take all other
necessary precautions ; insomuch that, thanks be to God,
no .misfortune has befallen me as yet, though I proclaim
that I am a sophist, and though I have practised that art
for a great many years, for by my age I should be the
father of you all ; so that nothing can be more agreeable
to me, if you are inclined to it, than to speak to you in
the presence of all that are in the house.

I immediately perceived his object, which was to elevate
himself in the opinion of Prodicus and Hippias, and to
take advantage of our having addressed ourselves to him,
as persons enamoured of his wisdom. Then I said to
oblige him : But should not Prodicus and Hippias be
called, that they may hear us ? Yes certainly, said Protagoras; who desired no better. And Callias, catching our
words upon the rebound, said, shall we prepare seats for
you, that you may speak more at your ease ? That
seemed to us to be a very good thought ; and, being impatient to hear such able men discourse, we soon obtained
seats from the house of Hippias. As soon as this was
done, Callias and Alcibiades returned, bringing with them
Prodicus, and all those that were with him. When we
were all seated, Protagoras, addressing his discourse to me
said, Socrates, now you may tell me, before all this good
company, what you had already begun to say respecting
this young man.

Protagoras, said I, I shall pass no other compliment
upon you, than what I have already done, and I shall
tell you plainly why we are come hither. Hippocrates
has an earnest desire to enjoy your conversation, and
he would willingly know what advantages he shall reap
from it. This is all we have to say.

Then Protagoras, turning towards Hippocrates, My dear
. child, said he, the advantages which you shall reap from

me, are, that from the first day of this correspondence you
shall return at night more learned than you were the
morning you came ; the next day the same, . and every
day you shall find that you have made some new progress.

But, Protagoras, said I, there is nothing extraordinary
in this ; for you yourself, how old and learned soever you
may be, if any body teach you what you knew not, you
will also become more knowing than you were. Alas !
that is not what we demand. But suppose Hippocrates
should suddenly change his mind, and apply himself to that
young painter who is lately arrived in this city, Zeuxippus
of Heracleus ; he addresses himself to him as he does now
to you, that painter promiseth the same things as you
have done, that every day he shall become more learned,
and make new progress. If Hippocrates asks him, in
what shall I make so great a progress ? Will not Zeuxippus
answer him, that he will make a progress in painting ?

Suppose he should be disposed to join himself in the
same manner to Orthagoras the Theban, and that after
having heard the same promises as he has heard from
you, he should ask the question ; in what he should become every day more learned ? Will not Orthagoras answer him, that it is in the art of playing upon the flute ?
The matter being so, I pray you, Protagoras, to answer
us likewise as positively. You tell us, that if Hippocrates
join himself to you, from the first day, he will return more
learned, the next day still more so, and every day after
make new progresses, and so on all the days of his life.
But explain to us wherein it is he will become so learned,
and the advantages he shall reap from this learning.

You have reason, Socrates, said Protagoras ; that is a
very pertinent question, and I dearly love to answer those
who put such questions to me. I tell you then, that
Hippocrates needs not fear, with me, any of those inconveniences which would infallibly happen to him with
all our sophists ; for all of them do notably prejudice
young people, in forcing them, by their fine discourses, to
learn arts which they care not for; as arithmetic, astronomy,
geometry, music: [and in saying that, he looked upon Hippias, designing as it were to point him out :] whereas with

me a young man will learn only the science for which he has addressed himself to me ; and that science is nothing but prudence, which teaches one to govern his house well, and which, as to things that regard the republic, renders us capable of saying and doing all that is most advantageous for it.

If, said I, I conceive you aright : it seems to me, that you would speak of politics, and that you pretend to be able to make men good citizens.

It is so, said he ; that is the thing that I boast of.

In truth, said I, Protagoras, that is a wonderful science you possess, if it be true that you have it, and I shall not scruple to tell you freely what I think. I have hitherto thought, that it was a thing that could not be taught ; but since you say that you teach it, how can we but believe you ? In the mean time, it is just that I should give you the reasons why I believe it cannot be taught, and that one man cannot communicate that science to another.* I am persuaded, as are all the Greeks, that the Athenians are very wise. I see in all our assemblies, that when the city is obliged to undertake some new buildings, they call all the architects before them, to ask their advice ; that when they design to build ships, they send for the carpenters that work in their arsenals ; and that they do the same in all other things that are required to be taught and learnt : and if any one, who is not of the profession, take upon him to give advice, though he be ever so fine, rich, and noble, yet they do not so much as give ear to him : but laugh at, and hiss him, until such time as he retires, or is carried off by the officers, by order of the senate. This is the manner of the city's conduct in all things that depend upon art.

But when they deliberate upon those things that relate to the government of the republic, then every body is heard alike. You see the mason, locksmith, shoemaker, merchant, the seaman, the poor, rich, noble, the wag-

---

* The first reason of Socrates, founded upon the practice of all men, is this. Upon things that are to be taught, they ask advice only of those who have learnt them ; but upon virtue they advise with every body : a clear proof that they are persuaded that virtue is not acquired.

P

goner, &c. rise up to give their advice, and no one takes it ill; there is no noise then, as on other occasions, and none of them is reproached for intruding to give advice in things he had never learnt, and in which he had not had a master; an evident demonstration, that the Athenians do all believe that wisdom cannot be taught. And this is what is not only seen in the general affairs relating to the republic, but also in private affairs, and in all families: for the wisest and the ablest of our citizens cannot communicate their wisdom and ability to others.

Without going farther, Pericles has carefully caused his two sons, to learn all that masters could teach them; but as to wisdom, he does not teach them that; he does not send them to other masters, but they feed in common in all pastures, like beasts consecrated to God,* that wander without a guide, to see if of themselves they can light by good fortune upon those healthful herbs, *wisdom* and *virtue*. It is true, that the same Pericles, being tutor to Alcibiades and Clinias, separated them, and placed Clinias with Ariphron, to the end that that wise man might take care to bring him up and instruct him. But what was the issue of it? Clinias had not been six months there, before Ariphron, not knowing what to do with him, returned him to Pericles.

I could quote you an infinite number of others, who, though they were very virtuous and learned, yet they could never make their own children, nor those of others, the better for that. And, when I think of all those examples, I confess, Protagoras, that although I continue of this sentiment, that virtue cannot be taught;† yet when

---

* This passage, which is very fine, had not been intelligible, if I had translated it verbatim; for the Greek says all this is one word, ὥσπερ ἄφετοι. It was therefore requisite to explain the figure, which is excellent, Socrates compares men to those beasts which the antients sometimes consecrated to the gods. As those beasts had no guides but the gods themselves, so it is the same with men, chiefly as to what relates to virtue. Not only God, to whom they are consecrated by their birth, can conduct them to the pure springs, healthful waters, and rich pastures. It is the same notion as David had in Psalm 20. *In loco pascuæ ibi me collocavit.*

† This is an incontrovertible truth: for who is it that can correct him whom God hath abandoned, because of his vices? Who can make that straight which is thus made crooked?

I hear you speak as you do, it makes me waver, being persuaded that you have great experience, that you have learned much of others, and that you have found out many things yourself that others are ignorant of. If, therefore, you can plainly demonstrate to us, that virtue is of a nature to be taught, do not conceal so great a treasure: I conjure you to communicate it to us.

Well, said he, I will not conceal it from you: but say; shall I, as an old man, speaking to young people, demonstrate it to you by way of a fable,* or shall I do it by a plain and coherent discourse?

At these words, most of those who were present cried out, that he was the master, and that the choice was left to him.

Since it is so, said he, I believe that a fable will be most agreeable.

† There was a time when the Gods were alone, before there were either beasts or men. When the time appointed for the creation of these last came, the Gods formed them in the earth, by mixing the earth, the fire, and the other two elements, whereof they are composed, together. But, before they brought them to the light, they ordered Prometheus and Epimetheus‡ to adorn them, and to distribute to them all qualities convenient. Epimetheus begged of Prometheus to suffer him to make this distribution; which Prometheus consented to.

Behold, then, Epimetheus in his office! He gives to some strength without swiftness, and to others swiftness

* Fables were the strength of the sophists. It was by these that Natural Religion, if we may so speak, was supplanted; and that Paganism, which is the corruption thereof, was introduced in its stead: wherefore St. Paul exhorts the faithful with so much care to avoid fables. When a man refuses to hearken to the truth, he, of course, gives ear to fables.

† In this fable, which is very ingenious, are traced the great footsteps of truth; as, that God was everlasting before the creation of man; that there was a time destined by Providence for that creation; and that man was created of the earth, in which were hid the seeds of all creatures.

‡ By Prometheus, is here meant the superior angels; to whom, some think, God entrusted the care of man in the creation, though they act solely by his spirit; for they only execute his orders. And, by Epimetheus, are meant the elementary virtues, which can give nothing but what they have received, and which go astray when they are not led and guided by the Spirit that created them.

without strength. To these he gives natural arms, and denies them to others, but at the same time gives them other means to preserve and defend themselves; he assigns caves and holes in the rocks for the retreat of those to which he gives but small bodies; or otherwise, by giving them wings, he shows them their safety is in the air. He makes those understand to whom he has allotted bulk, that that bulk is sufficient for their preservation. Thus he finished his distribution with the greatest equality he possibly could, taking particular care that none of those kinds should be extirpated by the other.

After having provided them with means to defend themselves from the attacks of each other, he took care to provide them against the injuries of the air, and the rigour of the seasons: for this purpose he clothed them with thick hair and very close skins, capable of defending them against the winter's frost and the summer's heat; and which, when they have occasion to sleep, serve them instead of a bed to lie upon, and a covering over them; he also provides their feet with a firm and thick hoof, and a very hard skin.

That being done, he assigns to each of them their food, viz. to one herbs, to another the fruits of the trees; to some roots, and one kind he permitted to feed upon the flesh of other creatures: but lest that kind should come at last to extirpate the others, he made it less fruitful, and made those that were to nourish them singularly prolific. But as Epimetheus was not very wise and prudent, he did not take notice that he had employed all his qualities to the use of irrational creatures, and that man was still wanting to be provided for; he therefore knew not on what side to turn himself, when Prometheus came to see what partition he had made. He saw all the creatures perfectly well provided for; but found man quite naked, without weapons, shoes, or covering.*

. The day appointed to take man out of the bosom of the earth, and to bring him to the light of the sun, being come, Prometheus therefore knew not what to do to make man capable of preserving himself. At last, he made use

---

* Epimetheus had given him all that he could give; for man, being gifted with reason, ought to furnish himself with all things necessary for his preservation.

of this expedient: he robbed Vulcan and Minerva of their wisdom relating to arts;* he also stole the fire; for without fire this wisdom could not be possessed; it would have been quite useless: and he presented them to man. After this manner, man received wisdom sufficient to preserve his life, but he did not receive the wisdom which relates to politics:† for Jupiter had it, and Prometheus had not the liberty to enter into the sacred mansion of this master of the Gods.‡ The way to it was defended by terrible guards:§ but, as I just now told you, he slipped into the common room, where Vulcan and Minerva were at work, and having robbed that God of his art, which is practised by fire, and this Goddess of her art, which relates to the design and conduct of the works, he gave them to man, who by this means found himself in a condition to provide all things necessary for life. It is said that

* Vulcan and Minerva are the two causes of arts. Vulcan (the fire) furnishes the instruments and the operation, and Minerva (the spirit) gives the design and knowledge by the imagination, which is, as it were, a ray that she sends from above; for arts are only imitations of the spirit and of the understanding, and they only give the form, and adorn the matter upon which they act.—*Procl.*

† According to this fable, the knowledge of arts preceded politic and moral virtues in the soul of man. This is a false tradition.

‡ This mansion of Jupiter is called here by a word which signifies fortress, and by which the ancient theologues, says Proclus, understood the upper region of the heaven and the *primum mobile;* from whence they conceived, that God gave motion to all things, and communicated his light, and his fruitful irradiations to the inferior gods for the creation of beings, without being subject to any cause. And it is of this fortress that Homer would speak, when he says, that Jupiter keeps himself at a distance upon the highest pinnacle of the heavens.

§ Those terrible guards which defend the way to this fortress of Jupiter, serve, according to Proclus, to point out the immutability of his decrees, and his indefatigable watchfulness for the support of that order which he has established. We may also say, that those guards are to let us know, that all the celestial spirits cannot enter into the secrets of Providence, but in so far as God wills to call them to it by his goodness. Wherefore Jupiter says in Homer (book first of the Iliads), that the other gods cannot enter into his counsels, and that they can know nothing, but what he pleases to communicate to them. Those guards may also have been feigned from the cherubims that God placed at the entrance of the terrestrial paradise, and who defended the same with a flaming sword.

Prometheus was afterwards punished for this robbery, which he committed only to repair the default of Epimetheus.

When man had received such divine advantages, he became the only one of all the creatures, who, because of his kindred, that linked him to the Divine Being, thought that there were gods. Who raised altars and erected statues to them; he also settled a language, and gave names to all things. He built himself houses, made himself clothes, shoes, and beds, and procured himself food out of the bowels of the earth.

But notwithstanding all the helps that men had from their very birth, still they lived dispersed; for there was yet no city. Therefore they were miserably devoured by the beasts, as being every where much feebler than they. The arts they had were a sufficient help to them to nourish themselves, but very insufficient for defence against enemies, and to make war with them; for they had not as yet any knowledge of politics, whereof the art of war is one part.

They therefore thought only of gathering themselves together, for their preservation, and of building cities. But they were no sooner together, than they did one another more mischiefs, by their injustice, than the beasts had formerly done them by their cruelty. And those injustices proceeded only from this, that they had not yet any idea of politics. Therefore they were soon obliged to separate themselves; and were again exposed to the fury of the beasts.

Jupiter being moved with compassion, and also fearing that the race of man would be soon extirpated, sent Mercury* with orders to carry shame and justice to men, to the end that they might adorn their cities, and confirm the bonds of amity.

Mercury having received this order, asked Jupiter, how he should do to communicate unto men shame and justice, and if he should distribute them as Prometheus had dis-

* The ancients therefore knew this truth, that God could make use of the ministry of an angel or god, to acquaint men with his will, to cure their weaknesses, and to communicate virtues to them.

tributed the arts. For, added he, the arts were distributed thus : he who has the art of physic given him, is
able alone to serve many particular persons. It is the
same also with all other artists. Will it therefore be
enough if I follow the same method, and if I give shame
and justice to a small number of people ? Or shall I distribute them indifferently to all ? To all, without doubt,
replied Jupiter, they must all have them : for if they are
communicated only to a small number, as other arts are,
there will never be either societies or cities. Moreover,
thou shalt publish this law in my name, that every man,
who has not shame and justice, shall be cut off as the
plague of cities.

This is the reason, Socrates, why, when the Athenians
and other people consult about affairs relating to arts,
they listen only to the counsel of a small number, that is
to say, of artists. And if any others, who are not of the
profession, take upon them to give their advice, they
do not allow him, as you have very well observed, and
as indeed is but reasonable. But when they treat of
affairs relating to policy, as this policy ought always to
rest upon justice and temperance, then they hear every
body, and that with very good reason ; for every one must
have these virtues, otherwise there can be no cities. That
is the only reason of this difference, which you have so
well argued against.

And, that you may not think that I deceive you, when
I say that all men are truly persuaded that every person
has a sufficient knowledge of justice, and of all other
politic virtues, I will give you a proof which will not suffer
you to doubt it ; if, for example, a man should boast that
he is an excellent player upon the flute,* without knowing
anything of it, every one would treat him with derision. On
the other hand, when we see a man, who, as to justice
and other politic virtues, says before every one, and
testifies against himself, that he is neither just nor virtuous, though on all other occasions there is nothing more

* This is a false reasoning of the sophist. We plainly perceive
when a man knows not how to play upon the flute ; but it is not
so easily seen whether a man be just, or only counterfeits justice.

commendable than to tell the truth, yet in this case it is taken for a sign of folly: and the reason of it is said to be, that all men are obliged to say that they are just, even though they are not; and that he, who at least cannot counterfeit a just man, is a perfect fool, seeing there is no person who is not obliged to participate of that virtue. You see then, that it is with good reason every one is heard speak when politics are spoken of, because we are persuaded, that there is no man who has not some knowledge of it.

Now that the world is persuaded, that civil virtues are neither the present of nature, nor an effect of chance, but the result of reflection and of precept, is what I am about to demonstrate to you.

You see that no person blames us for the faults and vices, which they are persuaded are natural to us, or which come to us by chance, no one admonishes us, or chastises us on this account. On the contrary, they pity us. For who would be so mad as to undertake to reprehend a man who is deformed, for being so? Is not every one persuaded, that the defects of the body, as well as its beauties, are the work of nature, or an effect of fortune, which often changes what nature has made? But it is not the same as to other things which are the result of application and study; when any one is found who has them not, or who has vices opposite to those virtues which he ought to have, then we are really angry with him: he is admonished, reproved, and chastised. Among these vices are injustice, impiety, and, in a word, all that is opposite to politic and civil virtues. As all these virtues are to be acquired by study and labour, every one condemns those who have neglected to learn them.

This is so true, Socrates, that if you will take the pains only to examine what that means, TO PUNISH THE WICKED, what force it bears, and what end is proposed by this punishment; that alone is sufficient to persuade you of this truth, that virtue may be acquired.

For no one punishes a miscreant, merely because he has been wicked, unless it be some savage beast, who punishes to satisfy his own cruelty. But he who punishes with

reason, does not do it for past faults, for it is impossible
to recall what has been done; but for faults that are
to come, to the end that the guilty may not relapse, and
that others may take example by their punishment. And
every man who has this for his end, must of necessity be
persuaded, that virtue may be taught. For he punishes
only for future good. Now it is plain, that all men who
punish the wicked, whether it be in private or in public,
do it only for this end; and your Athenians do it as well
as others. From whence it follows, by a most just and
necessary consequence, that the Athenians are persuaded
as well as other people, that virtue may be acquired and
taught. Thus it is with a great deal of reason that your
Athenians give ear in their counsels to a mason, a smith, a
shoemaker, &c. and that they are persuaded that virtue
may be taught. Methinks this is sufficient proof.

The only scruple that remains, is, that which you make
about great men; for you ask whence it comes that great
men teach their children in their infancy all that can be
taught by masters, and make them very learned in all
arts; and that they neglect to teach them those virtues
which cause all their grandeur and high character. To
answer you that, Socrates, I shall have no farther recourse
to fables, but shall give you very plain reasons.

Do not you believe, that there is one thing above all, to
which all men are equally obliged, or otherwise there can
be neither society nor city? The solution of your difficulty depends upon this one point : for if this only
thing exists, and that it be neither the art of a carpenter,
nor that of a smith, nor that of a potter; but justice,
temperance, holiness, and, in a word, all that is comprehended under the name of virtue; if that thing exists,
and all men are obliged to partake thereof, insomuch that
every particular person who would instruct himself, or do
any other thing, is obliged to guide himself by its rules,
or renounce all that it desires; that all those who will not
partake thereof, men, women, and children, must be reproved, reprehended, and chastised, until instructions or
punishments reform them; and that those who will not
be reformed, must either be banished or punished with
death. If it be so, as you cannot doubt, and that not-

withstanding this, those great men, of whom you speak,
should teach their children all other things, and should
neglect to teach them this thing, I mean virtue ; it must
then be a miracle if children, so much neglected, become
persons of worth, and good citizens.   I have already
proved to you, that every one is persuaded that virtue
may be taught in public and private.   Since then it may
be taught, do you think that fathers teach their children
other things, the ignorance of which is neither attended with death nor the least penalty ; and that they
neglect to teach them those things, the ignorance whereof
is usually attended by imprisonment, exile, confiscation of
goods, and, in a word, by the utter ruin of families ?
For this is the thing that happens to those who are
not brought up virtuously.   Is there not a greater likelihood that they will employ all their pains and all their
applications, to teach them that which is so important
and so necessary ?   Yes, without doubt, Socrates ; and
we ought to think, that those fathers, taking their
children in their younger years, that is, as soon as they
are capable of understanding what is said to them : never
cease all their lives to teach and reprehend them, and not
the fathers only, but also the mothers, nurses, and preceptors, they all chiefly endeavour to make children honest
and virtuous, by shewing them in every thing they do,
and say, that such a thing is just, and such a thing unjust;
that this is handsome, and that unhandsome ; that this is
holy, and that impious.   If children voluntarily obey these
precepts, they are rewarded and praised; and if they do
not obey them, they are threatened and chastised ; they
are propt up and set right, like trees that bend and become
crooked.

When they are sent to school, it is earnestly recommended to their masters not to apply themselves so much
to teach them to read well, and to play well upon instruments, as to teach them virtue and modesty.   Therefore
those masters take very great care of it.   When they can
read, instead of giving them precepts by word of mouth,
they make them read the best poets, and oblige them to
get them by heart.   There they find excellent precepts for
virtue, and recitals which contain the praises of the great-

est men of antiquity, to the end that those children being inflamed with a noble emulation, may imitate and endeavour to resemble them.

The poets and those who teach youth to play upon instruments, take the same pains; they train up young people to modesty, and take particular care that they do nothing amiss.

When they understand music, and can play well upon instruments, they put into their hands the poems of the lyric poets, which they make them sing and play upon the harp, to the end that numbers and harmony may insinuate themselves into their souls, whilst they are yet tender; and that being thereby rendered more soft, tractable, polite, and, as we may say, more harmonious and agreeable, they may be capable of speaking well, and doing well: for the whole life of man has need of number and harmony.

Not being satisfied with these means alone, they send them also to masters of exercise, to the end that having a sound and robust body, they may the better execute the orders of a masculine and sound spirit, and that the weakness of their constitution may not hinder them from serving their country, whether it be in war, or in other functions. And those who send their children most to masters, are such as are best able to do it; that is to say, the richest: insomuch that the children of the rich begin their exercises the earliest, and continue them the longest; for they go thither in their tender years, and do not cease till they are men.

They have no sooner quitted their masters, than their country obliges them to learn the laws, and to live according to the rules they prescribe, that they may do all things by reason, and nothing out of conceit and fancy. And as writing-masters give their scholars, who have not yet learnt to write straightly, a rule to direct them; so the country gives laws to men, that were invented and established by ancient legislators. It obliges them to govern and submit to be governed, according to their laws; and if any one goes astray, it punisheth him; and this punishment is called with you, as in many other places, by a word which properly signifies *to reform;* as justice reforms those who turn aside from the rule which ought to guide them.

After so much pains taken, both in public and private, to inspire virtue, are you amazed, Socrates, and can you have the least doubt that virtue may be taught? This should be so far from surprising you, that you ought, on the other hand, to be very much surprised if the contrary should be true.

But you will say, how comes it to pass, that many of the greatest men's children become dishonest? Here I have a very plain reason, that has nothing surprising in it, if what I have already supposed be firm and unshaken; that is to say, if every man is indispensably obliged to have virtue, to the end that societies and cities may subsist. If it be so, as without doubt it is, consider the other sciences or professions that men are employed in, and you shall see that what I advance is true.

Let us suppose, for example, that this city could not subsist unless we were all players on the flute:* is it not certain, that we should all addict ourselves to the flute, that both in public and private we should teach one another to play upon it; that we should reprehend and chastise those who should neglect to play, and that we should no more make that science a mystery to them, than we do that of justice and law? For does any body refuse to teach another justice? does any one keep that science secret, as he does others? No, certainly. And the reason of it is this, that the virtue and justice of every particular man is useful to the whole body. That is the reason why every one is always ready to teach his neighbour all that concerns law and justice. If it were the same in the art of playing on the flute, and that we were all equally ready to teach others, what we know of it, do you think, Socrates, that the children of the most excellent players upon the flute, would always become more perfect in that art than

---

* This sophist always mistakes himself. It is not the same with virtue as with other arts; a man is an able artist, though he has not acquired the highest perfection in art; but a man is not virtuous unless he has all virtue : for if one part of it be wanting, all is wanting. Protagoras will immediately fall into a manifest contradiction.

the children of the worst players? I am persuaded you believe nothing of the kind.

The children who would be found to be the most happily born for that art, would be those who should make the greatest progress therein, and who should render themselves the most famous for it; the rest would fatigue themselves in vain, and would never gain any name by it; as we frequently see the son of an excellent player upon the flute to be an indifferent scholar; and the son of a blockhead to become an able musician: But they are all superior if we compare them with the ignorant, and with those who never handled a flute. We must hold it for certain, that it is the same in the present case; such an one as would appear to you now to be the most ignorant of those who are brought up in the knowledge of the laws, and in civil society, would be qualified to teach justice, if you should compare him with people who have neither education, law, tribunal, nor judges, who are not forced by any necessity to apply themselves to virtue; who, in a word, should resemble those savages which Pherecrates * caused to be acted last year, at the country-feasts of Bacchus.† Believe me, if you were among men like the misanthropes that that poet introduces, you would think yourself very happy to fall into the hands of an Euribates and a Phrynondas, ‡ and you would sigh for the wickedness of our people, against which you declaim so much. But your distemper comes only from too much ease: because every body teaches virtue as they can, you are pleased to cry out, and say, that there is not so much as one master that teacheth it. It is just as if you

* The poet Pherecrates had acted a play, whereof the title was ἄγριοι, *The Savages*. And there is some appearance of probability that he represented therein the unhappy life that the first men led before they were united by society; and his aim was, to let the Greeks see that there was no happiness for them, but to be well united, and faithfully to execute the treaty of peace, which had so lately terminated a long and fatal war.

† At the country-feasts of Bacchus. He says the *country-feasts*, because there were other feasts of Bacchus that were celebrated in the city the beginning of the spring, and the country-feasts were celebrated the latter end of autumn in the fields.

‡ Euribates and Phrynondas were two notorious profligates, who had given occasion for the proverbs, "An action of Euribates," "To do the actions of Euribates," "It is another Phrynondas."

should seek in Greece for a master who teacheth the Greek tongue, you would find none : Why? because every body teacheth it. Indeed, if you seek for one who can teach tradesmen's sons the trade of their fathers with the same capacity as their fathers themselves, I believe, Socrates, that such a master would not easily be found; but there is nothing more easy than to find one who can teach the ignorant. It is the same with virtue and all other things. And how little soever be the advantage that another man has over us, to push us forward, and to make us advance in the way of virtue, it is always a very considerable thing, and for which we ought to think ourselves very happy. Now, I am certainly one of those who have all the necessary qualities for that; for I know better than any other person in the world, all that must be done to make an honest man; and I can say, that I do not rob them of the money which I take; nay, I deserve more, even in the opinion of my scholars. Wherefore this is the bargain that I usually make: when any body has learned of me, if he desires he pays me what others usually give; if not, he may go into a temple, and after having sworn that what I have taught him is worth so much, deposit the sum which he designs for me. Socrates, this is the fable, and the simple reasons I have thought fit to make use of to prove to you, that virtue may be taught; and to let you see, that we must not be astonished that the children of the greatest men are commonly very little worth, and that those of the ignorant and the poor succeed better, since we have seen that the sons of Polycletus, who are of the same age with Xantippus and Paralus, are nothing, if compared with their father; and so of many other children of our greatest masters.

Protagoras having finished this long and fine discourse, I, after having been some time at a stand, as a man charmed and ravished; looked upon him as if he should still continue to speak; but finding that he had actually done, and having at length resumed courage, I turned towards Hippocrates. In truth, Hippocrates, said I, I cannot express how much I am indebted to you, for having obliged me to come hither, for I would not for all the world, but have heard Protagoras: hitherto I believed that it was not by the help and care of men that we became honest; but now I am persuaded that it is a thing purely human. There is however one small difficulty remaining, which Protagoras will no doubt easily resolve. If we should consult some of our great orators upon such matters, perhaps they would entertain us with similar discourses, and we might believe that we heard a Pericles,* or some of those who have been the most eloquent; and after that, if objection were made to them, they would not know what to answer, and though no one should ask them ever so little upon what they might have already said, their answer would have no end; they would be as a brass kettle, which being once struck, keeps its sound a long time, unless one puts his hand upon it, and stops it; so our orators when once touched resound without end. It is not the same with Protagoras, for he is not only very capable of holding long and fine discourses, as now appears, but also of answering precisely, and in a few words, the questions that are put to him; and can start others, and wait for and receive the answers, which few people are capable of doing.

Now, then, said I to Protagoras, there wants but a small thing to answer me, and I shall be satisfied. You say, that virtue can be taught; but I pray you to remove the scruple which you have left in my mind.† You have said that Jupiter sent shame and justice to men; and in your whole discourse you have spoken of justice, temperance, and sanctity, as if virtue were only one thing which included all these qualities. Explain to me then, if virtue be one, and if justice, temperance, and sanctity, are only its parts; or if all these qualities which I have now named be only different names of one and the same thing. This is what I desire of you.

There is nothing more easy, Socrates, than to satisfy you

* This is a difficult passage, if we have no regard to the time, that is to say, if we do not observe the date of the dialogue. It is that which deceived Henry Stephens, who translated it as if Pericles were still alive, whereas he had been dead eight or nine years.

† Socrates does not trouble himself to answer all the sophisms of Protagoras, which are too gross; but he goes at once to the main point of the question, which consists in knowing the nature of virtue; for virtue being well known, it will be clearly seen that it is not possible for MEN to teach it.

in that point: for virtue is *one thing*, and these are *its*
parts.

But, said I to him, are these its parts, as the mouth, nose,
ears and eyes are the parts of the face?   Or are they parts
like parts of gold, that are all of the same nature as the
mass, and different from each other only in quantity?

They are without doubt parts of it, as the mouth and the
nose are parts of the face.

But, said I, do men acquire some one part of this virtue,
and others another?   Or is there a necessity that he who
acquires one must acquire all?

By no means, answered he.   For you see every day people who are valiant and unjust, and others who are just
without being wise.

For valour and wisdom are only parts of virtue.

Assuredly, said he, and wisdom is the greatest of its parts.

And is every one of its parts different from another?

Without doubt.

And every one has its properties: as in the parts of the
face the eyes are not of the same use with the ears, and
have different properties and faculties; and so of all the
other parts, they are all different, and do not resemble each
other either in form or quality. Is it the same of the parts
of virtue?   Does no one of them in any wise resemble
another? and do they absolutely differ in themselves and
in their faculties?   It is evident that they do not resemble
each other at all, if it be the same of them as of the example
which we have made use of.

That is very certain, Socrates, and the example is just.

Then said I to him, virtue has no other of its parts
which resemble knowledge, justice, valour, temperance, or
sanctity.

No, without doubt.

Come then, let you and I examine to the bottom the nature of every one of its parts.   Let us begin with justice:
is it any thing or nothing?   For my part, I think it is
something: what do you think?

I also think it to be something.

If then any body should apply himself to you and me,
and should say to us, Protagoras and Socrates, explain to
me, I pray you, what is that which you just now called
justice? Is it something that is just or unjust?

I should answer that it is something that is just; would not you answer the same?

Yes, certainly.

Justice consists then, he would say, according to you, in being just?

We would say yes: is it not so?

Without doubt, Socrates.

And if he should ask us, after that; Do not you also say, that there is sanctity? Should not we answer him in the same manner that there is?

Assuredly.

You maintain, he would reply, that it is something; what is it then? is it to be holy, or to be profane? For my part, I confess, Protagoras, that at this question I should be in a passion, and should say to the man, speak sense, I pray you; what is there that can be holy, if sanctity itself be not holy? Would not you answer thus?

Yes indeed, Socrates.

If after that the man should continue to question us, and should say, But what did you just now say? Have I misunderstood you? It seemed to me, that you said the parts of virtue were all different, and that one was never like another. For my part, I should answer him, you have reason to allege that it was said; but if you think it was I who said it, you are mistaken; for it is Protagoras who affirmed it. I only asked the question: doubtless he would not fail to apply himself to you, Protagoras; he would say, Do you agree to what Socrates says? Is it you alone that assure me, that none of the parts of virtue are like to one another? Is that your opinion? What would you answer him, Protagoras?

I should be forced to confess it, Socrates.

And after this confession, what could we answer him, if he should continue his questions, and say, According to you then sanctity is neither a just thing, nor justice a holy thing; but justice is profane, and sanctity is unjust. Is then the just man profane and impious? What should we answer him, Protagoras? I confess, that for my part, I should answer him, that I maintain justice to be holy, and sanctity to be just: and if you yourself did not prevent me, I should answer for you, that you are persuaded that justice is the same thing with sanctity, or at least a thing very like it. See then if you would answer so, and if you would confess it to me.

I could not confess it, Socrates; for that does not seem to me to be true, we ought not so easily to grant that justice is holiness, and that sanctity is justice; there is some difference between them; but what will you make of that? If you will have it so, I consent that justice is holy, and that sanctity is just.

Now, said I to him, if I will is not the question; it is not as I will, it is you or I, it is our persuasion and our principle; that IF does nothing but darken the truth and render proofs useless; it must therefore be removed.

However, we may say, answered he, that justice resembles sanctity in something; for one thing always resembles another in some sort; white itself has in some measure a resemblance to black, hard to soft; and so of all other things which seem to be the most contrary to each other. Those very parts which we have agreed have each different properties and faculties, and that one is not like the other, I mean the parts of the face; if you look to them narrowly, you will find that they in some measure resemble one another: and after this manner you may very well prove, if you will, that all things are alike. However, it is not just to call things alike, that have but a small resemblance; as it is not just to call those things unlike that differ but little from each other: To speak properly, as a slight resemblance, does not render things alike, so a small difference does not make them unlike.

Being amazed at this discourse of the sophist, I asked him: Does then the just and holy seem to you to have only a slight resemblance to each other?

That resemblance, Socrates, is not so small as I have said, but at the same time it is not so great as you say.

Well, said I, since you seem to be in so ill a humour against this sanctity and justice, let us leave them, and take some other subject. What do you think of folly? is it not entirely contrary to wisdom? *

* Socrates is going to prove, that temperance and moderation are the same thing with wisdom, seeing they are contrary to folly; for

It seems so to me.

When men have governed themselves well and profitably, do not they seem to you to be more temperate and more moderate than when they do the contrary?

Without doubt.

Are they not then governed by moderation?

It cannot be otherwise.

And those who have no good government over themselves, do they not act foolishly, and are in no wise moderate in their conduct?

I agree with you in that?

Therefore is not acting foolishly contrary to acting moderately.

It is agreed.

That which is done foolishly, does it not come from folly? and does not that which is done discreetly proceed from moderation.

That is true.

Is not that which proceeds from force, strong; and that which proceeds from weakness, feeble?

Certainly.

Is it not from swiftness that a thing is swift; and from slowness that a thing is slow?

Without doubt.

And all that is done the same, is it not done by the same? and is not the contrary done by the contrary?

Yes, doubtless.

Oh! said I, let us see then, is there not something that is called beauty?

Yes.

This beauty, has it any other contrary than ugliness?

No.

Is there not something that is called good?

Yes.

This good, has it any other contrary than evil?

No, it has no other.

Is there not in the voice a sound which is called acute?

Yes.

one contrary can have but one contrary: and thus temperance moderation and wisdom, are similar parts of virtue.

And that shrill, has it any other contrary than grave ?
No.

Every contrary then has but one contrary, and no more?
I confess it.

Let us make a recital then, of the things wherein we are agreed.

We have agreed,

1. That every contrary has but one only contrary.

2. That contraries are made by contraries.

3. That that which is done foolishly, is done after a quite contrary manner to that which is done discreetly.

4. That that which is done discreetly proceeds from moderation, and that which is done foolishly proceeds from folly.

It is agreed.

That therefore which is done a contrary way, ought to be done by the contrary : that which is done discreetly, is done by moderation, and that which is done foolishly, is done by folly of a contrary way, and *always* by contraries ?

Certainly.

Is not moderation then contrary to folly ?
So it seems to me.

You remember, however, that you agreed just now, that wisdom was contrary to folly.

I confess it.

And that one contrary had but one contrary.

That is true.

From which then of these two principles shall we recede, my dear Protagoras ? Shall it be from this, that one contrary has but one contrary ? Or from that which we asserted just now, that wisdom is some other thing than temperance and modesty ; that each of them are parts of virtue, and that as they are different, they are also unlike, both by their nature and effects, as the parts of the face ? Which of these two principles shall we renounce ? for they do not agree, but make a horrible discord. Ah, how is it possible they should agree, if there be a necessity that one contrary must have but one only contrary, and cannot have more; and that it be found in the mean time, that folly has two contraries, which are wisdom and temperance? Yes, Protagoras has agreed to it, whether he will or not. Wisdom and temperance then must of necessity be but one and the same thing, as we found that justice and sanctity were a little while ago. Now I ask you; a man, who does an unjust thing, is he prudent in being unjust?

For my part, Socrates, said he, I should be ashamed to confess it. However, it is the opinion of the people.

Well, would you have me apply myself to the people, or shall I speak to you?

I beg you, said he, direct yourself only to the people.

That is the same, said I, provided you answer me. For it imports nothing that you think this or that; I examine only the opinion.

Upon that Protagoras, disdaining to be thus questioned, answered by saying, that the matter was difficult. But at last he took his part, and resolved to answer me. Then I said, Protagoras, Answer, I pray you, to my first question: do you think any of those who commit injustice are prudent?

I think there are some, said he.

Is not to be prudent, to be wise?

Yes.

Is not to be wise, to have right aims, and to take the best part even in injustice itself?

I grant it.

But do the unjust take the right side when they succeed well, or the contrary?

When they succeed well.

You affirm then, that there are certain good things.

Certainly.

Then do you call those things that are profitable to men, good?

Yes, by Jupiter; and frequently I do not stick to call those which are not profitable to men, also good.

The tone in which he spoke this shewed that he was exasperated in a high degree, and ready to be transported with anger. Seeing his condition, I wished to make the best of him, therefore I interrogated him with greater precaution and discretion; Protagoras, said I, do you call good, those things that are profitable to men, or those that are no ways profitable?

Not at all, Socrates.* For I know many that are absolutely useless to men, as certain drinks, certain foods,
certain medicines, and a thousand others of the same nature; and I know others that are useful to them. There
are some that are indifferent to men, and excellent for
horses. Some are only useful to cattle, others only to·
dogs. Such a thing is of no use to animals, and very
good for trees. Moreover, that which is good for the
root is often bad for the twigs, which if you should cover
with it, would die. Without going further, oil is the
greatest enemy to all plants, and to the skin of all cattle,
but it is very good for the skin of man. It is so true,
that that which is called good, is various; that oil itself,
of which I speak, is good for the exterior parts of man,
and very bad for the interior. For that reason the physicians absolutely forbid the sick to take it, or at least give
them but very little, and only enough to correct the bad
smell of certain things which they give them.

Protagoras having thus spoken, all the company clapped
their hands, as if he had said wonders: I said to him,
Protagoras, I am a man naturally very forgetful, and, if
any body makes long discourses to me, I immediately
forget the subject of the dispute. Now as if I were somewhat deaf, and you had a mind to discourse with me, you
would speak a little louder to me than to others; even so
I desire you to accommodate yourself to this fault that I
have. And since you have to do with a man whose memory is very bad, shorten your answers, if you intend that
I should follow you.

Would you have me abridge my answers? Would
you have me make them shorter than they ought to
be?

No, said I.

But who shall be judge of it, and to what measure shall
we make it? must it be mine or yours?

I have always heard, Protagoras, that you were a very
able man, and that you could render others capable of
making as long and as short discourses upon all subjects

* Protagoras judges what Socrates is about, and to avoid being
caught by him, he throws himself into all these distinctions;
where, in commenting upon an impertinent science, he puts off the
chief question.

as they pleased ; and as no one enlargeth so much as you
when you think fit, so nobody can explain themselves
in less words. If then you have a mind that I should
enjoy your conversation, make use of few words, I conjure you.

Socrates, said he, I have had to do with many people
in my life, and even with the most renowned ; you cannot
but have heard of my disputes : but if I had done, what
you would have me do now, and had suffered my discourses to be cut short by my antagonists, I should
never have obtained such great advantages over them, and
the name of Protagoras would never have been so famous
amongst the Greeks.

By this answer I found that this manner of answering
precisely to questions did not suit him, and that he
could never submit to be questioned. Seeing then that
I could no longer join in that conversation ; Protagoras,
said I, I do not press you to dispute with me, and to follow
a method that is disagreeable to you; but if you have a mind
to speak to me, it is your part to proportion yourself to me,
and speak so that I may be able to follow you : for as all
the world says, and as you yourself admit, it is equally
easy to you to make long or short discourses. For my
part, it is impossible for me to follow discourses that are
long. I wish I were capable of it; but no man makes
himself. And seeing that it is indifferent to you, you
ought to show that complaisance towards me, to the end
that our conversation may continue. At present, farewell:
I am just going, what pleasure soever I might without doubt
have taken in your curious discourses : At the same time
I rose, as having a mind to retire ; but Callias taking me
by the arm with one hand, and with the other holding me
by my cloak: We will not suffer you to depart, Socrates,
said he ; for if you go, all is done, there will be no more
conversation. I conjure you then in the name of God to
stay; for there is nothing I would so willingly hear as
your dispute : I beg it of you, do us this favour.

I answered him standing, as I was ready to go ; Son of
Hipponicus, I have always admired the love you have
for science, I admire it still, and I commend you for it.
Truly I would with all my heart do you the favour you ask

me, if you demanded a thing that was possible. But as if you should command me to run a race with Crison of Himera,* or some of those who run the race six times together, or with some courier; I would say, Callias, I demand nothing more than to have all the swiftness necessary; I could wish it as much as you, but that is impossible. If you would see Crison and me run, you must obtain of him, that he will proportion himself to my weakness; for I cannot go very swift, and it lies on him to go slowly. I tell you the same on this occasion, if you have a mind to hear Protagoras and me, desire him to answer me in few words, as he began to do: for otherwise, what sort of conversation will it be? I have hitherto heard men say, and always believed it, that to converse with one's friends, and to make harangues, were two very different things.

Nevertheless, Socrates, said Callias, methinks that Protagoras demands a very just thing, seeing he desires only to be permitted to speak as much as he shall think fit, and that you may have the same liberty; the condition is equal.

You are deceived, Callias, said Alcibiades, that is not at all equal. For Socrates confesses he has not that abundance, that affluence of words; that he yields that advantage to Protagoras. But as for the art of dispute, and to know how to question and answer well, I shall be much surprised if he yields it either to Protagoras or any one. Let Protagoras then confess, in his turn, with the same ingenuity, that he is more weak in that point than Socrates, that will be enough; but if he boasts that he will oppose him, then let him enter the list with equal arms, that is to say, by questioning, and being questioned, without enlarging and deviating upon every question on purpose to entangle the discourse.

As for Socrates, I will engage for him, that he will forget nothing; he jeers us when he says he is forgetful. So it seems to me that his demand is reasonable, for every one should speak and tell his sentiments in all disputes.

* This Crison of Himera had won the prize of the race of a furlong three times successively.

At these words of Alcibiades, Critias directing his discourse to Prodicus and Hippias, said, Methinks, my friends, that Callias has declared himself openly for Protagoras; and that Alcibiades is one who strives to dispute, and to exasperate men's minds. As for us, let us not fall out one with another in taking part, some with Protagoras, and others with Socrates: let us rather join to entreat of them, not to part in such a way, but continue this agreeable conversation.

You speak extremely well, Critias, said Prodicus; all those who are present at a dispute, ought to remain, but not be indifferent; for these two things ought not to be confounded: to be neuter, is to give to each party all the attention which he requires; and not to be indifferent; is when one reserves his vote for him who is in the right. For my part, if you would follow my advice, Protagoras, and you, Socrates, here is a thing wherein I would willingly have you agree, that is, to dispute and not to quarrel; for friends dispute between themselves for their better instruction, and enemies quarrel to destroy one another. By this means your conversation would be very agreeable and very profitable to us all. First the advantage, which on your side you would reap therefrom, would be, I do not say our praise, but our esteem: now esteem is a sincere homage, which causes a soul to be sincerely touched and affected; whereas praise is frequently but a vain and deceitful sound, which the mouth pronounces contrary to the proper sentiments of the heart. And we, the auditors should get thereby, not that which is only a certain pleasure, but a real and sensible satisfaction.* For satisfaction is the contentment of the mind, which is instructed, and which acquires wisdom and prudence; whereas pleasure is only, properly speaking the tickling of the senses.

Most of the auditors highly applauded the discourse of Prodicus, and the wise Hippias afterwards beginning said: My friends, I look upon you all, as so many kinsmen, friends, and citizens, of one and the same city; not

* By this passage it appears, that the Greeks made some difference between εὐφραίνεσθαι and ἥδεσθαι, that by the first they meant the delights of the mind, and by the other pleasures of the body. This was not always exactly observed: but these words are determined to this sense by their root.

Q

by law but by nature, for by nature every thing is tied to
its like.   But the law, which is a tyrant over men, forceth
and layeth violent hands upon nature on many occasions.
It would be a very shameful thing, if we, who know the
nature of things perfectly, and who pass for the ablest
among the Greeks, should come into Athens, which for
science ought to be looked upon as the august Prytaneum
of Greece, and assembled in the greatest and richest
house of the city, do nothing there worthy of our reputation, than to spend our time in wrangling about trifles,
like the most ignorant of men.   I conjure you then, Protagoras and Socrates, and I advise you, as if we were
your arbitrators, to adopt a temperate and medium
course.   And Socrates, do not you stick too rigorously to
the plain and concise method of a dialogue, unless Protagoras will acquiesce therewith.   Leave him some liberty,
and slacken the reins to discourse, that it may appear to
us more magnificent and sublime.   And you Protagoras, do
not swell the sails of your eloquence, so as to carry you
into the broad ocean, and lose sight of shore.   There is a
medium between those two extremes.   Therefore, if you
will give ear to me, you shall chose a moderator, or
president, who shall oblige you both to keep within
bounds.

     This expedient pleased all the company.   Callias told me
again, that he would not suffer me to go, and they pressed
me to name the president myself : I declined it, saying it
would be a shame for us to have a moderator of our discourses.   For, said I, he whom we shall choose, shall be
either our inferior or our equal.   If he be our inferior, it is
not just that the most incapable, should give laws to the
most learned ; and if he be our equal, he will think as well
as we, and that choice will become altogether useless.

     But it will be said, you shall name one who is more learned
than you ; it is easy to say so, but in truth I do not think
it possible to find a more able man than Protagoras :
and if you should choose one who is not so, and whom
you pretend, however, to be more able, you yourselves see
what injury you do to a man of that merit, in subjecting
him to such a moderator.   But, as for my part, that in no
way concerns me, it is not my interest that makes me speak,
I am ready to renew our conversation to satisfy you.   If

Protagoras will not answer, let him question; I will answer, and at the same time endeavour to show him the manner how I think every man who is questioned ought to answer. When I have answered him as often as he shall have thought fit to question me, he will give me leave to question him in my turn, and he will reply to me after the same manner. If he scruples to answer me, then you and I will join to beg that favour of him, which you desire of me at present; which is, not to break the conversation; and for that there is no necessity to name a moderator, for instead of one, we will have many, for you shall all be moderators.

All said that this was what ought to be done.

Protagoras was not much for it; but was obliged to submit, and to promise that he would question first, and that when he should be weary of questioning, he should permit me to do so, and should answer in his turn precisely to the question.

Then he began after this manner.

Methinks, Socrates, that the best part of erudition consists in being very well versed in reading the poets:* that is, to understand all they say so well, as to be able to distinguish what is well said, and what is ill said; to give reasons for it, and to make every body sensible of it. Do not fear that I am going to remove myself far off from the subject of our dispute, my question shall rest upon virtue. All the difference will be, that I shall transport you into the country of poetry. Simonides says in some place, directing his discourse to Scopas, the son of Creon, the Thessalonian: " It is very difficult to become truly virtuous, and to be in virtue as a cube ; that is to say, that neither our carriage, our actions, or our thoughts, shall shake us, or ever draw us from that state of mind." Do you remember that passage, or shall I relate it to you at length?

There is no need, said I, I remember it, and have studied it with great care.

* The Sophists boasted that they understood all the poets perfectly well: we are about to see the difference in that point between a Sophist and a man who is truly learned.

You did right; but do you think that piece is well or ill done?

It seems to me to be perfectly well done; it is full of sense.

But would you call it well done, if the poet contradicts himself?

No, certainly.

Oh! said he, another time examine things better, and look into them more narrowly.

As for that, my dear Protagoras, said I, I believe I have sufficiently examined it.

Since you have so well examined it, you know then that he says in the sequel: "The saying of Pittacus does not please me at all, though Pittacus was one of the sages, for he says that it is difficult to become virtuous." Do you comprehend that the same man said this, after what he had said but a little before? ·

Yes, I do.

And do you think that these two passages agree?

Yes, Protagoras; said I, and at the same time, lest he should go upon some other thing, I asked him, Do not you find that they agree?

How shall I find that a man agrees with himself when he says contrary things? At first he fixes his principle, that it is difficult to become virtuous. And in a minute after he forgets that principle; and in relating the same motto, spoken in his own sense by Pittacus, that it is very difficult to become virtuous; he blames him, and says in plain terms, that that sentiment does not please him in any wise, and yet it is his own. Thus when he condemns an author, who said nothing but what he had said himself, he manifestly cuts his own throat: He must of necessity speak ill either there or here.

He had no sooner spoken, but a great noise was raised, by the auditors applauding him. As for me, I confess it, like a fencer who had received a hard blow, I was so stunned that I neither saw nor heard; my brains being turned with the noise they made, as also with what I heard him say. In fine, for I must tell you the truth, to gain time to dive into the meaning of the poet, I turned myself towards Prodicus, and directing my discourse to him;

Prodicus, said I, Simonides is your countryman; it is therefore just that you should come to his assistance, and I call you to it, as Homer feigns that Scamandre being vigorously pressed upon by Achilles, calls Simois to his succour, saying to him:

"Let you and I repel this terrible enemy."

I say the same to you, let us take care lest Simonides be turned topsy-turvy by Protagoras. The defence of this poet depends on your ability, which enabled you to distinguish so subtilly between will and desire, as two different things. It is that same ability which has furnished you with so many fine things that you just now taught us. See then if you can be of my opinion, for it does not at all appear to me that Simonides contradicts himself. But tell me first, I pray: Do you think, that to BE, and to BECOME, are one and the same thing, or two different things?

Two very different things, assuredly, answered Prodicus.

In the first verse then, Simonides declares his thoughts in saying, that it is very difficult to become truly virtuous.

You say true, Socrates.

And he blames Pittacus, not, as Protagoras thinks, for having said the same thing as he, but for having said something very different from it. In effect, Pittacus has not said as Simonides did, that it is difficult to BECOME virtuous, but to BE virtuous. Now, my dear Protagoras, to be and to become,* are not the same thing, even in the judgment of Prodicus. And if they be not the same thing, Simonides does in no wise contradict himself. Perhaps then Prodicus himself and many others, entering into Simonides's thoughts, might say with Hesiod, "that it is very difficult to become virtuous."† For the gods have placed labour before virtue; but when a man is come to the pinnacle where it dwells, then though it be very difficult, it is easy to possess it.

Prodicus having heard me speak thus, applauded extremely. But Protagoras answering said, Socrates, your explanation is still more vicious than the text, and the remedy worse than the disease.

* For *to be* denotes a fixed state, and *to become* denotes an alteration, or a going from one state to another.
† It is a passage of Hesiod in his Poem: Works, v. 287.

Then I have done very ill, according to your reckoning, Protagoras, answered I; and I am a pleasant physician indeed; seeing that in designing to cure a distemper, I make it worse.

It is just as I tell you, Socrates.

But how so?

The poet, said he, would be impertinent and ignorant, if he had spoken of virtue as of a thing which is vile and despicable, or easy to possess, for everybody agrees that it is very difficult.*

Being amazed at this quibble; in truth, said I, Protagoras, we are very happy that Prodicus is present at our dispute. For I fancy that you are very well persuaded that the science of Prodicus is one of the divine sciences, as you call those of the ancient times, and not only as old as Simonides, but also much more ancient. You are certainly very accomplished in many other sciences; but as for that, you seem to me but little instructed in it. For my part, I may say that I have some tincture of it, because I am one of Prodicus's disciples. Perhaps you are not aware that Simonides does not gives the word difficult† the sense which you give it; and it may be with that word as with those of dreadful, terrible.‡ At all times when I

* Protagoras changes sides here, according to the custom of the sophists; and instead of demonstrating the pretended contradiction of Simonides, he throws himself upon Hesiod, who says, that it is easy to possess virtue; and in that he puts a very ridiculous quibble upon him. This is the character of the sophists. They were very ignorant at the bottom; but with some reading, which had spoiled their minds, and which they supported with abundance of impudence, they made themselves admired by fools.

† At all times, when a word seems to signify something contrary to the design of the poet, all the different significations which that word can have in the passage in question, ought to be examined into. This is of very great use in criticism, as Aristotle hath well observed. Socrates makes use of it here in *appearance* to defend Simonides, but in *effect* to make these sophists perfectly ridiculous.

‡ Socrates cunningly makes the impertinence of those sophists appear here, in the criticism which they made upon words: for example, upon the word δεινὸς, they would not have it used in a good sense, because it was never used but in speaking of things that are bad, as poverty, prison, sickness. But these sophists ought to have observed this difference, that this word is always truly taken in an ill sense, when applied to inanimate things, but that it may be taken in a good sense when applied to persons. Homer, who understood and wrote his language better than all those sophists, has more than once

make use of them in a good part, and say; for example, to
praise you ; Protagoras is a terrible man, Prodicus always
finds fault, and asks me, if I am not ashamed to call that
which is laudable, terrible: for, says he, that word is
always taken in an ill sense.   This is so true, that you
shall find nobody who says, terrible riches, terrible peace,
terrible health: but every one says, a terrible sickness,
a terrible war, a terrible poverty, that word always de-
noting evil, but never good.   How do you know but that
perhaps by the epithet difficult,* Simonides and all the
inhabitants of the isle of Ceos intend to express something
that is bad, vexatious, or the like.   Let us ask Prodicus.
For it is reasonable to ask of him an explication of the
terms which Simonides made use of.   Tell us then, Prodicus, what would Simonides say by that word difficult?

He means bad.

Behold then, said I, my dear Prodicus, why Simonides
blames Pittacus for having said that it is difficult to be
virtuous, imagining, without doubt, that he meant thereby
that it is a bad thing to have virtue.

Do you think, Socrates, answered Prodicus, that Simonides meant any other thing, and that his aim was not to
upbraid Pittacus, who neither knew the force nor the difference of terms, but spoke coarsely, like a man born at
Lesbos,† and accustomed to barbarous language?

Do you, Protagoras, understand what Prodicus says?
and have you anything to answer?

joined δεινὸς, with αἰδοῖος, venerable. As in the beginning of the
8th book of the Odysses, in speaking of Ulysses ; for δεινὸς, as our
word terrible, signifies often, astonishing, extraordinary, &c.

* The snare which Socrates lays here for the sophists would be
too plain, if the word χαλεπός difficult, did never signify bad, vexatious, but it is taken in this last sense by all the poets. Homer himself has used it in that sense, as in the beginning of that fine Ode of
Anacreon, χαλεπόν το μή θιλῆσαι. ' It is a vexatious thing not to
love.' It is that which deceives Prodicus, whose ignorance he makes
to appear in going about to persuade him, that perhaps it was the
inhabitants of the isle of Ceos, who used that word in this sense.
Prodicus being deceived, would value himself upon this remark, and
acting the great critic, he says that Simonides reproaches Pittacus,
who was a man of Lesbos, whose language was gross and barbarous,
for having used that word ignorantly. Protagoras is a little more
cunning.

· † The language of the Lesbians was barbarous. Rudeness of language usually accompanies clownishness of manners.

I am very far from your opinion, Prodicus, said **Protagoras**; and I take it for a truth, that Simonides understood nothing more by that word DIFFICULT, than what we all understand; and that he meant not that it was bad, but that it was not easy; and that it must be acquired with much pains and labour.

To tell you the truth, Protagoras, said I, I doubt not in the least but that Prodicus knows very well what Simonides's meaning is. But he plays upon you a little, and lays a snare for you, to see if you will fall into it, or if you have the cunning to avoid it, and to maintain your opinion. For here is an indisputable proof that Simonides does not call difficult that which is bad, because he adds immediately after, and God alone possesses that precious treasure. For if he had meant that it is a bad thing to be virtuous, he would never have added, that God alone has virtue; he would have hesitated to make so bad a present alone to the Divinity. If he had done it, Prodicus, far from calling Simonides a divine man,* would not fail to call him a blasphemer and a profligate. But since you are something curious to know if I am well versed in that which you call the reading of the poets, I am going to tell you the meaning of that small poem of Simonides; or if you had rather explain it to me, I will willingly listen to you.

Protagoras hearing me, would willingly take me at my word: But Prodicus and Hippias, with the rest, besought me, not to defer giving them that satisfaction.

I am going, said I, to endeavour to explain to you

* Here is a very small fault; yet it fails not to corrupt the text extremely, and to alter the sense of it. To follow the letter, we should have rendered it, very far from calling him a man of Ceos; for the Greek says, καὶ οὐδαμῶς κεῖον, and not in the least a man of Ceos. But there is nobody but will agree that it ought to be read καὶ οὐδαμῶς θεῖον, and not in the least a divine man, for Simonides was called so. What sense would a man of Ceos bear in opposition to blasphemer and profligate? But it will be said, the piety of the men of Ceos might be so recommended; and so famous, that perhaps they might say a man of Ceos, for a pious man. It was quite contrary. The inhabitants of the isle of Ceos were an impious people, witness the law they made to put to death all the old men above 60 years of age; and that when they were besieged by the Athenians, they put to death all those who were not able to bear arms; which struck the Athenians with so much horror, that they raised the siege to stop the current of such horrible impiety..

my sentiments upon that piece of Simonides. You must
know, then, that philosophy is very ancient among the
Greeks, particularly in Crete and Lacedemon.* There are
more sophists there than in all the world beside; but they
conceal themselves, and make as if they were simple and
ignorant people, just like the sophists you spoke of, that
it may not be discovered that they surpass all the Greeks
in learning and science: That they may be only looked
upon as brave men, and only superior to others by their
courage and contempt of death. For they are persuaded,
that if they were known for what they are, everybody
would apply themselves to that study, and the art would
be no longer valued. Thus by concealing their ability,
they deceive through all the towns of Greece, those who
affect to follow the Lacedemonian way of living. The
most part, in imitation of them, cut their ears, have only
a cord for their girdle, use the hardest exercises, and wear
their garments so short, that they do not cover half their
body. For they persuade themselves, that it is by such
austerities, that the Lacedemonians have made themselves
masters of Greece: and the Lacedemonians are so jealous of
the science of their sophists, that when they have a mind
to discourse with them freely, and are weary of seeing
them in secret and by stealth, they turn out all those apes
that counterfeit them, that is to say, all those strangers
they find in their towns,† and then discourse with the
sophists without admitting any stranger to their conversations. Neither do they suffer their young people to
travel into other towns, for fear they should forget what
they have learnt: and the same thing is done in Crete.
Among those great teachers, there are not only men, but
also women: and a certain mark that I tell you the truth,

---

* He put Crete with Lacedemon, because Lycurgus had brought
back from Crete to Lacedemon many of the Laws that were made
by Minos, and had drawn from thence the idea of the government
which he had established. See the remarks of Plutarch upon the
Life of Lycurgus, tom. i. p. 199.

† Lycurgus shut up the gates of Sparta against all strangers whose
curiosity only drove them thither, and came not for any advantage
or profit: he also forbid travelling. Plutarch gives very fine reasons
for it, p. 248.

and that the Lacedemonians are perfectly well instructed in
philosophy and learning, is, that if any one will discourse
wth the most pitiful fellow of the Lacedemonians, he will
at first take him for an idiot; but in the sequel of the conversation, that idiot will find means pertinently to plant a
short and quick repartee, full of sense and strength, which
he will shoot like an arrow from a bow. Insomuch, that
he who had so bad an opinion of him, will find himself
but a child in comparison to him. Also abundance of
people in our age, and in past ages, have conceived that to
Laconize, consists much more in philosophising than in
the love of exercise, and that it belongs only to a man
who is well instructed and well educated to speak such
fine sentences. Of this number were Thales of Miletum,
Pittacus of Mitylene, Bias of Priene, our Solon, Cleobulas
of Lynde, Myson of Cheyn, a town of Laconia, and Chilon
of Lacedemon. All those sages were zealous followers of
the Lacedemonian learning, as appears still by some of
their works that have been preserved. Being one day
altogether, they consecrated to Apollo, as the first fruits
of their wisdom, those two sentences which are in every-
one's mouth, and caused them to be written in letters of
gold upon the portals of the temple of Delphos : ' Know
thyself, and know nothing too much.'

Why is it that I speak of those pieces of antiquity?   It
is to let you see that the characteristic of the ancient
philosophy was a certain laconic brevity. Now, one of
the best sentences that was attributed to Pittacus, and
which the sages most boasted of, is deservedly this, " It
is difficult to become virtuous." Simonides, then, as
emulating Pittacus in that career of wisdom; conceived
that if he could overthrow this fine sentence, and triumph
over it as over a champion that had acquired universal
applause, he would thereby obtain immortal renown. It
is this sentence then he carps at, and it is with a design
to destroy it, that he hath composed this whole poem,
at least I believe so; let us examine him together, and see
if I am right.

First, the beginning of this poem would be senseless, if
to express only that 'it is difficult to become virtuous,' the
poet should say, It is difficult, ' I confess, to become vir-

tuous ; for that word, *I confess*, is added without any sort
of reason, unless we suppose that Simonides had considered the sentence of Pittacus, in order to quarrel with it.
Pittacus having said, "That it is difficult to be virtuous :"
Simonides opposeth it, and corrects that principle in saying, " That it is difficult to *become* virtuous, and that it is
truly difficult." For observe well, that he does not say that
it is difficult to become truly virtuous ; as if among the
virtuous there might be some who were truly virtuous,
and others who were virtuous without being truly so :
that would be a foolish discourse, and not worthy of a
wise man, like Simonides. Therefore there must needs
have been a transposition in this verse, and the word truly
must be transposed and put out of its place to answer
Pittacus. For it is as if there were a kind of dialogue
between Simonides and Pittacus. The latter saying, " My
friends, it is difficult to be virtuous." Simonides answers ;
" Pittacus, you advance a false principle, for it is not difficult to *be* virtuous : but it is difficult, I confess, to *become*
virtuous, so as not to be shaken, and to be firm in virtue,
as a cube on its basis ; and that neither our carriage, our
thoughts, nor our actions, can draw upon us the least
reproach or blame ; that is truly difficult." Thus it is
plain that he has reason to put the words, *I confess*, there :
and that the word *truly* is very well placed at the end.
The whole sequel of the poem proves that this is the true
sense ; and it would be easy to make it appear that all its
parts agree together, that they are perfectly well composed,
and that all possible grace and elegance is found in them,
with abundance of strength and sense ; but it would carry
us too far to run through it ; let us content ourselves to
examine the idea of the poem in general, and the aim of
the poet to make it appear that he only proposes to himself by all that poem, to refute that sentence of Pittacus.

This is so true, that a little after, as if to give a reason
for what he had said, "That to become virtuous, is a
thing truly difficult;" he adds, "However that it is possible
for some time ; but after one is become so, to persist in
that state, and to be virtuous, as you say ; Pittacus, that
is impossible, and above the strength of man : this happy
privilege is only for God alone, and it is not humanly pos-

sible for a man to remain firm and unmoved when an insurmountable calamity falls upon him."

But what sort of people are they which insupportable calamities afflict, so that they are no longer themselves! For example : Of those who sit at the helm of a ship. It is evident that they are not the ignorant, or the idiots, for the ignorant are cast down even in a calm. As one does not throw to the ground a man that is lying upon it, but one that is standing upright ; so calamities only deject and change an able man, and they never alter one who is ignorant. A terrible tempest, which agitates of a sudden, astonishes and overcomes a pilot ; irregular and stormy seasons astonish and overcome the husbandman ; a wise physician is confounded by accidents, that he could not foresee with all his art of physic : in a word, it is the *good* that happen to become *wicked*, as another poet testifies in this verse : " The good are sometimes good, and sometimes wicked."

But it never happens to the wicked to become wicked, he is always so. It is only the learned, the good, and the wise, to whom it happens to be wicked when a frightful and sudden calamity overtakes them. And it is humanly impossible that it can be otherwise. And you, Pittacus, say, "that it is difficult to be good;" say rather, "that it is difficult to become so," and yet that it is possible : But to persist in that state, is what is impossible, for you must agree that every man who does good, is good; and that every man who does ill, is wicked. What is it then to do good: for example, in learning? and who is the man that you call good in that? Is it not he who has knowledge, and who is learned? What is it that makes a good physician? Is it not the knowledge to cure or comfort the sick? And is not that which makes an ill physician, his want of skill to cure? Whom, then, shall we call a bad physician? Is it not evident that a man must in the first place be a physician, before we can give him that name? and that in the second place he must be a good physician, for it is only the good who is capable of becoming a bad physician? In effect, we who are ignorant in physic, though we should commit faults in that art, yet we should never become *bad physicians*, seeing we are no physicians at all.

He that does not know what architecture is, can never properly be what is called a bad architect, for he is no architect : and so in all other arts. Every man, then, who is no physician, whatever faults he commits in acting the physician, is not, however, in a strict sense, a bad physician. It is the same of the virtuous man ; he may become vicious, without doubt, whether it be by age labour, sickness, or by any other accident ; but he cannot become vicious, unless he was virtuous before. Therefore the only scope of the poet in this work is to make it appear that it is not possible to be, and to persevere always in that state ; but that it is possible to become virtuous, as it is possible to become vicious. The virtuous are absolutely those whom the gods love and favour. Now the sequel of the poem makes it plainly appear, that all this is said against Pittacus. For he adds : " Wherefore I shall not fatigue myself to seek that which is impossible to find, and I shall not consume my life in flattering myself with the vain hopes of seeing a man without blame and entirely innocent amongst us mortals, who live upon what the earth presents to us. If I were happy enough to find him, I should quickly tell you." And in all his poem he carps so much at this sentence of Pittacus, that he says a little after : " For my part, every man who does not a shameful action voluntarily, I praise him, I love him. I do not speak of necessity, that is stronger than the gods themselves:" all this is also spoken against Pittacus. In effect Simonides was too well taught to refer this voluntarily to him, who commits shameful actions, as if there were people who did ill voluntarily. For I am persuaded that of all the philosophers, there is not one to be found, who says that men sin voluntarily. They all know that those who commit crimes, commit them whether they will or not. Therefore Simonides does not say, that he will praise him who does not crimes voluntarily ; but this voluntarily has reference to himself. He says, that he will praise him voluntarily, and with all his heart : for he was persuaded that it frequently happens that an honest and a good man is *forced* to love and to praise certain people. For example, a man has a very unreasonable father and mother, and unjust and cruel country, or some other such like thing.

If that happens to a wicked man what does he? First, he is very glad of it, and afterwards his chief care is to complain publicly, and to make the ill humour of his father and mother, and the injustice of his country known every where, in order thereby to free himself from the just reproaches that might be made against him for the little care he has of them, and for having abandoned them; and under this very notion, he multiplies the subjects of his complaint, and adds a voluntary hatred to that forced enmity. The conduct of an honest man is far different on such occasions: his sole care is to hide and cover the faults of his father and country; far from complaining of them, he hath so much command of himself, as always to speak well of them. If any crying injustice has forced him to be angry with them, he himself is their mediator to himself; he argues with himself for them and reposes to himself all the reasons that can be brought to appease him, and bring him back to his duty; and he is never at peace until being master of his resentment, he has restored them his love, and can praise them as before. I am persuaded that Simonides has frequently found himself under an obligation to praise a tyrant, or some other considerable person.* He has done so in spite of himself. This then is the language he speaks to Pittacus. " When I blame you, Pittacus, it is not because I am naturally inclined to blame ; no one shall ever see me quarrel with any person, who may be of use to his country. I do not love to find fault, for the *race of fools* is so numerous, that if any man should take upon him to re-prehend them, he would never have done. We must take all that for good and fine, wherein we find no shameful mixture, or scandalous blot." When he says, we must take all that for good, &c. It is not the same as if he said, we must take all that for white, wherein we find no mixture of black, for that would be altogether ridiculous. But he would have them to understand, that he contents

---

* He speaks this, because Simonides had kept a friendly correspondence with Pausanias, King of Lacedemon, who gained the battle of Platæa, and with Hioro the wisest of all the ancient tyrants.

himself with a mediocrity, and that he reprehends and blames nothing wherein this mediocrity is found. For we must not hope to meet with perfection in this world. "Wherefore, saith he, I do not look for a man who is altogether innocent among all those who are nourished by the products of the earth. Were I happy enough to find him, I should not hide him from you, but should quickly shew him to you. Till then, I shall praise no man as being perfect. It sufficeth me that a man be in this laudable mediocrity, and that he do no ill. These are the people whom I love and praise." And as he speaks to Pittacus, who is of Mitylene, he speaks in the language of the Mitylenes, "voluntarily I praise them, and I love them." This word *voluntarily* has no reference to what precedes, but to what follows. He means that he praises those people of his own accord, whereas there are others whom he praises of necessity. "Thus then, Pittacus, continues he, if you had kept yourself in that mediocrity, and told us things that were probable, I should never have reprehended you, but in lieu thereof you impose upon us for truths, principles that are manifestly false, and which is worse, about very essential things ; wherefore I contradict you." Behold then, my dear Prodicus, and my dear Protagoras, what, in my opinion, is the meaning and the scope of this poem of Simonides.

Hippias answering, said, Indeed Socrates you have perfectly well explained the hidden meaning of that poem : I have also a short speech to make to you to confirm your explication. If you please I will communicate my discoveries to you.

That is very well, said Alcibiades, interrupting him, but it must be another time. At present it is reasonable that Protagoras and Socrates make an end of their dispute, and that they stand to the treaty they have made. If Protagoras inclines still to question; Socrates must answer. And if he has a mind to answer in his turn, Socrates must question.

I leave it to Protagoras's choice, said I, let him choose which is most agreeable to him. But if he would be advised by me, we should leave for the present the farther consideration of the poets and poetry. I confess that I should be better pleased to dive with Protagoras into the depths of the first question I proposed, for in conversing

thus of poetry, we do as ignorant and vulgar people,
when they feast one another ; for not being able to discourse among themselves of fine things, and to maintain
conversation, they are silent, and hire at a great charge
singers and players upon flutes to hide their ignorance
and clownishness.* Whereas when honest men, who have
been well instructed, eat together, they do not send for
singers, dancers, and players ; they find no trouble to entertain one another without all these fopperies and vain
amusements. They reciprocally speak and hear, and prefer the harmony of such discourse to all music. It ought
to be the same in this kind of conversation, especially,
when it is between people who value themselves as most of
those do who are here ; they have no occasion for strange
voices, nor for poets, of whom they cannot ask a reason for
what they say, and to whom most of those who cite them
attribute some one sense, some another, without being
ever able to come to an agreement. That is the reason
why able men ought to avoid those dissertations upon
the poets, and entertain themselves in sounding and examining one another, by their discourse, and give a proof of the
progress they have made in the study of wisdom. That is
the example which, I think, you and I ought rather to
follow. Leaving the poets then, let us discourse, or if ·I
may so say, let us fence together to see how far we
are in the right. If you have a mind to question me, I
am ready to answer; if not, give me leave to propose the
question, and let us endeavour to bring the enquiry which
has been interrupted, to a satisfactory termination.

When I had spoken ·thus, Protagoras knew not which
part to take, and made no answer. Wherefore Alcibiades
turning towards Callias, said, Protagoras does well in not
declaring what he will do, whether he will answer or pro-
pound.

Let him enter the list, said Callias; or else say
why he will not, that we may know his reasons. and
that thereupon Socrates may dispute with another, or

* The musicians and players upon instruments were introduced to
feasts by unintellectual peeple who were incapable of entertaining
themselves. Does not the violent passion that is now observed for
music proceed from the same defect ? Perhaps we sing only because
we cannot discourse.

chat some one of the company may dispute with the first who shall offer himself.

Then Protagoras being ashamed, as I thought, to hear Alcibiades talk so, and to see himself solicited by Callias, and by almost all those who were present, at last resolved to enter into dispute, and desired me to propose questions to him.

I began to say to him, Protagoras, do not think I will converse with you upon any other design than to search into the bottom of some matters whereof I still daily doubt; for I am persuaded that Homer hath very well said, " Two men who go together see things best, for one sees what the other sees not." In effect : we, poor mortals, when together, have a greater facility for all that we have a mind to . say, do, or think. A man alone, though never so able and witty, seeks always some one to whom to communicate his thoughts, and assist him until he has found what he sought. Behold also why I converse more willingly with you than with another, being very well persuaded that you have better examined than others all the matters that an honest man ought in duty to search into the bottom of, and particularly all that relates to virtue. Alas ! to whom should one address himself rather than to you ? First, you value yourself on being a very honest man; and besides that, you have an advantage that most honest men have not, that is, that being virtuous, you can also make those virtuous who frequent your company: You are certain of doing it, and rely so much upon your wisdom, that whereas the other sophists hide and disguise their art, you make public profession, in all the cities of Greece, that you are a sophist; you give yourself out publicly to be a master in the sciences and in virtue ; you are the first who have set a value upon yourself, and put a price upon your precepts : Why then should we not call you to the examination of things that we enquire after, and which you know so well ? Why should we not be impatient to ask you questions, and to communicate our doubts to you ? For my part, I cannot refrain, and ardently desire that you would explain to me the things that I have already asked, and such as I have yet to ask.

The first question I proposed to you, I remember it very well, was, if science, temperance, valour, justice, and sanctity; I say, if these five names are applicable to one and the same subject, or if every one of these denote a particular essence, a thing which has its distinct properties, and is different from the other four. You answered me, that these names were not applicable to the one only and the same subject, but that each of them served to denote a thing separate and distinct, and that they were all parts of virtue, not similar parts, as those of gold, all which resemble the whole mass whereof they are parts, but dissimilar parts, as the parts of the face which are all parts of it without any resemblance to each other, and without resembling the whole, whereof they are parts, and which have every one their different properties and functions. Tell me then if you are still of this opinion ; and if you have altered it, explain your present thoughts to me ; for if you have changed your opinion, I will not hold you with rigour, but leave you an entire liberty to retract ; and shall not in the least be surprised that you have propounded those principles at first, as it were to try me.

But I tell you most seriously, Socrates, answered Protagoras, the five qualities which you have named, are parts of virtue. To speak the truth, there are four of them which have some resemblance to each other : but valour is very different from all the rest, and by this you may easily know that I tell you the truth ; you shall find an infinite number of people who are very unjust, very impious, very debauched, and very ignorant ; and yet at the same time they are *valiant* to admiration.

I stop you there, said I, for I must examine what you have advanced. Do you call those who are *bad*, valiant ? Is that your meaning ?

Yes, and those who venture headlong where others fear to go.

Let us see then, my dear Protagoras, do not you call virtue a fine thing ? And do not you boast of teaching it as something that is fine ?

Yes, and as something that is *very* fine, otherwise I have lost my judgment.

But is that virtue fine in part and ugly in part, or is it altogether fine ?

It is altogether fine.

Do not you find some people who throw themselves headlong into wells and deep waters?

Yes, our divers.

Do they do it because it is a trade they are accustomed to and expert in, or for some other reason?

Because it is a trade they are expert at.

Who are those who fight well on horse-back? Are they such as know how to manage a horse well, or those who cannot?

Doubtless those who can manage a horse

Is it not the same with those who fight with a buckler?

Yes, certainly, and in all other things, those who are expert in them are more brave and courageous than those who are not, and the same troops, after having been well disciplined and inured to war, are far different from what they were before.

But, said I, you have seen people who without having been thus disciplined, are notwithstanding very brave, and very courageous upon all occasions?

Yes, certainly, I have seen some, and these most brave.

Do not you call those people who are so brave and so bold, *valiant men?*

You do not consider, Socrates, what you say; then valour would be an ugly and shameful thing, for such men are fools.

But I say, have not you called bold men, valiant men?

Yes, so far.

And nevertheless now these bold men seem to you to be fools, and not valiant; and just now, quite the contrary, you then thought the most learned, and the most wise to be the most bold. If they are the most bold, then according to your principles, they are the most valiant; and consequently science is the same thing as valour.

You do not well remember, Socrates, what I answered to; you demanded if valiant men were bold, I answered, yes. But you did not at all ask me if bold men were valiant; for if you had, I should have made a distinction, and have told you that they are not at all so.* Hitherto

* It is an evasion of the sophist drawn from the rule of universal affirmative propositions, which are not convertible but by adding some restriction to the attribute, which become the subject.

my principle, that the valiant are bold, remains in its full strength, and you have not been able to convict it of any falsehood. You make it appear very well that the same persons are more bold when they are instructed and well trained, than before they had learned any thing; and that disciplined troops are more bold than those that are not disciplined; and from thence you are pleased to conclude, that valour and science are but one and the same thing. By this way of arguing, you will also find that strength and science are but one and the same thing. For first, you will ask me after your usual way of gradation. Are the strong, puissant?* I should answer you, yes. Then you would add, are those who have learned to wrestle more puissant than those who have not learned? And the same wrestler, is he not more puissant after having learned, than he was before he knew any thing of that exercise? I should still answer, yes. And from those two things which I should have granted, you would believe, that by making use of the same proofs, you might lawfully draw this consequence, that by my own confession, science is strength. Wait, I pray you; I have not granted, neither do I grant that the puissant are strong, I only say that the strong are puissant. For puissance and strength are far from being the same thing. Puissance comes from science, and sometimes from choler and fury; whereas strength comes always from nature and from the good nourishment, that is given to the body. It is thus that I have said that boldness and valour were not the same thing; that there have been some occasions wherein the valiant were bold, but that it could not be inferred from thence that all the bold were valiant. For men become bold by exercise and art, and sometimes by anger and fury, just as they become puissant. But

* To understand Protagoras's way of arguing, we must know that by strength, he means the natural disposition of a robust body; and that by puissance, he means a supernatural vigour like that of a frantic person, who in his fits breaks chains, and he also means acquired vigour, like that of a champion. This is the reason why he grants that the strong are puissant, and denies that the puissant are strong, for strength is natural, and puissance springs from habit, or from an impulse of the mind. But at last it is nothing but a mere quibble, wherein the sophist even contradicts himself, as will be seen immediately.

valour proceeds from nature, and the good cultivation of the soul.*

But do not you say, my dear Protagoras, that certain people live well, that is to say, agreeably, and that others live ill, that is to say, disagreeably?

Without doubt.

And do you say that man lives well, when he spends his life in troubles and grief?

No assuredly.

But when a man dies after having spent his life agreeably, do not you think he lived well?

Yes, I do.

Is it not then a good thing to live pleasantly, and a very bad thing to live disagreeably?

It is according as one delights in what is decent and honest, said he.†

What, Protagoras, said I, will you be of the opinion of the vulgar, and will you, with them, call certain things that are agreeable, bad, and some others that are disagreeable, will you call good?‡

Yes, certainly.

How, say you? Are those agreeable things, bad in that which makes them agreeable, independently from all that may happen? And these disagreeable things, are they good after the same manner independently of all consequences?

---

* He means that the more men are disciplined, or transported with anger, the more bold they are. He compares boldness to puissance, and valour to force. But he does not see that in confessing that valour proceeds from the good nourishment given to the soul, he acquiesceth with Socrates's principle, that valour is nothing but science. Socrates is going to lead him another way.

† Protagoras is ashamed of what he just now confessed, for he sees the consequence of it; therefore he contradicts himself all of a sudden, and he acknowledges that a man who spends his life in honest things, and who delights therein, lives agreeably, even though the said things be painful. Socrates makes good use of his confession, and is going to pursue this principle which will overthrow the sophist immediately.

‡ For the vulgar are persuaded that there are some agreeable things that are bad, and some disagreeable things that are good. But they reckon them good or bad only by their consequences; for if considered in themselves, we always find the things that are agreeable, to be good, and those that are disagreeable, bad.

Yes, just so.*

Then they are not bad, in so far as they are disagreeable.†

In truth, Socrates, said he, I know not if I ought to make my answers as simple and as general as your questions, and if I ought to assert absolutely, that all agreeable things are good, and that all disagreeable things are bad. Methinks, that not only in this dispute, but also in all others that I may have, it is best to answer, that there are certain agreeable things that are not good, and that among the disagreeable, there are certain things that are not bad; and that there is a third or medium kind which is neither good nor bad.

But do not you call those things agreeable that are joined with pleasure, and which give pleasure?

Most certainly.

I ask you then if they are not good, in so far as they are agreeable, that is to say, is not the pleasure they cause something of good?

To that, said he, I answer as you, Socrates, daily answer others, that is, that we must examine it, and if it agrees with reason, and we find that the agreeable and the good are but one and the same thing, we must acquiesce therewith, if not, there is an open field for dispute.

Which do you like best then, Protagoras, said I, will you be pleased to lead me in this inquiry, or shall I lead you?

It is most reasonable that you should lead me, for you began.

I will do it, said I, and here is perhaps a method that will make the thing appear plain: As a master of exercise, or a physician seeing a man whose constitution he would know, in order to judge of his health, or the strength and good disposition of his body, does not content himself with looking on his hands and face, but says to him, Strip

* This sophist confesses one thing here, whereof he is not in the least persuaded; he also retracts it in the following answer, for he foresees very well that this confession would carry him too far. He knows not how to rid himself out of the difficulty and confusion he is in.

† It is a necessary consequence of what this sophist confessed just now. For if disagreeable things are good independently from what may follow, they cannot be bad because they are disagreeable.

yourself, I pray you, that I may judge of your state with
the more certainty; I have a mind to use the same conduct
with you in our inquiry; after having known your sentiments of good and of agreeable, I must still say to you,
my dear Protagoras, do as that master of exercise does, discover yourself a little more, and tell me your thoughts of
science. Are your ideas of that, like those of the vulgar,
or are you of other sentiments? For it is the opinion
of the vulgar in reference to science or knowledge, that
it is a thing neither strong, capable of conducting, nor
worthy to command: They cannot fancy to themselves
that it has any of these qualities: and they persuade
themselves, that when science is found in a man, it is not
that which leads and conducts him, but quite a different thing: That it is sometimes anger, sometimes pleasure, sometimes sadness, at other times love, and frequently fear. In a word, the vulgar take science to be
a vile slave, always insulted and domineered over, and
dragged along by the passions. Are you of the same
opinion with them? Or do you think on the contrary,
that science is a fixed thing, that it is capable of commanding man, and that it can put him into a state never to be
conquered by any passion, so that all the potentates upon
earth shall never be able to force him to do anything but
what science shall command, and that it is alone sufficient to deliver him.

I do not only admit all that you have said of science,
answered Protagoras, but I add, that it would seem worse
in me than in any other man, not to maintain that it is the
strongest of all human things.

You have reason, Protagoras. However, you know very
well that the vulgar do not believe us upon this subject,
they consider that most men know to little purpose what
is most just, and what is best, for they do nothing of
it, and frequently act quite contrary. Those of whom I
have asked the cause of so strange a conduct, have all
told me, that these people are overcome with pleasure,
or by sadness, or vanquished, and carried away by some
other passion. I am apt to believe that those whom I have
consulted, are deceived in that, as in many other things.
But, let us see: let us endeavour to show them plainly
what this unhappy inclination is, and wherein it consists,

which occasions them to be overcome by pleasures, and prevents them from acting that which is best, though they know it : For perhaps, if we should say to them, friends, you are deceived, and you have a false principle, they would ask us in their turn, Socrates, and you, Protagoras: What! is it not a passion, to be overcome by pleasures? Tell us then what it is, from whence it comes, and wherein it consists?

What, Socrates! said my opponent, are we obliged to stand to the opinions of the vulgar, who speak at random all that comes into their heads?

However, answered I, this may serve in some measure to make us understand the coherence that valour has, with the other parts of virtue. If therefore you will stand to what you at first agreed, which is, that I should lead you that way which I should think the best and shortest, then follow me; or if you think fit, I will give over.

On the contrary, said he, Socrates, I pray you to continue as you began.

Resuming my discourse then: If those same people said I, should persist to ask us, what do you call that state of mind which is overcome by pleasures? What should we answer? For my part, this is the way I should take to answer them. I should immediately say, my friends, hearken, I pray you, and Protagoras and myself will endeavour to give a satisfactory answer to your question. Do you think that any other thing happens to you than what really happens, when you are enticed by the pleasures which seem very agreeable, you yield to the temptation, although you know very well that those pleasures are very bad and very dangerous? They would not fail to answer, that it is nothing else. We should afterwards ask them, Why say you that those pleasures are evil? Is it because they give you a sort of pleasure in the moment that you enjoy them? Or is it because in the sequel they engender diseases, that they throw you headlong into poverty, and draw after them a thousand misfortunes? Or suppose they should not be followed by any of those mischiefs, would you still call them bad, inasmuch as they cause man to rejoice; and that to rejoice in vice is the most deplorable of all vices? Let us consider, Protagoras, what other thing could they answer to us, than that they are not bad, by reason of the pleasure they occasion at the time of enjoyment, but because of the diseases and other accidents which they draw after them ?

I am persuaded, said Protagoras, that this is what almost all of them would answer.*

Does not, said I, all that which destroys our health, or which causeth our ruin, vex us ? I fancy they would agree to it.

Without doubt, said Protagoras.

Then should I continue : You think, my friends, that these pleasures are not bad because they terminate in sorrow, and deprive men of other pleasures which they desire to enjoy ? They would not fail to acquiesce therein.

Protagoras consents to it.

But, say I, if we should take the contrary side, and should ask them, My friends, you say that disagreeable things are good, how do you understand it ? Will you speak by example of bodily exercises, of war, of cures that the physicians perform by incision, by purgations, or by strictness of diet ? Do you say that these things are good, but that they are disagreeable ? They would be of that opinion.

Without doubt.

Why do you call them good ? Is it because at the moment, they cause the greatest pain ? Or, because by their operation, they occasion health and a good habit of body, and are the preservation of cities. Without doubt they would make no scruple to take the last part : Protagoras acquiesced therein.

But suppose I should go on and ask if all those things which I have named are good, for any other reason, than because they end in pleasure, and that they remove and chase away vexation and sadness ? For what other motive should oblige you to call those things good, but the removing of vexation, and the expectation of pleasure ? I cannot see any.

* And consequently Protagoras has spoken against his own proper sentiments, when he answered, that certain agreeable things were bad by the very same thing that made them agreeable, and independent from all that might happen, and that certain disagreeable things were good after the same manner, independent of all that may follow. We must observe this wonderful art whereby Socrates makes Protagoras contradict himself so plainly, without ever surprising or offending him.

R

Nor I neither, said Protagoras.

Therefore do not you seek after pleasure as a good thing, and avoid vexation as an evil?

Without contradiction.

And consequently you take vexation for an evil, and pleasure for a good? You call pleasure itself an evil, when it deprives you of certain pleasures that are greater than those which it procures for you, and when it causes you troubles more sensible than all its pleasures. For if you should have any other reason to call pleasure an evil, and if you should find that it had any other end, you would make no difficulty to tell us of it, but I am sure you cannot do so.

They cannot find any, said Protagoras.

Is it not the same thing with grief or pain? Do not you call it good when it delivers you from certain evils that are greater than those which it occasions you, or when the pleasures it procures, are greater than its vexations? For if you could propose to yourself any other end than what I have told you, for calling pain good, you would without doubt tell it us; but you cannot.

That is very true, said Protagoras.

Suppose, continued I, you should ask me, why I turn the thing so many ways? I should say, pardon me, my friends, this is my manner of examining into subjects on all sides. For first, it is not easy to demonstrate to you what that is which you call *to be overcome by pleasures;* and on the other hand, there is no other means of making certain and sensible demonstrations. But you are still at your liberty to declare unto me, if you find GOOD to be any other thing than pleasure, and EVIL to be any other thing than pain and sadness. Tell me, would not you be very well satisfied to spend your time agreeably, and without vexation? If you are contented therewith, and if you cannot find that good and evil are any other thing than what I say, hearken to what follows.

That being presupposed, I maintain that there is nothing more ridiculous than to say as you do, that a man knowing evil to be evil, and being able to prevent its commission, ceaseth not to commit it, because he is hurried along by pleasure. And, on the other side, that it is no less absurd to advance as you do; that a man knowing good,

yet refuseth to do it, because of some present pleasure that
diverts him from it. The ridiculousness that I find in
these two propositions will visibly appear to you, if we do
not make use of many names, which will only serve to con-
fuse us ; as *agreeable, disagreeable, good, evil.* Seeing
therefore we speak but of two things, let us make use only
of two names : let us at first call them by the names of
good and *evil ;* and afterwards we shall call them by those
of *agreeable* and *disagreeable.* That being granted, let us
say, that a man knowing evil, and being sensible that it is
so, ceaseth not to commit it. We shall certainly be asked,
why does he commit it ? We shall answer him, because
he is overcome. And by what is he overcome, they will
say ? We cannot now answer by the agreeableness of it,
that is to say, by pleasure, for it is a word that is banished,
and in lieu thereof, we have agreed to make use of the
word *good.* Therefore we must make use of this term only,
and we must answer, that the man commits evil only because he is overcome and surmounted. By what ! We
must cut short the words, *by good.* If he who questions
us has ever so little inclination to raillery, and if he be a
man that can push us home ; you see what a fine field
we give him. He will laugh immediately with all his
might, and will say to us: In truth that is a very pleasant
thing, that a man who knows evil, and is sensible that it
is so, and being able to forbear doing it, ceaseth not to
commit it, because he is *overcome by good.* He will ask:
Do you think that good is incapable of surmounting evil?
Or is it capable of it ? Without doubt we will answer it is
not capable of it ; for otherwise he whom we said was
overcome by pleasure would not have sinned. But for
what reason is good, incapable of surmounting evil? Or
why has evil the strength to surmount good? Is it not
because one is greater and the other less? Or because
one is more numerous and the other less? For we have
no other reasons to allege.

Then it is evident from this, he would add, that according to you, to be overcome by good, is to choose the
greatest evils instead of the least good. Now let us change
those names by calling *this good and evil* by the names of
agreeable and *disagreeable.* And let us say that a man

does, we have hitherto said evil, but let us now say *disagreeable things*. A man then does things that are *disagreeable*, knowing that they are so, he does them because he is overcome and surmounted by those that are *agreeable*, and these notwithstanding are unable to overcome and surmount. And what is it that makes pleasure incapable of surmounting grief? Is it not the excess or the defect of the one in reference to the other? that is to say, when the one is greater or less than the other ; when one is more or less flat and dull than the other.

But if any should object to us that there is a great difference between a present pleasure, and a pleasure or a pain that is to come and expected : I ask upon that head ; Do they differ by any other thing than by pleasure or pain? They can differ in nothing else. Now, I say, that a man who knows how to balance things well, and who puts agreeable things on the one side, and disagreeable things on the other, as well these that are present, as those that he may foresee are to come, knows very well which are the most numerous. For if you weigh the agreeable with the agreeable, you must always choose the most numerous, and the greatest ; if you weigh the disagreeable with the disagreeable, you must choose the least in number, and the smallest ; and if you weigh the agreeable with the disagreeable, and that the last are surmounted by the first; whether it be, that the present are surmounted by the absent, or the absent by the present, we must always choose the greatest, that is, the first, the *agreeable :** and if the latter, or the *disagreeable* weigh down the scales, we must beware of making so bad a

* This is Socrate's answer to the foregoing objection. Pleasure and pain differ only in the number or degree of the pains and pleasures. Therefore it is ridiculous to think that a man should be so much an enemy to himself, as voluntarily to prefer a small present pleasure to a great pleasure he is sure of, and to run after a pleasure which he sees is followed by a certain pain. For it is agreed that every man seeks the good and shuns the evil. All that is in question is to take a balance, and to weigh the good and evil, as far as they are known. This is not done, which is a sure token that they are not known, and consequently it is the want of knowledge, that is to say, ignorance, that precipitates us into evil. This is without all doubt.

choice.* Is not that all the art to be used? Yes, doubtless, they would say. Protagoras also agreed to it.

Since that is so, I would say; answer me, I pray; Does
not an object appear greater near at hand than at a distance? Do not you understand a voice better when it is
near you, than when it is far off?

Without doubt.

If therefore our happiness consisted always in choosing
and doing that which is *least*, what should we do all
our life-time, to assure us of happiness? Should we
have recourse to the art of measuring, or should we content ourselves with appearances, and with a simple
glance of the eye? But we know that the sight has
often deceived us, and that when we have judged by
the eye, we have been often obliged to change our opinion
when the question to be decided has been, which is the
greatest? Whereas the art of measuring has always
removed these false appearances, and by making the
truth appear, has set the mind at ease, which relied upon
this truth. What would our disputants say to that?
Would they say that our safety depends upon the art of
measuring, or upon any other art?

Upon the art of measuring, without doubt.

And if our safety should depend upon the choice of
even and odd, every time that one must choose the least,
and compare the most with the most, or the least with the
least, and the one with the other, whether they be near or
at a distance, upon what art would our safety depend? Is
it not upon the art of Arithmetic? For the art of
measuring, which teacheth us nothing but the greatness of
things, is no longer the business in question; it would be
requisite to know the even and the odd, and nothing but
the knowledge of Arithmetic can teach us that? Would
not our people agree to it?

Assuredly, said Protagoras.

That is well then, my friends. But since it has appeared to us that our safety depends upon the good choice

---

* Our safety depends upon the good choice between pleasure and
pain. We are only unhappy because we deceive ourselves in our
choice. Our misfortunes proceed only from our ignorance, for no
body desires to be unhappy

which we should make between pleasure and pain, that is
to say, between that which in these two kinds is the
greatest or the least, the most numerous or the least, the
nearest or the farthest off :   Is it not true that the art of
measuring is the art of examining the largeness of things,
and of comparing their different resemblances?

It cannot be otherwise.

Then the art of measuring must be an art and a
science: *They could not disagree to it.   We shall examine
hereafter what that art is, which at the same time is an
art and a science : now that the art of measuring is a
science, we agree, and that suffices for a demonstration
upon the question you have proposed to us ; for you and
I have agreed, that there is nothing so strong as science,
and that wherever it is found, it is victorious over pleasure,
and all other passions.   At the same time you have contradicted it, in assuring us, that pleasure is often victorious, and that it triumphs over man, even when he knows
the poison of it.   Now Protagoras, and Socrates, if that
be not to be overcome by pleasure, tell us what it is, and
what you call that inclination which carries us away.

If we should have answered you at the time that we
called it ignorance, you would have laughed at us.   Laugh
on now, and you will laugh at yourselves.   For you have
confessed that those who deceive themselves in the choice
of pleasure and of pain, that is to say, of good and evil,
are not deceived, but for want of knowledge; you further
agreed that it was not only for want of knowledge,
but for want of that science which teacheth to measure.
Now every action wherein one is deceived for want of
knowledge, you know very well yourself, that it is through
ignorance, and by consequence it is a very great ignorance
to be overcome by pleasure.   Protagoras, Prodicus and
Hippias, boast that they can cure this ignorance, and you
because you are persuaded, that this unhappy inclination
is some other thing than ignorance, will not apply yourself, and will not send your children to those Sophists

---

* It is an art, because there are rules and a method; and it is a
science, because its objects are things necessary, and immaterial, and
because it makes its demonstrations by infallible arguments built upon necessary principles that are incontestable and certain.

who are such excellent masters; as holding it for a
certain truth that *virtue cannot be taught*, and thus
save the money which you would be obliged to give
them. It is that opinion which causes all the misfortunes, not only of the republic, but also of particular
persons.

That is what we would answer to those honest people. But I apply myself now to you, Prodicus and
Hippias, and I ask you as well as Protagoras, if you
think what I have just now said to be true or false?

They all agreed that they were very evident truths.

You agree then, said I, that *agreeable* is that which
is called *good*, and *disagreeable*, that which is called *evil*.

Prodicus agrees to it, as do also the others.

Then what do you think of this, my friends, said I,
are not all actions fine, which tend to make us live agreeably, and without pain? And is not a fine action at the
same time good and useful?

They agree to it.

If it be true that agreeable is good, and that it is
the good, then it is not possible that a man knowing
that there are better things than those which he does,
and knowing that he can do them; should notwithstanding do the evil and leave the good. Therefore, to be
overcome by pleasure, is nothing else than to be in
ignorance; and to overcome pleasures is nothing else
than to have knowledge.

They acquiesced therein.

But, said I to them, what do you call it to be in
ignorance? Is it not to have a false opinion, and to
deceive one's self in things that are very essential and
important?

Without doubt.

It follows then from this principle, that no person
runs voluntarily into evil, nor into that which he takes
to be evil. And that it is not at all in the nature of
man to run after evil, as evil, instead of after good.*
And, when forced to choose one of two evils, you

* For it is certain that our will never inclines to any thing but
that which pleaseth it most. And there is nothing but good, or
what it takes for such, that pleaseth it.

will find no one who would choose the greatest, if it were in his power to take the least.

That seemed to all of us a manifest truth.

Then, said I, what call you terror and fear? Speak Prodicus. Is it not the expectation of an evil: whether you call it terror or fear?

Protagoras and Hippias acquiesced, that terror and fear were nothing else: Prodicus confessed it of fear, but denied it of terror. But that is no matter, my dear Prodicus, answered I. The only important point is to know if the principle which I just now asserted be true. If it be so, all your distinctions are useless. In effect, who is the man who would run after that which he dreads, when he might follow that which he fears not? That is impossible, by your own confession; for from the time that a man fears a thing, he confesseth that he believes it to be bad; and there is no one who voluntarily seeks after and receives that which he considers as evil.

They agreed to it.

These foundations being laid down: Prodicus and Hippias, said I, now Protagoras must justify and prove the truth of what he has asserted; or rather I must grant him quarter for what he advanced at first, for he said that of the five parts of virtue, there is not one that resembles another, and that they had each of them their own qualities and a different character. I will not insist upon that, but let him prove what he said afterwards, that of those five parts, there were four which had some resemblance to each other, and one which was altogether different from the other four, that is to say, *valour*.

He added, that I should know that truth by this evident mark, that is, said he, Socrates; that you shall see men who are very imperious, unjust, debauched, and ignorant, and yet have an heroic valour; and you will thus understand, that valour is extremely different from the other parts of virtue.

I confess that at first I was very much surprised at this answer, and my surprise hath been greater since I examined the thing with you. I asked him if he did not call bold and resolute men, valiant? He told me, that he gave that name to those bold spirits who run headlong into danger.

You remember it very well, Protagoras, that was the answer you made me?

I do remember it, said he.

Tell us then wherein are the valiant bold, is it in things that the timorous undertake?

Certainly not.

Is it in others?   In those things that the brave undertake?

Assuredly.

Do not cowards run on upon those things that seem to be safe, and the valiant upon those that seem to be terrible?

So people say, Socrates, answered Protagoras.

You say true, Protagoras; but that is not what I ask you, I would know your sentiment.   Wherein do you say are the valiant bold?   Is it in things that are terrible, or in that which they think such?

Do not you remember, Socrates, that you have plainly made it appear already, that this was impossible.

You are in the right, Protagoras, I had forgotten it. Then it is a thing demonstrated, that no one runs upon things that he finds to be terrible, because it is most certainly an ignorant thing to suffer one's self to be overcome by passion.

I agree to it.

But on the other side, the brave and the coward run upon things that seem to be safe and without danger, and by that means cowards do the same thing as the brave.*

There is a great difference, Socrates; the cowards do the contrary to what the brave do; without going further, the one seeks war, the other flies from it.

But do they find it to be a fine thing to go to war?

Yes, certainly, most fine.

---

* It is a necessary consequence of what Protagoras just now confessed, that the brave do not run upon terrible things because it is an evil.   Then they run upon things that are safe, and that appear to be without danger; and by consequence they do the same thing as cowards.   But here is the difference between cowards and brave men, that the brave acting always by knowledge, are never deceived in the side they choose; for they certainly know what is terrible, and what is not.   Whereas the cowards acting by ignorance, and fixing safety where danger is, and danger where safety is, are always deceived.   How many great truths are cleared up by this principle

If it be fine, it is also good, for we have agreed that all actions that are fine, are good.

That is most true, said he, and I have always been of that opinion.

I am very glad of it. But who are those who will not go to the war which they find to be so fine and good.

They are cowards, said he.

In the mean time, said I, to go to war being a fine and a good thing : Is it not also agreeable ?

It is a sequel of the principles which we have agreed to?

'Do cowards refuse to go to that which is finer, better, and more agreeable, although they know it to be what it is ?

But, Socrates, if we should confess that, then we overthrow all our first principles.

How, said I, do not the brave run upon all that they think to be the finest, the best, and the most agreeable ?

It cannot be denied.

Then it is evident that the brave have not a *shameful fear* when they fear, nor a *shameful assurance* when they are firm and assured ?

It is true.

If they are not shameful, then they are fine and honest: Is it not so ? And if honest, then they are good ?

Yes.

And are not the cowards, though rash and furious, quite the contrary ? Have they not unworthy fears and shameful assurances ?

I confess it.

And from whence come those unworthy fears and shameful assurances ? Is it not from ignorance ?

That is certain.

But, what do you call that which makes cowards to be cowards ? Do you call it valour, or cowardice ?

I call it cowardice, without doubt.

Then all cowards appear to you to be so, because of their ignorance.

Most assuredly.

Then it is that ignorance which makes them cowards ?

I agree to it.

You have agreed that it is cowardice that makes cowards ?

I have.

According to you, cowardice is the ignorance of things that are terrible, and of those that are not? Protagoras made a signal that he agreed to it. At the same time valour is opposite to cowardice? He made the same sign of approbation.

And consequently the knowledge of things that are terrible, and of those that are not; is opposed to ignorance of the same things? He gave another sign of his consent.

Is ignorance cowardice?

He hesitatingly passed this over.

And is not the knowledge of things that are terrible, and of those that are not, valour? seeing it is contrary to the ignorance of the same things?

Upon that he gave no sign, and said not another word.

How, said I, Protagoras, will you neither grant me what I demand, nor deny it?

Come to an end speedily, said he.

Then I ask you only one question more. I ask you if you still think as you lately did, that there are men who are very ignorant, and yet very brave?

Seeing you are so pressing, said he to me, and that you will oblige me to answer you still, I will do you that pleasure. I tell you then, Socrates, that which you ask me seems impossible, according to the principles that we have established.

I assure you, Protagoras, said I, that I propose all these questions to you with no other design, than to examine narrowly into all the parts of virtue, and to know well what virtue really is: For I am persuaded that this being well known, we should certainly find what we seek for, and what we have discoursed so much upon: the one in saying that virtue cannot be taught, and the other in maintaining that it can. And at this close of our dispute, if I durst presume to personate virtue, I should say that it mightily upbraids and laughs at us: saying, You are pleasant disputants, Socrates and Protagoras! You, Socrates, after having maintained that Virtue cannot be taught, are contradicting yourself, by endeavouring to show that all is science, as justice, temperance, valour, &c., and that is to conclude that virtue can be taught: For if knowledge be

different from virtue, as Protagoras endeavours to prove,
it is evident that virtue cannot be taught; whereas, if it
passes for a science, as you would have it acknowledged,
men will never apprehend that it cannot be taught.* And
Protagoras, on the other hand, after having maintained
that it can be taught, contradicts himself also, by endeavouring to persuade us that it is some other thing than
knowledge.

But let us leave the fiction.   For my part, Protagoras, I
am heartily sorry to see all our principles so horribly confounded; and I could passionately wish that we were able to
disentangle, and explain them ; that after having searched
into all the parts of virtue, we might plainly shew what it
is in itself, and that leaving our chief question at last to
another hearing, we might determine if virtue could be
taught or not : For I am very much afraid that your Epimetheus has deceived us in our examination, as you say he
deceived, and forgot us in the distribution he made.   I
will also tell you frankly, that in your fable, Prometheus
has pleased me much better than that lover of confusion
Epimetheus : and it is by following his example that I take

---

* That is founded upon this erroneous opinion which is very
common, that every science can be taught.   Socrates clearly proves
it to be an error, for by maintaining that virtue is a science, he asserts at the same time, and proves after a most solid manner that
man cannot teach it.   It is not difficult to see what he aims at: He
means that it can be learned of no one but God; for he is the God of
sciences, *Deus Scientiarum*, as he is called in the Holy Scripture;
(1 Kings ii. Psal. cxix. 66. Psal. xciv. 10.) wherefore David says to
him, "Lord, teach me knowledge;" and he assureth us, that it is he
who teacheth it to men, *qui docet hominem scientiam*.   If that be
true of knowledge, it is also true of valour, seeing Socrates hath already proved, that valour and knowledge are but the same thing.
Plato was not the first heathen who had the idea of those excellent
truths; above three hundred years before him, Homer had said (in the
first book of his Iliad) when he brings in Agamemnon speaking to
Achilles, "If thou be so valiant, from whence comes thy valour? Is it
not God who gave it to thee?"   And almost three hundred years before Homer, David had said, (Psal. xviii. 34, and cxliv. 1.) "it is God
who teacheth my hands to war," *qui docet manus meas ad prælium*.
But one will say, why does not Socrates explain his meaning?   It is
because a philosopher ought to fix what virtue is; before he explains
from whence it comes, and who are the masters that teach it; for
virtue being known, its author is also consequently known, and the
proof is made.

all care and precaution to frame my life well, employing myself solely in those inquiries, and if you will join me, as I told you before, I would most willingly dive into the bottom of all these matters.

Socrates, said Protagoras, I extremely commend your good intentions, and your way of treating upon subjects. I can boast that I have no vice; but above all, that I am far from envy; no man in the world is less inclined to it than myself: And as for you, I have often said, that of all those I converse with, you are the person whom I admire the most, and that there is none of all those of your age, but whom I think infinitely below you; and I add, that I shall not in the least be surprised that you should be some day among the number of those great persons who have rendered themselves famous for wisdom. But we shall speak another time of these matters, and it shall be when you please. At present, I am obliged to leave, upon other business.

We must then, Protagoras, said I, put off the dispute to another time, seeing you will have it so; besides, I should have gone long since, where I am expected; but I remained to oblige Callias, who deserved it of me. That being said, every one retired whither his affairs called him.

THE

INTRODUCTION TO SOCRATES'S APOLOGY.

IN Eutyphron we saw how Socrates attacked the superstition of the Athenians and the plurality of their Gods, by
exposing the ridiculousness of the fable, with which their
divinity was stuffed; and by that means endeavouring to
bring them to the knowledge of the true God. They were
a people devoted to idolatry, and always upon their guard
against innovations; witness the Acts of the Apostles;
(ch. 17. 18.), where we see the Athenians, who were disturbed at the preaching of St. Paul, cryed out, "He seemeth
to be a setter forth of strange Gods." Now a people thus
disposed, could not but be alarmed by a doctrine so opposed to their errors. But that was not the first cause of
their hatred to Socrates. The virtue and generous liberty
of that wise man, procured him many secret enemies, who,
in order to get rid of a public censor, that always exposed
their vices, decried him underhand, as being an impious
fellow, that meddled with suspected sciences. Aristophanes
was the most efficient instrument in spreading that calumny. His comedy of the Clouds had such an absolute
influence upon the people, that it moved them to receive the accusation brought against this philosopher
more than twenty years before. The cause being formally
brought to a trial, Socrates was obliged to appear before
his judges, and answer both of these different sorts of accusers. It was above all upon this occasion, as being the
last act of his life, that he admirably kept up the character
of a philosopher, endowed with a divine spirit, and a con-
summate wisdom; who never did an unadvised action, nor
spoke so much as one word amiss. Even death itself,
when threatened and presented to his view, could not

move him to depart one moment from the paths of virtue and justice. He speaks positively of his innocence,
and does not stoop to the base methods of begging votes,
that were then in use. He employs neither the artifice
nor varnish of human eloquence : he has no recourse to
supplications and tears ; he does not bring his wife and
children to soften the judges with their groans and lamentations. His defence does not savour of any thing that is
cringing, cowardly, base or little. His discourse is high,
masculine, generous, and becoming a philosopher. He
gave in his defence with so much plainness and simplicity,
that some of the ancients took occasion from thence to
say, that he did not clear himself of the charge. It is
true, he did not speak as persons upon their trial used to
do. He contented himself with speaking to the judges as
in common discourse, and with proposing some questions
to his accusers ; so that his part was rather a familiar conversation, than a studied harangue. However, even this
his careless Apology was true and to the purpose. Plato,
who was then present, afterwards gathered it into a body;
and without adding any thing to the truth, formed it into
a discourse, set off with an eloquence almost divine, and
which, to my mind, infinitely surpasses the greatest masterpieces of that nature yet known. No other work exhibits
so much candour and ingenuity, joined with so much force.
But, after all, the most admirable thing in this discourse is
not its eloquence, but the fine sentiments it is full of.
Here generosity, reason, piety, and justice, are displayed
with all their splendour; and the maxims scattered throughout may justly be esteemed sacred. Who would not
wonder at this lesson of Socrates ? viz. "That a prisoner
arraigned ought not to make it his business to raise the
pity of the judge ; that he ought to affect him by his
reasons, and not by his requests ; and procure an absolution by justice, not by favour : for a judge is not placed
on the bench to oblige people by violating the laws, but to
do justice pursuant to them : he swears to this purpose,
and his oath ought to be inviolable. Now an honest man
should not solicit his judge to be guilty of perjury ; and
a judge should not suffer himself to be inveigled : else,
two innocent persons will become two criminals." He

teaches, that an honest man ought always to stand to his
post, let the impending danger be ever so great : that he
ought to obey his superiors, and part with his life when
they demand it. For, says he, there is nothing more
criminal and scandalous, than to disobey superior powers,
whether Gods or men. He teaches us not to fear death, but
shame only, which pursues men more swiftly than death itself. He is of opinion, that our ordinary exercise should
be, discoursing of virtue, and putting ourselves to the test
of its rules ; for a life without examination, is no life at
all. In one word, this Apology is a perfect model of the
due conduct of an honest man in all the conditions of life,
and especially of the manner how a person unjustly accused ought to defend himself.

Several persons who assisted.in the court upon this occasion, drew up Socrates's Apology ; in which every one
produced the arguments that occurred to his memory, or
those that affected him most ; and all of them kept true
to the lofty and magnanimous temper of this philosopher.
After all the rest, Xenophon compiled one from the relation
of Hermogenes, the son of Hipponicus, for he himself was
not then at Athens. Time has robbed us of them all.,
except Plato's and Xenophon's ; but it is apparent that the
one of these is much inferior to the other. In the first
we meet with all the force of the greatest disciple of Socrates, a disciple that was present, and came near to the true
original : whereas the other presents us with the hand of
a disciple that was absent, and goes upon an imperfect
copy. However, even this imperfect copy is evidence
that the passages related by Plato are true ; for Xenophon
does not only go upon the same ideas of things, but likewise assures us, that Socrates spoke as he says he did.

" Do but observe," says Montagne,* " by what reasons
Socrates rouses up his courage to the hazards of war; with
what arguments he fortifies his patience against calumny,
tyranny, and death. You will find nothing in all this
borrowed from arts and sciences. The simplest may there
discern their own means and power. It is not possible
more to retire, or to creep lower. He has done human

* Book 3. Chap. 12.

nature a great kindness, in shewing it how much it can do
of itself.   His plea is plain and simple, but yet of an un-
imaginable height.   His way of arguing is equally admirable for its simplicity and its force.   It is an easier matter
to speak like Aristotle, and live like Cæsar, than to speak
and live as Socrates did.   Here lies the greatest difficulty,
and that degree of perfection, which no art can improve."

But before I launch into the Apology, it will be necessary
to say something of the familiar Spirit that governed Socrates, which has made so much noise in the world. Some
looked upon it as fiction ; others gave very different accounts of it.

It is needless to observe, that the opinion of Plato,
assigning to every man, from his very birth, a particular
genius, or angel, to take care of him, is in accordance with
the truth taught in holy Scripture, where we hear of men
conducted by angels, and Jesus Christ himself saying, that
" the angels of little children do see the face of God in heaven without interruption."   Upon which account, Origen
accuses those as calumniators, who would brand the FAMI-
LIAR of Socrates for a fable.*   A certain proof that he was
truly guided by a good Genius, is, that all his life long he
was pious, temperate, and just ; that in all cases he always
took the right side; that he never injured any man ; that
he always proclaimed war against vice; and attacked
false religions; that the whole business of his life was to
make men more honest; and acquaint them with truth and
justice.

The only difficulty is, to know how this Familiar gave
him to understand his meaning, and what was the nature of
that divine voice.   Doubtless inspiration was the manner
of conveyance.   And Plutarch naturally leads us to that
thought, where he speaks of the miracles recounted in
Homer, who often introduces Deities coming to succour men, and to inspire them with the knowledge of what
they ought to do or avoid.   His words are these:†   "We
must either deny the Deity the title of a moving cause,
or any principle of our operations ; or else own that it has
no other way of succouring men, and co-operating with
them, than by calling up and determining the will, by the

---

* In the 6th book against Celsus   † In the Life of Coriolanus.

ideas conveyed into the mind.   For it does not push or
act upon our bodies; it influences neither our hands nor
our feet; but by virtue of certain principles and ideas, which
it calls up within us, it stirs up the active faculty of our
soul, and either pushes on our will, or else checks it, and
turns it another way."

But some will ask, how then could it be a Voice?   It
was a Voice; that is, an impression upon the imaginative faculty of the soul: such as happens often while one is asleep,
and sometimes when awake; when one fancies that he
hears and sees, though at the same time he hears nothing
and sees as little.   This was the opinion that Plutarch
entertained: for he says,* that Socrates was a man of a
clear head, and of an easy and calm temper; that is, he was
not moved by trouble, nor disquieted by passion, and consequently was entirely disposed to listen to the suggestions
of that Genius, which, by virtue of its light, alone influenced the understanding part of the soul, and made the
same impression upon it that a voice does after it has passed
through the organs of the body.   It was this voice that
Homer so admirably describes, when, speaking of the
dream that came upon Agamemnon, he says, that "a divine
voice surrounded him."

There is yet another difficulty behind : It is, why this
Voice had only the power of diverting Socrates, and never
of urging him on to any thing: for Marsilius Ficinus is certainly wrong in pretending to give such a mysterious account of the matter, as if the Genius of Socrates never pushed
him on, because he was not of a martial spirit, and always
dissuaded him, because he was naturally heavy; as if the
Divine Being had only given him the light to deny, and not
to affirm.   This is the way to elude the argument, by split-
ting upon greater difficulties, or pinning the controversy
upon idle and frivolous distinctions.   The more reasonable and natural account of the matter is, that Socrates
was virtuous to the last degree, and always bent to take
up with whatever he considered fair and honest; that
upon other scores, he had no business to mind, but
to live a simple and uniform life, and consequently had no
occasion but to be reserved and backward, when soli-

* In his treatise of the Genius of Socrates.

cited either to pass a false judgment, or to make a wrong step.

In the Latin translations, this Apology is involved in much obscurity, because the translators have not taken care to divide it, and did not perceive that it was made at three several times, which are distinctly noted, in the present translation.

THE

APOLOGY OF SOCRATES.

I KNOW not, Athenians, what impression the harangues of my accusers have made upon you: for my part, I confess that they have almost made me forget myself; so artfully are their reasons coloured and set off. And yet, I can assure you, they have not spoken one word of truth.

But of all their calumnies, that which surprises me most, is, that they counsel you to beware of being seduced by my eloquence,* and endeavour to work you into a great opinion of it. For certainly it is the height of impudence, not to fear the shame of having the lie given them; which I am about to do, by shewing that I am not at all eloquent, unless they call him eloquent who can speak nothing but the truth. If that be their plea, I own myself a great orator, but not after their fashion; for I am now about to discover to you the naked truth, in common and simple expressions, without the quaint turns and picked expressions which set off their discourses. For I have this confidence in myself, that I speak the truth, and none of you ought to expect any thing else from me: it would be very unsuitable for one of my age to appear before you like a school-boy, with a studied harangue upon a fabulous subject.

Wherefore the only favour I beg of you, is, that when

* They cried up his eloquence, in order to aggravate the injustice they charged upon him; alleging, that he confounded the ideas of justice, and taught the way of putting a good face upon bad causes.

you find my defence given in the most ordinary and common terms, such as I am always wont to make use of in my interviews with you on the exchange and public banks, and the other places where I often used to meet you; my request is, that when you find it so, you would not be surprised or incensed against me, for I am about to speak of the matter of fact, just as it stands.

Though I am now seventy years old, this is the first time that I ever entered this hall; I am a stranger to it, and unacquainted with its language and customs. Now were I a foreigner, you would readily grant me the favour of making my defence in the language and manner of my own country. In like manner I beg of you, as a stranger to this hall, and I think my petition is just, that you would grant me the same favour, and overlook my manner of expression, which perhaps is not so good as others (though, after all, it is possible that it may be better) and only mind whether I speak justly or not: for that ought to be the chief view of a judge, as the greatest virtue of an orator consists in speaking nothing but the truth.

It is but reasonable that I should begin by answering the charges of my first accusers, and afterwards come up to the latter in their order : for I have had a great many accusers before this court these several years, and none of them have advanced any thing but what is false. I am more afraid of my old accusers than of Anytus and his accomplices. It is true, the latter display a great deal of eloquence; but the others are more to be regarded, since they have accosted you from your infancy, and persuaded you into a belief of what calumnies they pleased.

They told you, there was one Socrates, a wise man, that inquired into the motions of the heavens, and the hidden treasures of the earth; who has such a dexterous way of perplexing the ideas of justice and truth, that he can make a bad cause appear good.

The men who spread these false rumours are my most dangerous enemies; for those who listen to their surmises are persuaded that philosophers taken up with such inquiries, believe no Gods. Besides, these accusers are very numerous, and they have had a long while to concert their plot; they are now grown old, and took occasion to prepossess you with that opinion, in an age that generally is too credulous : for you were for the most part but infants, or at most in the first years of your youth, when they laid their accusation against me before you, and carried it on without opposition : and which is yet more unjust, I am not allowed to know my accusers.   They get off with setting a comedian at the head of the charge, while all those, who through envy or malice have wrought you into a belief of these falsehoods, and continue still underhand to throw the same calumnies about; these men, I say, are allowed to lie concealed : so that I have neither the power of calling them to account before you, nor the pleasure of refuting them in your presence; and the only way of defending myself is, to fight with a shadow, and speak against I know not whom.

Wherefore consider, Athenians, that I am now to encounter two sorts of accusers, those who arraigned me a great while ago, and those who summoned me lately; and I entreat you to believe that I lie under a necessity of giving my answer first to the former sort.

Now is the time then, that I am to defend myself, and in so short a space of time, I am to endeavour to root out of your minds a calumny, that you have entertained a long while, and which has taken deep root in your minds.   I wish with all my heart that my defences could promote your advantage as well as my own, and that my apology might serve some more important design, than that of justifying myself : but I perceive the difficulties that lie in the way; and am not so blind, as not to see, where all this will terminate.   God's will be done.   My business is to obey the law, and defend myself.

To return to the origin of the charge, upon which I am so much decried, and which inspired Melitus with the boldness to arraign me before you; let us see what was the plea of these my first accusers : for their charge must be put into form, and affidavits made.*   It is this : Socrates is an impious man; with a criminal curiosity he pretends to penetrate into all that passes in the heavens,

---

* Socrates treats the calumnies of Aristophanes and his first enemies, as if it were a just charge formally presented upon oath; for both the accuser and the prisoner were obliged to swear, that they would advance nothing but truth : and this they called ἀντωμοσία.

and to fathom what is contained in the bowels of the earth. He has the way of giving the ascendant to injustice; and is not content to reserve these secrets to himself, but communicates them to others.

This is the accusation : the heads of which you have seen in the comedy of Aristophanes, where one Socrates is represented as hung up in a basket, giving out that he walks upon the winds; with many other such foolish pretensions. Now these are secrets that I am altogether a stranger to; I never gave my mind to these sublime sciences : not that I despise them, or contemn those who are well versed in them, if any such there be, lest Melitus should thereupon charge me with new crimes : I would only give you to know, that I never meddled with these sciences, as most of you can bear witness.

Since you have so often conversed with me, and that there is so great a number of you who know me, I conjure you to declare, if ever you heard me speak of these things, either directly or indirectly. This may furnish you with certain evidence, that all the other articles of my indictment are of a piece with this. And further, if ever you heard that I either taught, or required a reward for so doing, I will prove it to be a base calumny.

Not that I disparage those who do so; such as Gorgias of Leonti, Prodicus of Ceos, and Hippias of Elia. For these great men have a wonderful talent of persuading and retaining all the youth of whatever city they go to; young men that might apply themselves to which of their own countrymen they have a mind to, without any charge, are so influenced by them, that they quit their own countrymen, and adhere to them only, paying large sums, and acknowledging infinite obligations besides. I have likewise heard, that there is yet another very ingenious master in this city, who came from Paros; for I met him the other day in the house of a person who spends more upon sophists, than all the other citizens put together; I mean Callias; where happening to speak of Callias's two sons, I addressed myself to him in this fashion : had you two young horses, would not you want to put them into the hands of some skilful man, and pay him well, for making them handsome, and giving them all the good qualities they ought to have? And would not this skilful man be some good groom, or expert horseman? Now you have two children; what master have you pitched upon for them? Whom have we in our city, that is well versed in human and politic virtues? For doubtless you have considered that question already, upon the account of your children. Tell me then, if you know of any? Yes, doubtless, replied Callias. Who is it, said I; what country is he of; and what are his demands? It is Evenus, replied he, from Paros: he demands fifty crowns. Whereupon I told him, Evenus was happy, provided it was true that he knew the art, and could impart it to others.

As for me, gentlemen, were I possessed of such endowments, I should be proud of them, and glory in them: but such is my misfortune, I have no title to them. I perceive you will be ready to reply,* "But what then have you done, Socrates, and what occasioned these calumnies you are charged with? Had you never done more than your fellow-citizens, nor meddled with further business, these reports of you would never have had a being. Tell us, therefore, how the matter stands, that we may not pass an unadvised sentence." This, I admit is a just objection: wherefore I will endeavour to lay before you the occasion of my being so much decried and talked of. Give ear to me, and assure yourselves, that I will speak nothing but truth.

The disrepute I lie under, is only occasioned by a sort of wisdom within me. But what is this wisdom? Perhaps it is merely human prudence, for I run a great risk of being possessed of nothing more; whereas those men I just mentioned, are superhumanly wise.

I can say nothing to this last sort of wisdom, because I am a stranger to it; and those who charge it upon me, mean only to injure my reputation. But I beg that you Athenians would not be startled, if I seem to speak a little favourably of myself: I shall not advance anything upon my own authority, but shall produce an unexceptionable

* Thus the words τόσον τί ἐστὶ πρᾶγμα are to be rendered; and not as De Serres does, viz., "Quænam hæc est tua res?" What is your business then? The judges knew very well what was Socrates's business, and consequently cannot be supposed to put that question to him. But it is very probable they might ask him what it was that brought him thither, or what he had done to merit those calumnies. Marsilius Ficinus was better acquainted with the spirit of the Greek language, for he rendered it, " Quodnam tuum est opus?"

author to vouch on my behalf. For a witness of my wisdom, such as it is, I refer you to the god himself that presides at Delphi. You are all acquainted with Chære-phon, who was my companion from my infancy, and had the like intimacy with most of you. He accompanied you in your exile, and returned along with you. So that you cannot but know what sort of a man Chærephon was, and how earnest in all his undertakings. One day, being at Delphi, he had the boldness to ask the Oracle (once more I beg you would not be surprised with what I am about to say). I say he put this question to the Oracle, whether there was a wiser man in the world than Socrates? The priestess answered, that there was none. His brother, who is yet alive, can assure you that this is true. Wherefore, I entreat you, Athenians, to consider seriously the reason why I present you with an account of all these things: for, it is only to show you the cause of those false rumours, that have been raised against me.

When I heard the Oracle's answer, I put the question to myself; what does the God mean? What is the hidden sense that lies couched under these words? For, I am sensible, that I am entitled to no wisdom, either small or great. What then does the God mean by calling me the wisest of men, since a Deity cannot lie? Thus I continued a long time in suspense about the meaning of the Oracle, till at last, after a great deal of trouble, it came in my mind to make this trial. I went to one of our citizens, who passes for the wisest man in the city, and hoped that by fixing upon him, as being a wiser person than myself, I should refute the Oracle. When I examined this man, who was one of our greatest politicians, and whose name, I know, is a sufficient recommendation; I found that all the world looked upon him as a wise man, and that he had the like thoughts of himself, but in effect was not such. After this discovery, I made it my business to convince him, that he was not the man he took himself to be. Now this was the occasion which rendered me odious to this man, and to all those who assisted at that inter-view.

When I parted with him, I reasoned within myself, and said: I am wiser than this man. It is possible, that nei-ther he nor I know anything that is good or valuable: but still there is this difference; he is possessed with an opinion of his own knowledge, though at the same time he knows nothing; but I, as I know nothing, so I pretend to know as little. So that upon this account, I thought myself a little wiser than he, because I did not think that I knew what I did not know.

After that I visited another who passes with some for a wiser man than the former; but found him in the same circumstances, and by that discovery gained new enemies. However, this did not discourage me. I continued to make the same experiment upon others. I was sensible that by so doing, I drew hatred upon myself, which gave me some trouble, because I dreaded the consequences. But I was convinced that I was bound to prefer the voice of God to all other considerations, and to apply myself to the most reputable men, in order to find out its true meaning. And now that, O Athenians, I must tell you the truth, the whole result of my inquiry was this: all those who passed for the wisest men, appeared to me to be infinitely less disposed to wisdom, than those who were not so esteemed.

To continue the account of my adventures, in order to refute the Oracle: having visited all the great statesmen, I addressed myself to the poets, both tragedians, dithyrambicks* and others; I made no question, but I should find myself far more ignorant than they. I took up some of their most elaborate performances, and put the question to them, what was their meaning, what plot or design they carried on in these pieces; as if I meant to be instructed. Indeed, Athenians, I am ashamed to ell you the truth: but after all, since I must do so, there was not one man of the whole company that was not better able to discourse of, and assign reasons for the poems, than their respective authors. Thus in a little time, I discovered that poets do not carry on their work by the measures of wisdom, but by a sort of enthusiasm, and by certain impulses of Nature, like prophets and diviners who speak of a great many

* The poets, who compiled hymns to the honour of Bacchus, were so called. These dithyrambs were full of a sublime rage, and consisted of bold and new-coined words. And accordingly, in order to be successful in compiling them, there was a necessity of being transported with fury and enthusiasm. See our remarks upon the 2nd Ode of the 4th book of Horace.

fine things which they do not understand. The poets seemed to me to be cast in the same mould; and at the same time, I perceived, that by reason of their poetry, they looked upon themselves as the wisest of men, and admirably well versed in all other things, that have no relation to their pursuits, and which they do not at all understand. Then I turned my back upon them, being convinced that I was above them, for the same reason that entitled me to a preference before the great politicians.

Having done with the poets, to conclude my inquiry, I addressed myself to the tradesmen. When I accosted them, I was fully convinced, that I understood nothing belonging to their profession, and that I should find them to be men of clear understandings and ready parts: and indeed, I was not deceived. They knew all that I was ignorant of, and upon that score were infinitely wiser than I. But after all, O Athenians, the wisest among them seemed to fall into a similar error to that of the poets.* For every man of them presumed so far upon his success in the way of his business, that he fancied himself admirably well skilled in greater matters: and this extravagant fancy alone obscured their other commendable qualities.

Then I put the question to myself, arguing on the behalf of the Oracle; whether I should rather choose to continue such as I was, without either the knowledge of that sort of men, or their ignorance; or to be entitled to both, and reduced to the same class as they? I answered, both for myself and for the Oracle, that it was infinitely preferable to continue as I was. This, sirs, is the source of that dangerous and mortal enmity, which raised all the calumnies I am now charged with, and denominated me *the Wise*. For all who hear me, believe that I know all things; and by virtue of that knowledge, am enabled to discover and expose the ignorance of others. But I am of opinion that there is none truly wise but God himself; and that the Oracle meant so, in giving us to know, that the utmost extent of human wisdom is no great matter; or rather, that it is just nothing. And as for the Oracle's

* This presumption of the Athenian tradesmen, is a sufficient evidence of the spirit of the people of Athens. They loved to meddle with, and judge of every thing.

mentioning Socrates, doubtless my name was only proposed as an instance; signifying to all men, that the wisest among them, is he, who like Socrates, disclaims all wisdom in himself.

Having fixed upon this truth, I proposed to fortify the idea yet more, and to obey God, in carrying on my enquiry, not only among my own countrymen, but likewise among strangers; in order to try if I could meet with any who were truly wise; and if I found none, I proposed to act the part of an interpreter to the Oracle, and convince the world that they are strangers to wisdom. This my design does so engross both my time and thoughts, that I have not leisure either to meddle in public business, or to take care of my private affairs: and thus, by reason of that continual worship which I render to God, my circumstances are so narrow in the world.*

Besides, a great many young men, who are descended from high families, and have time at command, do willingly follow me, and take so much pleasure in observing the method in which I confute all other men, that they afterwards endeavour to imitate me in baffling those they engage with: and it is not to be doubted but that they meet with a plentiful harvest, by reason of the infinite number of vain men, who fancy they know all things, though at the same time they know nothing, or at most but little.

All those whom they convince of their ignorance, have their eyes upon me, and not upon them; and proclaim, that there is one Socrates, a profligate and infamous wretch, who corrupts the youth: and if any one asks them what Socrates does, or what he teaches, they know nothing of the matter; but to avoid being at a stand, they have recourse to those frivolous reproaches that are commonly cast upon philosophers, viz. that he penetrates into the heavens, and the bosom of the earth; that he believes in no God, and colours bad causes with a good countenance. For they dare not tell the truth, that Socrates is too hard for them, and exposes them for making

* By the worship and service done to God, he means the pains he took in convincing the world that they have no wisdom, and that God alone is entitled to it.

a show of knowing what they do not know. Thus it
came to pass, that my ambitious, violent, and numerous
enemies, supported by a mutual union, and backed by an
irresistible eloquence, did a long while since suggest to
you the calumnies they had forged against me ; and now
have inveigled Melitus, Anytus, and Lycon. Melitus
stands by the poets; Anytus represents the politicians
and tradesmen ; and Lycon appears for the orators. Thus
you see I have reason to tell you in the beginning of
my discourse, that I should look upon it as a miracle, if
in so short a space, I could repel a calumny that has
had so much time to take root, and fortify itself in your
minds.

This, Athenians, is the whole, and the naked truth. I
conceal nothing from you, and I disguise as little : though
at the same time I am not ignorant, that all my advances
upon this score do but exasperate the wound. But even
that, is sufficient evidence that I speak the truth, and
point to the true source of those imputations. As often as
you will take the pains to canvass them, whether now or
at any other time, you will be fully convinced that it is so.
And this, I consider a sufficient apology against my first
accusers.

I am now come to the latter, and shall endeavour to
answer Melitus; who, if the world would take his word
for it, is a very honest man, and a passionate lover of his
country. To draw up the indictment in form, as I did in
answer to the first; the purport of it is this : Socrates is
guilty of unjust things. He corrupts the youth, by not
believing the Gods of his country, and introducing new
Deities. To examine each article apart :

His plea is, that I am guilty of injustice, in corrupting the youth. And I, on the other hand, allege that
Melitus is a very unjust man, for arraigning men on purpose to make a show of taking much care of things that
he never troubled his head with. This charge I am about
to make good. I challenge you then, Melitus : tell me,
is there nothing you mind so much as the promoting
the good and integrity of young men, as far as is possible ?

Mel. No, surely there is nothing.

Soc. But pray tell our judges, who it is that can render

your youth better? For it is not to be questioned, but that you can tell who it is, since you make that so much your business. In effect, since you have found out and impeached the person that corrupts them, you ought to tell who is able to set them right. Pray speak . . . . You see, Melitus, you are confounded, and know not what to answer. Does not this cover you with shame? Is not this a convincing proof that you never regarded the education of youth? But once more, who is it that is best able to improve youth?

Mel. The laws.

Soc. That is not the thing, my friend. I ask you, who it is? Who is the man? For it is a plain case, that the chief thing that the man must be versed in, is the laws.

Mel. I tell you, Socrates, that these judges are the men.

Soc. How do you mean, Melitus? What! are these judges the only men able to instruct and improve youth?

Mel. Most certainly.

Soc. But are all these judges able so to do? or is it only a particular number of them?

Mel. All of them.

Soc. You talk strangely: you have found out a great number of good preceptors for us. But pray, is the whole audience able likewise to better the youth, or not?

Mel. They are all able.

Soc. And what do you say of the senators?

Mel. The senators can also do it.

Soc. But, my dear Melitus, do those who harangue the public assemblies corrupt the youth? or are they able in like manner to better them?

Mel. They are all likewise able.

Soc. It will follow then, that all the Athenians are able to instruct the youth without me; and that it is only I who corrupt them. Is not this what you mean?

Mel. It is so.

Soc. I must needs admit, that by this means you convict me of a very great misfortune. However, pray go on and answer me: do you think, that horses are in the same condition? Can all men make them better, and is it only one man that has the secret of spoiling them? Or is not just the contrary the case, that is, that only one,

or a small number of men, know how to do it, and that
the rest of mankind, when they attempt to improve them,
only spoil them?   And is it not the same with all other
animals?   Certainly it is: whether Anytus and you agree
to it or not: for it would be an infinite happiness and
advantage to youth, if there were only one man in the
world who could corrupt them, and every one besides were
able to redress their errors.   But indeed, Melitus, you have
shewn that the education of youth never much disquieted
you; and of this you now give sufficient proof to the world.
However, pray Melitus, answer me to this point; does a
man benefit more by living with honest men, or with
knaves?   Return me an answer, my friend, for I put no
difficult question.   Is it not true, that wicked men do
always deteriorate the character of those who frequent their
company, and that good men always improve and benefit
those with whom they associate.

Mel. Yes, doubtless.

Soc. Is there any man, who would choose rather to
be injured, than benefited by those he converses with?
Answer me, for the law enjoins you to do so.

Mel. No: there is none.

Soc. But now that you charge me with corrupting and
debauching the youth, do you allege that I did it willingly
and knowingly, or against my will?

Mel. Willingly and knowingly.

Soc. How then, Melitus, does your wisdom, in the age
you are now of, so far surpass mine, that you know
very well that wicked men do always prejudice, and
good men benefit those who frequent their company; and
yet that I should be so ignorant as not to know, that if I
mislead any of my followers, I run the risk of being prejudiced by them, and at the same time continue to draw
that evil upon myself both willingly and knowingly?   In
this point, Melitus, I do not believe you at all; neither do
I think that any man in the world can believe you.   For
one of these things must be true, namely, either that I do
not corrupt the youth at all; or, if I do, that it is against
my will, and without my knowledge.   Now, turn the case
upon which of these two you will, it is plain that you are
a calumniator.   Put the case that I corrupt the youth
against my will, the law does not arraign men for involun-

tary crimes. But it orders that such men as are guilty of
them, should be taken aside, informed of them, and privately reproved for their errors; for it is plain that if I
am fully instructed, I shall cease to be guilty of what
I have committed against my will. Now you have neither
counselled me, nor instructed me; but have arraigned me
before a tribunal, which the law has provided for those
who deserve punishment, and not for those who stand only
in need of information and instruction. This is a convincing proof of what I before alleged, namely, that Melitus never burthened himself much with the thought of
these things.

But, after all, pray say how is it that I corrupt the
youth. According to your information, it is by teaching
them to disown the Gods acknowledged by their country,
and to honour strange ones. Is not this your plea?

Mel. It is.

Soc. Then, Melitus, I conjure you, in the name of all
those Gods whose interest is now concerned, to explain
your meaning more clearly, both to me and to our judges;
for I am at a loss to know, whether you allow that I teach
the youth to believe in any Gods, and only turn their
respect from the Gods of their own country, to foreign
ones; or whether you charge me with believing no God at
all; or that, whilst shaking the belief of others, I am
still persuaded that there are Gods: so that atheism is
not my crime.

Mel. I charge you with acknowledging no God.

Soc. You are a strange man! How can you talk so?
What! do not I believe as other men do, that the sun and
moon are Gods?*

Mel. Certainly, Athenians, he believes in no God; for
he says the sun is a stone, and the moon a piece of earth.

Soc. My dear Melitus, you think you are speaking to
Anaxagoras, and treat our judges very contemptuously, in
thinking them so void of learning, as not to know that the
books of Anaxagoras the Clazomenian, are stuffed with
such stories. Besides, would the youth be at the trouble

* Socrates threw in this ironical expression, in order to expose
the ridiculousness of the religion of the Athenians, who looked upon
the sun and moon as Gods, which are only the work of God's hands.

of learning from me such things as are contained in the
public books which are sold every day for a drachma in
the orchestra? This would furnish them with a fair opportunity of deriding Socrates, for attributing to himself such
things as are not only none of his, but likewise absurd and
extravagant. But pray tell me, do you allege that I own
no God?

Mel. Yes, I do.

Soc. You advance incredible things, my dear Melitus,
and are not consistent with yourself. Suffer me to tell
you, Athenians, that Melitus seems to me to be very
insolent, and that he has laid this accusation out of
a youthful presumption to insult over me : for he is
come hither, as it were, to try me, in proposing a riddle,
saying within himself, I will see if Socrates, who passes
for so wise a man, will be able to discern that I banter
him, and advance contradictory things, or if I can deceive him and all the audience. In effect, his information
presents us with a palpable contradiction : as if he had
said, Socrates is guilty of injustice in owning Gods, and
in owning no Gods. That is the notion I have of it. I
beg you would listen to me, and, pursuant to my first request, would not be incensed against me for addressing
you in my ordinary way of speaking.

Answer me, Melitus ; is there any man in the world
that believes that there are human things, and yet denies
the being of men? Pray answer, and no not make so
much noise. Is there any man who believes that there are
certain rules for managing of horses, and yet believes there
is no such thing as a horse? Is there any man that
troubles himself with tunes for a flute, and yet believes
that no man can play upon it? If you will not answer for
yourself, I will reply for you? There is no such man.
But pray answer me this point : is there any man that
believes divine things, and yet denies the being of a
God?

Mel. No, certainly.

Soc. What pains have I taken to wrest that word from
you ! You acknowledge then, that I believe and teach the
being of Deities. So that whether they be new or old,
you still own that I believe in Deities. And to this pur-

pose you swore in your information.* Now, if I believe
that there are deities, I must necessarily suppose that there
are Gods. Is it not so? Yes, doubtless. I take your
silence for consent. But do not we take these deities or
demons, for Gods, or the children of Gods? Answer me.

Mel. Yes, doubtless.

Soc. And, by consequence, you acknowledge that I believe there are demons, and that these demons are Gods.
You have now a fair proof of my allegation; namely, that
you proposed to me a riddle, in order to divert yourself to
my cost, in alleging that I owned no gods, and yet believe
there are demons. For if demons are children of God,
or bastards, if you will; since they are said to be born of
Nymphs or other women :† Who is the man that admits
the children of gods, and yet denies the being of the gods
themselves? This is as great an absurdity, as if one spoke
of colts and eaglets, and yet denied the being of horses or
eagles. So that Melitus, it is plain, that you laid this
accusation against me, in order to make trial of my parts;
or else you must own that you have no lawful pretence for
citing me before this tribunal. For you will never con-

* These passages are more important than at first view they
seem to be. Whoever believes that there are such creatures as the
children of gods, believes that there are gods. The acknowledging
of angels implies the belief of gods; which is the thing that Socrates points to. These inferior gods are children and ministers of
the supreme God, the God of gods. Now Socrates admitted an infinite number of these subordinate beings, which he looked upon as
a continued chain descending from the throne of God to the earth,
and as the bonds of commerce between God and men, and the medium which unites heaven and earth. This notion of his might be
taken from Homer's mysterious chain; or perhaps he had heard of
Jacob's ladder, the top whereof reached to heaven, when the foo
stood upon the earth; upon which the angels of God ascended and
descended. Gen. 28. 12.

† Socrates speaks thus in compliance with the opinion of the
people, who believed the demons owed their being to the correspondence of the gods with their nymphs or women. Now upon
this occasion, it was not his business to attack that error. It is
certain, that Socrates was not of that opinion; for he had learnt of
Pythagoras, that demons, or angels and heroes, that is, devout men
and saints, are the sons of God, because they derive from him their
being; as light owes its original to a luminous body. And in his
Timæus, speaking of the generation of angels, or demons, he says,
" it is above the reach of human nature."

vince any man who has one grain of sense, that the same man who believes there are such things as relate to the gods and demons, does yet believe that there are neither demons, nor gods, nor heroes. That is altogether impossible. But I need not enlarge my defences before you, Athenians : what I have already said will suffice to make it evident that I am not guilty of "unjust things," and that Melitus's charge is groundless.

As for what I told you in the beginning, about drawing the hatred of the citizens upon me, you may rest satisfied that it is just so ; and that if I die, I owe my death, not to Melitus, nor to Anytus, but to that spirit of hatred and envy that reigns among the people, which has ruined so many honest men, and will still continue to bring others to the like fate. For it is not to be hoped that my death will conclude the tragedy. Were it so, my life would be but too well spent.

But perhaps some will say, are not you ashamed, Socrates, that you applied yourself to a study that now pnts you in danger of your life ? To this objection I will give you a satisfactory answer. Whoever is the man that puts it to me, I must tell him, that he is much mistaken, in believing that a man of valour ought to regard the considerations of life or death. The only thing he ought to regard is, that his actions be just, and such as become an honest man. Otherwise it would follow from your proposition, that the demi-gods who died at the siege of Troy, were all of them imprudent, especially the son of Thetis, who was infinitely more careful to avoid shame than death ; insomuch that his mother seeing him impatient to kill Hector, accosted him, in these terms : "My son, if you revenge the death of Patroclus, by killing Hector, you will certainly die yourself."* But her son was so little moved by her threats, and so much contemned death, that he was infinitely more afraid to live like a coward, and not resent the death of his friends. "May I die immediately," (said he) "provided I do but punish the murderer of Patroclus; provided I be not exposed to contempt, and accounted a useless burden to the earth."

Now what do you think ? Does the valorous man stand

* In the 2nd book of the Iliads.

upon the consideration of danger or death? It is a certain truth, Athenians, that every man who has chosen to himself an honourable post, or is put into it by his superiors, ought to stand fast, fearlessly amidst all the dangers that surround him, without considering death, but bending his whole care to what is more terrible, namely to avoid shame.

So that I should be guilty of a monstrous crime, if, after the faithful services I have done, in exposing my life so often in the points I was preferred to by our generals, at Potidæa, Amphipolis, and Delium, I should now be so transported with the fear of death, or any other danger, as to abandon the post in which God has now placed me, by enjoining me to spend my life in the study of philosophy, and in examining myself and others. That indeed would be a criminal desertion, and would justly occasion the arraignment of me before this tribunal, as being a profligate man, that owns no gods; disobeys an oracle, fears death, and believes himself wise. For to fear death, is nothing else but to believe ourselves to be wise when we are not ; and to fancy that we know what we do not know. In effect no body knows death ; no one can tell but it may be the greatest benefit of mankind : and yet men are afraid of it, as if they knew certainly that it were the greatest of evils. Now, is it not a scandalous ignorance, for men to fancy they know what they do not know ?

For my part I differ in that point from all other men ; and if in any thing I seem more wise than they, it is in this, that as I do not know what passes in the regions below, so I do not pretend to know it. All that I know is this, that there is nothing more criminal or .scandalous, than to be guilty of an unjust thing, and to disobey those who are better than ourselves, or placed above us, whether Gods or men. So that I shall never dread or endeavour to avoid those evils of which I am entirely ignorant, and which, for any thing I know, may really be good. But I shall only dread and avoid those evils which I certainly know to be such,

Now, after all the solicitations of Anytus, in repre senting to you the necessity of bringing me to a trial and now that I am upon it, that you cannot dispenswith my life, lest your sons who are already so much addicted to my doctrine should be entirely corrupted : supposing, I say, that after all these remonstrances, you should say to me, Socrates, we have no regard to the allegations of Anytus ; we dismiss and absolve you, but upon this condition, that you shall give over the pursuit of your philosophy; and in case you be found guilty of a re- lapse, you shall certainly die. If you fix my absolution upon these terms: I answer you, Athenians, that I honour and love you, but that I will rather obey God than man ; and that while I live I will never abandon the exercise of philosophy, in admonishing you according to my usual custom, and addressing myself to every one I meet, in this manner : Since you are so honest a man, and a citizen of the most famous city in the world, equally renowned for wisdom and valour, are not you ashamed to make it your whole business to amass riches, and to purchase glory, credit, and honour; and at the same time to slight the treasures of prudence, truth and wisdom, and not to think of improving your soul to the highest perfection it is capable of ? If any man denies this to be his case, and maintains, that he minds the concerns of his soul, I will not take his word for it, but will still interrogate and ex- amine him : if I find that he is not truly virtuous, but only makes a show of being such, I will make him ashamed of his ignorance, in preferring vile and perishing things to those which are infinitely more valuable, and which will never depart from us.

In this fashion will I discourse the young and the old, the citizens and foreigners ; but above all, you citizens, for whom I am most concerned. For, be it known, that I am commissioned by God so to do ; and I am fully persuaded that your city never enjoyed so great an advantage, as this my continued service. All my busi- ness is to persuade you, both young and old, that you ought not to doat so much upon your body, your riches, and other things, but should love your souls. I ever tell you, that virtue does not flow from riches ; but on the contrary, that riches spring from virtue ; and that all other advantages accruing to men, whether in public or private stations, take rise from the same fountain.

If by speaking these things I corrupt the youth, then

of necessity the poison must lie in those maxims : for if they allege that I advance any thing different from these, they either are mistaken, or impose upon you. After that, I have only to say, that whether you do as Anytus desires or not ; whether you dismiss me, or detain me ; I shall never act contrary to them, though I were to die for it a thousand times. Be not disturbed, Athenians, at what I have said, but vouchsafe me the favour of a patient hearing : your patience will not be in vain, for I have several other things to acquaint you with, which may be of use to you. You may assure yourselves, that if you put me to death, who love your city so passionately, you will prejudice yourselves more than me. Neither Anytus nor Melitus can hurt me : it is impossible they should. For God does not permit that the better sort of men should be injured by those who are worse. All men may kill us, or put us to flight, or assail us with calumnies ; and doubtless Anytus and the rest look upon these things as great evils, but, for my part, I am not of their opinion. In my mind, the greatest of all evils is the doing what Anytus does in persecuting an innocent person, and endeavouring to take away his life by flagrant injustice.

So that upon this occasion, Athenians, it is not out of love to myself, but out of love to you, that I make this defence. Do not sin against God by your sentence, and prove unmindful of the present he has made you. For if you condemn me to death, you will not easily find another citizen, whom God has united to your city. For, God has appointed me to rouse and spur you up, and to be always among you : and upon my word you will scarce light on another that will perform the office as I have done. If you believe this, you will dismiss me.

But perhaps, like men awakened when they have a mind to sleep, you will be uneasy, and reject my advice, and in compliance with Anytus's passion, will condemn me upon very slight grounds. Let it be so. But then you will pass the remainder of your lives in a profound lethargy, unless God take a particular care of you, and send you another man to reprove you.

But to show that it is God who united me to your city, I present you with an infallible proof, viz. that there is something more than human in my neglecting my own private affairs for so many years, and devoting myself wholly to your interest, by taking you aside one after another, like a father, or an elder brother, and incessantly exhorting you to apply yourselves to virtue.

Had I reaped any benefit or advantage by my exhortations, you might have something to say : but you see, my very accusers, who with so much impudence revile me, have not had the face to charge me with that, nor to offer the least evidence of my demanding any reward ; and besides, my poverty is an evidence for me that cannot lie.

Some may think it strange that I should have busied myself so much in giving advice privately, and yet had not the courage to appear in the conventions of the people to counsel and assist my country. The thing that hindered me from doing so, Athenians, was this familiar Spirit, this divine Voice, that you have often heard of, and which Melitus has endeavoured so much to ridicule. This Spirit has stood by me from my infancy: it is a Voice that does not speak but when it means to take me off from some resolution. It never presses me to undertake any thing, but it always thwarted me when I meant to meddle in affairs of state : for had I embarked in such matters, I had long before now been out of the world, and had neither benefitted you nor myself : pray be not disturbed if I speak my mind without disguise : *Whoever offers frankly and generously to oppose the whole body of a people, whether you or others, and endeavours to prevent the commission of iniquity in the city; will never escape with impunity.* It is absolutely necessary that he who stands up for justice, should live a plain private life, and remote from public stations. This I will make good, not by words, but by matter of fact ; upon which I know you lay much stress.

Give ear to the relation of my adventures, and you will find that I am incapable of yielding to any man, in an unjust thing for fear of death, and that by reason of my not complying, I must unavoidably fall a sacrifice to injustice. I am about to talk of things that indeed are disagreeable, but at the same time are very true, and such as have been transacted in your own councils.

You know, Athenians, that I never bore any magistracy, but was only a senator.* Our Antiochian tribe was just come in their turn to the Prytanæum, when, contrary to all the laws, you at the same time resolved to indict the ten generals, for not taking up and interring the bodies of those who were killed or drowned in the sea-fight at the Isles of Arginusæ :† and would not condescend to try them *separately :* a piece of injustice that you were afterwards sensible of, and regretted. Now I was the only senator, who upon that occasion dared to stand up and oppose the violation of the laws. I protested against your decree, and notwithstanding all your menaces and outcries, and the advances of the orators that were preparing an accusation against me, I chose rather to endanger myself on the side of the law and justice, than to suffer myself to be frightened by chains, or death, into a tame compliance with such horrid iniquity.‡

This happened under the popular form of government : but after the establishment of Oligarchy, the thirty Tyrants§ sent for me and fourteen more to the Tholus,‖ and ordered us to bring Leon from Salamina, in order to be put to death ;¶ for by such orders they meant to cast the odium of their ill actions upon several persons. Upon this occasion I gave them to understand, not by words, but by deeds, that I made no account of death, and that my only care was to avoid the commission of impiety and injustice. Notwithstanding the greatness of these . thirty Tyrants, all their power did not influence me to violate the law, and betray my conscience.

Upon our departure from the Tholus, the other four went to Salamina, and brought off Leon ; and as for

* The people of Athens were divided into tribes, and 50 men were chosen by turns out of each, who governed 35 days; and were called the Prytani, or senators.

† This battle was fought by Callicratides the Lacedemonian general, against the ten Athenian generals, who obtained the victory. *Vid. Zenoph. lib. I. Histor. Græc.*

‡ Xenophon gives the same testimony of Socrates.

§ The 30 Tyrants were set up in the first year of the 34th Olymp. being the 64th or 65th of Socrates's age.

‖ The Tholus was a sort of clerk's office, where the Prytani dined, and the clerks sat.

¶ In the 2nd year of the 39th Olymp.

me, I retired to my house: and doubtless my disobedience had been punished by death, had not that form of government been soon after abolished. There are witnesses enough to vouch for the truth of all that I advance.

You see then, that the thing I always aimed at, whether in public or private, was never to go along with any man, no not with tyrants themselves, in an unjust thing.

As for the young people, whom my accusers would have pass for my disciples, I affirm, that I never made a trade of teaching. Indeed, if any persons, whether young or old, were at any time desirous to see me and hear my principles, I never declined to gratify them: for as I do not speak for money, so I will not hold my peace for want of it. I am at all times equally free to the rich and the poor, and willing to give them all possible leisure for asking me questions; or if any of them choose rather to hear me, I give them satisfaction by answering my own questions: Now if any of these be found either good or bad, I am neither to be praised nor blamed; for I am not the author either of their good or bad qualities. I never engaged to teach them any thing, and in effect I never did teach them. If any of them boast that he ever heard from me privately, or was taught any thing besides what I avow publicly to the whole world, you may assure yourselves he does not speak the truth.

Ye have now heard, Athenians, the reason why most people love to hear me, and converse so long with me, viz. that they take a singular pleasure in seeing those men baffled who pretend to be wise, and are not so. I have likewise told you, that I received my orders so to do from God himself, by oracles, dreams, and all other methods which the Deity makes use of to make known his pleasure to men.

If I did not speak truth, you might easily convict me of a lie: for had I debauched the minds of youth; of necessity those who are now old, and conscious of my having done so, would rise up and prosecute me; or if they did not, to be sure their fathers, uncles, or brethren, would find it their duty to demand vengeance upon the corrupter of their sons, nephews, or brethren. Now, I see many of those here present, particularly Crito the father of this Critobulus, a man of the same city and age with myself; Lysanias the Sphecian, father to this Eschines; Antypho, a citizen of Cephisia, and father to Epigenes; and several others whose brethren assist at this meeting, at Nicostratus, son to Zotidas, and brother to Theodotus. It is true Theodotus is dead, and so has no occasion for his brother's assistance. Besides these, I see Paralus, the son of Demodocus, and brother to Theages; Adimantus, son to Aristo, and brother to Plato, who is now before you; Aiantodorus, brother to Apollodorus:* and a great many more, of whom Melitus should have selected at least one or two for witnesses.

If it was an oversight in him, there is yet time enough; I allow him to do so now: let him name them. But you will find, Athenians, it is quite otherwise; all these men, whose children, whose brethren, Melitus and Anytus allege I have debauched and entirely ruined; these very men, I say, are all on my side. I do not offer to take shelter under those whom I have misled: perhaps they may be said to have reasons for defending me. But I put the case upon men advanced in years, and near relations to those young men. What other reason should move them to protect me, but my innocence? These men know that Melitus is a liar, and that I advance nothing but truth. Such, Athenians, are the arguments that may be urged in my defence: and the others, which I pass over in silence, are of the same weight and force.

But perhaps there may be some among you, who calling to mind their being formerly arraigned in the same place where I now stand, will be incensed against me, upon the account, that when they were in much less danger, they made suppliant addresses to their judges; and to move their compassion more effectually, presented their children, with their friends and relations, in this place; whereas I have no recourse to such artifices, notwithstanding that in all probability I am encompassed with the greatest dangers. It is possible, I say, that the consideration of this differ-

* This Apollodorus was likewise present. He was a man of a very weak head, but one that loved Socrates entirely. When Socrates was condemned and going to prison, he cried out, "That which afflicts me most, Socrates, is to see you die in innocence." Socrates stroking his head with his hand, smiled, and said, My friend, would you rather see me die in guilt."

ence may excite their anger against me, and move them to condemn me.

I am unwilling to believe that there are any such here; but if there be, the most reasonable excuse I can plead, is this: I have relations as well as they. To use Homer's expression, " I am neither sprung from oak nor stone, but am born like other men." I have three sons, the eldest of whom is yet young, and the other two are but infants: and yet I shall not bring them hither to get myself cleared upon their account.

Now, what is the reason that I will not do it? It is neither a proud stiffness of humour, nor any contempt of you; and as for my fearing or not fearing death, that is another question: it is only with respect to your honour, and that of the whole city, that I decline it. For it is neither handsome nor creditable, either for you or me, to make use of such means at my years, and under such a reputation as I have: it is no matter whether it is merited or unmerited; since it is sufficient that by an opinion generally received, Socrates has the advantage of most men. If those who pass among you for men of an uncommon rank, superior to the rest for wisdom, courage, or any other virtue, should stoop to such unaccountable base and mean actions, as if they were apprehensive of some great evil accruing to them upon your condemning them to die, and expected immortality by virtue of your absolution: if these men, I say, should be guilty of such meanness, they would affront the city extremely; for they would give strangers occasion to imagine, that the most virtuous men among the Athenians, those who are entitled to honours and dignities, by way of preference to all others; are nothing different from the lowest-spirited and most pusillanimous. Now this, Athenians, you ought to prevent; you that are possessed of some reputation and authority. And supposing that I designed to do any such thing, you should give me to understand that you would sooner condemn one that means to excite your compassion by such tragical scenes, and by that means to expose your city to ridicule : than one who with tranquillity and repose, patiently awaits whatever sentence you shall be pleased to pronounce.

But not to regard the city's glory, which is sensi-

THE APOLOGY OF SOCRATES.

bly wounded by such indignities; justice itself forbids supplicating the judge, or extorting an absolution by requests. A judge ought to be persuaded and convinced. He is not placed upon the bench to oblige men by violating the laws, but to do justice pursuant to the laws. He is sworn so to do by an oath that ought to be inviolable. It is not in his power to favour whom he pleases: he is obliged to do justice. We ought not therefore to bring you into a custom of perjury; and you ought to hinder those who attempt it: for both those who tempt you, and you who comply, do equally wound justice and religion, and both are involved in the guilt.

Wherefore, Athenians, do not you expect that I will have recourse to such things as I take to be neither creditable, just nor pious; especially upon this occasion, where I stand arraigned of impiety by Melitus. Should I move you by prayer, and force you to break your oath, that would be evidence that I taught you to believe no gods; and thus in offering to justify myself, I should entangle myself in the very charge of my adversaries, and prove against myself that I believe in no gods. But I am very far, Athenians, from being of that principle. I am more convinced of the being of a God, than my accusers are; and am so well satisfied in the point, that I resign myself to you and to God, that you may judge as you think fit, both for yourselves and for me.

[Socrates having spoken in this manner, the judges put it to the vote, and he was found guilty by thirty-three voices. After which Socrates again began to speak]

I am not at all troubled, Athenians, at the sentence you have now pronounced. Several things keep me from being disturbed; especially one thing, viz. that I was fully prepared beforehand, and have met with nothing more than I expected: for I did not think to have come so near to an absolution, but expected to be cast by a greater majority of votes. Finding now that I am only condemned by thirty-three votes, I fancy I have escaped Melitus's prosecution; and not only so, but I think it is evident, that if Anytus and Lyson had not joined in the accusation, he had lost his 1,000 drachms, since he had not the fifth part of the

votes on his side.*   Melitus then thinks I deserve death!
and as for me, what punishment shall I allot to myself?†
You shall see plainly, Athenians, that I will choose
what I deserve.   Now what is it that I must condemn myself to, for not concealing what good I have learnt in my
life-time, and for slighting what others court very earnestly,
I mean riches, care of domestic affairs, offices, dignities; and
for never embarking in a party, or engaging in any office,
which things are commonly practised in this our city?   I
always looked upon myself as a man of more honesty and
goodness, than to preserve my life by such pitiful shifts.
Besides, you know I never would engage in any profession
that did not enable me at once to promote both your advantage
and my own'; and that my only aim was, to be always in
readiness to procure to each of you in private, the greatest
of all good things, by persuading you not to set your
mind upon your possessions, until you had taken care of
yourselves in studying wisdom and perfection; just as a
city ought to be taken care of, before the things that belong to it; and in like manner, every other principal thing
is entitled to a preference in our thoughts, before its
appurtenances.

After all these crimes, what is my demerit?   Doubtless,
Athenians, if you proportion the reward to the merit, I
deserve some considerable good.   Now what is it that is
suitable for a poor man that is your benefactor, and wants
leisure and opportunity for exciting and exhorting you?
Nothing suits better with such a man, than to be enter-

* An accuser was obliged to have one half of the votes, and a
fifth part more, or else he was fined in 1,000 drachms, i. e. 100 crowns.
Vide Theophrast. in his Book of Laws; and Demosthenes against
Androtion.

† To understand this, we must know, that when the criminal was
found guilty, and the accuser demanded a sentence of death; the
law allowed the prisoner to condemn himself to one of three punishments, viz. perpetual imprisonment, a fine, or banishment. This privilege was called ὑποτιμᾶσθαι; and was first enacted on the behalf
of the judges, that they might not scruple to pass sentence upon
those, who by condemning themselves, owned their guilt. Socrates
was caught in this snare; but Xenophon testifies that he did not
condemn himself at all, and would not allow his friends to do it, because it was in effect an acknowledgment of the crime. Only, in
obedience to the laws, and in order to proclaim his innocence,
instead of punishment, he demanded a reward worthy of himself.

tained in the Prytanæum ; that is more due to him than
to those of you that have brought off the trophies of victory from the horse and chariot races in the Olympic
games.   For these victors purchase you a seeming happiness by their victories: but as for me, I make you really
happy by mine.   Besides, they stand not in need of such
a supply ; but I do.   In justice therefore you ought to ad-
judge me a recompence worthy of myself.

Perhaps you may again charge me with arrogance and
self-conceit, in speaking thus to you, as you did when I
spoke against the supplications and prayers of prisoners.
But there is nothing of that in the case : pray hear
me.

It is one of my maxims, that knowingly and willingly,
we ought not to do the least harm to any man.   My time
is so short that I cannot upon this occasion fully recommend and enforce it upon you.   If the same law prevailed
here that is observed elsewhere, enjoining that a trial upon
life and death should last, not one, but several days, I am
persuaded I could make you sensible of its importance.
But how is it possible adequately to defend myself in so
short a space of time.   However, being convinced that I
ought to injure no man, how should I behave towards myself, if I owned myself worthy of punishment, and passed
sentence against myself ?   What ! shall I be afraid of the
punishment adjudged by Melitus ; a punishment that I
cannot positively say whether it is good or evil; and at the
same time choose another sort of punishment which I am
certain is evil ?   Shall I condemn myself to perpetual imprisonment ?   Why should I live always a slave to the
eleven magistrates ?   Shall it be a fine, and continuing in
prison till I pay it ?   That is just one, for I have nothing
to pay it with.   It remains then that I should choose
banishment ; and perhaps you will confirm my choice.
But indeed, Athenians, I must needs be much blinded by
the love of life; if I did not perceive that, since you who
are my fellow-citizens could not endure my conversation
and principles, but were always so galled by them, that
you were never at ease till you got rid of me, much more
will others be unable to brook them.   That would be a
decent way of living for Socrates, at these years, to be ex-

pelled Athens, and wander from city to city like a vaga-
bond! I am very well satisfied, that wherever I went
the younger sort would listen to me just as they do here :
But if I thwart them, they will solicit their fathers to
expel me.

But perhaps somebody will say : Why, Socrates, when
you go from hence, cannot you hold your peace, and live
quietly? I see plainly, that to persuade you to any thing,
is a difficult task : for if I tell you that my silence would
be disobedience to God, and upon that account I cannot
hold my peace :* you will not believe me, you will look
upon the whole story as a mysterious irony. And if on
the other hand I acquaint you, that a man's greatest happiness consists in discoursing of virtue all the days of his
life, and entertaining himself with all the other things you
have heard me speak of, either in examining himself or
others ; you will believe me yet less. However, it is just
as I tell you, though you cannot believe it. But, after all,
I am not accustomed to think myself worthy of any
punishment. Indeed, if I were rich, I would amerce my
self in such a sum as I might be able to pay. But I am
not in a condition, unless you would allow the fine to be
proportioned to my indigency ; and so perhaps I might
make shift to pay a mina of silver.† Indeed Plato, who
is here present, and Crito, and Critobulus, and Apollodorus
would have me stretch it to 30 minas,‡ which they will
answer for : and accordingly I amerce myself in thirty
minas, and I give you them for very creditable surety.

[*Socrates having amerced himself in obedience to the laws,
the judges took the matter into consideration, and
without any regard to the fine, condemned him to die.
After the sentence was pronounced, Socrates began again
thus:*]

INDEED, Athenians, your impatience and precipitancy
will draw upon you a great reproach, and give the envious

---

* It were impossible in Socrates to disobey God, and conceal the
truths he was obliged to reveal. What a noble example is this in a
Pag:n!

  † 10 Crowns.   ‡ 300 Crowns.

occasion to censure your city, for condemning that wise man, Socrates : for to heighten the scandal, they will call me wise, though I am not. Whereas, had you staid but a short while, my death had come of it self, and thrown into your lap what you now demand. You see my age has run the most of its round, and draws very near to a conclusion. I do not make this address to all my judges, but only to those that voted my condemnation. Do you think that I had been condemned, if I had thought it my duty to try every means for procuring my absolution; and if so, do you think I had wanted persuasive and touching expressions ? It is not such words that I have been wanting in, but in boldness, in impudence, and in a desire to gratify you, by telling you such stories as you like to hear. Doubtless you had been infinitely well pleased, to see me cry, groan, whine, and stoop to all the other mean shifts that are commonly made use of by prisoners at this bar. But upon this occasion, I did not think it my duty to stoop to any thing so base and scandalous ; and now that the sentence is past, I do not repent of avoiding the indignity, for I choose rather to die upon the defence I have now made, than to live by such prayers and supplications as you require. Neither civil nor military justice allows an honest man to save his life by base means. For in duels it happens often, that a man may easily save his life by throwing down his arms, and begging quarter of his enemy : and in like manner in all other dangers, a man that is capable of saying, or doing any thing, may hit upon a thousand expedients for avoiding death. To escape dying, Athenians, is not the greatest difficulty. Shame falls in upon us more swiftly, and is much harder to avoid. And accordingly in this juncture, I, who am stiff and old, am only overtaken by the slowest of the two ; whereas my accusers, who are vigorous and strong, are attacked by the swiftest ; I mean, infamy. Thus am I about to be delivered up to death by your orders, and they are surrendered by the orders of truth to injustice and infamy. Thus things are as they should be, and our shares are equally and justly divided.

In the next place I have a mind to foretel you, who have condemned me, what will be your fate ; for I am now just arrived at the point of time, that affords a man the steadiest thoughts,* and enables him to prophecy of things to come. I tell you then, that no sooner shall you have put me to death, than the vengeance of God shall pursue you with more cruelty than you have shown me.† By ridding yourselves of me, you design only to throw off the troublesome task of giving an account of your lives; but I tell you beforehand, you shall not compass your end.

A great number of persons will rise up and censure you. Though you perceived it not, it was my presence that has hitherto restrained them. But after my death, they will make you uneasy; and forasmuch as they are younger than I am, will prove more troublesome, and harder to be got rid of. For if you fancy to yourselves, that putting me to death is an effectual way to restrain others, and prevent their upbraiding you, you are mistaken.

That way of ridding yourselves of your censors, is neither honest nor practicable. A better way, which is at once very easy and honest, is not to stop their mouths, but to amend your lives. So much for those who voted my condemnation.

As for you, Athenians, who gave your votes for my acquittal, I would gladly discourse with you, whilst the head magistrates are busy, until I am carried to the place of execution: I beg therefore a short audience; for while we have time, why may not we confer together. I mean to represent to you a thing that has recently happened to me, and give you to understand what it imports. It is a marvellous thing, my judges, (for in calling you my judges, I am not mistaken) that the divine law, which has advised me so often; and upon the least occasion never failed to divert me from whatever I meant to pursue, that was unfit for me; this law has not given me any

---

* At the point of death men's thoughts are steadier, than in the career of life; because at that time passion is dethroned and the soul begins to retrieve its liberty. This was Homer's opinion: and there is no difficulty in tracing a higher source for it, than that poet.

† This prediction was fulfilled in a raging plague, that soon after laid Athens desolate; and all the misfortunes that overrun this unjust republic, and indeed all Greece; were taken for a certain mark of divine vengeance.

sign this day ; a day on which I have met with what most
men take to be the greatest of evils : it did not discover
itself to me, either in the morning when I came from my
house,* or when I entered this hall, or when I began to
speak.   At other times it frequently interrupted me in my
discourse ; but this day it has not thwarted me in any
thing I designed, either to say or do.   Now I am about to
tell you what this means.   It is very probable that what I
am now to encounter is a very great good ; for certainly
it is a mistake to look upon death as an evil.   And for an
evident proof of the contrary, let us consider, that, if I
had not been about to meet with some good thing to-day,
God, under whose care I am, would not have failed to
acquaint me, pursuant to his usual custom.   Let us
fathom the depth of this matter, in order to demonstrate,
that the belief of death being a good thing, is a well-
grounded hope.

One of these two things must be true ;† either death
is a privation of thought, or it is the soul's passage from
one place to another.   If it be a privation of thought,
and, as it were, a peaceful sleep undisturbed by dreams,
then to die is great gain. After one night of such tranquillity,
free from disturbance, care, or the least dream, I am
confident, that if a man were to compare that night with
all the other nights and days of his past life, and were to
confess in conscience and in truth, how many nights or
days of his whole life he had passed more happily than
that one : I am confident, I say, that not only a private
man, but the greatest king, would find so small a number,

---

* For Socrates was not imprisoned till after his condemnation.

† By this dilemma, Socrates does not call into question the immortality of the soul, but points to the two opinions of philosophers,
some of whom thought the soul died with the body ; and others,
that the former survived the latter.   Now he offers to prove that
death is not ill in either of these opinions : for, says he, if the soul
dies, it is annihilated, and consequently void of thought ; and if it
survives, we are happier after death than before.   Some decry Socrates's ratiocination, in alleging a third state of the soul, where
after death it stays to undergo the punishment due to its crimes.
But that is a mere quibble ; for Socrates speaks only of good men,
who having obeyed God, may expect a blessed immortality : for he
likewise taught, that the wicked suffer eternal punishment in the
world to come ; as we see in his Phedon ; and he did not in
the least pretend that wicked men had no occasion to fear death.

T

that it would be very easy to count them. Now if death does in any measure resemble such a night, then as I have just said to die is great gain.

If death be a passage from this place to another, and the regions below are a place of rendezvous for those who lived here; pray, my judges, what greater good can a man imagine? For if a man quits his counterfeit judges here, for true ones in the regions below, who, they say, administer justice with so much equity, such as Minos, Rhadamanthus, Æacus, Triptolemus, and all the other demi-gods, who were so just in this life; will not that be a happy change? At what rate, would not you purchase a conference with Musæus, Hesiod, and Homer?* For my part, if such a thing were practicable, I would die a thousand times to enjoy so great a pleasure. What transports of joy shall I encounter, when I meet Palamedes, Ajax the Telamonian, and all the other heroes of antiquity, who in this life were victims of injustice! How agreeable will it be to put my adventures in the balance with theirs! But the greatest and most valuable pleasure will consist in spending my time in putting questions and interrogatories to these great men, in order to strike out the distinction between the truly wise, and those who falsely fancy themselves to be such.† Who would not give all he has in this world for a conference with him, who led the numerous army against Troy, or with Ulysses, or Sisyphus, and a thousand other men and women, whose conversation and discoveries would afford us inexpressible felicity? These men are infinitely more happy than we, and invested with immortality. Upon which account, my judges, you ought to encounter death with steady hopes, as being persuaded of this certain truth, *That an honest man needs to fear no evil, either in this, or the future life, and that the god take care of all his concerns*: for what has now happened to me, is so far from being the effect of chance that I

---

* He ranks these three poets together, as being the authors of the pagan theology.

† Socrates here speaks of the wisdom they were really possessed of, or fancied themselves to possess in this world; and does not at all imply that any in a blessed state are capable of believing themselves wise when they are not

am fully convinced, it is infinitely advantageous for me to
die, and be rid of the encumbrances of this life.   And for
that reason, God, who regulates my conduct, did not
thwart me to-day.   So that I have no resentment against
my accusers, or those who voted my condemnation ; notwithstanding that they meant to do me no kindness, but
the contrary; which might afford me just ground of complaint.   One thing I have to beg of them, which is this ; that
when my children grow up, if they make them uneasy, as
I did, that you would punish them severely.*   But if
you find that they prefer riches to virtue, and take themselves to be somewhat, when in effect they are nothing ;
pray be not wanting in checking and exposing them,
for not minding those things which deserve all their
care, and for believing themselves to be what they are
not.   But now, it is right we should all betake ourselves
to our respective offices, you to live, and I to die.   But
whether you or I are going upon the better expedition,
is known to none but God alone.†

---

* Socrates is so well content to die for the sake of justice, that he
desired his judges to treat his children in the same manner, if
they proved so happy as to give them the same trouble that he
did; that is, if they made it their business to correct their injustice, idolatry, and all their other vices.

† Socrates did not speak this out of ignorance, for he knew very
well that the just were happier in their death, than the wicked in
their life.   But the people that had just condemned him, were not
in a condition to relish that maxim; upon which account, Socrates
tells them, that God alone knew ; and accordingly God quickly gave
them all to know the difference between the fate of Socrates, and
that of his judges.   The Athenians repented their putting to death
an innocent person, and publicly lamented the loss of him, whom
they had condemned by a public sentence.   The schools and
places of exercise were shut up; Socrates's statue was erected,
a chapel consecrated to his memory; and his accusers prosecuted.
Melitus was torn in pieces, Anytus was expelled the Heraclea,
where he sheltered himself, and all the abettors of the conspiracy
were looked upon as cursed, and excommunicated, and reduced to
such a depth of despair, that most of them laid violent hands on
themselves.

THE END.

'To those good with a spirit; the
ill shall flee. The good endure;
to those evil with pleasure, The evil
have endure, the pleasure flee."
                    Musonius the Stoic

J. BILLING, PRINTER, WOKING.

36
—
25